A Meeting of Minds

Relational Perspectives Book Series
Volume 4

Relational Perspectives Book Series

Stephen A. Mitchell and Lewis Aron
Series Editors

Volume 1
Rita Wiley McCleary
Conversing with Uncertainty: Practicing Psychotherapy in a Hospital Setting

Volume 2
Charles Spezzano
Affect in Psychoanalysis: A Clinical Synthesis

Volume 3
Neil Altman
The Analyst in the Inner City: Race, Class, and Culture Through a Psychoanalytic Lens

Volume 4
Lewis Aron
A Meeting of Minds: Mutuality in Psychoanalysis

In Preparation
Joyce A. Slochower
Holding and Psychoanalysis: A Relational Perspective

Barbara E. Gerson, editor
Therapists' Life Crises and Life Choices: Their Effect on Treatment

Karen J. Maroda
Surrender and Transformation: Mutuality in Relational Analysis

Stuart A. Pizer
Negotiation of Paradox in Psychoanalysis

Charles Spezzano and Gerald Gargiulo, editors
Soul on the Couch: Spirituality, Religion, and Morality in Contemporary Psychoanalysis

Emmanuel Ghent
Process and Paradox

Donnel B. Stern
Unformulated Experience

Peter Shabad
The Echo of Inner Truth: A Psychoanalytic-Existential Synthesis

Lewis Aron and Frances Sommer Anderson, editors
Relational Perspectives on the Body

A Meeting of Minds

Mutuality in Psychoanalysis

Lewis Aron

THE ANALYTIC PRESS

1996   Hillsdale, NJ   London

Published by
The Analytic Press, Inc.
Editorial Offices: 101 West Street
            Hillsdale, NJ 07642

Typeset in Goudy Oldstyle and Penguin by Laserset, Inc., New York City
Indexed by Bruce Tracy, Ph.D., Pine, Arizona

Library of Congress Cataloging-in-Publication Data
Aron, Lewis.
   A meeting of minds : mutuality in psychoanalysis / Lewis Aron.
        p.   cm.
   Includes bibliographical references and index.
   ISBN 0-88163-159-0
   1. Psychotherapist and patient. 2. Psychoanalysis. I. Title.
   [DNLM. 1. Psychoanalysis. 2. Physician-Patient Relations. WM
460 A769m 1996]
RC480.8.A76   1996
616.89'17–dc20
DNLM/DLC
For Library of Congress   96-4872
                                                              CIP

Printed in the United States of America
10 9 8 7 6 5 4 3 2

For Janie

To discover truth about the patient is always discovering it with him and for him as well as for ourselves and about ourselves. And it is discovering truth between each other, as the truth of human beings is revealed in their interrelatedness. While this may sound unfamiliar and perhaps too fanciful, it is only an elaboration, in nontechnical terms, of Freud's deepest thoughts about the transference neurosis and its significance in analysis [Loewald, 1980, pp. 297–298].

But it is a curious fact that unless the patient feels understood we feel that we have not fully understood him. Understanding would seem to be an act that involves some sort of mutual engagement, a particular form of the meeting of minds [Loewald, 1980, p. 382].

CONTENTS

Preface

Psychoanalysis seems to thrive when it is most besieged. It is indeed curious that, just at a time when our critics so assuredly pronounce the death of psychoanalysis, we psychoanalysts are enjoying a remarkably exciting period of renewed intellectual growth and clinical development. Psychoanalysis has become increasingly diverse and pluralistic; and what is most invigorating to students and practitioners of psychoanalysis is that, for the first time in its history, our discipline is strong enough to tolerate this pluralism of theoretical perspectives and hold together as a single, if not homogeneous, psychoanalytic science and profession (Wallerstein, 1988, 1995). The ferment within psychoanalysis has included the proliferation of competing psychoanalytic models as well as the careful reexamination, reformulation, and sometimes abandonment of fundamental and long cherished assumptions of traditional theory. In keeping with the best of our postmodern sensibilities, psychoanalysis has generated, and has been able to contain, multiple voices and multiple selves that can maintain an ongoing conversation and debate without silencing, excommunicating, or dissociating any of them. Psychoanalysis, it seems, has the capacity to transform and reinvent itself in response to contemporary intellectual and cultural demands, and it is this protean character of psychoanalysis as a discipline that gives it vitality and allows it to survive the continual pronouncements of its death and irrelevance.

Among the most significant developments on the contemporary American psychoanalytic scene has been the emergence and expansion of a distinctively relational approach to psychoanalysis. The relational approach places human relationships, rather than biological drives, at its theoretical center. The relational perspective approaches traditionally held distinctions dialectically, attempting to maintain a balance between internal and external relationships, real and imagined relationships, the intrapsychic and the interpersonal, the intrasubjective and the intersubjective, the individual and the social. Relational theory draws on and attempts an integration of ideas taken from the full range of current psychoanalytic schools of thought, including object relations theory, self psychology, interpersonal psychoanalysis, neo-Kleinian theory, and certain currents within contemporary Freudian (post-ego-psychological) thinking. Relational theory is based on the shift from the classical idea that it is the patient's mind that is being studied (where mind is thought to exist independently and autonomously within the boundaries of the individual) to the relational notion that mind is inherently dyadic, social, interactional, and interpersonal. From a relational perspective, in investigating the mind the analytic process necessarily entails a study of the intersubjective field. This distinction between the classical and the relational views of the mind and of the analytic process is often discussed under the problematic rubric of a shift from a one-person to a two-person psychology.

Where the classical view[1] depicts analysis as optimally operating as a one-way influence, with the analyst influencing and changing the patient and, by and large, *not* vice versa, the relational view emphasizes the inevitability of a mutual and reciprocal two-way influence between patient and analyst. In this book I trace the formation and proliferation of relational psychoanalysis, and I argue that what is most central and unique to the relational approach is the emphasis placed on various dimensions of mutuality in the psychoanalytic relationship.

What do I mean by mutuality? This book examines various aspects of mutuality in detail, but it may be best to begin with a common-sense, everyday meaning of the term. According to Webster's unabridged (2nd ed.), mutuality and reciprocity are synonymous; however, "the distinctive idea of *mutual* is that the parties unite by interchange in the same act; as, a *mutual* covenant. The distinctive idea of *reciprocal* is that one party acts by way of return and response to something previously done by the other party; as, a *reciprocal* kindness." When the word mutual is used, its meaning might be paraphrased by substituting "between" or "in common"; for instance, a mutual agreement is one we have between us and a mutual friend is a friend we have in common. The essence of the word mutuality seems to be a sharing in common or a sharing between people. If we feel mutual or reciprocal hate, then we share our hate, we have our hate in common, or we might say that there is hatred between us. Mutuality implies reciprocation, community, and unity through interchange. Lack of mutuality, by contrast, connotes difference and separateness, a lack of sharing. While I emphasize aspects of mutuality in psychoanalysis, it should be understood that psychoanalysis requires a dialectical relationship between mutuality on one hand and separateness, difference,

---

[1]By classical here, I mean the tradition of Freudian ego psychology that dominated American psychoanalysis in the 1950s and 1960s.

and autonomy on the other. Without some concept of autonomy, the meaning of mutuality would degenerate into merger or fusion.

The definition of mutuality does *not* include symmetry or equality. Two people may be said to have formed a mutual admiration society when they hold each other in high esteem or share reciprocal mirroring and idealization. There need be no assumption, however, of quantitative equality or functional symmetry for the term mutual to be applied. A teacher and a student may have mutual admiration for each other without our thinking that the quality or quantity of their admiration is identical or that their roles and functions are symmetrical. That a mother and an infant exert mutual influence in certain interactions does not imply that they influence each other equally or in identical ways (Beebe, Jaffe, and Lachmann, 1992).

Symmetry, in contrast, is a correspondence in form or arrangement on either side of a dividing line or plane. In mathematics, for example, we designate as symmetrical an equation whose terms can be interchanged without affecting its validity. Symmetry implies a degree of similarity and of quantitative equality between the two sides, whereas mutuality refers to a commonality and sharing that may be quite different in form, quantity, or degree for each party.

One of the central purposes of this book is to explore the many important ways in which mutuality plays a role in the psychoanalytic relationship. In the course of the book, I develop, elaborate, and distinguish among a wide variety of meanings to which the term mutuality refers: mutual alliance, mutual empathy, mutual resistances, mutual regressions, mutual transferences, mutual affective involvement, mutual participation, mutual enactments, mutual generation of data, mutual analysis, mutual regulation, and mutual recognition. I develop the point of view that psychoanalysis is in many respects a mutual process based on a mutual relationship. Nevertheless, I argue throughout that the relationship must simultaneously and inevitably remain relatively asymmetrical. By relatively asymmetrical, I mean to suggest that, while analyst and patient share a great deal and while influence and regulation move in both directions, that influence is not necessarily equal, nor do patient and analyst have equivalent or corresponding roles, functions, or responsibilities. Psychoanalysis, then, is mutual but inevitably asymmetrical—inevitably because it is the patient seeking help from the analyst and it is the patient coming to the analyst's office and paying the analyst; it is the analyst who is the professional and is invested as such with a certain kind of authority and responsibility.

Furthermore, I emphasize that mutuality of regulation or dyadic regulation must always be considered in conjunction with self-regulation. Mutuality as a principle needs to be balanced by self-regulation or autonomy. I elaborate on this in order to develop a more precise way of talking about the question of psychoanalysis as a one- or two-person psychology. This emphasis on the dialectics between a one- and a two-person psychology, between an emphasis on autonomy and mutuality, between agency and communion (Bakan, 1966), goes back to the very roots of relational psychoanalysis in the work of Sándor Ferenczi and Otto Rank.

In its clinical implications, the relational view of the psychoanalytic situation abandons the idea that the analyst has superior knowledge of the patient's psyche or psychodynamics. Instead, there is a strong commitment to viewing the analytic situation as, to borrow Winnicott's (1971a) term, a "potential space" (p. 47) for the mutually creative coconstruction of meaning. Meaning, in the analytic situation, is not generated by the analyst's rational (secondary) processing of the analysand's associations; rather, meaning is seen as relative, multiple, and indeterminate, with each interpretation subject to continual and unending interpretation by both analyst and analysand. Meaning is generated relationally and dialogically, which is to say that meaning is negotiated and coconstructed. Meaning is arrived at through "a meeting of minds."

Bion (1990) wrote, "In the practice of psycho-analysis it is difficult to stick to the rules. For one thing, I do not know what the rules of psychoanalysis are" (p. 139). Are there rules of psychoanalytic practice? Even guidelines? We now view the analyst as a participant in the analysis, but how should the analyst participate? If analysis is inevitably a mutual endeavor, then to what extent should analysts reveal their subjectivities? How much does the analyst self-disclose? How much does the analyst get caught up with the patient in the therapeutic action? How much is the analyst involved in enactments and interaction? How do we maintain our ethical responsibilities if there are no rules, no certainties, and no foundations? We have moved to a more egalitarian stance with our patients, but just how mutual a process is psychoanalysis? How symmetrical? How equal?

These are some of the questions with which this book struggles. Drawing on recent developments in psychoanalysis, particularly the elaboration of relational and social-constructivist arguments, I examine some of our fundamental clinical principles to see how they are being both preserved and transformed.

Just as meaning is mutually constructed within the analytic situation, so, too, psychoanalytic theories are coconstructed dialogically within the community of psychoanalysts, and it is the pragmatic results of these theories that determine their "truth." Mitchell (1993a) writes, "Ultimately, it is the community of psychoanalytic practitioners who provide the crucial testing ground, in the crucible of daily clinical work, for the relevance and efficacy of all levels of psychoanalytic theorizing" (p. 65).

This book is part of an ongoing conversation or dialogue with both external and internal others. I have written each part of the book in an attempt to argue with various analytic thinkers who, I also recognize, serve as external representatives, containers, for aspects of myself. Writing psychoanalytic theory has been a way for me to argue with myself and think through various positions. The title of the book, *A Meeting of Minds*, refers on one level to my own attempt to make up my mind, to reconcile opposing tendencies in myself, to resolve my own conflicts and ambivalences about a variety of psychoanalytic arguments. Perhaps it would be more useful to suggest not a reconciliation and the elimination of difference and conflict, but rather an ongoing conversation with myself. I am of more than one mind about most of the issues discussed in this book, and, having written it, I am no more unified or cohesive in my point of view. Nevertheless, it is hoped that there is much coherence even among my conflicting positions.

Chapter 1 begins by introducing the relational orientation as it has emerged in recent years to become one of the dominant American approaches to psychoanalytic theory and practice. Drawing on my personal experiences at the New York University Postdoctoral Program in Psychotherapy and Psychoanalysis, where the relational orientation was first institutionalized, as well as from my involvement with *Psychoanalytic Dialogues: A Journal of Relational Perspectives*, I tell the story of the development and growth of the relational orientation and examine some of its basic tenets. In this initial chapter, I examine the influence of some broad social movements, including feminism and postmodernism, on psychoanalysis.

In Chapter 2, I begin to explore the boundaries of relational theory. What is relational theory and how is it different from other traditional and contemporary psychoanalytic approaches? What are the relations between relational approaches and interpersonal theories, self psychologies, object relations theories, and contemporary Freudian theories? What are some of the current debates and disagreements within relational theory and among relational psychoanalysts? Here I ask, what do we mean by one- and two-person psychologies? Is relational theory a two-person psychology or does it embrace one- and two-person psychologies? How do these conceptualizations effect analytic technique?

In Chapter 3, I explore intersubjectivity as it is understood by various analytic theorists. I look at the patient's experience of the analyst's subjectivity. What do I mean by subjectivity, and what is the connection between the analyst's subjectivity and countertransference? How much does the patient know about the analyst's subjectivity? How much should the patient know? How does exploring the patient's experience of the analyst's subjectivity further the analytic interests of the patient? How do these understandings change our clinical practice?

Chapter 4, reevaluating the notion of interpretation, suggests that interpretations, as well as other analytic interventions, are always expressions of the analyst's subjectivity. What is an interpretation? What is the nature of its therapeutic action from a relational point of view? Are the data on which interpretations are based provided exclusively by the patient, or are psychoanalytic data generated mutually between patient and analyst? How and why do analysts transform elements of their subjectivities into interpretations? How much mutuality is there in the exchange of interpretations and in the sharing of insight?

In Chapter 5, I examine clinical aspects of mutuality in the psychoanalytic situation. What do I mean by mutuality? What are the various dimensions of mutuality that are relevant to psychoanalytic work? Here I will consider mutual transferences, mutual resistances, mutual regressions, mutual participation, and especially mutual recognition and mutual regulation.

Chapter 6 examines the dialectics between autonomy and mutuality (one-person and two-person psychologies) in psychoanalysis by tracing these emphases back to the dialogues and debates between Freud and Ferenczi, on one hand, and Freud and Rank on the other. I show how much of contemporary relational theory can be traced back to the early contributions of Ferenczi and Rank, with Ferenczi contributing the two-person focus on mutual analysis, Rank contributing to a focus on the creative analytic process giving birth to the self, and both thinkers highlighting the importance of the immediate affective experience and engagement within analysis. I use the concept of resistance to demonstrate how the contributions of these two thinkers taken together lead to a quite modern view of the clinical situation, with resistance viewed as a mutual creation and an affirmative interpersonal engagement.

In Chapter 7, I look at what have become newly accepted psychoanalytic terms, the concepts of interaction and enactment. I inquire into the relation between enactment, interaction, and projective identification. Why was it necessary to coin new technical terms? How have these terms added to our clinical conceptualizations? What are the implications of this understanding of enactment and interaction for how we conduct psychoanalysis? My examination of enactment will also highlight some of the subtle differences between various analytic theories. I make use of the concept of enactment to differentiate between relational analysts and contemporary liberal or "left-wing" (Druck, 1989) Freudian analysts, particularly one subgroup whom I identify as Freudian interactionists.

Chapter 8 returns to the question of the analyst's subjectivity, this time by asking more directly how, when, why, and where it is appropriate or clinically useful for analysts to directly reveal aspects of their experiences to their patients. Here we take up what is perhaps the most controversial topic in contemporary psychoanalysis, the issue of self-disclosure or self-revelation. I place the issue of self-disclosure within the context of mutual conflicts, in both patient and analyst, regarding the desires to know and be known by the other and desires to hide from and avoid contact with the other. Here, perhaps, lies the most profound aspect of mutuality between patient and analyst: the mutual and conflicted needs, of both patient and analyst, for both privacy and safety as well as for affirmation and contact.

In the Coda, I bring the book to a close by raising further questions about the implications of the relational approach for the analyst's ethics, values, and responsibilities and how these are handled in the clinical practice of psychoanalysis. If we accept that there is a certain mutuality inherent in the analytic process, and that in some respects patients may need to serve as therapists to their analysts, then how do we ethically protect patients from exploitation and how do we know when we are indulging our own needs rather then attending to patient's needs. In the light of the postmodern critique of foundations, on what do we base our ethical choices, values, and responsibilities? Where does relational psychoanalysis leave us in regard to our authority and our morality as psychoanalysts?

Acknowledgments

The great polarities of individual and community, agency and commu-nion, autonomy and mutuality are the subject matter of this book. It is fitting, therefore, that I should acknowledge that the ideas developed here have emerged out of an ongoing conversation among a commu-nity of relational psychoanalysts so that in some respects it is fair to say that they are not one individual's ideas, rather, they have developed in communal space and belong to the group. This is literally true in the sense that after an intellectually lively dialogue with a colleague or group discussion it is almost impossible to say who thought of a partic-ular idea, who first proposed it; the ideas develop in transitional space, between the individuals.

At the same time, however, the ideas elaborated here are very much my own; they belong to me, no one else proposes these ideas in precisely the way that I do; I have an individual investment in them, and I accept full responsibility for them. Because ideas can never quite be anyone's exclusive property it is never possible to be certain that you have not stolen ideas from someone else. I have tried my best, however, to credit individuals' contributions throughout the book. The one group of people who make the greatest contribution but who can never be credited explicitly are of course one's patients, they deserve acknowledgement; they have my gratitude, as do my students and supervisees.

My ideas have taken shape in a specific psychoanalytic community. The New York University Postdoctoral Program in Psychotherapy and Psychoanalysis has been my intellectual and professional home for the past 16 years. I want to acknowledge the help of the entire postdoc-toral community. I have been lucky enough to learn from faculty members, supervisors, students, and supervisees in all of the tracks (Freudian, interpersonal, relational, and independent). I know of no other program in the world that represents such a wide range of analytic perspectives and teaches them with such depth and compre-hensiveness. I consider myself truly fortunate to be a member of this community.

Stephen A. Mitchell has been my teacher, supervisor, mentor, colleague, and friend. While he has helped me with my writing from my first analytic paper, I am delighted that he is now officially my editor. I always learn from Stephen and with his great generosity he manages to make me feel that I am also teaching him. No one in the field could be a better model for the practice of mutuality while maintaining respect for the other's autonomy. Sitting in editorial meetings of *Psychoanalytic Dialogues* I feel a continual sense of privilege for being able to work, not only with Stephen, but with such an incredibly stimulating, thoughtful and productive editorial board. Everyone in this group read and commented on some portion of this book somewhere along the way, and I have grown enormously from my participation with them. I thank Neil Altman, Anthony Bass, Philip M. Bromberg, Jody M. Davies, Muriel Dimen, Emmanuel Ghent, and Adrienne Harris.

Donald Kaplan, Ph.D. was my esteemed teacher, supervisor, and colleague. He served as my model and guide in the years that I was in psychoanalytic training in the Freudian track of the Postdoctoral Program. Donald and I engaged in a continual dialogue and debate about all of the issues addressed in this book and it is a great sorrow to me that he did not live to see the completion of the project. A posthumous collection of Kaplan's papers has just been published (see Kaplan, 1995).

There are far too many individuals (and even institutes) for me to acknowledge and I am sorry that I can only thank them communally. Many of the ideas in this book were originally developed and elaborated in my lecturing around the country at local chapters of the Division of Psychoanalysis (39), American Psychological Association, as well as in lectures and papers presented at the annual meetings of this association. I thank Division 39 for providing me with a national forum within which to develop these thoughts.

Jessica Benjamin and Stuart A. Pizer carefully read and commented on most or all of final drafts of the book and helped me to fine tune it at a time that I was prepared to let it go as it was.

Carl Jung would have called it "synchronicity." Just as I had completed this book and was thinking about its cover, I received in the mail a copy of an art catalogue of paintings by David Newman, published in conjunction with the exhibition *Breaking the Tablets: Works by David Newman*, The Joseph Gallery, Hebrew Union College—Jewish Institute of Religion. On the back cover of the catalogue was the painting "Mutual Analysis." I learned from the artist's biography, in the catalogue, that aside from being an accomplished artist, David was a psychoanalytic candidate at the Manhattan Institute for Psychoanalysis. I quickly arranged to meet David to arrange permission to use this work on the cover of this book.

David's paintings often deal with the theme of hermeneutics and the interpretation of texts. I found myself drawn to his images of birds and animals tearing up parchment and biblical scrolls. The painting, "Mutual Analysis," that appears here, emphasizes both the erotics and the aggression in mutuality. I especially like that David portrays the dark side of mutuality, and that he does so with a sense of humor.

Portions of this book are based on or excerpted from earlier works that I published by myself and in collaboration with others. I am grateful to Adrienne Harris, Ph.D. for permission to use passages from our introductory essays in L. Aron and A. Harris (1993) *The Legacy of Sándor Ferenczi*, Hillsdale, NJ: The Analytic Press, and from our article, A. Harris and L. Aron (in press), Ferenczi's semiotic theory: Previews of postmodernism, to appear in *Psychoanalytic Inquiry*. I am grateful to Therese Ragen, Ph.D. for her help in preparing Chapter 6 of this book and for permission to use material from our earlier work, Abandoned workings: Ferenczi's mutual analysis. In: *The Legacy of Sándor Ferenczi*, ed. L. Aron & A. Harris. Hillsdale, NJ: The Analytic Press, pp. 217-226. I also wish to thank Dr. Esther Menaker for her help and encouragement about my ideas on the complementarity of Ferenczi and Rank in Chapter 6.

Chapter 2 contains material originally published in 1990 as "One-Person and Two-Person Psychologies and the Method of Psychoanalysis." *Psychoanalytic Psychology*, 7:475–485. Chapter 3 contains materials originally published in 1991 as "The patient's experience of the analyst's subjectivity." *Psychoanalytic Dialogues,* 1:29–51. Chapter 4 contains material originally published in 1992 as "Interpretation as Expression of the Analyst's Subjectivity." *Psychoanalytic Dialogues*, 2:475–507. In all of these cases the material has been extensively rewritten and reworked for this book.

Thank you to Paul Stepansky, Ph.D., Eleanor Starke Kobrin (Lenni), Joan Riegel, and the staff of The Analytic Press for all their help in bringing this book to completion.

Most importantly, I want to express my love and appreciation to my wife, Janie, and to my children, Benjamin, Raphael and Kirya, who are the joy of my life. Without Janie's continual support and willingness to carry the burden of family responsibilities on top of her own busy professional life, I would not have been able to write this book.

1 | The Relational Orientation

An Introduction

On the contemporary American psychoanalytic scene, the dominant alternative to classical theorizing has become an approach known as relational psychoanalysis.[1] While among individual psychoanalysts there have always been creative thinkers and maverick individualists who developed their own points of view, prior to the 1960s the American psychoanalytic establishment was overwhelmingly singular and unitary; its approach was dominated by Freudian structural theory and ego psychology. Beginning in the 1960s, and even more in the 1970s, schools of psychoanalysis outside the ego psychology tradition were introduced into this country. Analysts began to hear about the developments in neo-Kleinian psychoanalysis in England (with its emphasis on introjective and projective mechanisms as reflected in unconscious phantasy) and in British Middle Group or Independent school, object relations theory (with the special attention that it paid to the early maternal environment and the analyst's countertransference); and, from the United States, Heinz Kohut began to elaborate his own school of self psychology (which introduced a less moralistic tone regarding narcissism and allowed for the extension of psychoanalysis to more vulnerable patients).

Even from within the mainstream ego-psychological tradition, new ideas were emerging that emphasized relational considerations and challenged the prevalent positivist epistemology, as in the work of Hans Loewald (who reconceptualized drives as relational phenomena)

---

[1] Contemporary versions of classical theory have also moved in an increasingly relational direction, and so in this sense it seems an error to contrast "relational theory" with "classical theory." Current classical theorists are likely to argue that their versions of classical theory are indeed relational or contain relational concepts. Granted. Nevertheless, I argue in this book that even the most current versions of mainstream classical theory can be conceptually and clinically distinguished from the version of relational theory that is developed here.

and Roy Schafer (who drew on hermeneutics to critique the classical psychoanalytic metapsychology and who emphasized the active agency of the individual).

Building on the revisionist contributions of Harry Stack Sullivan and Erich Fromm, as well as of Karen Horney, Frieda Fromm-Reichman, and Clara Thompson (noted for their emphasis on interpersonal, social, and cultural forces), American interpersonalists had for a number of generations been building a rich and comprehensive alternative psychoanalytic vision.

Under the dominance of the ego-psychological paradigm, however, interpersonal theory had been viewed as outside of the scope of mainstream psychoanalysis. The breakup of the monopoly on psychoanalysis long maintained by the ego psychologists encouraged the increased acceptance within the psychoanalytic community of the interpersonal tradition and its contemporary expression, especially in the writings of Edgar Levenson (1972, 1983), whose compelling writing began to bring interpersonal sensibilities to the attention of the wider psychoanalytic community.

By the 1980s, it was only natural that new schools of thought would emerge that would draw on what had become a multiplicity of psychoanalytic models. It was also inevitable that these new schools of thought would reflect the impact of such intellectual developments as contemporary hermeneutics, postmodernism, poststructuralism, social-constructionism, and, most especially, a full range of feminisms. In keeping with the postmodern trend, psychoanalysis went from being coherent and unitary to being multiple and diverse. Robert Wallerstein (1995), a leading spokesperson for mainstream psychoanalysis, has referred to these developments in terms of the splintering of the "unquestioned hegemony of so-called classical ego psychology in America" (p. xiv). He speaks of relational developments (beginning with Sándor Ferenczi and especially as they became elaborated in British object relations theory) as having infiltrated American mainstream psychoanalysis, leading to what he calls a "sea change" in post-ego-psychological theory (p. 535). Wallerstein does an admirable job of describing the ego psychology consensus that existed in this country in the 1950s and its progressive fragmentation in recent decades. He explores this trend toward a plurality of perspectives in connection with the proliferation of relational and interactional perspectives in today's psychoanalytic world.

The relational approach to psychoanalysis developed out of the breakup of the hegemony of classical theory in this country; and, while its growth is still very much underway, and while there is still a great deal of lively diversity and debate within the relational community, the relational paradigm may be seen as a new integration of psychoanalytic concepts and approaches that offers a formidable alternative to classical psychoanalytic theorizing. To be clear, I want to suggest that, while in recent years classical or mainstream theory has clearly moved in an increasingly relational direction, nevertheless significant differences remain between current versions of classical theory and what has come to be referred to as relational psychoanalysis.

The best way I can explain the meaning and significance of relational theory in contemporary psychoanalysis is to describe its personal significance to me. A personal approach may best convey some of the reasons why the relational perspective has created so much excitement and enthusiasm in the field. The story I tell here is the story of the emergence of relational theory in the United States over the past decade. Although I relate it as part of the local history of a particular institute in New York City, it is, nevertheless, also the story of the popularization of relational theory across the country, particularly as it was disseminated at meetings and conferences of the Division of Psychoanalysis (39) of the American Psychological Association and at the local chapters of Division 39 around the country. Indeed, relational psychoanalysis may be regarded as a distinctive contemporary American school of psychoanalysis. The history of the development of the Relational orientation at the New York University Postdoctoral Program is a microcosm of the development of psychoanalytic theory in New York City and throughout the rest of the country.

It is, of course, no accident that I would begin a book about the relational model by describing my own subjective experience in developing my theoretical perspective. Stolorow and Atwood (1979) have explored the subjectivity of psychological knowledge and especially the subjective origins of universal metapsychological narratives. It seems to me perfectly appropriate that a work based on relational principles would begin by locating the development of the theorist's ideas within a historical and interpersonal context. The usefulness or pragmatic validity of the ideas that follow in this book must ultimately be judged on their own merits rather than on the basis of their subjective or historical-political origins. But they can be understood only as products of particular, local, cultural, historical, and social circumstances.

My own formal psychoanalytic training took place from 1980 to 1985 at the New York University Postdoctoral Program in Psychotherapy and Psychoanalysis in New York City (NYU Postdoc). The history of the NYU Postdoctoral Program is directly relevant to the emergence of the Relational orientation there in the 1980s and so I will provide some background.[2] My purpose is to describe the way in which the relational orientation first came into existence and how it became an important new paradigm in American psychoanalysis.

Psychoanalysis is unique among the intellectual disciplines in that it has grown outside of the university system. Perhaps this development has its roots back in turn of the century Vienna in Freud's ambivalent relationship to the University.[3] In the United States, psychoanalysis was taught at private training institutes, the most orthodox and official of which were affiliated with the American Psychoanalytic Association. Disdainful of Freud's commitment to the training of nonmedical analysts, these official institutes largely restricted admission to medical candidates. Exceptionally, however, independent institutes existed outside of this system and often promoted less orthodox approaches to psychoanalysis and teaching nonmedical trainees.

As far back as 1952, a small group of psychologists, Bernard Kalinkowitz, Erwin Singer, and Avrum Ben-Avi, put before New York University a proposal for a postdoctoral program in psychoanalysis. At the time they were matriculants at the William Alanson White Institute; the White Institute, not affiliated with the American Psychoanalytic Association, was the "home" of interpersonal theory. While these men appreciated the training that they were receiving at the White Institute, there were many problems they were hoping to resolve by beginning a new program. For one thing, they were insecure at White because there was always some question as to whether White would continue the training of psychologists. There were pressures within White to try to join the American Psychoanalytic Association; and, if the institute were to move in that direction, then psychologists would

---

[2] I do not mean to suggest that the relational perspective originated at the New York University, Postdoctoral Program in Psychotherapy and Psychoanalysis in any exclusive way. A good case could be made for example to tracing its development at the William Alanson White Institute in New York. I am highlighting its emergence at the NYU program *both* because I was very personally involved in that institution as well as because I believe that the "track system" at that program forced it to take shape with particularly sharp contours. This account is based on my own experience at that institute as a matriculant (or candidate), as a graduate, and as a faculty member and supervisor in the Relational Track of that program. I was actively involved in the formation of the track and have been on its various steering committees since its inception. In addition, I have relied very heavily in this account on notes and newsletter articles written by the founder and long-time director of the program, Bernard N. Kalinkowitz. For the impact of the program on relational psychoanalysis I have borrowed liberally from Ghent (1992a).

[3] Freud's ambivalence may have been due as well to the Viennese University's ambivalence toward him as a Jew.

have to be dropped from the training program. In fact, in the 1950s the few psychologists who were trained at White did not receive certificates as psychoanalysts as had their medical colleagues who had received identical training. Instead, the psychologists received diplomas saying that they had completed courses in clinical psychology, in spite of their having completed doctorates in clinical psychology years before.

The situation at White was, nevertheless, better than it was at the more conservative medical institutes, those affiliated with the American Psychoanalytic Association. In those years, and for a long time after, few psychologists were admitted to the medical institutes, and those who were admitted were taken on a research basis and were required to take an oath that they would not practice as psychoanalysts. This demand was, of course, completely hypocritical since these psychologists expected to practice clinical psychoanalysis and everyone "unofficially" knew that. So the motivation to begin a postdoctoral program in a department of psychology was an attempt to establish a home for psychologist/psychoanalysts where they would feel secure, could be full-fledged psychoanalysts, and could utilize their academic and research backgrounds as psychologists to inform their psychoanalytic studies, and where greater numbers of psychologists could be trained (since admission to other institutes was extremely limited).

Coming from an academic, university-based background, these psychologists wanted to have a university-based program in psychoanalysis that would be in line with the academic tradition and the empiric, open-minded approach of psychology. In a university setting, with a commitment to academic freedom of thought, the hope was to develop a program that fit into the long tradition of open discussion among a diversity of views. The hope was to build a psychoanalytic center that was not loyal to any one approach or founder, but that was instead committed to the academic values of free inquiry and intellectual expression, debate, comparison and contrast of theories, efforts at integration and synthesis, an expansion of approaches rather than a narrowing of them, and research.

By 1961, Bernard Kalinkowitz, who by then had become Director of the Doctoral Program in Clinical Psychology at New York University and had graduated from the White Institute, began the Postdoctoral Program in Psychoanalysis and Intensive Psychotherapy. The addition of the words intensive psychotherapy was a politically minded move that served the purpose of demonstrating to the New York State Department of Education that a university sponsored training program was willing to certify that the profession of psychology would assume responsibility for training psychologists as psychotherapists. Until that time (the late 1950s) no doctoral program in the state was willing to certify that their Ph.D. graduates were trained for the independent practice of psychotherapy!

The Postdoctoral Program at New York University was the first of its kind, housed in a department of psychology, a home for psychologist/ psychoanalysts, and established as a psychoanalytic program committed to diverse viewpoints and academic freedom. A distinguished faculty was put together that included psychiatrists and psychologists in spite of the fact that the program was essentially being boycotted by members of the medical establishment institutes.

The curriculum expressed the diversity of thought at the time. Courses were offered from the Freudian, Sullivanian, and Frommian traditions as well as in subjects that cut across points of view. It was a matter of principle that students never had to declare allegiance to one or another point of view but were encouraged to remain uncommitted, free to explore without prejudice the various offerings. Nevertheless, if students did want to specialize and follow a more "narrow" or "in depth" approach to one point of view, they were equally free to do just that. In striking contrast to what existed in other institutes at the time, and for many years later, the Postdoctoral Program was designed from the beginning to promote comparative study, high-level debate, and a critical examination of basic assumptions of various psychoanalytic points of view.

In spite of this promising beginning, keeping different psychoanalysts functioning under one roof without polarization was not easy. By the late 1960s students were complaining about the difficulty of getting into good courses and the amount of time spent in any given course criticizing and devaluing other approaches. Perhaps more important, there was a feeling on the part of many students and faculty that they wanted to be able to commit themselves to one point of view or another and learn that approach in greater depth and with more rigor. This need led, by 1970, to the establishment of a two-track system that consisted of a Freudian track of courses and an Interpersonal-Humanistic (I-H) track. The I-H track took its name by hyphenating the interpersonal label, which stood for Sullivan's theoretical legacy, with the term humanistic, which was the term Fromm had applied to his own outlook. It was always a great disappointment to the founder and director, Bernie Kalinkowitz, that the program had to be split up in this way. To have two tracks so deeply divided and separate went against the grain of his intent, which was to foster integration, synthesis, open debate, and comparative study.

By the time I began my training in 1980, these two tracks were well established, and there also existed a third, nonaligned track, later called the Independent track, which consisted of a small faculty committed to independence from the other groups as well as from any single theoretical position. While many students indeed felt nonaligned with either of the two major tracks, the nonaligned track did not have a large faculty, offered few courses, and did not have much political power in the program. The two major groups, the Freudian track and the I-H track had grown more and more apart from each other. They tended to have their own independent meetings and colloquium; they had separate curriculum, spoke different languages, and tended to read different journals. In this atmosphere of rigid polarization and lack of cross-track dialogue, many of us felt that we were not being encouraged to think for ourselves but, rather, were being asked to choose between party lines.

I remember that in the early 1980s a Freudian faculty member began his course by telling students that if any of them wanted to bring up an interpersonal perspective on a topic that he would welcome their remarks, but that he himself would not be able to contribute to the discussion because he had not read any of "their" writings in the past 20 years. How ironic and sad this was at an institute that had been established to promote open and free exchange of ideas!

But interesting and encouraging developments were taking place all around us in the psychoanalytic world. Self psychology was emerging as a new psychoanalytic paradigm. Kohut's (1971, 1977, 1984) work was being hotly debated by everyone in both tracks. Self psychology was extending the range of patients for whom psychoanalysis was thought to be possible. It reconceptualized the problem of narcissism and avoided speaking of narcissism moralistically in pejorative tones. As self psychology grew and expanded, it raised serious questions about classical metapsychology; and, by viewing psychopathology as arising in response to parental failures in empathy, it began to pay increased attention to the role of relations with others. Clinically, by pointing to failures in analytic empathy, self psychology found a limited (but at the time refreshing) way to attend to the analyst's contribution to the transference.

Freudian faculty tended to be quite ambivalent about Kohut's contributions; while some were dismissive of self psychology as a departure from analytic principles, many Freudian faculty were impressed with his efforts to understand a difficult treatment population and considered that his ideas were integratable with Freudian theory. They saw him as a "modifier" but not as a "heretic," to use Martin Bergmann's (1993) felicitous phraseology. On the other hand, other Freudian faculty were extremely critical of the direction that Kohut's theory was taking in moving away from drives and the body, emphasizing developmental arrest over conflict, minimizing the interpretation of resistance, and overemphasizing external social concerns. In short, to many Freudians, as self psychology developed in its own direction it proved indeed to be heresy.

Within the I-H camp a similar battle was being waged. Some I-H faculty looked positively on developments within self psychology; they felt that Kohut and his followers were launching an attack on the classical metapsychology that was similar in many respects to the criticisms that had long been made by members of their own community. On the other hand, many I-H faculty believed that self psychology remained a "one-person psychology," in which transferences were understood as developing on the basis of the inner organization of the patient's mind without due consideration being given to the impact of the interpersonal other, the analyst. These interpersonal critics viewed Kohut's pivotal notion of a selfobject as obscuring the recognition that selfobjects were indeed real other people in the person's life. Furthermore, self psychologists continued to advocate a rather conservative use of the self in the conduct of analysis. And interpersonalists saw in the term empathy another technical straightjacket, much as they had previously viewed the concept of neutrality. In summary, for many interpersonal analysts Kohut's self psychology had not gone far enough and remained incompatible with what they were teaching and developing. (We will see in later chapters that there has been much development within self psychology in the past decade that leaves all these arguments somewhat dated.)

So here we were at NYU Postdoc, designed to encourage academic freedom of thought, debate, and criticism. Where would this new school of self psychology be housed or contained? It was both claimed and disclaimed by the Freudian and Interpersonal tracks. It might have fit in nicely with the Nonaligned track, and indeed there was some attempt in that direction. But that track had little political power in the program to approve courses, faculty and supervisors, and furthermore the faculty of that track were committed, for didactic purposes, to not aligning with any single tradition within psychoanalysis. (I remember that my own personal response to the name Nonaligned was to think that I always felt multiply aligned, and when the name changed to Independent, I similarly felt that in contrast I was multiply dependent on a variety of theoretical positions.)

A similar dilemma concerned the growing popularity of interest in British object relations theories such as those of Balint, Fairbairn, Winnicott, Guntrip, Bowlby as well as contemporary writers of this independent tradition. There was some limited place for these thinkers in the Freudian track, although, while I was in the program, no course was offered about these thinkers by the Freudian track. There was once again a great deal of discomfort about the extent to which their contributions were in the Freudian psychoanalytic tradition versus the degree to which they were to be seen as heretics. The object relations tradition placed an emphasis on the developmental origins of psychopathology in the preoedipal phase and especially in the early mother–infant relation. Clinically, these theorists often focused on nonverbal phenomena, regressed states, and noninterpretive interventions, all of which were seen as a challenge to classical theory and technique. Certainly, it was easier to make a case for Winnicott as a modifier and extender since he continued to speak in the terminology of classical theory, while it was easier to present Fairbairn and Guntrip as radicals and heretics since they were more outspoken in their departures from orthodoxy.

On the side of the Interpersonal track a similar phenomenon occurred. There were those on the I-H side who welcomed the contributions by the British. They saw these contributions as parallel to their own attacks on classical theory, since interpersonalists had long criticized the centrality that classical analysts gave to the oedipal phase and had long disparaged the exclusive use of interpretation as a therapeutic tool. On the other hand, many I-H faculty condemned the object relationists for holding on to outmoded conceptions of drives, continuing to utilize Freudian terminology, advocating regression in the transference, and being preoccupied with internal structures ("internal objects") instead of attending to real interpersonal relations. Once again, as it had with Kohut and self psychology, the question emerged, Where do these theorists fit in to what had become an overly polarized split between the Freudian and the interpersonal community of analysts?

By 1985, when I graduated from the program, these were burning issues! And further excitement and controversy were developing as we began to hear more about the creative work of the neo-Kleinians, such as Betty Joseph, who was using the concept of projective identification (as it had been reworked by Bion, Meltzer, Rosenfeld, and others) to develop an approach to technique that examined the subtle interactions between patient and analyst. We were also exposed to a new generation of British Independent analysts (including Bollas, Casement, Coltart, and Klauber) as well as Independent analysts from the continent (such as McDougall and Green), who were expanding our understanding of countertransference and the clinical use of the analyst's subjectivity. Furthermore, we were beginning to read Lacan and his followers, who were finding ways to bring culture into the discourse of psychoanalysis by conceptualizing the unconscious in linguistic terms. Beyond this, we were starting to pay attention to the new findings of infancy research (Stern, 1985) that seemed to have a great deal to say to us as practicing analysts. And perhaps most important, we were exposed to feminist and postmodern cultural critiques of all of these theories, which demanded the reconceptualization of psychoanalytic theory and practice. All these influences pushed against the boundaries of the rigid framework of a two-track system.

I had studied with mostly the Freudian faculty and supervisors and considered myself a Freudian analyst when I graduated. But I was interested in and drawn to these new developments and to the evolution of contemporary interpersonal theory, particularly as reflected in the work of Edgar Levenson (1972, 1983), for whom what was talked about in psychoanalysis was always simultaneously being enacted between the participants.

Many of us were looking for a transitional theoretical space, a track that would integrate these new contributions and highlight what they had in common, a theoretical home where we could anticipate the future of psychoanalysis rather than continue fighting over its past. It seemed to me, and to many of my colleagues, that all these schools were moving in a similar direction, toward a focus on self–other relations, toward a less authoritarian stance on the part of the analyst, an interest in affect rather than in drives, and a clinical focus on the patient–analyst relationship and the way in which subtle interactions and enactments dominated the clinical situation. This was the background to the events that led up to the establishment of the Relational track. It is important to recognize that none of these developments were exclusive or unique to the NYU program. To the contrary, similar debates were taking place in one form or another throughout the psychoanalytic world. Because of the track system, however, these controversies took on a particularly concrete expression, making it easier to trace the emergence of a new paradigm. Let's consider some of the key ideas that were in the air in the mid-1980s.

In their influential book, *Object Relations and Psychoanalytic Theory*, Greenberg and Mitchell (1983) (both of whom were to become members of the Relational faculty) distinguished two distinct approaches to psychoanalytic theory: the drive-structure model and the relational-structure or relational model. According to their argument, theoretical positions in psychoanalysis are inevitably embedded in fundamental social, political, and moral contexts. The drive-theory perspective and the relational perspective are based on two essentially different views of human nature and are therefore fundamentally incompatible. Drive theory is derived from a philosophical tradition that sees man as an essentially individual animal and human goals and desires as essentially personal and individual. In contrast, relational theory is linked philosophically to the position that man is a social animal and that human satisfactions are realizable only within a social community. According to Greenberg and Mitchell, although there have been a variety of attempts to bridge the gap between these two world views by attempts at integration in hybrid theories, none of these efforts has been successful in reconciling the inherent incompatibilities. Grouped together by Greenberg and Mitchell as having developed broadly relational models were such diverse thinkers as Klein, Fairbairn, Winnicott, Balint, Sullivan, Fromm, Kohut, and Loewald.

In a series of writings, Merton Gill (1982, 1983a, b, 1984), long considered a leader in American ego psychology, documented his growing recognition of the contributions of the interpersonal school of psychoanalysis and gradually shifted toward an interpersonal view. Gill did not want to call what he was proposing interpersonal because he recognized that this label was too closely connected to the more narrow view of Sullivan and the White Institute. Similarly, to call it a self psychology would have aligned it too one-sidedly with Kohut's perspective. Gill (1983a) contrasted the energy-discharge point of view with what he called the person point of view. In this way he contrasted what he thought to be the most essential aspects of the two metapsychologies. On one side he put the energy-discharge model, or the more mechanistic aspects of the metapsychology. On the other side he put the person point of view, a less mechanistic and more humanistic conception of people's relating to each other. Gill described both Winnicott and Loewald as forerunners of this more person-centered approach. Gill's considerations were not only metapsychological. On the level of clinical practice, Gill and his collaborator, Irwin Z. Hoffman (Gill, 1982; Gill and Hoffman, 1982), suggested a reconceptualization of the meaning of transference that gave considerably increased attention to the interpersonal impact of the analyst on its development.

Hoffman (1983) has extended the implications of the work he began with Gill. Hoffman distinguishes between conservative and radical critics of the blank-screen model. He demonstrates that there is a new paradigm emerging in psychoanalysis, a radically social or interpersonal perspective that seems to cut across particular Freudian, Kleinian, or interpersonal schools or traditions. He includes in this group of thinkers such analysts as Gill, Levenson, Racker, Searles, and Wachtel. What these diverse thinkers have in common is their understanding that transference is not simply a distortion that emerges or unfolds from within the patient, independent of the actual behavior and personality of the analyst. Rather, the analyst is viewed as a participant in the analysis whose behavior has an interpersonal impact on the cocreation or coconstruction of the transference. Hoffman (1991, 1992a, b, 1993, 1994) later extended these ideas into what he calls a social-constructivist perspective.

Similarly, Stolorow and his colleagues (Stolorow, Atwood, and Ross, 1978; Stolorow and Atwood, 1979; Stolorow, Brandchaft, and Atwood, 1987) were espousing an intersubjective approach to psychoanalysis that emphasized a dyadic systems view of the psychoanalytic situation that had radical methodological and epistemological implications for the revision of psychoanalytic thought. In yet another attempt at theoretical integration, Morris Eagle (1984), who was to become a member of the Relational track, surveyed a wide variety of current theories in an attempt to place attachment and relationship at the center of psychoanalysis.

Also very much in the air in the mid-1980s was the topic of projective identification, which I have already mentioned in relation to the contributions of the neo-Kleinians. While the concept is problematic (and is taken up further particularly in Chapter 7), it is important to keep in mind that, especially as it was developed by Ogden (1979) in this country and by the neo-Kleinians in England, it became a pivotal concept linking the intrapsychic with the interpersonal, internal object relations with external interpersonal behavior. Because the concept of projective identification served as a bridge between these diverse realms of discourse, it played a critical role in furthering interest in the relational approach.

So, to return to the story of the development of the relational orientation at New York University, here we were, in a program that divided up the world of psychoanalytic theory and practice neatly between the Freudian and the interpersonal. Many of us, candidates, graduates, and faculty, began to feel more and more that we fit into neither camp. A "potential space" emerged as "transitional" between the Freudian and the interpersonal world views. By 1988 a new track, or orientation, was created. Five original faculty members (Philip Bromberg, Bernard Friedland, James Fosshage, Emmanuel Ghent, and Stephen Mitchell) met to consider what to call the track. This was an important but not an easy decision because the name needed to reflect that they were attempting to develop a broad umbrella track that would be inclusive in spirit and that would reflect the consensus that seemed to be emerging in the field. While they might have liked the term interpersonal because its literal meaning was appealing (they were all focused to a great degree on what went on between people in development, psychopathology, and treatment), nevertheless they were distinguishing themselves from the more narrowly defined Interpersonal track that already existed and that was quite ambivalent at best about what this new group was doing! (As we have seen, the Interpersonal track had various objections to aligning itself with these other traditions. The faculty of the Interpersonal track were determined to maintain the purity of their own perspective, rather than risk diluting their unique contribution by broadening their own position.) More important, the central objection to the word interpersonal was that it had unfortunately come to connote only external relationships between real people; the analytic position that was being developed by this new group, however, emphasized not only external interpersonal relations but intrapsychic, internal, fantasized, and imaginary relations. It was precisely because of this limitation of the term interpersonal that Greenberg and Mitchell (1983) had introduced the alternative term relational in their book.

This initial group of faculty also liked the idea of a point of view that emphasized the self. Some of the members of this faculty had indeed been highly influenced by Kohut and by developments in self psychology. To call the track a Self track, however, would have aligned them much too narrowly with the Kohutian school and its derivative approaches. They considered calling the approach an object relations approach. To do so however, would have been confusing too since it did not differentiate between the various object relational approaches (consider the significant differences between, for example, Klein, Fairbairn, and Winnicott) and also because some of the faculty were more oriented either to the interpersonal or to the self-psychological than to the British schools. They considered Gill's person point of view, but a person track or orientation would have sounded jarring. The term intersubjective was also appealing, but it had already come to be identified with the particular approach of Stolorow and his colleagues, which was viewed (perhaps not completely correctly) as a version of self psychology. Indeed, Stolorow's intersubjective approach has much in common with the relational approach.

The original faculty compromised on the term relational, borrowing it from Greenberg and Mitchell's (1983) book. At first no one was happy with the term because it seemed to minimize both the role of the self and the biologically given components of personality. It had the advantage, however, of seeming to borrow from the object relations tradition, the interpersonal relations tradition, and the self-selfobject relations tradition; and it clearly seemed to distinguish itself from the drive-theory perspective. So the term was adopted and the Relational track, or Relational orientation, was born and approved by the Postdoctoral Program in 1988. The most significant issue was not the name of the track so much as the process of working toward some shared theoretical assumptions and clinical sensibilities. This is a process that continues even now.

I began to teach in the Relational track in 1989, and by then it had met with enormous success and had generated considerable enthusiasm. A few other publishing events had generated increased excitement within our community. Mitchell (1988a) had seen the publication of his first individually authored book, *Relational Concepts in Psychoanalysis*. In this book, he persuasively elaborates his own version of an integrative relational approach to psychoanalysis. By focusing on relational concepts in the title of the book, he draws increasing attention to this point of view. (Chapter 2 features Mitchell's relational contributions.)

Jessica Benjamin (1988), also a member of the Relational faculty, published *The Bonds of Love*, which not only develops a feminist psychoanalytic approach, but also emphasizes the need for psychoanalytic theory to include *both* an intrapsychic *and* an intersubjective perspective. Benjamin's book is only one of a number of publications by a large group of feminist-psychoanalysts associated with the Relational track at NYU. This is important to note because women as people and feminism as an intellectual movement have been a major (often unacknowledged) influence on the development of relational theory. (I also review Benjamin's ideas at greater length in Chapter 3.)

Another publishing event of 1988 was critical: the release in English of *The Clinical Diary of Sándor Ferenczi* (Ferenczi, 1932), which had been suppressed for more than half a century. This controversial work (recordings of Ferenczi's clinical experiments with mutual analysis in the last few years of his life) brought to the attention of the analytic world the importance of Ferenczi's ideas for contemporary psychoanalytic thinking. Ferenczi had been an important influence on many of those psychoanalysts who were to develop relational perspectives in psychoanalysis, and so, with the rediscovery of Ferenczi's work, groups of analysts who until then had felt disconnected from each other found that they had an important shared progenitor. This led to a greater sense of identity among relational analysts (see Aron and Harris, 1993). (In Chapter 5, I review the contributions of Sándor Ferenczi, who, along with his at one time best friend and collaborator Otto Rank, may be considered the forebears of relational theorizing.)

In 1989, Emmanuel Ghent, who was in many ways the leader of the Relational group at NYU, published "Credo: The Dialectics of One-Person and Two-Person Psychologies," which highlighted the need for *both* one-person and two-person perspectives within a relational model of psychoanalysis. Ghent has gone on to publish several papers developing his own unique relational perspective drawing heavily on the work of Winnicott (Ghent, 1990, 1992a, b, c, 1993, 1994, 1995).

That is the story of the origins of the Relational Orientation as it began at NYU. The similarities to what had happened in Britain during World War II should be clear to any student of psychoanalytic history (see King and Steiner, 1991). Just as in Britain during and following the war, the psychoanalytic world split apart between the polarized perspectives of the Anna Freudians and the Kleinians, leading to the development of what was known as the British Middle Group, or, later, the Independent group of analysts, so too psychoanalysis in New York City, and especially at New York University, was split between the American ego psychology tradition and the interpersonal approach. This split had been reasonably stable for a few decades, but with the emergence of new theoretical developments it became increasingly polarized and unstable until enough tension was created to allow for the creative emergence of a new paradigm, the Relational Orientation. Along these lines, Spezzano (1995) has even referred to this new orientation as the "American Middle School" (p. 23).

The identity of relational analysts was consolidated further with the establishment of *Psychoanalytic Dialogues: A Journal of Relational Perspectives*. The journal became an overnight success in the psychoanalytic world not only because of its ecumenical approach and high literary and theoretical quality, but also because of the explosion of interest in the relational point of view and because of the willingness of the journal to present debates and encourage dialogue among a wide variety of approaches.

Another important forum for the spread of the relational approach has been the annual meetings and presentations to local chapters of the Division of Psychoanalysis of the American Psychological Association. This psychoanalytic society itself is a very recent development and the new relational orientation has had wide appeal to many of its members. While Division 39 has many classical analysts, many members have diverse, nonclassical orientations, and the rubric of relational theory offers them a more unified identity. Relational concepts and perspectives have become a very frequent topic for panels and symposia at Division 39 meetings. This could not have happened if the meetings of the American Psychoanalytic Association were still the only national forum for psychoanalytic discussion, which was the case until the mid- to late 1980s. Psychologists and analysts who began their training after the formation of the Division may not appreciate the dramatic way in which the Division meetings changed the face of American psychoanalysis by providing an alternative to the American Psychoanalytic Association and giving psychologist/psychoanalysts a recognized forum under the auspices of the American Psychological Association.

WHAT IS RELATIONAL THEORY?

But what is relational theory? What is a relational analyst? I have given an introduction to the "politics," or to the sociology, of psychoanalysis, but what is the substance? Here I want to present a brief overview of the essence of relational theory, while I continue to document the formation of the relational orientation as it was influenced by a number of extraanalytic social and cultural forces, particularly feminism and postmodernism. In the next chapter, we have a chance to examine the substance of relational theory in further detail and describe the boundaries of relational theory with other contemporary psychoanalytic points of view.

It is useful to begin by quoting Ghent (1992a) at some length since it was this statement that served as the platform with which the Relational orientation was created:

> There is no such thing as a relational analyst; there are only analysts whose backgrounds may vary considerably, but who share a broad outlook in which human relations—specific, unique human relations—play a superordinate role in the genesis of character and of psychopathology, as well as in the practice of psychoanalytic therapeutics.
>
> Relational theorists have in common an interest in the intrapsychic as well as the interpersonal, but the intrapsychic is seen as constituted largely by the internalization of interpersonal experience mediated by the constraints imposed by biologically organized templates and delimiters. Relational theorists tend also to share a view in which both reality and fantasy, both outer world and inner world, both the interpersonal and the intrapsychic, play immensely important and interactive roles in human life. Relational theorists do not substitute a naive environmentalism for drive theory. Due weight is given to what the individual brings to the interaction: temperament, bodily events, physiological responsivity, distinctive patterns of regulation, and sensitivity. Unlike earlier critics of drive theory, relational theorists do not minimize the importance of the body or of sexuality in human development. Relational theorists continue to be interested in the importance of conflict, although conflict most usually is seen as taking place between opposing relational configurations rather than between drive and defense. Relational theory is essentially a psychological, rather than a biological or quasi-biological theory; its primary concern is with issues of motivation and meaning and their vicissitudes in human development, psychopathology and treatment [p. xviii].

Ghent goes on to point out that in his way of thinking the intrapsychic is not a concept in opposition to the interpersonal, but, rather, the intrapsychic and the interpersonal complement each other. Speaking of the intrapsychic is a way of referring to the structuring or patterning of internal psychic experience or organization. Ghent suggests that "the more profound significance of the term relational is that it stresses relation not only between and among external people and things, but also between and among internal personifications and representations" (p. xx). Thus, the relational approach is an attempt to bridge theories that have traditionally emphasized either internal object relations or external interpersonal relations, the intrapsychic or the interpersonal, constitutional factors or environmental factors, one-person psychology versus two-person psychologies.

I mentioned earlier that Stolorow's intersubjective approach has much in common with the relational approach as it developed at NYU. Consider the following two descriptions of the basic thesis of the relational approach, as described by Mitchell (1988a), and the intersubjective approach as described by Stolorow and colleagues. Mitchell describes the relational model as "an alternative perspective which considers relations with others, not drives, as the basic stuff of mental life" (p. 2).

> In this vision the basic unit of study is not the individual as a separate entity whose desires clash with an external reality, but an interactional field within which the individual arises and struggles to make contact and to articulate himself. *Desire* is experienced always *in the context of relatedness*, and it is that context which defines its meaning. Mind is composed of relational configurations. The person is comprehensible only within this tapestry of relationships, past and present. Analytic inquiry entails a participation in, and an observation, uncovering, and transformation of, these relationships and their internal representations [p. 3].

Compare that statement with Atwood and Stolorow's (1984) definition of the essentials of their intersubjective approach:

> In its most general form, our thesis . . . is that psychoanalysis seeks to illuminate phenomena that emerge within a specific psychological field, constituted by the intersection of two subjectivities—that of the patient and that of the analyst. . . . psychoanalysis is pictured here as a science of the *intersubjective*, focused on the interplay between the differently organized subjective worlds of the observer and the observed. The observational stance is always one within, rather than outside, the intersubjective field. . . . [pp. 41–42].

> Clinical phenomena . . . cannot be understood apart from the intersubjective contexts in which they take form. Patient and analyst together form an indissoluble psychological system, and it is this system that constitutes the empirical domain of psychoanalytic inquiry [p. 64].

Stolorow, Atwood and Brandschaft (1994) have themselves pointed out that the new paradigm that has been brewing in psychoanalysis goes by several names, including relational-model theorizing, a dyadic-systems perspective, social constructivism, and intersubjectivity theory. Each of these models emphasizes the study of interacting subjectivities, relational configurations, social construction or coconstruction, reciprocal and mutual influence, and the interlocking nature of the transference-countertransference integration. Lachmann (1993) summarizes this paradigm shift by pointing out that, whereas the classical contributions to psychoanalysis entailed the recognition of unconscious motivation, the more recent approaches have recognized the interactive organization of experience.

Some of the similarities between the relational approach and Stolorow's intersubjective approach went unrecognized or were at least underemphasized because of the relationship between self psychology and intersubjectivity theory. While the relational group at NYU included a few self psychologists, most of the members of this group were more greatly influenced by interpersonal theory. This was particularly true of Mitchell and Greenberg, the most prolific writers of the group. Interpersonalists were quite critical of self psychology, viewing it as a one-person psychology. I think that this attitude led a number of relational analysts to overlook some of the similarities between their own relational model and Stolorow's intersubjective model. Only more recently has Stolorow (1992) made it clear that, although intersubjectivity theory was greatly influenced by self psychology, it was not an outgrowth of it but, rather, developed parallel to it. Intersubjectivity theory and relational theory are similar, but their terms and metaphors reflect their independent origins and their connectedness to other schools of psychoanalysis, self psychology and interpersonal theory, respectively.

Thus, relational theory is essentially a contemporary eclectic theory anchored in the idea that it is relationships (internal and external, real and imagined) that are central. Within the broad approach that has been designated as relational there are actually many different perspectives, and this is particularly evident at NYU. Stephen Mitchell's relational theory (whose center lies in the attempt to integrate Sullivan with Fairbairn and Winnicott) is not Emmanuel Ghent's (whose theory may be seen as more heavily weighted toward Winnicott with an emphasis on the individual's longing to surrender the pretense of false-self), and neither of the two hold quite the same view as Jay Greenberg (whose theory has been more heavily influenced by recent developments in ego psychology and emphasizes the universal preexperiential needs for safety and effectance). Philip Bromberg's position, which begins with interpersonal theory and incorporates aspects of object relations theory, particularly the importance of regression and dissociative states of consciousness, is different, as is that of Jessica Benjamin, who used Winnicott's work to elaborate an intersubjective theory that highlights mutual recognition; Doris Silverman's multimodel approach; James Fosshage's contemporary self psychology and intersubjectivity theory; Morris Eagle's broad integration with a focus on attachment; Michael Eigen's unique integration, which draws on Winnicott, Bion, and Lacan; that of Adrienne Harris, who draws on her background in developmental psychology and psycholinguistics, feminist theory, and Ferenczi studies; Beatrice Beebe's theory, which is rooted in her ground-breaking infancy research and on the theoretics of self psychology; the position of Neil Altman, who has pointed to the relevance of relational theory for extending psychoanalysis to the study of race, class, and culture; and that of Donnel Stern, who has employed Gadamer's hermeneutics to extend his strong interpersonal identity. I mention these writers especially because they have all been active together on the relational faculty at NYU, they have all published numerous articles or books on psychoanalytic theory, and they are all broadly relational; yet each of them holds quite a distinct theoretical position.

In the scholarly endeavor of comparative psychoanalysis, approaching the various schools of psychoanalysis as separate and distinct categories is seriously problematic and yet seemingly unavoidable. Elsewhere (Aron, 1993b), I compared this way of classifying analytic theories to the categorical approach of psychiatric diagnosis, which attempts to pigeonhole analytic theories into discrete groupings such as Freudian, Kleinian, or relational. I argued that it would be more useful to sort analytic theories along a wide spectrum of dimensions rather than categorically.

A study of the work of the previously listed analysts reveals that they are hardly a homogeneous grouping. Relational psychoanalysis is not a unified or integrated school of thought, nor is it a singular theoretical position. Rather, it refers to a diverse group of theories that focus on personal, intrapersonal, and interpersonal relations. An emphasis on relational dimensions of development and treatment cuts across all contemporary schools of psychoanalysis. Nevertheless, in this book, I do refer to these theories as relational. I do so with some ambivalence because I am cognizant of the dangers of seeming to establish a new school, cult, or sect within psychoanalysis. Classifying these theories under the rubric of relational psychoanalysis, however, serves didactic purposes because it helps to demonstrate certain trends and developments within American psychoanalysis over the past two decades.

Throughout this chapter I have been describing the development of relational theory on two different levels, the local institute level and the national (and even international) stage of psychoanalytic thought. I have focused in detail on the formation of the Relational orientation at the NYU Postdoctoral Program as a microcosm of the psychoanalytic world at large. I will turn now to the macrocosm, to shifts in psychoanalytic ideas more generally, and to an examination of two broad extraanalytic cultural and intellectual trends that played a decisive, and sometimes unacknowledged, role in the development of relational theory: feminism and postmodernism. These two broad trends in the history of ideas were often in the background as the relational approach came to dominate contemporary psychoanalytic discussion.

WOMEN, FEMINISM, AND PSYCHOANALYSIS

The entrance of great numbers of women into the field of psychotherapy and psychoanalysis, and the concomitant intellectual impact of feminism and the women's movement, has had a momentous impact not only on professional practice but on psychoanalytic theory itself. Ilene Philipson (1993) has documented the dramatic shift that has been occurring in the mental health field over the past two decades. Women have entered the profession of psychotherapy in huge numbers while the number of incoming men has declined steadily. Philipson argues that the shift from a drive to a relational model is deeply embedded in the gender recomposition of the field. While most of the writing of relational analysts has not acknowledged the influence of gender directly, it can be seen in the major shifts that have occurred in psychoanalysis accompanying the ascendancy of the relational model.

Many of the articles written in the past decade on relational theory and practice have been indirectly influenced by feminism and the infusion of women into the mental health professions. Those contributions, focusing on greater mutuality between patient and analyst and acknowledging the intersubjective dimension of treatment, are likely to have been influenced by feminist consciousness and by the feminist emphasis on egalitarianism. Contributions that have focused on a two-person psychology, on social constructivism, and on the analyst as conceptualized as inside of the very system that he or she is studying have been at least indirectly influenced by the feminist critique of the masculine ideals of objective science and lack of involvement with the object of investigation (Keller, 1985; Flax, 1990). Papers emphasizing attachment as a central aspect of clinical psychoanalysis and relatedness and empathy as just as important as independence and autonomy have similarly been influenced at least indirectly by the feminist critique of the idealization of independence and the isolated self of our culture. The shift in emphasis from the centrality of the Oedipus complex to preoedipal phenomena is also a development that has been influenced by the numerous and very powerful feminist critiques of the Oedipus theory within traditional psychoanalysis.

It is not common, however, to find clinical psychoanalysts who have introduced significant ideas into psychoanalysis proper, and particularly psychoanalytic technique, explicitly drawing on their knowledge of and involvement with feminist theory and the women's movement. Furthermore, such contributions have tended to be confined to areas that are directly concerned with feminism, such as the study of gender and sexuality or the clinical implications of male and female patients working with male or female analysts.

Listen for the gender markers in the following quotation describing the shift from the classical to the relational model:

> The tradition of abstinence, detachment, and objectivity as methods of eliciting frustration, anxiety, and insight is founded in an authority relationship between analyst and analysand. The therapist is the unquestioned authority figure who cures by reason of his prestigious training and superior insight. He skillfully identifies and eradicates a patient's resistances through timely and well-articulated interpretations, thus permitting the surfacing of memory and the renunciation of infantile wishes. The relational model therapist, however, eschews such an authority relationship in favor of a "real relationship" between therapist and client. The therapist is a participant in the therapeutic encounter far more than an observer. She not only acknowledges her own countertransference as a normative component of therapy but she utilizes it as a means of deciphering what her client is experiencing. Rather than emphasizing interpretation, she privileges the therapeutic relationship as curative rather than hierarchical in nature [Philipson, 1993, p. 115].

While this comparison of classical and relational theory appears to be overly polarized, perhaps intentionally to caricature each position, nevertheless it serves its purpose in alerting us to the gender issues embedded in these theoretical models. It is thought provoking to consider how much many of the conceptualizations proposed in the present book and how many of the changes in psychoanalysis over the past few decades that have accompanied the ascendence of the relational model are connected to the fact that the analyst of earlier decades was a man in a predominantly male profession (medicine) that was accorded high status; whereas today the analyst is more likely to be a woman in a predominantly female profession (psychology and social work) that is accorded declining status.

As for the men (and keep in mind that what it is to be a man has also changed and been destabilized), remember that we are largely teaching and supervising women and delivering papers and writing books for a largely female audience who themselves are treating mostly women patients. These material realities coexist with the impact of feminism as an intellectual enterprise on all contemporary knowledge. While there are certainly larger intellectual currents flowing within the culture which have influenced both feminism and psychoanalysis, nevertheless, feminism itself has had a direct influence on psychoanalysis that most often goes unacknowledged. Philipson (1993) has rightfully pointed out that, with the exception of the contributors to and readers of *Psychoanalytic Dialogues: A Journal of Relational Perspectives,* very few relational theorists have acknowledged the impact of feminism on psychoanalytic relational theory. The feminist-psychoanalytic group associated with the relational track at NYU is notable among those exceptions.

Beginning with Simone de Beauvoir's (1949) *The Second Sex,* feminists identified key Freudian concepts that they found misogynistic, including such ideas as penis envy, biological determinism, and the related ideas of female passivity, narcissism, and masochism. With the liberation movements of the 1960s and the development of feminism in the 1970s, feminists such as Betty Friedan, Shulamith Firestone, Kate Millet, and Germaine Greer agreed in making Freud a common target. They argued that women's social position and powerlessness were socially constructed rather than caused by their biology.

Strikingly, contemporary psychoanalytic feminism has its roots in this very history of challenge and attack on Freud. As feminist theory developed and matured, feminists (re)turned to Freudian concepts and to psychoanalytic theory. In Britain, Juliet Mitchell (1974) argued against the then fashionable feminist attacks on Freud and suggested, that to the contrary, Freudian insights, particularly as filtered through Lacan's reading of Freud, were essential to the liberation of women. In America, in the 1970s and 80s, Nancy Chodorow (1978, 1989) was arguing that the centrality of sex and gender in the categories of psychoanalysis made it particularly suitable as a source of feminist theorizing. She suggested that, because mothering is done almost exclusively in our culture by women, men's and women's selves tend to be constructed differently. Women's selves are constructed in relation to mothers and men's selves are more distanced and detached, based more on defensively constructed boundaries and denials of self–mother connection. Where Juliet Mitchell had grounded her arguments in Lacanian theory, Chodorow grounded her contributions in object relations theory, although she strongly acknowledged their origins in the political and theoretical work of Karen Horney.

Continuing the project of integrating object relations theory and feminism begun by Chodorow, a group of feminist-psychoanalysts led by Jessica Benjamin, Muriel Dimen, Virginia Goldner, and Adrienne Harris (all of whom were to become associated with the Relational track of the NYU Postdoctoral Program) individually and jointly developed, elaborated, and disseminated versions of feminist-psycho-analysis informed by and closely allied to the Relational orientation. The presence of a large group of feminist-psychoanalysts within the Relational track has led this group of analysts to be more receptive than other psychoanalytic groups to the contributions of feminism.[4]

Among the most important contributions of contemporary feminist theorizing is that of the feminist/postmodernists to the critique of positivist epistemology, the power relations embedded in the authority of knowledge, and the challenge to the very notion of objectivity (Flax, 1990; Nicholson, 1990). It is to this intersection of feminism and postmodernism that I turn now .

POSTMODERNISM, CONSTRUCTIVISM, AND PERSPECTIVISM

If feminist consciousness was one major background factor in the proliferation of relational theory, then postmodern consciousness was another. Here I examine social constructivism as one variant of post-modern discourse which has had a sweeping influence on current thinking in psychoanalysis.

The most detrimental side effect of Freud's understanding of psycho-analysis as an objective science was his attempt to eliminate "the subjective factor" (cited in Grubrich-Simitis, 1986, p. 271) from the analytic situation. Freud believed that the analytic procedure he had developed led to consistent and replicable observations that, when compiled and systematized, would lead in turn to a scientific theory of mind, development, psychopathology, and cure. The analytic instru-

---

[4] Another group of feminist-psychotherapists that has made a significant contribution to clinical practice is based at The Stone Center, Wellesley College. This group, interestingly enough, also refer to themselves as proponents of "self-in-relation" theory or simply relational theory (see, for example, Surrey, 1985). Their work was influenced by the writings of Jean Baker Miller (1976), an interpersonally influenced analyst. Their emphasis on "mutual empathy" is taken up in Chapter 5. I mention them here to alert the reader that, although this group's work is also referred to as "relational" theory, it is not closely related to the body of relational theory taken up in this book. In my view, whatever commonality exists is largely based on the origin of some of these ideas in the earlier work of Nancy Chodorow (1978).

ment, like a microscope, had to be free of distorting influences, so that observations would be replicable by any observer who could use the instrument properly. The "subjective factor" was equated with arbitrariness. If analysts introduced their own personalities into their clinical work, than it could *not* be claimed that the resulting findings were objective or scientific.

Freud's determination to eliminate the subjective factor was characteristic of 19th-century scientific and scholarly thinking. In the search for general, universal laws and all-encompassing principles, scholars and scientists strove to achieve an objective view as opposed to expressing the perspective of a particular person. Freud's insistence on the neutrality, anonymity, and abstinence of the analyst is a reflection of the principle of scientific detachment that insists on the rigid demarcation between the observer and the observed. The analyst, as observer/scientist, is removed from the world of investigation, rather than situated at any point within it. Therefore, it can be assumed that the analyst acquires an objective view, a "view from nowhere" (Nagel, 1986), implying a totalistic view, objectivity, a view from everywhere simultaneously.

In recent years the impact of postmodernism has reverberated throughout the social and human sciences.[5] In broad and general terms, postmodernists oppose the uncritical acceptance of philosophical foundationalism; the Enlightenment heritage, with its emphasis on reason and rationality; and the methodological suppositions of modern science. In a postmodern world, theory is not thought of as innocent or detached, and truth is not conceptualized as neutral or objective. Truth claims are often seen as the product of power struggles in which the truth serves the interest of those with the most power. Hence, in its more radical forms, the distinction between truth and propaganda is undermined by postmodernists. Postmodern truth is perspectival, plural, fragmentary, discontinuous, kaleidoscopic, and ever-changing. Postmodern discourse rejects the totalizing metanarratives or masternarratives of 19th-century modernism, which claim to be scientific and objective, favoring pluralistic, decentered explanatory narratives.

---

[5] My brief remarks on postmodernism are intended to situate recent developments in psychoanalysis within a wider intellectual context. For readable introductions to postmodernism, see Sarup (1993), Best and Kellner (1991), and Resenau (1992). For a splendid introduction to the interrelationship among psychoanalysis, feminism, and postmodernism, see Flax (1990). For feminism, poststructuralism, and psychoanalysis, see Weedon (1987). For an interesting collection of readings on psychology and postmodernism, see Kvale (1992). For more on postmodernism and psychoanalysis, see Barratt (1993), and for a lively debate on the values and limitations of postmodernism on psychoanalysis, see Chessick (1995) and Price (1995).

Postmodern theory provides a critique of "representation"; the belief that our ideas and theories mirror or reflect reality. Instead, postmodernism takes the "relativist" position that theories provide only partial perspectives on their objects and emphasizes that our theories are historically and linguistically mediated. A variety of postmodern theories have tried to understand reality in constructivist and contextualist terms, with a focus on the social and linguistic construction of a perspectival reality. Furthermore, these theories are critical of the notion of a rational and unified subject and speak instead of a socially and linguistically decentered and fragmented subject.

While postmodernism has exerted a widespread influence in academic circles, none of the psychoanalysts whose contributions I discuss in this book have embraced postmodernism in its more extreme forms. Resenau (1992), in her discussion of the impact of postmodernism in the social sciences, makes a useful (although oversimplified and overly dichotomized) distinction between two broad general orientations within postmodernism: the more extreme, skeptical, and cynical postmodernism, and the more moderate, affirmative, and optimistic postmodernism. The more extreme, skeptical postmodernists tend to be influenced by Continental European philosophers, especially Heidegger and Neitzche, and emphasize the dark side of postmodernism, despair, the demise of the subject, the end of the author, the impossibility of truth, radical uncertainty, and the destructive character of modernity. The more moderate, affirmative postmodernists tend to be more indigenous to Anglo-North American culture and are more oriented to process, emphasizing a nondogmatic, tentative, and nonideological intellectual practice.

> These [affirmative] post-modernists do not, however, shy away from affirming an ethic, making normative choices, and striving to build issue-specific political coalitions. Many affirmatives argue that certain value choices are superior to others, a line of reasoning that would incur the disapproval of the skeptical post-modernists [Resenau, 1992, p. 16].

In short, skeptical postmodernists take these arguments to their extreme and lead us into a vicious circle of absolute uncertainty and extreme relativism; affirmative postmodernists are less concerned with categorical, epistemological rigor and more moderately offer a substantial contribution of revision and positive renewal. While these two groupings are greatly oversimplified, the distinction is useful to us here for understanding the impact of postmodernism on American relational analysts.

Smith (1994), in an attempt to take a "reasoned stance toward postmodernism" (p. 408), proposes that humanistic psychologists can abandon logical positivism, welcome social constructionism, accept cultural and contextualist criticism, and even embrace an interpretive hermeneutic framework without abandoning a conception of science as a social enterprise committed to an ideal of truth that can be evaluated pragmatically. Affirmative postmodernists argue that one can take these critiques seriously without foresaking the aspirations of ethical struggle toward the truth and the good. To whatever degree post-modernism has influenced a current generation of American relational analysts, it is clearly the more moderate, affirmative, and optimistic versions of postmodernism that are having this impact. It is arguable that this more moderate, affirmative stance may be better catego-rized as part of the tradition of critical modernism rather than of postmodernism.

In several brilliant and highly influential papers, Irwin Z. Hoffman (1983, 1987, 1990, 1991, 1992a, b, c, 1993, 1994, 1995; Gill and Hoff-man, 1982) has elaborated the psychoanalytic perspective that he calls "social-constructivism," which while not explicitly identified as a post-modern theory clearly conveys a distinctively affirmative postmodern sensibility. Hoffman emphasizes the analyst's inevitable personal par-ticipation in the analytic project. According to Hoffman, the patient's experience and understanding of the analyst as well as the analyst's experience of and understanding of the patient are "constructions" based both on their individual histories and characteristic organi-zational patterns and on their perceptions of the participation of the other. These constructions are not to be judged as right or wrong, accu-rate or distorted, transference or real relationship, but are better viewed as plausible constructions, one way among many to organize experience.

Hoffman's psychoanalytic social-constructivism is loosely related to a much larger intellectual movement known by a variety of names including social-constructivism and social-constructionism and consisting of epistemological developments associated with the post-modern turn. In contemporary psychology, social-constructionism (Berger and Luckmann, 1966) expresses the recognition that people actively construct ideas about themselves and their worlds of experi-ence and behavior in a social context.[6] Hoffman (1991) differentiates between the metapsychological shift from drive theory to a relational approach, on one hand, and the epistemological shift from positivism to constructivism, on the other. Hoffman (1991, 1995) has repeatedly argued that these two dimensions need to be distinguished since a

---

[6] For a description of their similarities and differences as well as for the intellectual history behind these ideas, see Gergen (1994).

theory may be relational and yet maintain an objectivist and positivist epistemology. As we will see in the next chapter, Hoffman's social-constructivism has been enormously influential for contemporary relational theorists and has been incorporated by Mitchell (1988a, 1993a) in his integrative relational approach to psychoanalytic theory.

Drawing on the writings of Mitchell and Hoffman, I have been using the terms relational-perspectivism and relational-constructivism to make explicit my effort to link together the epistemological shift from positivism to constructivism and the shift within psychoanalytic metapsychology from the drive-discharge, energic, one-person model to the relational, or two-person, perspective. I agree with Hoffman that the principles are conceptually distinct and that in practice not all relational theorists have taken a constructivist or perspectivist position. I would argue, however, that perspectivism is a potential consequence of any intersubjective or two-person psychology. To the degree that you take seriously that there are two separate subjectivities within the analytic dyad, two perspectives on the interaction—not one subject and one object, one irrational patient and one rational authority; not one transferentially distorting reality and one judging what is real, but two people each, with his or her own subjectivity; two observing-participants (Hirsch, 1987)—to that extent they each have a plausible perspective on the psychoanalytic interaction. Hence, these two seemingly separate dimensions are not completely independent; they are not "orthogonal" dimensions. As Gill (1995) pointed out, a relational view may or may not be constructivist, but the classical view is certainly positivist.

My preference is to use the word relational rather than social because the term social carries too much of the baggage of "social psychology" in connoting a behavioral or superficial level of analysis. Thus, it was characteristic of the classical critique of the early interpersonalists that they were denigrated as promoting a form of "social" psychology. "Social" is too often taken to mean external relationships, whereas the term relational has been associated with theorists who focus on both internal and external relations or on relations as they are psychically experienced rather than as they occur behaviorally or from the point of view of an external observer.

The terms perspectivism and constructivism are often used interchangeably. Perspectivism is the philosophical view that the external world may be understood through alternative systems of concepts and beliefs and that there is no authoritative independent criterion for determining that one such system is more valid than another. Perspectivism emphasizes that reality is always vast and ambiguous and that everyone has his or her own plausible viewpoint on reality, that all knowledge is perspectival, and that there are always perspectives other than one's own. Along these lines, I have come to think of psychoanalytic "neutrality" as the analyst's openness to new perspectives, a commitment to take other perspectives seriously, and a refusal to view any interpretation as complete or any meaning as exhaustive.

Levenson (1972) introduced perspectivism to psychoanalysis as a central organizer of his interpersonal approach. While relationalists and interpersonalists vary in their epistemological positions and specifically in how radical or conservative they are in their perspectivism, they all share a perspectivist epistemology if only in their shared emphasis on the contextual nature of clinical perception and interpretation (Fiscalini, 1994). In recent years, with the powerful impact of postmodernism and deconstructionism in academic circles and in cultural discourse more generally, most relational and interpersonal analysts have become increasingly radical in their perspectivism. As Fiscalini (1994) and Mitchell (1995a) have suggested, a more radical version of perspectivism or constructionism seems to contradict the traditional interpersonal emphasis on establishing, through a detailed inquiry, the "reality" of what happened in a patient's interpersonal life. Ironically, while Levenson (1972, 1983) did more than any other theorist to promote perspectivism within psychoanalysis, his commitment to a more traditional (modernist) interpersonal emphasis on establishing the "truth" of what happened to people has brought him criticism from Greenberg (1987), who suggests that Levenson relied too heavily on objectivism, and from Hoffman (1990), who derides Levenson's "special kind of disclaimed positivism" (p. 296). (See Levenson, 1990, for his response to this charge.)

On the other hand, Leary (1994), criticizing social-constructivism for its ahistoricism, argues for contemporary psychoanalysis to maintain a dialectical position between positivism and postmodernism. He writes: "Narrative reconceptualizations nod to historical reasons but these are then reinterpreted as present-day tellings. In key respects, postmodernism purges the analytic situation of the need to grapple with history, with things that once were and had an effect" (p. 457). Leary persuasively argues for the congruence of relational, interactional, intersubjective, and social-constructivist conceptualizations of psychoanalysis with postmodern theory. In depicting these trends as encouraging an extreme, anything goes, posture on the part of the analyst along with radical uncertainty and relativity of what the analysts can know, however, she seriously misreads Hoffman's thinking. Leary's critique would have benefited from an acknowledgment of the distinction, made by Resenau (1992), between radical and moderate or affirmative postmodernists. Leary conflates the arguments of relationalists, intersubjectivists, and social-constructionists with those of the more extreme postmodernists, instead of recognizing their far more moderate and affirmative point of view.

My preference for the term perspectivism or perspectivalism over constructivism or constructionism is based on the confusion created by the implications of radical constructivism and skeptical postmodernism. As both Hoffman (1992c) and Gill (1995) have suggested, they do not intend to imply a radical constructivism in which the certainty that an external reality exists is questioned, but only to argue that what we understand of reality is only a construction that we make of reality. "A construction is subject to the constraints of reality even if we cannot say what the reality is" (Gill, 1995, p. 2). Donnel Stern (1992), who has championed a constructivist approach to interpersonal psychoanalysis, similarly argues that, just because we claim that both patient and analyst play a substantial role in constructing what they agree to be the truth, we need not deny that reality itself has its own structure apart from that which we impose on it.

Even with all the caveats regarding the distinction between radical and critical constructivism, and even with all that has been written concerning how constructivism does not necessarily lead to the slippery slopes of relativism nor that what happened historically does not matter, it seems to me (in agreement with Orange, 1992) that the terms constructivism and constructionism continue to mislead people. I am sympathetic to Hoffman's (1992c) point, however, that the term constructivism gives added emphasis to people's active construction of their interpersonal worlds and highlights the patient's and analyst's mutual responsibility for shaping their interaction. All things considered, I prefer to avoid the confusion created by the term constructivism, and so I more often speak of relational-perspectivism. Social-constructivism is an important ingredient in the integrative relational position articulated by Mitchell (1988a, 1993a) and being extended here, a point that I develop further as I examine Mitchell's contributions in Chapter 2.

It should be clear that this narrative of the development of the relational orientation is a personal and especially a social-political one. I have thus far only hinted at a new theory or way of working. I have a great deal to say about theory and practice throughout this book. I must emphasize, though, that I think the history of developments in psychoanalysis must be understood on the level of local politics and personalities. Psychoanalysis as an intellectual endeavor is part of an ongoing conversation between people. A theoretical work must always be understood as part of an argument written to someone or in response to someone. Neither a theoretical nor a clinical paper can be understood outside of its interpersonal context.

From a social-constructionist perspective, theoretical knowledge is a product of social relationships (Gergen, 1994), and therefore the philosophy of science has been largely replaced on the intellectual agenda by a sociology of knowledge. Perhaps it is not surprising that I began this book by advocating a relational or social approach to teaching and understanding the development of psychoanalytic theory. In the next chapter, I will look in more detail at the substance of relational theory and its boundaries with other schools of thought.

2 | Relational Theory and Its Boundaries
One- and Two-Person Psychologies

STEPHEN MITCHELL'S RELATIONAL APPROACH

A large community of American psychoanalysts has been drawn together by enthusiasm for a relational approach to psychoanalysis. As we saw in Chapter 1, relational psychoanalysis is not so much a unified theoretical system as it represents a community of psychoanalysts who share a common clinical and theoretical sensibility. There are currently numerous relational models being elaborated in psychoanalysis, and many analysts who may not even think of themselves as relational are nevertheless using relational concepts in their thinking. Among the various psychoanalytic models proposed in recent years, the relational approach that has been most widely influential in America is that of Stephen Mitchell (Mitchell, 1988a, 1993a, 1995; Greenberg and Mitchell, 1983). When contemporary analysts refer to or criticize relational theory, it is generally Mitchell's work that they have in mind. I feature Mitchell's contributions here because I believe his work to be the most systematic, comprehensive, and compelling of the various relational integrations and because his work has been most personally influential on my own thinking and practice.

Mitchell's relational-conflict model represents a sophisticated, eclectic approach within psychoanalysis. Mitchell feels free to include a wide range of analytic theorists within the relational framework that he is building, even when these theorists are self-identified as belonging to other psychoanalytic traditions. Thus, he has borrowed from the contributions of such writers as Mahler, who maintained a general allegiance to the concept of drive, but who, according to Mitchell, developed perspectives that largely supplant it. He has drawn on the work of authors like Winnicott and Loewald, who wrote in drive-model language but who redefined the notion of drive or placed drives in a less central place in their theories. And, of course, he has included within his relational framework contributions from those like Sullivan and Fairbairn, who explicitly broke from the drive-theory framework.

A theorist's self-identification as a Freudian, an interpersonalist, an object relationist, or a self psychologist is of no consequence to Mitchell as he attempts to build an integrated relational approach. He employs relational concepts independently of where they originated. Mitchell does not deny that there are biological urges that are important in life, but he objects to viewing these "drives" as psychological bedrock, as the ultimate explanatory concepts of psychoanalytic theory. Mitchell argues that one can be critical of drive theory without necessarily minimizing the importance of the innate, the biological, sexuality, or the body. His critique simply displaces the drives from their position at the very center of the psychoanalytic explanatory system.

Mitchell (1993a, b) has identified the relational turn in psychoanalysis as revolutionary. He writes, concerning recent developments in psychoanalysis,

> I portray these developments as revolutions. My purposes are deliberately provocative. I want to emphasize discontinuities because I believe that an excessive preoccupation with traditionalism has impeded the recognition, working on and working through of the often stunning changes that have occurred in psychoanalytic thought in recent decades [Mitchell, 1993a, p. 8].

With this tone, Mitchell has contributed to the idea that relational theory is a heresy, a sharp break with the classical tradition, a new school of psychoanalysis. I am much more sympathetic to Mitchell's remarks later in the same paragraph: "Yet the psychoanalytic tradition, for which I have a deep love and respect, is best served by a framework that balances continuities with discontinuities, preservation with change, gratitude for what has preceded with an openness to moving on" (p. 8). I think that Mitchell is at his best when he moves back and forth between these positions, dialectically maintaining the tension between relational theory presented as revolutionary and relational theory depicted as evolutionary.[1]

Much of the success of relational theory in the past decade may be attributed to Mitchell's brilliant synthetic strategy. He argues that, for many years, leading psychoanalytic theorists expressed dissatisfaction with certain aspects of Freud's work. As soon as analysts dissented too much, mainstream psychoanalysis excommunicated them from the analytic community. Each dissident then established his or her own

---

[1] Mitchell (1993b) carefully considers the pros and cons of the evolutionary and revolutionary strategies of change in psychoanalysis.

heretical school of psychoanalysis, each with something important to contribute. But none of them, isolated from each other, was comprehensive enough to stand as a compelling alternative to Freudian theory. Mitchell, however, addresses what no one before seems to have noticed, namely, that these diverse schools all seemed to share certain key ideas. What many revisionist schools shared was that they tended, each in its own way, to be critical of Freudian drive theory and alternatively to emphasize the centrality of relationships between people, real and imagined, internal and external. This commonality was not obvious by any means because each school had developed in relative isolation from the other schools, often under historically diverse circumstances, in geographically separate locales, and under different cultural and linguistic circumstances. They tended to develop their own terminologies and journals, and adherents of one school were often not well read in the literature of the other approaches. Mitchell's point is that none of these schools individually could stand as a viable theoretical alternative to the comprehensiveness of Freudian thought, but, if their insights were brought together, a composite relational theory might be comprehensive enough to offer a viable alternative to the classical framework. Mitchell does not claim to have completed a finished theoretical system; rather he has attempted to formulate an approach that enables the analytic community to begin to work out such a system.

The relational approach uses the concept of the relational matrix, the web of relations between self and other, as the overarching framework within which to house all sorts of psychoanalytic concepts. Thus, Mitchell can bring together within one model those theorists, like Winnicott and Kohut, who have emphasized *the self*; those theorists, like Fairbairn and Klein, who have emphasized *the object*; and those theorists, like Bowlby and Sullivan, who have emphasized *the interpersonal space between self and other*. By elaborating the relational matrix of self and other, Mitchell is able to bring together concepts from diverse schools which in many other ways are contradictory and incompatible.

One way of viewing Mitchell's achievement is to think of his having forged a multinationalistic coalition consolidating diverse nations, some of which have conflicting interests in regard to other matters, but uniting them against a common adversary (classical theory). He has brought into one relational confederation a wide variety of alternative (nonclassical) analytic schools, in the hope that, even with their individual weaknesses, together they would be able to overcome the force of classical theory. To this end he is willing to overlook and minimize the differences between these groups so as to further the aims of the coalition. A younger generation of analysts, not as embroiled in older loyalties and allegiances, not pulled as much by their nationalistic impulses, might be willing to put their differences aside for a time and present a unified alternative to classical orthodoxy. Of course, there would be some elements from within each group that would resist fighting under anyone's flag but their own, wanting to maintain their national independence. (These militaristic metaphors are meant to capture the sense of struggle and conflict that goes on between theoretical and political analytic camps, nevertheless, they are not meant to depict hostile motivations.) I believe that, while there is a certain healthy competitiveness and rivalry between the various schools, there has also been a growing sense of good will and dialogue between the positions.

Mitchell has done more than just bring together a loose confederacy of relational theories. He has added his own emphases and sensibilities and structured his theory along certain lines. Mitchell's synthesis goes beyond any of the individual relational theories. The whole is more than the sum of its parts. In bringing these theories together, Mitchell modified them by adding two important principles, neither of which is necessarily relational: a focus on conflict and personal agency and a social-constructivist epistemology.

Conflict and Agency

First, drawing on the classical tradition, Mitchell (1988a) consistently emphasizes conflict in his approach. Unlike in the drive model, however, "in the relational-conflict model, the antagonists in the central psychodynamic conflicts are relational configurations" (p. 10). Mitchell's emphasis on conflict is an attempt to preserve an aspect of the classical tradition that was underemphasized by many previous relational theorists. Some relational theorists had emphasized developmental deficits or developmental arrests and had thereby neglected the individual's conflicts. In eliminating a focus on conflict, people were often depicted as the passive victims of their childhood traumas. Analysis then took on the role of "reparenting" them, providing reparative experiences, a form of "replacement therapy" (Guntrip, 1971, p. 191) to make up for what they had been cheated out of in childhood. Hence, Mitchell's distinction between "relational-deficit" approaches and his own "relational-conflict" approach. In his own relational synthesis, Mitchell did not want to minimize the person as agent of his or her own life. Influenced both by the classical model, particularly as it had been transformed by Loewald and Schafer, as well as by the existential tradition, Mitchell has attempted a relational synthesis that highlights the individual's conflicts, will, and agency.

Classical critics have greatly misunderstood Mitchell in this regard. Bachant, Lynch, and Richards (1995) write, "Appreciably diminished in Mitchell's perspective is an understanding of the intrapsychic dimension of conflict, of those factors *in the person*, engendered by unconscious wishes and fears from the earliest phases of life, that interact with how the environment is experienced" (p. 77). Similarly, Wilson (1995) writes:

> Mitchell argued that his is a conflict theory because it stipulates conflict between a person and his or her environment. This is quite different from what most contemporary analysts define as intrapsychic conflict—namely ideational conflict between mental elements warding each other off, not a theory of rough-and-tumble human life [p. 18].

These tendentious readings ignore Mitchell's main points. In Mitchell's relational-conflict theory, people are viewed as inevitably conflicted, not only torn between loyalties to different figures in their lives, but divided in their feelings toward and identifications with various aspects of each person in their lives. Furthermore, following Fairbairn, Mitchell makes clear that these conflicts are internalized and continually divide people's selves, leaving the internal world constituted by a variety of internal structures in conflict with one another.

A careful reading of Bachant, Lynch and Richard's (1995) and Wilson's (1995) critiques, reveals that the problem for them is that Mitchell views conflict differently than they do. Like any theoretical construct, "conflict" will have different meanings in different theoretical contexts. The Freudian conception of conflict is embedded in a framework of drives, and so those authors ask, where is the emphasis on "unconscious wishes and fears"? Mitchell places great emphasis on unconscious wishes and fears (the title of his 1993 book, *Hope and Dread in Psychoanalysis*, reflects just this emphasis), but what is emphasized in Mitchell's theory is the relational context of these wishes and fears, rather than their origins in biological drive. What is central for Mitchell is conflict between various relational configurations. Similarly, Bachant, Lynch, and Richards ask where those factors are "*in the person*," where the "intrapsychic dimension of conflict" is. But to look for these terms in Mitchell's approach is to prejudge the issue (see Mitchell, 1993b). The very point of Mitchell's contribution is to argue that conflict is not best regarded as "intrapsychic" or located "in the person," but rather that conflict may best be conceptualized as relational (i.e., both intrapersonal and interpersonal) and that it is central to psychoanalysis and inevitable and universal in human life. Mitchell's (1988a) version of relational theory points out that "*conflict is inherent in relatedness*" (p. 160). Other relational theorists (Greenberg, 1991; Hoffman, 1995) have also addressed the centrality of conflict within their own theoretical perspectives and have developed and elaborated their ideas about this quite explicitly.

In the criticisms of Mitchell's work by a number of contemporary Freudian authors,[2] we encounter an obstacle that makes defining the relational approach very difficult, namely, that, to a great degree, relational theory is defined in opposition to or as an extension of classical theory or American ego psychology. The tricky problem is that it is not clear that classical theory understood drives in precisely the way relational theorists describe, nor is it apparent that classical theory did not attend to personal relations as well. As a matter of fact, it is clear (as Mitchell acknowledges) that classical theorists always considered relations with others, object relations, to be critically important. Hence the question becomes, Are relations with others important to relational theorists in a way that is significantly different from how they were important to classical theorists? And even if classical theory was based on drive theory, and even if it did place less emphasis on interpersonal relations, nevertheless, it has clearly progressed and evolved so that contemporary Freudian theory might include these emphases. These arguments lead classical authors to object that relational theorists compare their own theory to an outdated and distorted classical theory.

Practitioners of classical theory feel misunderstood; they object that relational critics have set up a straw man to attack. While I can certainly understand that classical analysts feel challenged and even threatened by the growing popularity and increasing dominance of the relational paradigm in American psychoanalysis, there is no excuse for the shabby scholarship and disdainful tone of many of these critics toward Mitchell and other relational theorists. In attempting any comparative psychoanalysis, it is probably unavoidable that both sides will feel that their positions are being unfairly caricatured. It is quite clear, however, that Mitchell has carefully studied the classical and contemporary Freudian literature, has cited it extensively, and has been deeply influenced by Freudian authors; the reverse cannot be said. Freudian critics of relational theory appear to have hardly read the relational literature. Their familiarity with it is superficial at best, and they have treated it out of context and with little evidence of having studied it with any seriousness. One might not agree with Greenberg and

---

[2] My discussion here of Freudian critics of the relational approach is largely drawn from the special section of *Psychoanalytic Psychology* devoted to "Contemporary Structural Psychoanalysis and Relational Psychoanalysis," especially, Sugarman and Wilson, 1995; Wilson, 1995; Bachant, Lynch, and Richards, 1995.

Mitchell's (1983) interpretation of Freudian theory, but one would be hard pressed to say that it was not a serious and scholarly study of that tradition. So far, at least, critics of the relational model have not treated it with comparable or appropriate seriousness of purpose.

Social-Constructivism

To return now to our overview of Mitchell's relational integration, the second catalyst Mitchell uses in his cooking of concepts to create a relational stew is the epistemology of hermeneutics and constructivism. As I discussed in Chapter 1, these postmodern epistemological trends have criticized the archeological and reconstructive model of psychoanalysis. Instead of seeing the psychoanalytic method as exposing what is there, hiding behind the surface, buried in the depths, it sees the analytic method as a particular way of organizing what is there into uniquely psychoanalytic patterns. "To say that human experience is fundamentally ambiguous is to say that its meaning is not inherent or apparent in it but that it lends itself to multiple understandings, multiple interpretations" (Mitchell, 1993a, p. 58). Mitchell was influenced here by Spence (1982) and Schafer (1983) among others who have employed hermeneutics—the study of the principles of interpretation—in reformulating psychoanalytic theory.

According to hermeneutic philosophers Ricoeur (1970) and Habermas (1971), Freud suffered from a "scientistic self-misunderstanding" in regarding psychoanalysis as a natural science. According to these theorists, psychoanalysis is fundamentally a study of meanings rather than a search for causal connections.[3] Spence (1982) argued that the psychoanalytic process is not one of archeological reconstruction but is, rather, an active construction of a narrative about the patient's life. The analyst assembles, on the basis of psychoanalytic theory, a coherent picture of the patient's life that takes on a "narrative truth" rather than being a "historic truth." Patient and analyst, from Spence's hermeneutic perspective are pattern makers rather than pattern finders. Similarly, Schafer (1983) emphasizes that reality is always mediated by narration, that the narrative arrived at in psychoanalysis is constructed on the basis of the analyst's theory. It is not that the theory guides the analyst in "uncovering" what is already there in the patient's mind, in "the unconscious." Rather, the analyst's theory guides the analyst in shaping and organizing the patient's free associative material.

---

[3] For critical discussions of the value of hermeneutics, see Grünbaum (1984), the collection by Messer, Sass, and Woolfolk (1988), and a two-part Symposium: "What Does the Analyst Know?" (1993).

In Chapter 1, I introduced the general principles of social-constructivism as they have been articulated by Irwin Z. Hoffman (1991). While Hoffman (1983) has expressed criticism of both Sullivan's original interpersonal theory as well as Levenson's more contemporary version of interpersonal theory (see the debate between Hoffman, 1990, and Levenson, 1990), nevertheless social-constructivism is in many respects compatible with the clinical sensibilities of the interpersonal tradition and may indeed be seen as an extension of the work of Sullivan and Levenson (along with the perhaps even more important neo-Kleinian contributions of Racker, 1968). It is these compatibilities between Hoffman's social-constructivism and interpersonal and relational theories that made Hoffman's approach so appealing to Mitchell. Since Hoffman's contributions have played a significant role in the development of Mitchell's relational approach, I want to distinguish Hoffman's view from that of analysts like Schafer and Spence, who have long been advocating the revisioning of psychoanalysis as a hermeneutic, or narrative, enterprise. Like them, Hoffman proposes the abandonment of positivism as the fundamental paradigm for psychoanalysis. Positivism, or objectivism, encourages the belief that the analyst can eliminate the impact of his or her own subjectivity and observe from a detached perspective the object of scientific investigation, from outside the system, thus discovering "objective truth" that is reliably independent of the observer's subjectivity. Constructivism emphasizes that the observer plays a role in shaping, constructing, and organizing what is being observed. The term social emphasizes that therapy is a social, two-person process, but, more importantly, that all knowledge is derived socially.

Hoffman's position is decidedly more radical than either Schafer's or Spence's. Hoffman's contribution is unique in his fundamental emphasis on the analyst's continual personal participation. Whereas Schafer and Spence are more inclined to emphasize that the analyst's *theory* plays a continual influence, Hoffman's argument places more emphasis on how the analyst's *personality* plays a continual influence. Hoffman (1992a) considers the arguments of those like Schafer and Spence to represent a "limited constructivist view" (p. 290). Hoffman is critical of Schafer in this regard because Schafer (1983) continues to believe that an "analytic attitude" purified of personal factors, uncontaminated by the analyst's subjectivity, may be obtained through "continuous scrutiny of countertransference" (221). But in Hoffman's (1992a) social-constructivist view, "it is the current of countertransference that is continuous, not its scrutiny" (p. 291).

Bruner (1993) has similarly criticized Spence in this regard. Spence's writing, like Schafer's, suggests that if one takes into account the analyst's subjectivity, theoretical bias, and cultural surround, then one can get to the facts. Bruner, pointing to this underlying assumption in Spence's (1993) work, refers to him as a "closet positivist" (Bruner, 1993, p. 12). Hoffman's description of this as a "limited constructivist view" and Bruner's calling Spence a "closet positivist" are both reactions to Spence's and Schafer's belief that, with enough countertransference analysis, with enough stripping away of the impact of the analyst's subjectivity, something like "the facts" can be "objectively" reached.

To return again to Mitchell's relational-conflict model, his (Mitchell, 1988a) synthesis brought together the wide range of relational theorists, those who emphasized the self, those who emphasized the object, and those who focused on the interaction between self and other. He brought these theorists together whether they emphasized deficit or conflict, positivism or constructivism; and he reworked them into a complex synthesis that maintained a continual emphasis on conflict (and with conflict, personal agency); perspectivism, hermeneutics, and constructivism; and an overarching two-person (field-theoretical) perspective. Building on this earlier work and now incorporating the contributions of a wider community of relational analysts, Mitchell (1993a) has synthesized two broad revolutions in recent psychoanalytic thought: a revolution in theory concerning what the patient needs, and a revolution in epistemology concerning what the analyst can know. Concerning what the patient needs, Mitchell suggests that in recent psychoanalytic theory (following the shift from drive to relational theory) the emphasis has shifted from insight and renunciation of infantile wishes to the development of meaning and authenticity. Concerning what the analyst can know, postmodern influences (including social-constructivism) have led us to be skeptical of objective, universal knowledge and to emphasize instead a facility with a variety of story lines and theories all deeply embedded in our own personal subjectivity.

RELATIONAL THEORY AND ITS BOUNDARIES

It is not only the Freudians who have been critical of Mitchell and others who are building a relational approach. Purists from within the interpersonal, object relational, and self psychology perspectives have raised objections as well. Mitchell has been chided by some for synthesizing approaches that, they point out, are incompatible. Whereas Mitchell emphasizes the commonalities of the interpersonal school with the object relations school, Summers (1994) argues that there is a sharp division between these two schools. Object relations theorists tend to emphasize the role of early relationships in organizing the internal structuralization of mind, whereas interpersonal theorists, he asserts, tend either to disregard development or to view development as nothing but a series of relationships. "In the conceptualization of the treatment process," Summers writes, "the interpersonalists place far greater emphasis on the analyst's role in shaping the interaction than do even those theorists who propose an interactional extension of object relations theories" (p. 337). Furthermore, from the point of view of Summers's object relations theory, interpersonal theory minimizes not only developmental issues but concepts of psychopathology as well. According to Summers, because interpersonalists view all personal difficulties as inherent in relationships, they tend to depreciate conceptualizations of psychopathology. Furthermore, interpersonal theory abandons all notions of internal structure and therefore cannot describe the structural basis of psychopathology. Summers therefore objects to Mitchell's relational synthesis since he sees Mitchell as adopting too many of the limitations of interpersonal theory. In short, Summers favors the purity of an object relations perspective and emphasizes the disadvantages of a hybrid of object relations theory and interpersonal theory.

Summers greatly exaggerates the deficiencies of interpersonal theory. Stern (1994), for example, extensively documents the many ways interpersonal theorists use structural concepts. Summers's criticisms, however, are actually similar to those leveled against interpersonal theory by Mitchell and other relationalists themselves. Indeed, as we discussed earlier, one of the major reasons that Mitchell advocates bringing these two theories together is precisely because he believes that the structural and developmental concepts that are minimized in interpersonal theory may be supplemented by object relations conceptualizations. Summers's preference, insofar as he emphasizes the difficulties with interpersonal theory, is to maintain a more purely object relations theory. Mitchell's preference, since both interpersonal and object relations theories have their limitations, is to bring them together and use each to correct the flaws in the other.

There are indeed significant differences between interpersonal theory and object relations theory, just as there are profound differences between self psychology and interpersonal theory and self psychology and object relations theory. For that matter, none of these schools of thought is homogeneous. One can point to significant differences between Fairbairn's and Winnicott's object relations theory, among the numerous contemporary versions of self psychology, and between Sullivan's and Fromm's interpersonal theories. These schools are built upon certain choices and assumptions; they are constructions. Mitchell never minimizes the differences between interpersonal theory and object relations theory. He explicitly acknowledges that in certain respects they are incompatible.

What are the benefits and risks of emphasizing the similarities of relational theories versus the differences between them? My own feeling is that it is strategically useful to emphasize their similarities. By doing so, we have created a movement within psychoanalysis that allows analysts of very diverse schools of thought to recognize that they have something in common, namely, the shift away from a focus on drive theory and toward more relational considerations. Students have become interested in a broad approach to psychoanalysis that serves as an alternative to the classical model. This recognition of our commonalities does not prevent us from examining the very interesting differences between us once what we share has been acknowledged.

My larger point is again a constructivist one. These are personal choices. We can (1) construct a model that emphasizes the sharp differences between classical theory and relational theory; (2) we can emphasize differences between relational models; or (3) we can emphasize the way in which classical theory always was a relational theory. My pragmatist leanings suggest that, rather than ask which of these is more true or valid, we need to ask what the practical consequences are of constructing our theories one way versus another.[4] Clearly, I believe that Mitchell's strategy was very useful for the field. The construction of a relational model that offers an alternative to the classical model has led to incredible intellectual excitement within the field. There are, however, difficulties created by the establishment of any "school," and we will be dealing with these for a long time to come.

Merton Gill (1994) viewed relational theory as essentially a derivative of interpersonal theory, and I am largely in agreement with this view. Like interpersonal theory, relational theory places its emphasis on interpersonal relations, real and imagined. However, Edgar Levenson, perhaps the foremost spokesperson for contemporary interpersonal theory and a major influence on Mitchell, has been quite critical of Mitchell's relational synthesis. Levenson's (1991, 1992) critique of "the new psychoanalytic revisionism" seems to come down to his belief that relational approaches, unlike his own interpersonal approach, generalize and even universalize the important motivations and developments

---

[4] As elaborated by Rorty (1979), William James suggested that truth is "what is better for us to believe" rather than "the accurate representation of reality. . . . Or, to put the point less provocatively, they show us that the notion of 'accurate representation' is simply an automatic and empty compliment which we pay to those beliefs which are successful in helping us do what we want to do" (p. 10).

in human life. He depicts his own brand of interpersonalism as being the only psychoanalytic school of thought that pays attention to the particularities of the individual's life, rather than generalizing on the basis of a universal developmental theory.

Levenson's (1991) argument is very similar to that of another lead-ing interpersonal theorist, Herbert Zucker, who is also extremely criti-cal of the attempt at theoretical synthesis undertaken under the umbrella of relational theory. Zucker (1989) argues that relational the-orists, both of the British object relations school and the American self psychology school, posit a single drive as the basis of human motivation and elevate that single drive to an all-explanatory principle. For Zucker, even though relational theory shifted its emphasis away from the classical drives of sex and aggression to that of an object-seeking drive, it nevertheless maintains much in common methodologically with classical theory, in that both theories reduce human complexity to a single or limited set of explanatory principles. It is the granting of near-total explanatory power to a particular category of motivation that is the methodological weakness of drive theories of any type, according to Zucker.

Consider the following as an example of the subtleties and complexi-ties of dialogue across psychoanalytic schools of thought. This example demonstrates how relational theory can be meaningfully understood only as arising historically out of the dialectic between Freudian and interpersonal points of view, as we examined in Chapter 1. In his modern-day Freudian critique of relational theory, Wilson (1995) claims that the solutions offered by relational theorists risk locking the analyst into an environmental position. He writes: "The clinician who maps the mind this way is limited to interventions that are pulled to the external, with little or no anchoring in the internal. The give-and-take of relationship factors is the priority, and the mind disappears from view" (p. 17). But, as we have previously questioned in regard to conflict, is it that relational theory ignores conflict, or is it that there is a shift in how conflict is conceptualized? Similarly, is it that mind disappears from view, or is it that the very nature of mind is thought about in a new way? As we have seen, it was precisely out of the concern that interpersonal theory was mistakenly being used to support such an environmentalist position, focusing only on external relations rather than on internal ones, that the relational group came about. Ironically, classical analysts are here criticizing relational analysts for precisely the same thing that relational analysts were criticizing in interpersonal theory. Mitchell's (1988b) point was that object relations concepts could complement interpersonal theory just because it contributed ideas about how the private, inner world was organized.

Now, on the other side, interpersonalists like Zucker (1989) criticize relational analysts for making too much of concepts of inner organization, such as "internal objects." For Zucker, "Even taken as a metaphor, the conception is reminiscent of classical methodology, of the id and the ego, of independent agencies endowed with intrinsic energy operating mechanistically outside of self and volition" (p. 411). Zucker fears that such a theory leads to an emphasis in which internal objects supersede experience. In comparing the Freudian critique, and the interpersonal critique we begin to see how relational analysts, in their attempt to take what is valuable from both sides of the theoretical spectrum, leave themselves vulnerable to attack from both sides. The development of psychoanalytic theory can be understood dialogically only as evolving out of ongoing conversation. Freudians, object relations theorists, interpersonalists, and relationalists often have a hard time understanding each other because they have such different histories and live in diverse psychoanalytic cultures. To contemporary structural theorists like Wilson (1995), relationalists seem to focus on external social relations and neglect principles of conflict and inner organization. To interpersonalists like Zucker (1989), relationalists are too caught up with concepts of inner organization like internal objects and therefore are liable to neglect interpersonal experience. Each view developed in relation to and in reaction to the other. They can begin to talk to each other only as each understands more about the others' histories, cultures, languages, and traditions. The type of scholarship required for comparative psychoanalysis (Schafer, 1983) requires long and deep immersion in the foreign cultures of other psychoanalytic traditions, not a quick reading of someone else's book with an eye to finding its flaws.

We have seen that for Freudian critics, relational theory is too similar to interpersonal theory in its neglect of conflict (as they define conflict between drive and defense) and in its avoidance of mapping out inner psychic organization. Similarly, for an advocate of object relations theory like Summers (1994), Mitchell, like interpersonal theorists, neglects the structure of psychic organization and therefore abandons a theory of psychopathology. For the interpersonalists, the problem with relational theory is that it has not gone far enough in its movement away from classical methodology. While it has shifted away from Freud's dual-drive theory of sex and aggression, it has nevertheless retained a narrow explanatory system, with a focus on object seeking, on one hand, and maintenance of the self, on the other. In essence, while relational theorists believe that what they have in common, and what distinguishes them from classical theory, is precisely their rejection of drive theory and their replacement of it with a focus on interpersonal relations, these interpersonal critics have pointed out that relational analysts have essentially maintained a form of drive theory that, while different from Freud's, still reduces the enormous complexity of human behavior. As a consequence of maintaining this reductionistic methodology, they further suggest, relational analysts underemphasize the reality of the analyst–analysand interaction and instead overemphasize fantasy, internal objects, and psychic reality.

This is a challenging critique, but I believe that these interpersonal theorists underestimate the extent to which they too must make use of generalizations and reduce the complexity of human behavior and the degree to which relational theorists do indeed attend to the interpersonal interaction within the analysis. One problem is that both Levenson and Zucker mistakenly confuse Mitchell and his colleagues' more recent relational integrations with those of their forerunners in traditional object relations theory. As Summers (1994) has pointed out, contemporary relational theorists focus on the transference–countertransference as a mutual coconstruction in a way that classical object relations theorists never have. Levenson and Zucker have not realized just how much interpersonal theory has been used by relational thinkers in building their new model. Interestingly, the Freudian critiques, as well as Summers's critique from the object relations side (which implies that relational theory is too close to the interpersonal), and Levenson and Zucker's critique from the interpersonal side (which implies that relational theory is too close to the classical/object relational) establish the sense of tension with which relational theory continually struggles.

In a most interesting way, the complexity of relational theory becomes apparent when one studies the objections raised by its critics. Relational analysts have not been impervious to their critics, and in recent years there has been an attempt on the part of some leading relational analysts to conceptualize a coherent motivational theory that does not reduce behavior to a single motivational factor. Greenberg (1991), for example, elaborates on the dangers of single-motivational systems. Greenberg agrees that theorists like Kohut and Fairbairn implicitly have proposed single-drive systems in which behavior is explained in terms of a single motivational thrust. In these systems, intrapsychic conflict is indeed minimized because, if there is a single drive, then conflict can result only from incompatibility between the individual and the external environment. Greenberg therefore argues for a new dual-drive theory and suggests that behavior be understood as resulting from the interplay of two broad motivational systems, the need for effectance and the need for safety. By positing a purely psychological dual-drive theory, Greenberg can continue to explain the inevitability of intrapsychic conflict.

In a critical review of Greenberg's proposal, Hoffman (1995) argues against the reduction of fundamental motives to just two drives. Instead, he argues that we are better off with a multiple-drive theory that might include a variety of polarities. Thus, we could have a drive theory that included several independent axes. Examples would include, in addition to effectance versus safety, love versus hate, and object seeking or attachment versus a need for separation. This multiple-drive framework would retain the benefit of thinking along the lines of the great polarities in life and would therefore maintain a clinical focus on conflict but would have the advantage of not arbitrarily reducing all conflict to one fundamental issue.

Emmanuel Ghent (1992a), another leading relationalist, has suggested yet another drive theory as a central polarity in life. Angyal (1965) distinguished between the dual tendencies of autonomy (the drive to make things happen, assertion, competence, and mastery) and homonomy (the drive to surrender oneself to something greater than oneself). Earlier, Buber (1947) had made a distinction between these dual tendencies in positing an "originator instinct" (the need to make things) and the "instinct for communion" (the need to enter into mutuality). (In Chapter 5, I will look more carefully at Buber's ideas concerning mutuality.) Building on these broad categories of motivation, as well as on Sullivan's (1953) distinction between needs for security and needs for satisfaction, Ghent (1992a) suggests that there are two basic opposing motivational thrusts in all living beings. He refers to them as "expansive versus conservative, centrifugal versus centripetal, growth-oriented versus status-quo oriented, and so on" (p. xxi). These drives are conceptualized as being in certain circumstances adversarial and at other times quite complementary, but adopting this framework leads to a focus on the inevitability of internal human conflict.

Many relational analysts have also been persuaded by Lichtenberg's (1989) motivational theory, which brings together the findings of infancy research and psychoanalytic clinical studies, especially those of self psychology. Lichtenberg posits five motivational systems: the need for psychic regulation of physiological requirements; the need for attachment and affiliation; the need for exploration and assertion; the need to respond aversively through antagonism, withdrawal, or both; and the need for sensual enjoyment and sexual excitement. All these motivational systems, although based on innate needs, become psychological motives in the course of infant–caregiver interactions.

Were the interpersonal critics right all along? Was relational theory just a way to reintroduce drive theory while pretending to be more interpersonal? Once you introduce such nonoperational concepts as internal objects and psychic reality, can drives be far behind? Relational theorists turn this question back onto the interpersonalists (for an example of one such debate, see Levenson, 1991; Mitchell, 1992; Ghent, 1992c; Fosshage, 1992, and Levenson's, 1992, reply; also see Greenberg, 1987, and Levenson, 1987b). Can it really be that interpersonalists work without some implicit theory of drives? Is it really possible that interpersonal analysts do not have some implicit ideas about what people are struggling with that amount to a "universal" or "general" theory of human behavior? Do not interpersonalists assume that people universally need to relate to other people, and does not the avoidance of anxiety work pretty much like a basic motive or drive? Can anyone listen to the ambiguities and complexities inherent in any clinical narrative and not "reduce" this complexity along some theoretically biased lines so as to make it comprehensible? And no matter how you organize the material in order to understand it and keep it manageable, do you not do that along some theoretical lines that you have brought to the analytic situation? So, are relationalists more reductionistic if they choose to articulate the fundamental motivational lines that they construct as central? Can interpersonalists eliminate any notion of drives without becoming antitheoretical or obscuring the degree to which underlying theoretical bias shapes their own clinical interactions?

I do not wish to debate the pros and cons of these varying relational proposals regarding human motivation. They are each interesting to me, and I certainly agree on the importance of not reducing motivation to any single factor as well as with the value of recognizing the great polarities of life and the inevitability of human conflict. My point, however, is that relational theory began with the assumption that the one thing that relational analysts had in common, as opposed to classical theorists, was that relational analysts had moved away from drive concepts and had replaced drives with relations as the central explanatory concept in psychoanalysis. But relational analysts do *not* have even this in common. Rather, we are at a point now where relational analysts are arguing about which drives to emphasize and how best to conceptualize them. Of course, relational analysts do have in common their rejection of Freud's very specific dual-drive theory. Even for those relational theorists who use drive constructs, drives are not defined in biological terms, as they were in Freud's theory, but rather are thought of as purely psychological constructs. For relational analysts, the actualization of these drives as human needs and the specific form that these needs take derive from the qualities of interpersonal experience (Ghent, 1989). Relational theory attempts to maintain the tension between one- and two-person psychologies, inherent motivations (conceptualized in purely psychological terms) and relations, the intrapsychic and the interpersonal, the bodily and the social. It is precisely because it tries to keep this tension, pulling from a variety of traditions in order to do so, that it is subject to misunderstanding and attack from all sides. It is to these complementarities that I now turn.

ONE-PERSON AND TWO-PERSON PSYCHOLOGIES

Relational theory has been identified as a two-person psychology in contrast to classical theory, which is treated as a one-person psychology. What is meant by a one-person and a two-person psychology? In what sense is relational theory a two-person psychology? In what sense is it legitimate to think of classical theory as a one-person psychology? Would it make more sense to think of relational theory as maintaining both one- and two-person psychologies? Is this even a meaningful or useful way to categorize psychoanalytic theories? Does the distinction between one- and two-person psychologies aid in our efforts at comparative psychoanalysis, or does it further obscure our vision?

In his 1950 review of changing aims and techniques in psychoanalysis, Michael Balint, Sándor Ferenczi's analysand and disciple, argued that, because of Freud's "physiological or biological bias," he unnecessarily limited his theory by formulating the basic concepts and aims of psychoanalysis in terms of the individual mind. Balint pointed out that, in the psychoanalytic situation, relations to an object are of overwhelming importance, and he proposed therefore that classical psychoanalytic theory be supplemented by a theory of object relations.

John Rickman, also an analysand of Ferenczi, wrote: "The whole region of psychology may be divided into areas of research according to the number of persons concerned. Thus we may speak of One-Body Psychology, Two-Body, Three-Body, Four-Body and Multi-Body Psychology" (cited in Balint, 1950, p. 123). Balint borrowed Rickman's terms to make the point that the clinical psychoanalytic situation is a two-body experience and that it cannot be adequately conceptualized in terms of classical theory, which hardly goes beyond the domain of one-body psychology. A two-body, or object relations, theory was needed to describe events that occur between people.

Classical Theory

The theory of instinctual drives is the cornerstone of Freud's metapsychology, and Freud's fundamental conceptualizations are formulated with drive theory as an underlying assumption. Implicit in drive theory is a view of the human being as a biologically closed system seeking to discharge energy in order to maintain homeostasis. From the perspective of classical psychoanalytic theory, the fundamental unit of study is the individual, and therefore all that is interpersonal must ultimately be traced back to the vicissitudes of drive and defense, to the intrapsychic, and to the realm of a one-person psychology.

Many analysts mistakenly believe that, while Freudian metapsychology is based on a one-person psychology, the clinical theory has always been a two-person one. How could it be otherwise when there has always been so much emphasis in the clinical theory on transference and the importance of the analyst as an object? Thus, Modell (1984) suggests that "transference and countertransference phenomena have never been considered anything but events occurring within a two-person context" (p. 3). The view of Freud's clinical theory as having always been a two-person psychology receives support in a number of statements of Freud's.

> A correctly executed psycho-analysis is from this point of view a social process, a "mass structure of two," according to an utterance of Freud, in which the analyst must take the place of the whole heterogeneous environment, particularly of the most important persons in the surroundings of the patient [Ferenczi and Rank, 1924].

That in some of his clinical remarks Freud may have recognized that psychoanalysis was a "social process" that constituted a "mass structure of two" does not negate that Freudian metapsychology inevitably constructed the object of psychoanalytic investigation as the individual mind, a one-person psychology. In my view, this artificial distinction between the clinical theory and the metapsychology obscures the recognition that the most fundamental psychoanalytic clinical concepts and procedures were formulated and historically understood as one-person phenomena. Transference was not conceptualized as an interpersonal event occurring between two people but, rather, was understood as a process occurring within the mind of the analysand. "The long-held view of transference," Gill (1994) writes, "was not one of a relationship between two people, but rather of the distorted view of the analyst by the analysand" (p. 36). Transference was thought to be determined by the patient's developmental history and was viewed in terms of displacements from the past. It was thought that if the analyst was analyzing correctly, being technically neutral and anonymous, then the transference would spontaneously unfold and would not be distorted by the personality of the analyst. This is clearly a "one-person" conceptualization of the nature of transference. I believe it can be easily demonstrated that all our fundamental clinical notions have been conceptualized as intrapsychic events, explicable in terms of the psychology of one person.

In an exchange regarding this topic, Donald Kaplan (1988, personal communication) objected to my portrayal of classical psychoanalysis as a "one-person psychology." He wrote:

> I barely recognize your version of so-called classical psychoanalysis. I have only the faintest idea, for example, what you mean by a one-person psychology, since I always read Freud, even before 1914, as a three-variable psychology and always think of the clinical situation as an oedipal triangle—the patient, the analyst, and the profession to which the analyst is married, a marriage creating primal scene issues for the patient.

Kaplan's argument is essentially that, inasmuch as the clinical situation is always understood as recreating an oedipal triangle, it does not make any sense to refer to psychoanalysis as a one-person psychology. The problem with this line of reasoning is the same as we just encountered in discussing transference. Yes, transference has always clearly involved both patient and analyst in the consulting room; but our theory refers the process back to the mind of the individual patient. Similarly, Kaplan's oedipal understanding of the primal scene issues created by the analytic situation refers back to the oedipal dynamics of the patient. Let me illustrate.

An analyst ends a session at the correct time. The patient experiences this ending as an oedipal defeat, a reenactment of exclusion from the primal scene. The analyst, wedded to his or her profession, is more committed to Freud than to the patient, the patient thinks. So the patient is thrown out of the room because of the analyst's devotion to another. What would be emphasized in the interpretation is how the patient's mind works to create oedipal scenarios out of whatever experience is available.

While I am impressed with the value of searching for oedipal meanings in the patient's material, it seems to me that a two-person or relational position would have to push the inquiry further. On hearing this material, I would be interested not only in the patient's oedipal dynamics and genetic history, but also in the following questions: What is the nature, extent, and quality of this particular analyst's marriage to his or her theory? Is this particular analyst rigidly attached to a theory that really does interfere with a deeper engagement with the patient? What has the patient observed about the analyst's commitments, values, rigidities, attachments? If the patient views the analyst as married to his or her profession, then what does the patient observe about the quality of that marriage? In what ways could the patient plausibly construe that he or she has been rejected, slighted, cut-off, or excluded by the analyst?

It is not enough for the content of the analysis to be concerned with three psychological variables. The analyst may always be thinking in terms of three psychological variables and may be focusing on transference and even countertransference issues, but all these can be referred back to the mind of the subject, as if the environmental context were irrelevant or at most served as a hook on which to hang the contents of intrapsychic projections. Central to a relational, two-person model is the idea that the seemingly infantile wishes and conflicts revealed in a patient's associations are not only or mainly remnants from the past, artificially imposed onto the therapeutic field, but are, rather, reflections of the actual interactions and encounters with the unique, individual analyst, with all of his or her idiosyncratic, particularistic features. The implication of a two-person psychology is that who the analyst is, not only how he or she works but his or her very character, makes a real difference for the analysand. The analyst's personality affects not only the therapeutic alliance or the so-called real relationship, but also the nature of the transference itself. From the perspective of a two-person psychology, the impact of the analyst needs to be examined systematically as an intrinsic part of the transference, which is thought to be based on the mutual contributions of both participants to the interaction.[5]

The classical approach views free associations as determined by unconscious dynamic conflict, which in the absence of interference from the analyst or resistances from within, will spontaneously unfold. A major proponent of the classical approach is Jacob Arlow, for whom free associations reveal the conflicting forces of the mind and how past efforts to resolve these conflicts are repeated in the present. He writes that "the stream of the patient's free associations is the record of the vicissitudes of the analysand's intrapsychic conflicts" (Arlow, 1987, p. 70). The associations reflect the patient's intrapsychic experience, derived from the past, and how this inner experience intrudes on the present.

---

[5] Kaplan and I maintained an ongoing dialogue, and in his rejoinder to my reply he concluded that he and I (and Freudian and relational analysts generally) "read things entirely diffferently. I am not right where you are wrong. It is rather that we constitute each other's boundaries. What you regard as constants (parameters) in my commitment to things are actually the variables that describe my subject matter. This is a rather ordinary problem" (personal communication, March 26, 1989). In this view, classical and relational theory represent figure and ground to each other.

For Arlow (1980), the function of the psychoanalytic situation, and in particular of free association, "is to ensure that what emerges into the patient's consciousness is as far as possible endogenously determined" (p. 193). It is as if the patient's developmental history of conflict between drive and defense spontaneously emerges and can be studied through the flow of the free associations. The associations are not seen as largely or predominantly determined by the current interpersonal relationship with the analyst, if the analyst is analyzing correctly.

For Arlow and other classical theorists, use of the free association method is conceptually dependent on the metapsychological foundation of drive theory. The purpose of the psychoanalytic situation is to minimize external stimuli so as to allow the spontaneous unfolding, from within, of derivatives of drive and defense. Paul Gray (1994) argues that the analyst uses the free association method to keep the focus on the patient's "mind" rather than on the patient's "life" or "behavior." Patients, as a result of this focus on ego resistances, learn to study the way their own minds work and thus benefit from increased ego autonomy. The problem I have with this line of argument is that it too easily accepts the differentiation between "mind" and "life" or "behavior," as if "mind" existed inside the person, maintaining a relatively isolated or independent—"ego autonomous"—existence. A relational view, by contrast, emphasizes that mind itself is a relational construct and can be studied only in the relational context of interaction with other "minds." The very distinctions made by Gray (1994) between mind and behavior, mind and life, mind and interaction assume a model of mind as a one-person psychology. It is precisely this model that is challenged by a two-person, relational perspective.

With a model of mind as an open system, always in interaction with others, always responsive to the nature of the relationship with the other, comes a very different model of the analytic relationship. In the relational, or two-person, model, the analytic relationship and the transference are always contributed to mutually by both participants in the interaction. One can no longer think of associations as solely emerging from within the patient; all associations are responsive to the analytic interaction, even if the analyst remains silent, hidden, or "neutral." The traditional notions of anonymity and neutrality were intended to enable the transference, free associations, and other aspects of the analysand's psychological life to make their appearance in the analysis without interferences. Free associations and the patient's transference are thought to "emerge" from within and to "unfold" spontaneously. Wachtel (1982) has argued that the language of "emerging" and "unfolding" is "a verbal sleight of hand" that

obscures the realization that psychological events are never just a function of inner structures and forces, but are always derivative of interaction with others. A two-person psychology, a relational view of transference, a heightened sensitivity to the interactional elements in the
analytic situation, and a radical critique of the blank-screen model of
the analyst's functioning (Hoffman, 1983), all point to the interactional component in each of the patient's associations. The free association method may be of immense clinical value, but in no way does it
eliminate the influence of the analyst or minimize the effect of the
ongoing interaction on the associative process. My objection to those
who portray the analytic situation as "a standard, experimental set of
conditions" (Arlow, 1987, p. 76) is that the method of free association
continues to be used as a rubric under which to hide the extent to
which the analyst affects every aspect of the patient's associations. That
is, the two-person nature of the analytic situation is obscured.

Is my depiction of the classical position regarding transference as a
one-person psychology a distortion? Do classical analysts pay more
attention than I credit them for to the analyst's contribution to the
transference? Bachant, Lynch, and Richards (1995) suggest that I
overly dichotomize the classical and the relational positions. They
suggest that my description of the classical analyst as lacking any
awareness that transference is an interpersonal process does not accurately reflect the contemporary classical position on transference. But I
have never suggested that classical analysts are oblivious to the interpersonal, only that their theory lends itself to minimizing the interpersonal factor so as to highlight the intrapsychic factor. As evidence of
their position, they cite Brenner as writing, "The 'real personality' of
the analyst is important only in so far as a patient perceives it and
reacts to it. It is a stimulus to a patient's mental activity like any other"
(cited in Bachant et al., 1995, p. 78). But as Gill (1995) was quick to
point out in response, "Brenner's almost exclusive emphasis on how
the analyst's reality is experienced in the patient's *psychic* reality belies
their contention" (p. 95). Clearly, while one can always find isolated
quotes and references to demonstrate that classical authors *do* take
into consideration the interpersonal impact of the analyst, the thrust of
classical theory is in the direction of minimizing the significance of this
input or at least *not* making it central to their methodology. If I do
"dichotomize" classical and relational theory, as Bachant, Lynch, and
Richards (1995) suggest, it is with a specific didactic purpose in mind. I
think that there are different emphases reflected in classical and relational theory, and, since I believe that these emphases are clinically
significant, I am trying to highlight them.

Self Psychology

It is not only classical Freudian theory that may be described as a one-person psychology. The history of the development of psychoanalytic ideas shows that even today's best-known relational theories did not begin as fully developed two-person psychologies. Indeed, it may be asserted that each of today's most popular relational approaches began as a one-person psychology. Let us examine self psychology as an example of a contemporary "relational" theory that began as a one-person psychology and that for some theorists remains a one-person psychology. As I have discussed, Mitchell's strategy in constructing his relational integration was to include contributions from self psychology as one pole of the relational continuum. Self–other relations are central to his theory: some theorists focus their contributions on the object; some, on the self; and some, on the interaction between the two. Kohut's (1971, 1977, 1984) important contributions are seen to add to the self pole of the relational matrix.

Self psychology makes an important contribution to clinical psychoanalysis in its emphasis on the need for the analyst to be responsive and empathic; in recognizing the vital experience of emotional attunement in the analytic process; and in its rich description of selfobject transferences. Self psychology, however, from its beginnings with Kohut's work and continuing in the work of its more "conservative" practitioners, maintains an emphasis both on a one-person psychology, by placing the self in a superordinate position, and on the individual's talents and ideals. More important, however, self psychology in its conservative form maintains the classical view that who the analyst is as a unique character is irrelevant to the process of the analysis. Kohut (1977) wrote that the patient's transferences are defined by "preanalytically established internal factors in the analysand's personality structure" (p. 217). The analyst's contribution to the process is, according to Kohut, limited to making "correct" interpretations on the basis of empathy with the patient. Goldberg (1986) has stated that

> Self psychology struggles hard not to be an interpersonal psychology . . . because it wishes to minimize the input of the analyst into the mix . . . it is based on the idea of a developmental program (one that may be innate or prewired if you wish) that will reconstitute itself under certain conditions [p. 387].

In this version of the self-psychological model, the analyst is restricted to being a selfobject, focusing only on what the patient (as subject) needs from the analyst (as object). It is important to recognize that, in this respect, this version of self psychology does not differ from the classical model (see Hoffman, 1983; Bromberg, 1989; Ghent, 1989). Both the classical model, with its focus on drive and defense, and this conservative version of self psychology, with its reliance on the notion of a "developmental program," require that the psychoanalytic situation remain free of the contaminants of the analyst's subjectivity so that the patient's transferences can "unfold" in pure form from within. The presuppositions of a one-person psychology demand that the only "psychology" in the consulting room that should matter is that of the patient. The patient's subjectivity, the patient's transferences, the patient's psychic reality are there to be examined. The subjectivity of the analyst is to be kept out of the equation so as to produce an objective experimental situation.

Evelyne Schwaber (1981, 1983, 1992, 1995) has consistently and eloquently argued for a listening perspective that empathically focuses on the patient's psychic reality. While Schwaber's point of view is not, strictly speaking, self-psychological, she has been enormously influenced by Kohut's approach, thus I believe it is appropriate to discuss her clinical approach in this context. Her point is a perspectival one; she argues for always taking the patient's perspective, rather than the analyst's, as our data base. Her framework is one of interaction and coparticipation, but, as a perspectivist and not a constructivist, she views truth as being discovered rather than created in the psychoanalytic situation. There is, however, some slipperiness in her argument. She acknowledges—even emphasizes—that the analyst's subjectivity and theoretical prejudice must have an impact on what can be observed and that we must use our subjectivities to locate the subjectivity of another. Nevertheless, she insists on formulating her theory as a one-person psychology because it is the patient's perspective exclusively that must be considered for an approach to be defined by her as psychoanalytic. She emphasizes interaction, but it is interaction exclusively as it is experienced by the patient that is the focus of psychoanalysis. She writes, "Sustaining the focus on the patient's intrapsychic world, psychoanalysis remains, paradoxical as it may seem for its coparticipatory elements, a one-person psychology" (Schwaber 1995, p. 558). For Schwaber, the term countertransference indicates a "retreat from the patient's vantage point." I am sympathetic to the emphasis that Schwaber wants to put on privileging the patient's perspective. Nonetheless, she seems to me to contradict herself when, on one hand, she says that we can discover another's subjectivity only by using our own, but also argues for "vigilantly guarding against the imposition of the analyst's point of view" (Schwaber, 1981, p. 60). A similar argument is made by Pizer (in press).

For Schwaber, psychoanalysis is defined by studying what the inter-action means to the subject—hence, a one-person psychology—whereas I would say that psychoanalysis studies the meaning of the interaction as it is coconstructed by or negotiated between the patient and the analyst—hence, a two-person psychology. Schwaber's main argument is that as analysts we too often fail to maintain a focus on the patient's inner reality; we fail to see things from the patient's perspec-tive. Renik (1993b) objects, I believe rightly, to Schwaber's position. Renik argues that, if we take seriously the analyst's subjectivity, then it is impossible to maintain the patient's perspective independent of our own for even an instant. "It seems to me, . . ." he writes, "we are always completely personally involved in our judgements and decisions, and it is precisely at those moments when we believe that we are able to be objective-as-opposed-to-subjective that we are in the greatest danger of self-deception and departure from sound methodology" (p. 562).

Along lines very similar to Schwaber's, Ornstein and Ornstein (1995) aver that "analysts guided by the principles of self psychology do not *demand* that patients experience them in their own uniqueness and 'otherness'" (p. 423n, italics added). This statement is somewhat ambiguous because it hinges on the meaning of the word "demand." A two-person psychology would not necessarily dictate a confrontational clinical stance; it would, however, highlight the ways in which the analyst's very presence acts as a *demand* on the patient.

The interpersonal wing of the relational camp tends to object to self psychology because they view it as a one-person psychology that focuses on the patient's unfolding of a narcissistic transference based on early history (see Bromberg, 1989). To these interpersonal critics, the concept of empathy seems to position the analyst outside of the analytic arena of participation with the patient, and the concept of the selfobject seems to obscure the importance of real others. Mitchell (1988a) himself, while drawing on Kohut's important contributions, argues against the "developmental-arrest" perspective that is so central to self psychology. He maintains that it reifies the damage experienced by patients and leaves them more likely to perceive themselves as having been passive recipients of inadequate care in the past and to feel justified in their victimization in the present, even with their analysts.

From the self-psychological side, interpersonalists and relationists are viewed as insisting on their own view of the patient's functioning and not adopting the patient's perspective; they are thought to be overly confrontational with patients, "demanding" that patients experience them as separate individuals; they are thought to work from an "experience-distant" theoretical framework; and they are thought to neglect the selfobject dimensions of the transference. To complicate matters, self psychology has developed considerably since Kohut's initial contributions, and self psychologists today are hardly in agreement about their own commonalities and differences (for example, there is little agreement about what is meant by a selfobject), let alone how they compare with other schools. One of the differences among contemporary self psychologists concerns the degree to which they view self psychology as representing a one-person psychology. Two volumes of papers deal with these issues of comparative psychoanalysis (Detrick and Detrick, 1989; Bacal and Newman, 1990), and a Symposium: Self Psychology After Kohut (1995) has been devoted to just this topic.

Of course, many self psychologists believe that they have moved beyond Kohut's narrow one-person psychology to embrace a broader relational framework. For example, Bacal (1995a) has attempted to build a bridge between self psychology and object relational theorizing by arguing that, while self psychology leaves the other implicit in its theorizing, object relations theories leave the self implicit in their theorizing. Each theory therefore needs the other to be complete. Similarly, as we saw in Chapter 1, Stolorow and his colleagues have elaborated an intersubjective position precisely because they are critical of the one-person psychological aspects of self psychology. Stolorow (1995) has expatiated a variety of ways in which Kohut maintained "relics of the doctrine of the isolated mind" (p. 394) that persists in much of contemporary self psychology. Stolorow's position, which gives prominence to the contextual interaction of subjectivities with reciprocal, mutual influence, is therefore much closer to a relational perspective than that of some other self psychologists.

OBJECT RELATIONS THEORY

The approaches constituting what is known as the British object relations school also vary in regard to their commitment to a one- or two-person psychology. The metaphors of the analyst as "good enough mother" and "holder" (Winnicott, 1986) or as "container" (Bion, 1959) and "metabolizer" of the patient's pathological contents have been extremely useful in drawing attention to nonverbal and subtle exchanges and to the ways in which the analyst needs to respond to these "primitive communications." The danger with these "developmental-arrest" metaphors, however, is not only that the patient may be infantilized and deprived of a richer and more complex adult kind of intimacy, as Mitchell (1988a) correctly points out, but that the analyst is similarly instrumentalized and denied subjective existence. The mother, and the analyst, instead of being seen as subjects, are transformed into the baby's, and the patient's "thinking apparatus" (Bion, 1970). The blank screen has simply been replaced with an empty container, free of the analyst's personal psychological insides (Hoffman, 1983; Levenson, 1983; Hirsch, 1987). In parallel to this, Chodorow (1989) has pointed out that most object relations theorists still take the point of view of the child, with mother as the object, and do not take seriously the problem of the subjectivity of the mother (p. 253).

Renik (1995) offers a penetrating critique of the work of Christopher Bollas, who is himself a leading current exponent of the British Independents. Bollas (1987) has been known for attending to the analyst's subjectivity and even for restrained, disciplined, and selective sharing of countertransference experiences with patients. In championing the recognition of the analyst's subjectivity as a resource for understanding the patient's impact, however, Bollas has once again diminished recognition of the analyst's subjectivity as a force in its own right, with its own consequences. Bollas adopts the traditionally British emphasis on the analyst as container, receiver, recipient of projective identification, who is thought to create a potential space within which patients create the analyst that they need. Bollas suggests that analysts look inward, into their own subjectivity, to find their patients within themselves. Renik's (1995) point is that, in Bollas's formulation, the analyst's unique, individual psychology is diminished. Bollas assumes that the patient's use of projective identification or unconscious communication has the power to override the analyst's subjectivity or be imposed on it, rather than the patient's psychology being intermingled with the analyst's. In a more fully developed, two-person psychology the analyst looking either inward or outward can find only a commingling of two psychologies.

INTERPERSONAL THEORY

It is striking that even interpersonal theory did not begin as a fully two-person psychology. While contemporary interpersonal analysts (Levenson, 1972, 1983; Wolstein, 1983) stress the analyst's personal contributions to the patient's transferences, this was not true of Sullivan's clinical position. Sullivan (1953, 1954) saw the therapist as an "expert" on interpersonal relations who would function as a "participant-observer" in conducting the analytic inquiry, and he assumed that the therapist, as the expert, could avoid being pulled into the patient's interpersonal entanglements (Hoffman, 1983; Hirsch, 1987). Sullivan's interpersonal theory, while interpersonal in its examination of the patient's life, was asocial in its neglect of the subjectivity of the therapist as inevitably participating in the analytic interaction. Sullivan's description of the principle of participant-observation soon led to attention's being paid to the analyst's subjective experience and the patient's perceptions of the analyst's experience, which became the focus of attention for later interpersonal analysts.

In spite of his limited focus on the analysis of transference and countertransference, Sullivan's development of an interpersonal theory of psychiatry and the later elaborations of this theory into an interpersonal psychoanalysis by Clara Thompson, Erich Fromm, and Frieda Fromm-Reichmann, along with the parallel work by Suttie and Balint in London, were the earliest attempts to construct a two-person or field theory of psychoanalysis. It is notable that each of these theorists was influenced by the pioneering contributions of Sándor Ferenczi (whose work is examined in Chapter 6).

Today, within the interpersonal community there is room for disagreement about whether interpersonal theory is exclusively a two-person psychology or whether it is also a one-person psychology. While Levenson (1972, 1983) clearly highlights the field-theoretical, two-person dimension of interpersonal theory, Wolstein (1990) has articulated a contemporary interpersonal theory that emphasizes not only the experiential and the empirical, but specifically the experience of the psychic center of the interpersonal self. Downplaying any attempt to universalize his own metapsychological position, Wolstein focuses on a one-person psychology within an interpersonal context: "From this psychic center of the self arise the gritty therapeutic elements of agency and responsibility, the irreducible subjectivity that may be termed the first person, singular and active, in the study of ego, object, or interpersonal relations" (p. 248). Thus Wolstein's theory places the self in a superordinate position within an interpersonal, two-way, coparticipant psychological inquiry into unconscious experience. Compared with Levenson's brand of interpersonalism, Wolstein's may be said to advocate a more balanced one- and two-person psychology. While Levenson's model has been very influential among relational analysts for its emphasis on the interactive dimensions of the therapeutic relationship, Wolstein's seems to me a useful complement to Levenson's in his underscoring the need for both one- and two-person psychologies.[6]

---

[6] For an interesting depiction of the range of contemporary interpersonal positions, see Fiscalini, 1994. It may be surprising to note that, according to Fiscalini the relational position represents one group within the contemporary interpersonal school.

ONE- AND TWO-PERSON PSYCHOLOGIES: COMPLEMENTARY OR CONTRADICTORY?

Modell (1984) is among the earliest theorists to have explicitly proposed an integration of one- and two-person psychologies. He suggests that the traditional intrapsychic context of psychoanalysis is complementary to a two-person intersubjective psychology, and he argues that psychoanalysis needs both theories. By limiting itself to the study of "the mind," conceptualized as residing "inside" the person, Freudian theory, in Modell's view, is forced to explain interpersonal events by referring back to the mind of the individual through the use of such concepts as internalization and representation. Just as Balint (1950) saw the one-body theory as an inevitable outcome of Freud's physiological or biological bias, so too Modell believes that the focus on the individual's mind inevitably followed from Freud's early neurological investigations and his commitment to materialist, natural science ideals.

Greenberg and Mitchell (1983) distinguish between the drive model, which "establishes individual pleasure seeking and drive discharge as the bedrock of human existence" (p. 404), and the relational model, which establishes relational configurations as the bedrock of existence. Mitchell (1988a) has argued that this distinction between a monadic theory of mind (a one-person psychology) and an interactional relational theory of mind (a two-person psychology) is crucial to understanding psychoanalytic concepts. According to Greenberg and Mitchell (1983), the two models are both all-encompassing theoretical structures, each of which is independently capable of explaining all the data generated by the psychoanalytic method. Each model is a complete and comprehensive account of human experience. They rest on fundamentally different and incompatible premises, and neither theory is reducible to the other. Ultimately, Greenberg and Mitchell believe, it is a matter of personal choice as to which model is more appealing and which vision of human nature more compelling.

Mitchell (1988a, 1993a) has consistently taken the position that there is a radical choice to be made here. He views the movement within psychoanalysis over the past two decades as nothing short of a "paradigm shift." He writes: "Mind has been redefined from a set of predetermined structures emerging from inside an individual organism

---

This is a reversal of my perspective, which views interpersonal theory as a wing of the broader relational movement. Clearly, the difference in our respective emphases may be taken as one more demonstration of perspectivism, a principle with which we both agree.

to transactional patterns and internal structures derived from an inter-active, interpersonal field" (Mitchell, 1988a, p. 17). Nevertheless, even Mitchell acknowledges that interpersonal experience inevitably has its impact on a child, who brings to the interaction his or her own temper-ament and constitutional endowment, and therefore the interpersonal is always filtered through the individual's particular capacities to take in experience. In this sense, Mitchell's two-person psychology includes within itself an implicit recognition of a one-person psychology. Mitchell has suggested that biology can enter human experience only insofar as it is mediated through interaction. This relational approach is a far cry, however, from eliminating the influence of the body. The body, Mitchell argues, is not represented in the mind in a direct or unmediated way; rather, bodily meanings and sensations are con-structed in a linguistic, interactional field (Mitchell, in press).

Sex and aggression, the dual drives of classical theory, are not neglected by Mitchell, although his approach to them is quite different from that of classical analysts. Once again, the relational position needs to be understood historically in terms of the way it attempts to balance the Freudian and the interpersonal traditions. When I was in analytic training, a joke often told was that if a patient talked to a Freudian about intimacy, then the analyst interpreted in terms of sex, and if a patient talked to an interpersonalist about sex, then the analyst responded in terms of intimacy. This joke captures some truth in the way in which the two theories prioritized aspects of human life. Rela-tional theory attempts to maintain the tension between these two posi-tions. Mitchell (1988a) suggests that sex is *not* simply to be attributed to the relational context, but rather that physiological, bodily surges of sexuality take on meaning to the individual in a specific relational context. Similarly, Mitchell (1993a) addresses the importance of physi-ology and biology in understanding human aggression. In my view, Mitchell's position does not in any way neglect individual or innate factors in development, nor does it neglect the role of individual talents, capacities, bodily factors, physiology, or generally what is known as the psychology of individual differences. Rather, Mitchell views the self within an interpersonal context and construes biology as entering experience only indirectly through the mediation of social forces. His relational, two-person psychology subsumes what are gener-ally considered to be aspects of a one-person psychology. Nonetheless, he undoubtedly gives greater emphasis to two-person factors.

In turning to the questions of whether one- and two-person psychologies are complementary or contradictory, whether we need both a one-person and a two-person psychology or whether the two-person psychology replaces the one-person psychology, we would do well to begin by considering a passage from Freud that illuminates his thinking psychoanalysis is a "mass structure of two." While Freud can be easily quoted to support almost any position, in this passage Freud (1921) "deconstructs" the dichotomy of one- and two-person psychologies and asserts the dialectical relation between the individual and the social:

> The contrast between individual psychology and social or group psychology, which at first glance seems to be full of significance, loses a great deal of its sharpness when it is examined more closely. It is true that individual psychology is concerned with the individual man and explores the paths by which he seeks to find satisfaction for his instinctual impulses; but only rarely and under certain exceptional conditions is individual psychology in a position to disregard the relations of this individual to others. In the individual's mental life someone else is invariably involved, as a model, as an object, as a helper, as an opponent; and so from the very first individual psychology, in this extended but entirely justifiable sense of the words, is at the same time social psychology as well [p. 69].

Ghent (1989) has described the history of psychoanalysis as constituted by dialectical shifts between one-person and two-person psychologies. He put forth his own belief in the need for an enlarged theory that encompasses an integration of both one-person and two-person psychologies. Gill (1994) endorsed Ghent's integrative approach. Blatt and Blass (1992) have suggested that self-definition and relatedness are each primary dimensions in personality development. Similarly, Slavin and Kriegman (1992) use the framework of evolutionary biology to argue for maintaining the dialectical tension between a classical and a relational view.

The major difficulty in attempting to sort out the contradictory versus complementary nature of one- and two-person psychologies is that the referents for these terms remain unclear. Sometimes the question of one-person and two-person psychologies is equated with the dichotomy experiential versus the innate, but just as often people use these terms to distinguish the intrapsychic and the interpersonal, terms that are themselves ambiguous at best. At other times, the terms one- and two-person psychologies may be used to refer to self-regulation and mutual regulation as these terms are used by infancy researchers such as Beebe, Jaffe, and Lachmann (1992), who believe that it is most useful to think of the dyadic system as organized by an integration of stable, individual characteristics *and* emergent dyadic properties. I agree with Lachmann and Beebe (1995), who suggest that the distinction between self- and mutual regulation is a finer and more useful one and cuts across that between one- and two-person psychologies. Furthermore, the distinction between self- and mutual regulation does not imply such an either-or implication.

I am suggesting that the terms one- and two-person psychologies have been used so broadly, to cover so much conceptual ground, that it is hard to know what anyone means by advocating a position that requires only one or both perspectives. David Bakan (1966) distinguished between

> the terms "agency" and "communion" to characterize two fundamental modalities in the existence of living forms, agency for the existence of an organism as an individual, and communion for the participation of the individual in some larger organism of which the individual is a part. Agency manifests itself in self-protection, self assertion, and self-expansion; communion manifests itself in the sense of being at one with other organisms. Agency manifests itself in the form of separations; communion in the lack of separations. Agency manifests itself in isolation, alienation, and aloneness; communion in contact, openness, and union [pp. 14–15].

Earlier, we saw that Ghent (1989) drew on Buber's (1947) distinction between the originator instinct and the instinct for communion to build his own dialectical relational theory of one- and two-person psychologies. In some ways the terms one- and two-person psychologies are consistent as well with Bakan's (1966) distinction between agency and communion. A comprehensive psychoanalytic theory needs, of course, to take both modalities into account. All the dichotomies that we have been discussing are probably best approached in dialectical terms. That is, dividing up the world into the innate and the experiential or the intrapsychic and the interpersonal is certainly simplistic, since each of these terms contains, organizes, and defines the other. As is clear from the passage that I quoted from Freud (1921), he clearly saw that the individual contained the social and the social the individual. Any tendency relational theory has to emphasize the superordinate position of a two-person psychology is predominantly as a corrective to classical psychoanalysis's focus on elements of a one-person psychology.

Complicating matters a bit more, Altman (1995) has suggested that we speak *not* of a one- or a two-person psychology, but of a three-person psychology! Altman rightly points out that a wider social-systems perspective can enrich our understanding of both the individual and the dyad. Family therapists and systems theorists similarly suggest that speaking of a two-person psychology is limiting in its neglect of contributing factors from the wider social system. A good example of a three-person psychology would be in thinking through the therapeutic relationship as it operates in a particular clinic or in conjunction with a specific insurance company, factors that Racker (1968) took into account in discussing "indirect countertransference" (p. 161).[7]

To conclude this discussion of one-, two-, and three-person psychologies and relational theory, it seems clear that we need to think in terms of both/and rather than either/or, that we need to think dialectically about the individual and the social, the innate and the learned, the body ("drives") and the interpersonal, autonomy and mutuality, intrasubjective and intersubjective, agency and communion. To view relational theory as representing only one of these polarities is to misconstrue the intent of relational authors and to misunderstand the very purpose that the term relational was coined to serve. Remember, from Chapter 1, that the term relational was specifically introduced by Greenberg and Mitchell (1983) as broader than interpersonal so as to contain these tensions within it. It was meant to bridge the perceived gap between British school object relations theory and American interpersonal theory. Relational theory was, from the outset, formulated as a dialectical theory and includes the deconstruction of these various polarities. Perhaps the most important aspect of the term relational is precisely that it *includes* the *relation* between the individual and the social, internal objects and external interpersonal relations, self-regulation and mutual regulation. If relational theory has tended to emphasize that it is a two-person psychology, this is not because it eschews all elements of one-person psychologies, but rather because, in the history of psychoanalysis and in Western culture more generally, our bias has been so strongly in favor of an individual view and our values are so highly individualistic that a correction has been needed. As I have indicated throughout this discussion, our technical terms are all defined and used within an individualistic, one-person framework. We speak of the individual patient forming a transference; we speak of the individual's mind or psyche and of the individual's unconscious; we speak of the patient's resisting or even of the analyst's resisting. Until the advent of the relational perspective, we had no words for the relational unconscious, for the relationship's resisting, or the relationship's

---

[7] Systems theory and family therapy have been an important, if rarely acknowledged, influence on relational analysts. The younger generation of analysts, drawn largely from the professions of psychology and social work, have usually had some experience with family therapy before becoming analysts. Once one is exposed to systems theory (and anyone who trained in the mental health professions in the past two decades has been exposed to systems theory), it is very easy to view the analytic relationship as a dyadic system in which the individual (patient or analyst) can be understood only as a subsystem. This systems model is quite compatible with relational theory.

transference. Now our focus has shifted to a coparticipant model, to mutual construction, to *interaction*. Ultimately, we need to consider *both* how the individual determines relations *and* how the relationship determines individuals. Perhaps the term relational seems to be biased along the lines of the second of these considerations, but, given the prevalent bias in the first direction, some correction and compensation is necessary.

This discussion of relational theory and of one- and two-person psychologies leads to questions about a related term, intersubjectivity, a term that is also ambiguous. As I mentioned in Chapter 1, Freud cautioned against the introduction of "the subjective factor" on the grounds that it would detract from the objectivity, and hence from the scientific status, of psychoanalysis. Today, in the sciences and across all disciplinary pursuits, the polarization of subjectivity and objectivity has been questioned, the subjectivity of the investigator has been incorporated into disciplinary methodologies, and we have begun to investigate the nature and development of intersubjectivity. In the next chapter I turn to the various meanings of intersubjectivity, explore its theoretical and clinical implications, and investigate the patient's experience of the analyst's subjectivity, a psychic space where there comes to be a meeting of minds.

3 | The Patient's Experience of the Analyst's Subjectivity

Although many cultural, social, and scientific developments have contributed to a relational view of the psychoanalytic process, I believe that the shift to an intersubjective perspective has emerged predominantly out of our accumulated clinical experience in psychoanalytic work with patients. In this chapter, I highlight the clinical centrality of examining the patient's experience of the analyst's subjectivity in the psychoanalytic situation.

THE DEVELOPMENT OF INTERSUBJECTIVITY

Only with the recent development of feminist psychoanalytic criticism has it become apparent that psychology and psychoanalysis have contributed to and perpetuated a distorted view of motherhood (Dinnerstein, 1976, Chodorow, 1978, Balbus, 1982, Benjamin, 1988). In all our theories of development, the mother has been portrayed as the object of the infant's drives and as the fulfiller of the baby's needs. We have been slow to recognize or acknowledge the mother as a subject in her own right. In discussing the prevalent psychological descriptions of motherhood Jessica Benjamin (1988) writes:

> The mother is the baby's first object of attachment, and later, the object of desire. She is provider, interlocutor, caregiver, contingent reinforcer, significant other, empathic understander, mirror. She is also a secure presence to walk away from, a setter of limits, an optimal frustrator, a shockingly real outside otherness. She is external reality—but she is rarely regarded as another subject with a purpose apart from her existence for her child [1988, p. 24].

Benjamin argues that the child must come to recognize the mother as a separate other with her own inner world and her own experiences, and as being her own center of initiative, an agent of her own desire. According to Benjamin, this expanding capacity on the part of the child represents an important, and previously unrecognized, developmental achievement. Benjamin has proposed that the capacity for recognition and intersubjective relatedness is an achievement that is best conceptualized as a separate developmental line, and she has begun to articulate the complex vicissitudes involved in this advance. The developmental achievement she describes is radically different from that previously described in the literature. The traditional notion of "object constancy" is limited to the recognition of the mother as a separate "object." The focus of the intersubjective perspective is the child's need to recognize mother as a separate subject, which is a developmental advance beyond viewing mother only as a separate object. Dorothy Dinnerstein (1976) anticipated this intersubjective idea when she wrote, "Every 'I' first emerges in relation to an 'It' which is not at all clearly an 'I.' The separate 'I'ness of the other person is a discovery, an insight achieved over time" (p. 106).[1]

The term intersubjectivity has been used in a variety of ways by philosophers and by psychoanalysts. Benjamin's (1988) work on intersubjectivity emphasizes mutual recognition as an intrinsic aspect of the development of the self. Regarding the clinical psychoanalytic situation, Benjamin (1990) writes that "an inquiry into the intersubjective dimension of the analytic encounter would aim to change our theory and practice so that 'where objects were, subjects must be'" (p. 34). Benjamin, drawing on her background in critical theory, adopts the term intersubjectivity from Habermas, and other philosophers who deliberately formulated the concept of a subject–subject relation in contrast to the subject-object relation. For Benjamin (1992), intersubjectivity "refers to that zone of experience or theory in which the other is not merely the object of the ego's need/drive or cognition/perception, but has a separate and equivalent center of self" (p. 45). How it is that a person may come to recognize the other as an equivalent subject is the central problem that she, following Winnicott, attempts to address. She argues that we need to maintain a tension in our theory between relating to others as objects and relating to others as separate subjects. She uses the terms intrapsychic and intersubjective, respectively, to indicate these two realms, and she insists on maintaining both intrapsychic and intersubjective theory.

Winnicott (1954–1955) anticipated the importance of an intersubjective perspective and provided a preliminary hypothesis regarding the establishment of intersubjectivity. He expanded Melanie Klein's depressive position to include the development of the capacity for

---

[1] Viewing the other as an "I" or an "it" evokes Buber's (1923) *I and Thou*. I comment further on Buber, intersubjectivity and the "interhuman" in Chapter 5.

"ruth" (p. 265), which he contrasts to the state of "ruthlessness" that exists prior to the development of the capacity to recognize the other as a separate person. Winnicott (1969) elaborated a theory of "object usage," which describes the process by which the infant destroys the object, finds that the object survives destruction, and therefore is able to surrender omnipotence and recognize the other as a separate person. Turning his attention to the transaction between the internal world and the external surround, Winnicott (1951, 1958) developed the concepts of transitional objects and transitional phenomena in an attempt to explore the mediational processes operating between these worlds.

Outside of relational theory, the idea of intersubjectivity was already developing through the work of Lacan. It was perhaps Lacan (1988) who, in his seminars of the mid-1950s, first discussed the implications of intersubjectivity within the psychoanalytic situation. Lacan and his followers described the emergence of subjectivity as it was mediated by language and other cultural structures in the formation of personal experience. Lacan thus introduced his own way of integrating the psychological with the social domain into psychoanalytic thought.

Stolorow and his colleagues (1978) introduced the term intersubjec-tivity into American psychoanalysis. For them,

> intersubjectivity theory is a field theory or systems theory in that it seeks to comprehend psychological phenomena not as products of isolated intrapsychic mechanisms, but as forming at the interface of reciprocally interacting subjec-tivities [Stolorow and Atwood, 1992, p. 1].

They note that their use of the term intersubjective has never presupposed the attainment of symbolic thought, of a concept of oneself as subject, or of intersubjective relatedness in the sense used by Stern (1985). "Unlike the developmentalists," they write, "we use 'intersubjective' to refer to *any* psychological field formed by interacting worlds of experience, at whatever developmental level these worlds may be organized" (p. 3).

There are important differences in the ways the term intersubjec-tivity is used by Benjamin, Stolorow, and Stern. For Benjamin (1988), intersubjectivity is a developmental trajectory, in which recognition is inconsistently maintained. Intersubjectivity refers to a dialectic process where subjects recognize each other as separate centers of subjective experience, but also continually negate the other as separate subjects. For Stern, following Trevarthan and Hubley (1978, cited in Stern, 1985, p. 124), who were themselves influenced by the existential litera-ture of the mid-1970s (Natterson, 1991), intersubjectivity refers to the developmentally achieved capacity to recognize another person as a separate center of subjective experience with whom subjective states can be shared.

Stern's (1985) description of the developmental progression of the sense of self has begun to draw attention to the domain of intersubjective relatedness in which the nature of relatedness includes the recognition of subjective mental states in the other as well as in oneself. Recent theorizing about the construction of internal representations of self and others (Lichtenberg, 1983; Beebe and Lachmann, 1988a; Stern, 1989), has just begun to consider the child's emerging ability to attribute subjectivity or internal states to others and to explore the ways in which these internal states can be interpersonally communicated.

Stern (1983) writes that somewhere between the seventh and ninth month the child makes

> a momentous discovery, namely, that he or she can share with another a state of mind such as intention. In other words, the infant develops a "theory of interfaceable minds." This has several implications: that the infant has the ability to impute, unawares, an internal mental state to another; that he or she has some apperception, at the moment of a particular internal mental state; and that the interfacing, in the sense of sharing or reciprocally manifesting these two states is not only possible, but a goal to be sought [pp. 8–9].

Stern (1985) explains that traditional psychoanalytic, ego-psychological developmental theory neglected the creation of mutually held mental states because of its overriding emphasis on the emergence of a more autonomous self through the separation-individuation process. In contrast, Stern cites Vygotsky's notion of the "intermental," Fairbairn's conception of the newborn's innate interpersonal relatedness, MacMurray's philosophical idea of the field of the personal, and Sullivan's interpersonal field theory as examples of the thinking of influential theorists outside the psychoanalytic mainstream who were receptive to the study of intersubjectivity as a dyadic phenomena.

By contrast, for Stolorow and his colleagues, the term intersubjectivity is applied whenever two subjectivities constitute the field, even if one does not recognize the other as a separate subjectivity (Stolorow and Atwood, 1992). *The difference between Benjamin and Stern, on one hand, and Stolorow and colleagues, on the other, in their use of the term intersubjectivity is that Benjamin uses the term to describe a developmental achievement in which there is mutual recognition of each other's subjectivity. Her thinking includes the idea that intersubjectivity is a category that refers to a whole dialectic continuum that includes movement toward and negation of mutual recognition, whereas Stolorow and colleagues use the term intersubjectivity to indicate the principle of mutual regulation and unconscious influ-*

ence. Some theorists, like Hirsch (1993), have questioned the need for the term intersubjective as it is used by Stolorow by asking how it differs from the term interpersonal.

Where relational, interpersonal, and intersubjective theories intersect is in their shift of focus from the individual to the "realm of the between" (Gergen, 1994) or to the "transitional space" between analyst and analysand. G. H. Mead's (1934) early work, which was a significant influence on the interpersonal theory of Sullivan (1953, 1954), was a major contribution to this viewpoint. Mead suggested that self-consciousness derives from adopting the standpoint of the other toward the self. One's conceptions of oneself are dependent on the attitudes and actions of others; the self is radically intersubjective and interdependent. Sullivan (1953, 1954) developed this line of thinking in his conceptualization of psychopathology in terms of microsocial processes that trace symptoms to interpersonal, rather than intrapsychic, processes. Object relations theories, while continuing to emphasize psychic structure formations, turned their attention to the interrelatedness of the self and the other, while self psychology similarly centered on the relations between the self and the selfobject.

Pizer (1992) has linked the concept of intersubjectivity with the two-person process of negotiation. He speaks of "intersubjective negotiation" (p. 217) in the sense that we constantly influence one another, consciously and unconsciously, and in this way patient and analyst weave the complex tapestry of the transference–countertransference; through negotiation they reach a meeting of minds.

Contemporary Kleinians are also interested in the development of intersubjectivity. Projective identification, a central concept in Kleinian-Bionian theory, is assumed to occur extremely early in life. In emphasizing, following Bion (1959), projective identification as a form of primitive, preverbal, and presymbolic communication, these theorists must reconsider how early in life the infant might be thought of as recognizing the presence in the object of another mind.

> It may indicate that once mental life starts, it has an entirely mentalistic base—everything is a mind. A concrete physical reality develops only as a later awareness. This confounds more usual notions of the development of mind: from an earlier stage of physical perceptions towards a sensitivity to other minds at a much later, more mature level [Hinshelwood, 1994, p. 133].

Perhaps the capacity for intersubjectivity is not even a development, but is rather hard-wired into the human brain at birth, a preconception, in Bion's terms; or perhaps we should think of it as something that is hard-wired but appears maturationally, as in Chomsky's (1957, 1968) view of language. This way of thinking about the early development or innate capacity for intersubjectivity may have different implications than Stern's developmental model does and raises further questions about the difference between Stolorow's position and that of the developmentalists. Perhaps Hinshelwood is right in advising us to remain agnostic on the actual state of the newborn infant's mind!

Natterson (1991) presents a detailed comparison of a variety of uses of the term intersubjectivity in contemporary psychoanalytic theory. His own work moves in the direction of a radical and relentless inter-subjective analysis. Critical of Stolorow and colleagues, he argues that in their reported case studies they conflate the terms intersubjectivity and countertransference. According to Natterson, Stolorow and his followers limit their focus on intersubjectivity to the pathological aspects of the analyst's interaction with the patient. From Natterson's perspective, Stolorow's brand of intersubjectivity does not pay consis-tent enough attention to the therapist's continual influence on the treatment. For Natterson, "Nothing short of a complete inclusion of all psychological input and reactions of both participants will permit opti-mal understanding of the issue" (p. 99). Intersubjectivity must be carefully distinguished from the more traditional view of transference–countertransference in which the direction of influence remains largely from the patient to the analyst. The more traditional view pathologizes countertransference. For Natterson, intersubjectivity implies the "essential, initial, coequal role of the analyst in the analytic process" (p. 109).

While I am in general agreement with Natterson's argument—I too would emphasize the analyst's essential, continual, bidirectional, or mutual influence in the analysis—my own view is that Natterson is mistaken in referring to the mutual influence as "coequal," since mutual influence need not imply equal influence (I elaborate on this in Chapter 5). It does seem to me that speaking of the organization of the analyst's subjectivity or subjective experience has advantages over referring to the analyst's countertransference, and speaking of inter-subjectivity has advantages over referring to transference–counter-transference, because (1) the terms subjectivity and intersubjectivity do not imply the pathological, (2) because they do imply bidirectional, if not necessarily equal, influence, and (3) because these terms do imply a continuous, ongoing flow of influence, in contrast to countertransfer-ence, which implies an occasional or intermittent event.

More than any other psychoanalytic theorist writing today, Thomas Ogden (1986, 1989, 1994) has systematically formulated a theory of the interplay of subjectivity and intersubjectivity in development, psychopathology, and psychoanalytic treatment. Ogden traces the establishment of subjectivity to the distinction between the symbol and the symbolized. Subjectivity is seen as emerging in the space between the thought and the object of thought. "For symbol to stand independently of the symbolized, there must be a subject engaged in the process of interpreting his perceptions. . . . The achievement of the capacity to distinguish symbol and symbolized is the achievement of subjectivity" (Ogden, 1986, pp. 224–225).

In his elaboration of the dialectical nature of subjectivity, Ogden has built on the work of Freud, Klein, and Winnicott. For Freud, subjectivity was constituted by the dialectic between consciousness and unconsciousness. For Klein, the subject was defined by the oscillating movement between the paranoid-schizoid and depressive positions, and in Ogden's reading of Klein, in her concept of projective identification, she contributed to the understanding of subjectivity as it develops within a "complex system of psychological-interpersonal forces" (p. 8). At the heart of Winnicott's work is the notion that the subject comes to exist in the (potential) space between the mother and the infant. Ogden's conception of analytic intersubjectivity places central emphasis on its dialectical nature. His elaboration of the contributions of Freud, Klein, and Winnicott culminates in the development of his original concept, "the analytic third," neither subject nor object, but jointly created, intersubjectively, by the analytic pair. "The intersubjective and the individually subjective each create, negate, and preserve the other," and created out of the dialectical interplay of these forces is "the intersubjective analytic third" (Ogden, 1994, p. 64). Gerson (1995) has suggested that we speak of this mutual relation of minds as the "relational unconscious."

In spite of the boldness of Ogden's theoretical innovations, a reading of his work suggests that he is quite conservative technically, particularly in his advocacy of using the analyst's subjectivity primarily to understand the patient's experience. Ogden emphasizes the asymmetrical nature of psychoanalysis, writes forcefully against attempts at "mutual analysis," and does not advocate any active use of self-disclosure. But, more fundamentally, my reading of Ogden leaves me with the impression that he views his own subjectivity largely as reactive to the patient rather than as initiating particular forms of interaction; nor does he view the analytic participation as mutually influenced from the beginning. The relational-perspectivist view that I am propounding here assumes the mutual, even if unequal, participation of patient and analyst from beginning to end. For Ogden, subjectivity is paradoxically *both* always already present *and* a developmental achievement; in his elaboration of Klein's work on the paranoid-schizoid and depressive positions, both these positions exist from the beginning in dialectical relation to each other. "Even at the very beginning of life," Ogden

(1994) writes, "the infant has some rudimentary sense of otherness that he bumps up against. At the same time, there is an aspect of consciousness in which the infant and other are at one" (p. 198).

Elsewhere I (Aron, 1993a, 1995a) have argued for the oedipal stage and the internalized primal scene as a fundamental structure in the establishment of one's sense of self and of internal object relations, and I have referred to its role in the establishment of intersubjectivity. Prior to the oedipal stage, the child lives in a two-person world. The child relates to both the mother and the father, but to each of them differently; that is, the child has a separate and unique relationship with each parent. The child relates to only one parent at a time, however, even if alternating from one to the other in momentary glances. It is only in the oedipal stage of triadic object relations that the child perceives that he or she is part of a system that includes a separate relation between the parents from which the child is excluded. Britton (1989) uses the term "triangular space" (p. 86) to describe the internalization of this relation.

The Oedipus complex entails not just the child's viewing of the parental relationship as an excluded outsider, but also the myriad fantasies of the child in which the entire system of family relations is experimented with and internalized. The little boy or girl is at one moment the small, excluded child barred from the gratifications of adult sexuality, at another moment is the fantasied rival of the father for mother's love, and at the next moment loves father and is seeking a separate, private, and exclusive relationship with him. The child alternates between seeing himself or herself as outside of a two-person relationship, as the observer, or inside a two-person relationship, being observed by a third. Thus, it is in the oedipal stage that the child first alternates between observation and participation. This oscillating function, the moving back and forth smoothly between experiencing and observing, can come about only with the attainment of Piaget's period of concrete operations, because it requires maintaining two perspectives in mind at once (Flavell, 1963). The oscillating function is clinically important because the oscillating function becomes the basis on which a person can participate in an analysis.

From the standpoint of the development of intersubjectivity, it is critical that, in reversing the configurations of the oedipal triangle, the child comes to identify the self-as-subject with the self-as-object and the other-as-subject with the other-as-object. The child internalizes the image of the parent as an object and the image of the parent as a separate subject; but, just as important—because this involves the dialectical relations of subjectivity and objectivity—the child internalizes and identifies with the parent's image of the child (reflected appraisals)

(Sullivan, 1953, p. 17; see also Mead, 1934). Thus the child's identification with the parent's subjectivity includes, as one component, an identification with the parent's subjective image of the child as both a subject and an object. In effect, these ideas are consistent with Benjamin's (1988) view of intersubjective and intrapsychic complementarity.

Preoedipal and oedipal development is always interconnected. The development of intersubjectivity should not be seen as an early or exclusively preoedipal development, for example, one tied to the anal-rapproachment subphase, to be studied in isolation from later oedipal issues. Rather, I am suggesting that the establishment of subjectivity and of intersubjectivity continues to evolve with oedipal development.

Children are confronted with a multitude of tasks surrounding the establishment of self- and object constancy. They need to establish a sense of self as a center for action and thought, and they need to view this self in the context of other selves as an object among other objects (Bach, 1985). Similarly, they need to establish a sense of the other as a separate center of subjectivity as well as a view of the other as the object of their own subjectivity (Benjamin, 1988). These developments are of central importance to psychoanalysts since the analytic process consists of introspection and reflective self-awareness as well as of awareness of the self's interpersonal relations. Thus, one needs to develop a cohesive sense of self as a subjective self, a separate center of subjectivity, a sense of self-as-agent, an experiencing ego; and one needs to be aware of and be able to reflect upon oneself as an object of one's own investigation, as well as of oneself as an object of the wishes and intentions of others. Each of these two dimensions of self needs to be attained, and one needs to be able to recognize each of them as one's own self. When an analysand has not achieved these distinct senses of self or their integration, for example in the "narcissistic neuroses," the goal of analysis becomes to help the analysand achieve them.

A dramatic example of the failure to develop this integration is provided by Guntrip (1969), who tells of a schizoid woman who would punch herself in a perpetuation of the beatings by her mother. When Guntrip once said to her that she must feel terrified being hit like that, she stopped and stared and said, "I'm not being hit. I'm the one that's doing the hitting" (p. 191).

Postmodernist or poststructuralist thought has questioned the very existence of a unitary, cohesive, nonmultiple, essentially unique identity. Poststructuralism deconstructs and decenters the human subject and insists that the notion of a unique, bounded individual is socially and historically constituted. It is from this postmodernist perspective that Dimen (1991) and Goldner (1991) have challenged the idea of a unitary gender identity as anything other than a simplified version of a self from which opposing tendencies have been split off and repressed: "a universal, false-self system generated in compliance with the rule of the two-gender system" (Goldner, 1991, p. 259). The postmodernists insist on each of our "multiplicities" and view our "identities" with suspicion. Consequently, the term intersubjectivity should not be taken to mean relations between two cohesive subjects; rather, the terms intersubjective and interpersonal refer to relations among multiple personifications (Barratt, 1994; Bromberg, 1994, 1995; Mitchell, 1993a).

Sympathetic critics (e.g., Flax, 1990), however, have argued that postmodernists have erred by not distinguishing between a "core self" and a "unitary self." Flax proposes that "those who celebrate or call for a 'decentered' self seem self-deceptively naive and unaware of the basic cohesion within themselves that makes the fragmentation of experiences something other than a terrifying slide into psychosis" (pp. 218–219). Similarly, Rivera (1989) concluded that the idea of personality integration or unification is necessary but that personality integration prescribes

> not the silencing of different voices with different points of view—but the growing ability to call all those voices "I," to disidentify with any one of them as the whole story, and to recognize that the construction of personal identity is a complex continuing affair in which we are inscribed in culture in a myriad of contradictory ways [p. 28].

I am suggesting, in agreement with Flax and Rivera, that, instead of abandoning the notion of "identity," as the postmodernists would have us do, our understanding of subjectivity must include both "identity" and "multiplicity." Identity emphasizes a person's sense of continuity, sameness, unity, constancy, consistency, synthesis, and integration. Postmodernism is correctly concerned with the way in which the idea of identity obscures differences within and between human beings. While people certainly need a cohesive and integrated sense of self, they also need to be able to accept a lack of integration, and to tolerate—perhaps, enjoy—confusion, contradiction, flux, and even chaos in their sense of who they are. They need to accept their own internal differences, their lack of continuity, their multiplicity, their capacity to be different people at different times, in different social and interpersonal contexts. Thus, I am suggesting that, rather than abandon "identity" and "subjectivity," we maintain both identity and multiplicity as aspects of human subjectivity.

How is it that psychoanalysis, which is so concerned with individual subjective experience and with the development of the child's experience of the other, for so long neglected the exploration of intersubjectivity? Why has it taken so long for us to recognize that we must develop a conception of the other not only as object but also as separate subject? As separate psychic self? As separate center of experience?

The answer to this question brings us back to the nature of classical theory as a one-person psychology dominated by the metapsychology of drive theory. Classical metapsychology envisions the mind as a closed energy system fueled by biological drives pressing for discharge. The ego regulates, channels, and defends against these drives while attempting to find objects suitable to meet their fulfillment. From within this theoretical framework, the other person is "objectified"— seen as the "object" of the drive. Because the focus of the theory is on the vicissitudes of the drives, the role of the other is reduced to that of the object of the drives, and the most relevant variable is whether he or she is gratifying or frustrating. It is only with the shift in psychoanalysis away from drive theory and toward a relational theory that psychoanalysis could begin to study the other not as an object but as a separate subject. As Mitchell (1986b) has put it, "If the analytic situation is not regarded as one subjectivity and one objectivity, or one subjectivity and one facilitating environment, but two subjectivities—the participation in and inquiry into this interpersonal dialectic becomes a central focus of the work" (p. 38).

On a more deeply unconscious level, it may be that psychoanalytic theorists were unable to conceptualize early development intersubjectively because they were avoiding the recognition of the mother as a separate subject. Dinnerstein (1976), Chodorow (1978), and Benjamin (1988) have clarified the ways that our collective fear and envy of the mother lead us to objectify her as a means to control and devalue her.

INTERSUBJECTIVITY AND CLINICAL PRACTICE

The theory of intersubjectivity has profound implications for psychoanalytic practice and technique as well as for theory. Just as psychoanalytic theory has focused on the mother exclusively as the object of the infant's needs while ignoring the subjectivity of the mother, so too psychoanalysis, neglecting the subjectivity of the analyst as he or she is experienced by the patient, has considered the analyst only as an object.

The traditional model of the analytic situation retained the notion of a neurotic patient who brought his or her irrational childhood wishes, defenses, and conflicts into the analysis to be analyzed by a relatively mature, healthy, and well-analyzed analyst who would study the patient with scientific objectivity and technical neutrality. The health, rationality, maturity, neutrality, and objectivity of the analyst were idealized, and thus countertransference was viewed as an unfortunate, but (it was to be hoped) infrequent, lapse. Within the psychoanalytic situation, this bias, which regarded the patient as sick and the analyst as possessing the cure (Racker, 1968), led to the assumption that only the patient had transferences. It was as if only the patient possessed a "psychic reality" (see McLaughlin, 1981), the analyst being left as the representative of objective reality. If the analyst was to be a rational, relatively distant, neutral, anonymous, scientist/observer, an "analytic instrument" (Isakower, 1963), then there was little room in the model for the analyst's psychic reality or subjectivity, except as pathological, intrusive countertransference.[2]

As is well known, only in the most recent decades has countertransference been viewed as a topic worthy of study and as potentially valuable in the clinical situation. For Freud (1910), countertransference reflected a specific disturbance in the analyst elicited in response to the patient's transference and necessitating further analysis of the analyst. Contemporary theorists are more inclined to take a "totalistic" (Kernberg, 1965) approach to countertransference. They view it as reflecting all the analyst's emotional responses to the patient and therefore useful as a clinical tool. Rather than viewing countertransference as a hindrance to the analytic work which should be kept in check or overcome and which should in any event be kept to a minimum, most analysts today recognize the ubiquity of analysts' feelings and fantasies regarding patients and hope to utilize their reactions to understand their patients better. Psychoanalysis has thus broadened its data base to include the subjectivity of the analyst. It has not yet, however, sufficiently considered the patient's experience of the analyst's subjectivity.

In my view, referring to the analyst's total responsiveness as countertransference is a serious mistake because doing so perpetuates the defining of the analyst's experience in terms of the subjectivity of the patient. Thinking of the analyst's experience as "counter" or responsive

---

[2] Isakower's concept of the analyzing instrument has been valuable in highlighting the importance of unconscious communication between patient and analyst. The term "instrument," however, is problematic because of its mechanical and technical connotations, and it has now become an outdated artifact superseded by such concepts as intersubjectivity (Natterson, 1991).

to the patient's transference encourages the belief that the analyst's experience is reactive rather then subjective, emanating from the center of the analyst's psychic self (McLaughlin, 1981; Wolstein, 1983). It is not that the analyst is never responsive to the pressures that the patient puts on him or her. Of course, the analyst counterresponds to the impact of the patient's behavior. But the term counter-transference obscures the recognition that the analyst is often the initiator of the interactional sequences, and therefore the term coun-tertransference minimizes the impact of the analyst's behavior on the transference.

The relational-perspectivist approach I am advocating views the patient–analyst relationship as continually being established and reestablished through ongoing mutual influence in which both patient and analyst systematically affect, and are affected by, each other. A communication process is established between patient and analyst in which influence flows in both directions. This implies a "two-person psychology" or a regulatory-systems conceptualization of the analytic process. The terms transference and countertransference too easily lend themselves to a model that implies a one-way influence in which the analyst reacts to the patient. That the influence between patient and analyst is not equal does not mean that it is not mutual; the ana-lytic relationship may be mutual without being symmetrical. This model of the therapeutic relationship has been strongly influenced by the recent conceptualizations of mother–infant mutual influence pro-posed by Lachmann and Beebe (1988b, 1995). (I expand on it further in Chapters 4 and 5.)

Others have also proposed that we abandon the term counter-transference. Olinick (1969) suggested the alternative "eccentric responses" in the "psychology of the analyst," but I see no advantage to the pejorative word, eccentric. Bird (1972) sees transference as the basis for all human relationships and refers to it simply to "the analyst's transferences." This strategy, however, leads to terminological confu-sion, such as in Loewald's (1986) discussion of the importance of ana-lyzing the patient's countertransference to the analyst's transference (p. 280). McLaughlin (1981) convincingly argues for abandoning the term countertransference altogether: "The term countertransference particularly cannot accommodate the intrapsychic range and fullness of the analyst's experiences vis-à-vis his patient" (p. 656).

In a seminal paper, Hoffman (1983) draws together the work of theorists from a wide variety of psychoanalytic schools. These theorists share a radical social and perspectival conception of psychoanalysis that recognizes that patients make plausible inferences regarding aspects of their analysts' experience. Hoffman advances a view of psychoanalytic technique that makes central the analysis of the patient's interpretations of the analyst's experience. In many respects, much of this chapter may be seen as my efforts to grapple with and elaborate on the implications of Hoffman's contribution. While Hoffman titled his paper "The Patient as Interpreter of the Analyst's Experience," he continues to refer to the patient's interpretation of the analyst's countertransference. Because of my objections to the implications of the term countertransference, I prefer to describe the focus of this chapter as the patient's experience of the analyst's subjectivity.

Racker (1968) was one of the first to make the technical recommendation that "analysis of the patient's fantasies about countertransference, which in the widest sense constitute the causes and consequences of the transference, is an essential part of the analysis of the transferences" (p. 131). Gill (1983b) puts it simply and directly, although in my view this point has not received nearly the attention it deserves: "A consequence of the analyst's perspective on himself as a participant in a relationship is that he will devote attention not only to the patient's attitude toward the analyst but also to the patient's view of the analyst's attitude toward the patient" (p. 112).

Since, from a classical perspective, the analyst was viewed as participating with the patient in only a minimal way (Gill, 1983b), very little attention was given to the impact of the individual analyst and his or her character. Classical analysts did not consider that their patients would inevitably and persistently seek to connect with their analysts by exploring their own observations and inferences about their analysts' behavior and inner experience.

Wolstein (1983) has pointed out that resistances are defensive efforts by a patient to cope with a particular analyst and these resistances must therefore be patterned by the patient to accommodate to some aspect of the analyst's unconscious psychology. The patient can find a specific defense or resistance to be effective only if in some way it was designed to match the personality of his or her particular analyst. Therefore, the ultimate outcome of successfully analyzing resistances is that patients will learn more not only about their own psychologies, but also about the psychology of others in their lives, particularly about the psychology of their analysts. Wolstein (1988) writes:

> Nothing was more natural than for patients to turn the strength of this new awareness and reconstruction toward the psychology of their immediately enviorning others—especially their psychoanalysts—and describe the perceived aspects of countertransference against which they thought they had gone into resistance [p. 9].

The implications of Wolstein's point are enormous, for it means that, as resistances are analyzed, patients not only expose more of their own unconscious but also gain awareness of hitherto unnoticed, dissociated, or repressed aspects of the psychology of their analysts. But, in spite of extended training analyses, analysts might not be aware of some of what their patients notice. Some of the observations that patients make about their analysts are likely to be unpleasant and anxiety provoking. Therefore, analysts might hesitate to explore the patient's resistances because of their own anxieties and resistances (also see Racker, 1968; Gill, 1982; Hoffman, 1983).

Of course, it is often argued that patients fantasize about the analyst's psychology and that therefore the successful result of analysis of these fantasies is that patients learn more about their own psychology rather then about that of their analysts. These fantasies are not endogenously determined, drive-determined, autistic creations of the patient, nor are they purely the result of expectations derived from past interpersonal experiences. Rather, these fantasies may be seen as the patients' attempts to grapple with and grasp, in their own unique and idiosyncratic ways, the complex and ambiguous reality of their analysts (see Levenson, 1989). Ultimately, an analysis of these fantasies must contribute to a clearer understanding of both the patient's and the analyst's psychologies.

I believe that patients, even very disturbed, withdrawn, or narcissistic ones, always accommodate the interpersonal realities of the analyst's character and of the analytic relationship. Patients tune in, consciously and unconsciously, to the analyst's attitudes and feelings toward them, but insofar as they believe that these observations touch on sensitive aspects of the analyst's character, patients are likely to communicate these observations only indirectly through allusions to others, as displacements, or by describing these characteristics as aspects of themselves, as identifications (Lipton, 1977; Gill, 1982; Hoffman, 1983). An important aspect of making the unconscious conscious is to bring into awareness and articulate the patient's denied observations, repressed fantasies, and unformulated experiences of the analyst (Racker, 1968; Levenson, 1972, 1983; Hoffman; 1983).

All children observe and study their parents' personalities. They attempt to make contact with their parents by reaching into their parents' inner worlds. The Kleinians have vividly emphasized this tendancy of children through concrete metaphors of the infant's seeking literally to climb inside and explore the mother's body and to discover all the objects contained inside. Children imagine with what and with whom their mothers are preoccupied. They have some sense of how their mothers related to their own mothers, the children's grandmothers. A mother's internal working model of her relationship with her own mother affects her child's attachment to her (Main, Kaplan, and Cassidy, 1985). Children acquire some sense of the characters who inhabit their parent's inner worlds and of the nature of the relations among these inner objects. Most important, children formulate plausible interpretations of their parents' attitudes and feelings toward the children themselves. Children are powerfully motivated to penetrate to the center of their parents' selves. Pick (1985) states this thought in Kleinian language: "If there is a mouth that seeks a breast as an inborn potential, there is, I believe, a psychological equivalent, i.e. a state of mind which seeks another state of mind" (p. 157). There is a preexperiential motivational push, a drive, for a meeting of minds; although, as I argue later (in Chapter 8), there is also a drive to remain hidden, an isolate, unfound and untouched by others. These conflicting desires operate in both patient and analyst. Hence, intersubjectivity is always intensely conflictual.

If, as McDougall (1980), asserts, "a baby's earliest reality is his mother's unconscious" (p. 251), then a patient's psychic reality may be said to implicate the analyst's unconscious. Patients have conscious and unconscious beliefs about the analyst's inner world. Patients use their observations of their analysts—which are plentiful no matter how anonymous an analyst may attempt to be—to construct a picture of their analyst's character structure. Patients probe, more or less subtly, in an attempt to penetrate the analyst's professional calm and reserve. They do this probing not only to turn the tables on their analysts defensively or angrily, but also because people need to connect with others. And they want to connect with others where they live emotionally, where they are authentic and fully present. So they search for information about the other's inner world. (They do this conflictedly, however, because they also wish not to know or be known by the other.)

An analytic focus on the patient's experience of the analyst's subjectivity opens the door to further explorations of the patient's childhood experiences of the parent's inner world and character structure. Similarly, patients begin to attend to their observations about the character of others in their lives. This is an inevitable and essential part of how patients begin to think more psychologically in their analyses. The analytic stance being described considers fantasies and memories not just as carriers of infantile wishes and defenses against these, but as plausible interpretations and representations of patient's experiences with significant others (Hoffman, 1983). This point was anticipated by Loewald (1970) who wrote:

> The analysand in this respect can be compared to the child—who if he can allow himself that freedom—scrutinizes with his unconscious antennae the parent's motivations and moods and in this way may contribute—if the parent or analyst allows himself that freedom—to the latter's self awareness [p. 280].

In the clinical situation, I often ask patients to describe anything that they have observed or noticed about me that may shed light on aspects of our relationship. When, for example, patients say that they think that I am angry at them, or jealous of them, or acting seductively toward them, I ask them to describe whatever it is that they have noticed that led them to this belief. I find that it is critical for me to ask the question with the genuine belief that I may find out something about myself that I did not previously recognize. Otherwise, it is too easy to dismiss the patient's observation as a distortion. Patients are often all too willing to believe that they have projected or displaced these feelings onto their analyst, and they can then go back to viewing their analyst as objective, neutral, or benignly empathic. Insisting that there must have been some basis in my behavior for their conclusions, I encourage patients to tell me anything that they have observed. I often ask patients to speculate or fantasize about what is going on inside of me, and in particular I focus on what patients have noticed about my internal conflicts.[3]

For instance, a patient said that, when he heard my chair move slightly, he thought for a moment that I was going to strike him. I asked him to elaborate on what he thought I was feeling: What did he think was the quality and nature of my anger? What had he noticed about me that led him to believe that I was angry in this particular way? How did he imagine that I typically dealt with my anger and frustration? I asked the patient what he thought it was like for me to be so enraged at him and to not be able to express that anger directly, according to his understanding of the "rules" of psychoanalysis and professional decorum. I asked him how he thought I felt about his noticing and confronting me with my disguised anger.

---

[3] Elsewhere (Aron, 1989), I have suggested that, although patients are often reluctant to put these perceptions and observations into words, a particular value of studying patients' dreams is that "the analyst can use the dream themes to monitor not only the patient's transferences, but also the patient's perceptions of and fantasies about the analyst's countertransferences" (p. 125). Now, I speak of the analyst's subjectivity, rather than countertransference.

Rather than examining either the patient's own projected anger or the displaced anger of others in the patient's current or past life, I choose to first explore the patient's most subtle observations of me, which reflect my attitudes toward him as well as my character and personal conflicts. All of this ultimately needs to be explored, but, following Gill's (1983) recommendations, I begin with an analysis of the transference in the here-and-now, focusing on the plausible basis for the patient's reactions. I proceed in this way whether or not I am aware of feeling angry at that point. I assume that the patient may very well have noticed my anger, jealousy, excitement, or whatever before I recognize it in myself.

Inquiry into the patient's experience of the analyst's subjectivity represents one underemphasized aspect of a complex psychoanalytic approach to the analysis of transference. A balance needs to be maintained between focusing on the interpersonal and focusing on the intrapsychic, between internal and external object relations. While at times exploring patients' perceptions of the analyst deepens the work, at other times this path is used defensively, by both patient and analyst, to avoid the patient's painful inner experience (see Jacobs, 1986, p. 304, for a clinical illustration of this problem). For each time that I ask patients about their experience of me, there are other times when I interpret their concentrating on the interaction with me as an avoidance of their inner feelings and of looking into themselves. Of course, I need to remain open to the possibility that my interpretation is itself an expression of my own resistance to being probed. Ultimately, patient and analyst need to maintain a dialogue in which these meanings are negotiated between them. Agreement may or may not be reached, but the dialogue is essential. Intersubjective negotiation is the essence of relational practice.

While asking direct questions about the patient's observations of the analyst is often necessary and productive, the most useful way to elicit the patient's thoughts and feelings about the analyst's attitudes is to analyze the defenses and resistances that make these feelings so difficult to verbalize. Asking patients direct questions about their experience of the therapeutic relationship has the disadvantage that it may appeal to more surface and conscious levels of discourse. The analyst needs to listen to all of the patient's associations for clues to the patient's experience. Often patients fear offending their analysts and provoking the analysts' anger by confronting them with aspects of the analysts' character that have been avoided. Patients fear that they are being too personal, crossing the boundary of what the analyst is willing to let them explore. Patients are especially likely to fear that, if they expose the analyst's weaknesses and character flaws, the analyst will retaliate, become depressed or withdrawn, or crumble (Gill, 1982). Implicit in this fear is not only the patient's hostility, the patient's own projected fears, or simply the need to idealize the analyst, but also the patient's perception that the analyst's grandiosity would be shattered by the revelation of a flaw.

All of this is related to the ways in which the patient's parents actually responded to the child's observations and perceptions of them. How did the parents feel about the child's really getting to know who they were, where they truly lived emotionally? How far were the parents able to let the child penetrate into their inner worlds? Was the grandiosity of the parents such that they could not let the child uncover their weaknesses and vulnerabilities? To return to the rich Kleinian imagery of the infant's attempts in unconscious phantasy to enter into the mother's body, we may wonder whether the violent, destructive phantasies encountered are only due to innate greed and envy or whether they are not also the result of the frustration of being denied access to the core of the parent. Could these phantasies be an accurate reflection of the child's perceptions of the parents' fears of being intimately penetrated and known?

What enables patients to describe their fantasies and perceptions of the analyst is the analyst's openness and intense curiosity about the patients' experience of the analyst's subjectivity. Patients will only benefit from this probing if the analyst is truly open to the possibility that they will communicate something new to the analyst about themselves, something they have picked up about the analyst that the analyst was not aware of before. If, on the other hand, the analyst listens to a patient with the expectation of hearing a transference distortion and is not open to the likelihood and necessity of learning something new about himself or herself, then the analysis is more likely to get derailed or to continue on the basis of compliance and submission to authority. There is a tradition within psychoanalysis, although it has always remained on the periphery of the analytic mainstream, that has emphasized this mutual aspect of psychoanalysis. It began in the writings of Groddeck (1923) and Ferenczi (1932) and proceeded especially through the work of Harold Searles (1975, 1979). (I examine this tradition in detail in Chapters 5 and 6.)

When patients are encouraged to verbalize their experiences of the analyst's subjectivity, it is likely that they will put increased pressure on the analyst to verify or refute their perceptions. It is extremely difficult and frustrating for patients to be encouraged to examine their perceptions of their analysts' subjectivity and then to have their analysts remain relatively "anonymous." Once an analyst expresses interest in a patient's perceptions of the analyst's subjectivity, the analyst has tantalized the patient (Little, 1951) and will surely be pressured to disclose more of what is going on inside of himself or herself. Furthermore, how the analyst pursues the inquiry into a patient's perceptions of himself or herself is inevitably self-revealing. I assume that one reason analysts have historically avoided direct inquiry into their patients' experience of analytic subjectivity is that they recognized that pursuing this line of inquiry would unavoidably result in self-disclosure.

But self-revelation is not an option: it is an inevitability. Patients accurately and intuitively read into their analysts' interpretations the analysts' hidden communications (Jacobs, 1986). In unmasking the myth of analytic anonymity, Singer (1977) pointed out that the analyst's interpretations were first and foremost self-revealing remarks. It cannot be otherwise, since the only way we can truly gain insight into another is through our own self-knowledge; our patients know that.

Hoffman (1983) emphasizes that the psychology of the analyst is no less complex than that of the patient, as our patients know. He challenged what he termed "the naive patient fallacy," the notion that the patient accepts at face value the analyst's words and behavior. For analysts simply and directly to say what they are experiencing and feeling may encourage the assumption that they are fully aware of their own motivations and meanings. An analyst's revelations and confessions may tend to close off further exploration of a patient's observations and perceptions. Furthermore, we can never be aware in advance of just what it is that we are revealing about ourselves, and, when we think we are deliberately revealing something about ourselves, we may very well be communicating something else altogether. Is it not possible that our patients' perceptions of us are as plausible an interpretation of our behavior as the interpretations we give ourselves? If so, then it is presumptuous for us to expect patients to take at face value our self-revelations. Pontalis (1975 cited in Limentani, 1989) asks, "What is more paradoxical than the presupposition that: I see my blind spots, I hear what I am deaf to, . . . and (furthermore) I am fully conscious of my unconscious" (p. 258).

Analysts, we hope, have had the benefit of an intensive analysis of their own, but this training in no way insures that they have easy access to their unconscious or that they are immune from subtly enacting all sorts of pathological interactions with their patients. It is this recognition that has led to our contemporary acceptance of the inevitability of countertransference. Whereas in the past the idealized, well-analyzed analyst was thought to have no countertransference problem, today's idealized analysts are thought to be so well analyzed that they have immediate and direct access to their unconscious. But it is well to keep in mind that the trouble with self-analysis is in the countertransference! When analysis is viewed as a coparticipation (Wolstein, 1983) between two people who are both subjects and objects to each other, then the analyst can read the patient's associations for references to the patient's perceptions of the analyst's attitudes toward the patient. This approach provides additional data with which the analyst can supplement his or her own self-analysis. In this way, the analyst and patient coparticipate in elucidating the nature of the relationship that the two of them have mutually integrated.

Christopher Bollas is among the most creative analytic writers in the field today. While often referred to as Winnicottian, Bollas's approach is unique, expressed in his own idiom; and he is not to be pigeon-holed. Blending elements of many analytic approaches, including British object relations, classical, Kleinian, Lacanian, and interpersonal theories, his writings have been very influential for relational authors in America. Bollas (1989) advocates that the analyst establish him- or herself as a subject in the bipersonal analytic field. Bollas encourages analysts to reveal more of their internal analytic process to their patients, for example, describing to a patient how a particular interpretation was arrived at or sharing with the patient one's associations to a patient's dream. He argues that if the analyst's self-disclosure is congruent with who the analyst really is as a person, then the disclosure is unlikely to be taken as a seduction. In establishing themselves as subjects in the analytic situation, analysts make available to their patients some of their own associations and inner processes for the patient to use and analyze. It is important to note that Bollas's revelations have a playful and tentative quality. He does not take his associations or "musings" as containing absolute truth but, rather, puts them into the analytic field to have them used or even destroyed by the patient. Furthermore, Bollas is reserved and cautious in his approach because he is aware that an incessant flow of the analyst's associations could be intrusive, resulting in "a subtle takeover of the analysand's psychic life with the analyst's" (p. 69). While arguing that the analyst should be available to the patient as a separate subject, Bollas would certainly agree that we must be cautious in advocating an approach that focuses on the analyst's subjectivity because of the danger that analysts may insist on asserting their own subjectivity. Analysts may impose on patients their own need to establish themselves as separate subjects, thus forcing patients to assume the role of objects. This is not "intersubjectivity"; it is simply an instrumental relationship where the subject–object polarities have been reversed. I find Bollas's work particularly useful because in his emphasis on ordinary moments of therapeutic regression and on traditional analytic reserve, he balances his own focus, and that of most other relational theorists, on the therapeutic value of the analyst's expressiveness. Nevertheless, in spite of the high value that Bollas places on analysts's use of their subjectivities, and in spite of his cautious endorsement of self-disclosure, from my perspective Bollas pays too little attention to the analyst's personal contributions to the analytic process. For Bollas, the analyst's subjectivity is a means to search for the patient's subjectivity, and his work does not do justice to the impact of the analyst's subjectivities on a patient or on the patient's subjectivity as a reflection of the impact of the analyst.[4]

In my view, self-revelations are often useful, particularly those closely tied to the analytic process rather than those relating to details of the analyst's private life outside the analysis. Personal revelations are, in any event, inevitable; they are simply enormously complicated and require analysis of how they are experienced by the patient. We benefit enormously from the analytic efforts of our patients, but we can help our patients only if we can discipline ourselves enough to put their analytic interests ahead of our own.

The major problem for analysts in establishing themselves as subjects in the analytic situation is that, because of their own conflicts, they may abandon traditional anonymity only to impose their subjectivity on patients. They thus deprive patients of the opportunity to search out, uncover, and find the analyst as a separate subject, in their own way and at their own rate. While the patient's experience of the analyst needs to be central at certain phases of an analysis, there are other times, and perhaps long intervals, where to focus on the perceptions of the analyst is intrusive and disruptive; such a focus does not permit the patient, even temporarily, to put the analyst into the background and indulge in the experience of being left alone in the presence of the analyst. Analysts' continuous interpretations of all material in terms of the patient–analyst relationship, as well as their deliberate efforts to establish themselves as separate subjects, may be correctly experienced as an impingement stemming from their own narcissistic needs. To some degree this outcome is inevitable, and it can be beneficial for patients to articulate it when it happens (Aron, 1990a,b, 1991a, 1992b).

---

[4] It is interesting, from my perspective, that neither Bollas nor Ogden goes far enough in recognizing the impact of the analyst as a person on the unfolding of the patient's transference. This relative neglect may be because, while both are broadly relational, they tend to draw their influence largely from British psychoanalysis (Middle Group and Kleinian). My own clinical sensibility has been more heavily influenced by the contributions of the American interpersonalists.

Winnicott (1971a) suggested that psychoanalysis occurs in an intermediate state, a transitional space between the patient's narcissistic withdrawal and full interaction with reality, between self-absorption and object usage, between introspection and attunement to the other, between relations to a subjective-object and to an object, objectively perceived, between fantasy and reality. In my own clinical work I attempt to maintain an optimal balance between the necessary recognition and confirmation of the patient's experience and the necessary distance to preserve an analytic space that allows the patient to play with interpersonal ambiguity and to struggle with the ongoing lack of closure and resolution. A dynamic tension needs to be preserved between responsiveness and participation, on one hand, and nonintrusiveness and space on the other, intermediate between the analyst's presence and absence.

My manner of maintaining this tension is different with each patient and varies even in the analysis of a single analysand. I believe that each analyst–patient pair needs to work out a unique way of managing this precarious balance. The analysis itself must come to include the self-reflexive examination of the ways in which this procedure becomes established and modified. Analysis, from this perspective, is mutual but asymmetrical, with both patient and analyst functioning as subject and object, as coparticipants, and both working on the very edge of intimacy (Ehrenberg, 1992). The degree and nature of the analyst's deliberate self-revelation are left open to be resolved within the context of each unique psychoanalytic situation.

In my frequent attempts to present these thoughts to groups of colleagues and students, I have been struck by the overwhelming tendency on the part of my listeners to focus the discussion on the issue of the analyst's self-revelations. In my view, what is most important is not the analyst's deliberate self-disclosure but, rather, the analysis of the patient's experience of the analyst's subjectivity. The very expression by the patient of his or her perceptions of the analyst leads to the acknowledgment of the analyst as a separate subject in the mind of the patient. So why do analytic audiences focus on self-revelation?

Of course, one reason that analysts are interested in these issues is that until recently self-disclosure had never been considered acceptable as part of psychoanalytic technique, which has drive theory as its underlying foundation. As analysts have abandoned drive theory, they have had to rethink the basic principles of analytic technique anew. As analysts beginning with a new set of principles and assumptions must reconsider how they work, they have become interested in the therapeutic value, as well as in the dangers, of self-disclosure.

There are other reasons for the intense interest in self-disclosure as well. I believe that people who are drawn to analysis as a profession have particularly strong conflicts regarding their desire to be known by another; that is, they have conflicts concerning intimacy. In more traditional terms, these are narcissistic conflicts over voyeurism and exhibitionism. Why else would anyone choose a profession in which one spends one's life listening and looking into the lives of others while one remains relatively silent and hidden? The recognition that analysts, even those who attempt to be anonymous, are never invisible and that patients seek to "know" their analysts raises profound anxieties for analysts who are struggling with their own longings to be known and defensive temptations to hide. This recognition leads to the question of to what extent and in what ways it might be useful for the analyst purposefully to disclose aspects of the countertransference to the patient. If we admit that our patients do indeed observe a great deal about us no matter how anonymous we may try to be, then is it clinically indicated for the analyst purposefully to reveal aspects of themselves to their patients as part of the analytic work? This question has stimulated a heated controversy among analysts of all schools of thought.

Establishing one's own subjectivity in the analytic situation is essential and yet problematic. Deliberate self-revelations are always highly ambiguous and are enormously complicated. Our own psychologies are as complicated as our patients', and our unconsciouses no less deep. We need to recognize that our own self-awareness is limited and that we are not in a position to judge the accuracy of our patients' perceptions of us. Thus, the idea that we might "validate" or "confirm" our patients' perceptions of us is presumptuous. Furthermore, direct self-revelation cannot provide a shortcut to, and may even interfere with, the development of a patient's capacity to recognize the analyst's subjectivity. Nevertheless, I believe that there are clinical circumstances where self-disclosure is analytically useful, at least for some analysts (since technique is highly personal). In Chapter 8, where I explore the question of self-disclosure in more detail, I argue for a good deal of personal flexibility in deciding when, what, how much, and why to self-disclose. In this chapter, my goal is to highlight the importance of analyzing a patient's conflicts about knowing the analyst.

CLINICAL ILLUSTRATION

The following is an example of the impact of an analyst's inquiry into the patient's experience of the analyst's subjectivity. I was consulted by a young analyst trained in the classical tradition who was treating a patient who was himself a psychology graduate student. The analyst came to me for supervision specifically because he wanted to be exposed to a relational approach. He was about to deliver a scholarly paper, and the patient had seen a brochure advertising the conference presentation. For the past five weeks this had been the dominant topic of the patient's associations. The patient was conflicted about whether or not to attend the meeting and see and hear his analyst present the paper. He spent a good part of his sessions associating about his ambivalence concerning this decision.

His considerations included that he thought he would be envious of the analyst, that he would sit in the audience feeling resentful that it was his analyst giving a paper and not himself getting this admiration and recognition from the audience. He was concerned about seeing his analyst with other people. He wondered whom he would see his analyst talking to. Would the analyst be there with a woman, his wife perhaps? He was concerned that he would then feel jealous of the analyst's sexual relationship to a woman. At the same time, he thought that he would be filled with admiration for the analyst. He might sit in the audience feeling so impressed with the analyst that he would have a sexual fantasy about him; he would fantasize giving his analyst a blow job so as to absorb his analyst's strength and potency. On the other hand, he was sure that he would be tempted to find a fatal flaw in his analyst's presentation. He would be the one in the audience who would stand up at the end of the presentation and ask the most penetrating and devastating question, humiliating his analyst in front of everyone. He was thrilled that it seemed as though his analyst might become famous. He always wanted to be analyzed by a famous analyst so that he could tell people and they would all recognize the name and be impressed. He, though, was afraid to present papers even in class; he was afraid of the humiliation he would suffer if he were criticized.

I listened to the analyst as he presented the process notes of many of these sessions. I was indeed impressed that the analysis seemed in many ways to be going well. The patient, after all, was telling the analyst all sorts of personal fantasies directly concerning his relationship with the analyst. The analyst had created an environment safe enough that the patient could expose all these thoughts, including sexual, particularly homosexual ones, aggressive, competitive, rivalrous, jealous, admiring, loving, and hateful thoughts. Yet, listening to the session notes, I was struck by the level of intellectualization about the material. In fact, the patient seemed to be excited about producing this material, perhaps to please the analyst and even give him something to write a paper about. The analyst, I should say, had been helpful to the patient in asking him about his feelings as he associated and helping him to articulate these thoughts and fantasies, as well as his feelings.

I asked the analyst what he would in fact feel if the patient showed up to see him present the paper. The analyst deflected my question by answering that he really did not expect that the patient would come. I asked again: if he did come, what would it be like for you? He said he was not sure; he felt rather indifferent. He did not think that he would feel anything much one way or the other.

I suggested that in the next session, when the patient discussed his thoughts and feelings about this topic once again, he might find a suit-able moment to ask the patient the following question, or something like it, in his own words and style: "What do you imagine that it will be like for me to have you come hear the paper? Picture me up at the podium about to read the paper, I look out into the audience and I notice you are there. What do you imagine I feel at that moment?"

The analyst laughed when I made this suggestion. He wondered why it had never occurred to him to ask anything like that. It was not his style, he said. He thought it might direct too much attention to his feelings and detract from the patient's experience. But he would think about it. I told him that I certainly would not pressure him to make any intervention that felt uncomfortable to him. After all, he knew the patient better than I, and more important, his interventions and his style of working would have to fit his own character and personal style.

The next few consultations proved enormously interesting. Indeed, the analyst had asked the question as I recommended. He was not prepared for what happened next, not to the patient, but to himself. For the first time, the patient stopped finding it so easy to free associ-ate. All of a sudden, instead of being able to think of one idea after another about what it would be like to go to the presentation, now the patient felt blocked, uncomfortable, and intensely anxious. The analyst too began to feel anxious, but now his thoughts were racing concerning the upcoming talk. He began to imagine what it would be like to meet the patient at the talk, and he realized that, indeed, he would have feelings about it, many of them not at all unlike those of his patient.

He was able to work with the patient and show him that his difficulty associating now had to do with his fears of making the analyst more anxious by talking about him in a way that was much more personal. The analyst had gone from being the patient's object to being a sepa-rate subject, and this change had happened *not* because of a develop-mental step on the patient's part, but because the analyst had shifted his stance and opened himself up to his own subjectivity. While the analyst may have conveyed something of his own anxiety and conflict in pursuing this work, it was all done with relatively little direct self-disclosure of the content of his own reactions. Nevertheless, this intervention significantly shifted the analysis. This example illustrates the importance of exploring the patient's experience of the analyst's subjectivity; it also demonstrates the power of an intervention to have a mutual impact on both the patient and the analyst.

The exploration of the patient's experience of the analyst's subjectivity represents only one aspect of the analysis of transference. It needs to be seen as but one underemphasized component of a detailed and thorough explication and articulation of the therapeutic relationship in all of its aspects. The psychoanalytic encounter constitutes an intersubjective exchange that leads not simply to agreement or acquiescence, but rather to dialogue and connection, to a meeting of minds.

4 | Interpretation as Expression of the Analyst's Subjectivity

The thesis of this chapter is that all analytic interventions reflect aspects of the analyst's subjectivity. There are no therapeutic interventions delivered from a position of neutrality or transcendent objectivity; rather all interventions reflect the person of the analyst as a separate subject. In Renik's (1993b) words, "Every aspect of an analyst's clinical activity is determined in part by his or her personal psychology" (p. 553).

I suggest further that not only does every intervention reflect the analyst's subjectivity, but it is precisely the personal elements contained in the intervention that are most responsible for its therapeutic impact. In particular, I believe that it is the emotionally responsive aspects of the analyst's subjectivity that are communicated to the patient through the intervention that lead to its effectiveness. It is however, precisely because the subjective element is contained within a technical intervention that it is transformed from being simply an idiosyncratic emotional response on the analyst's part into an analytic intervention carrying a sense of dialectical objectivity, (to be discussed fully in the Coda), and it is this mix of the personal and the technical that potentially generates its transformative analytic power.[1]

I have been speaking of interventions rather then interpretations because a number of writers (see Bromberg, 1985; Maroda, 1991; Renik, 1993b) have objected to the use of the term interpretation within a relational context on the ground that it implies an active and authoritative analyst "giving" an "objective" *interpretation* to the relatively passive and less informed patient. These authors are rightly concerned that for contemporary analysts to continue to speak of interpretation may obscure the extent to which the term was originally embedded in the structural model of conflict. For Freud (1900), to interpret (*Deutung*) was to assign meaning (*Bedeutung*) to the patient's

---

[1] Elsewhere (Aron, 1991b, 1993a), I have elaborated on the therapeutic action of psychoanalysis and the concept of working through.

material (p. 96). The German *Deutung* is closer to the English term explanation than to interpretation (see Laplanche and Pontalis, 1973, p. 228). I will continue to speak of interpretation, however, because I believe that the word has other connotations that make it useful even within a relational framework.

I think of interpretation not in its ego-psychological meaning of an explanation or translation with the connotation of one who knows interpreting to one who does *not* know. Rather, I like the term interpretation because it can also be used to mean the expression of a person's conception of a work of art or subject, as for example, the pianists interpretation of a sonata or an actor's interpretation of a role. This use of the word interpretation emphasizes the individual's unique, personal expressiveness. I like to think of an analyst's interpretation as a creative expression of his or her conception of some aspect of the patient. Using the term in this way, I believe that an analyst may interpret with a sense of conviction even while eschewing certainty and abandoning positivist epistemological presuppositions (Hoffman, 1992a, b, 1993). My thesis, in any event, applies to interpretations as well as to all the analyst's interventions. I believe that all interventions, including interpretations, are expressions of the analyst's subjectivity and that it is precisely this that gives them whatever effectiveness they may have.

I propose a shift from the traditional view of interpretation as conveying information about the mind of the patient *from* the analyst *to* the patient to a view of interpretation as a bipersonal and reciprocal communication process, a mutual meaning-making process. Interpretation is a complex intersubjective process that develops conjointly between patient and analyst. A contemporary reinterpretation of the nature of psychoanalytic interpretation demands a deconstruction of several fundamental psychoanalytic terms, concepts, and principles. My use of the term interpretation is extremely broad and encompasses much of the process of interpersonal exploration and inquiry, as well as affective attunement and nonverbal responsiveness. This usage also moves in the direction of breaking up the neat distinction between verbal interpretations (which have traditionally been given higher status) and other verbal and nonverbal interventions (which have traditionally been less highly valued).

THE DATA OF INTERPRETATION

From the point of view of traditional psychoanalysis, an interpretation is an explanation that conveys knowledge about the patient's psychic life from the analyst to the patient (Lowenstein, 1951). From this perspective, everything that the patient says is to be regarded as an association. The patient never interprets, because by definition an interpretation conveys knowledge from the analyst to the patient. When patients insightfully explain aspects of their own behavior, it may seem as if they have interpreted their own behavior, but the analyst is to regard even these explanations as further associations, manifest content, which itself needs interpretation. At the same time, the analyst, from a traditional point of view (whether Freudian or Kleinian), should never associate, that is, speak his or her mind freely; rather, the analyst should interpret only. That is, the analyst may make other interventions, like clarifying or confronting, but these interventions are preparatory to the interpretation and should be kept to a minimum, subordinated to the primacy of interpretation as the mode of conveying knowledge to the patient. From this perspective, Etchegoyen (1991) states that what distinguishes the psychoanalytic field is that the observational data come from the patient, and the analyst "abstains rigorously from offering any data. . . . The aim of the analytic situation is to create a field of observation where the data are offered exclusively by the patient" (p. 502).

Etchegoyen, himself a Kleinian, has written what has already become a classic text on psychoanalytic technique that integrates the world's literature, drawn from four languages on the subject (although unfortunately excluding the American interpersonal literature). He is conveying the international consensus among psychoanalysts when he suggests that the analyst's task is to interpret, that is, to explain the patient's behavior and associations; it is not to add any new data. Therefore, if the patient has a particular impact on the analyst (if for instance, the patient always confuses the analyst), then for the analyst to tell the patient of that effect—that is, to communicate the counter-transference reaction directly—would be to provide the patient not with an explanation but with a new piece of data that itself is in need of an explanation. Etchegoyen's position is that this is contrary to the analytic method. Similarly, to tell a patient how you arrived at a particular interpretation, even if the explanation revealed nothing personal about your life, would not be an explanation of the patient's data but, rather, would provide the patient with information about you, about your thought processes, and in this sense would be self-revealing.

It is particularly interesting to note Etchegoyen's position that the data should flow in only one direction, because he is aware of the inter-subjective and mutual nature of the analytic situation. He recognizes as valid, for example, the Barangers' (1966) claim that the analytic situation is a bipersonal field. Nevertheless, for Etchegoyen, and most traditional analysts, even if the analytic situation is seen as an interpersonal field, that is, as mutual and reciprocal, and even if the object of investigation is the field itself, rather than the patient per se, the method of studying the field is that of a one-person psychology. As such, the method is limited to the analyst's acquiring data from the patient (unilateral data generation), rather than the two participant-observers sharing data with each other and than coparticipating in interpreting this mutually arrived at data (mutual data generation). In contrast to these mainstream approaches, the American interpersonal and relational approaches are distinguished by their use of methods that encourage the mutual generation of data by patient and analyst.

My objection to Etchegoyen's position is that, in sharpening the distinction between interpretation and data generation (association), he obscures the recognition that every interpretation by the analyst inevitably contains aspects of the analyst's subjectivity. In my view, even when the analyst attempts to interpret without revealing any personal associative material, something personal nevertheless emerges in the course of interpreting, if the interpretation is to be related and meaningful. Only the most hackneyed and barren of interpretations could be so (secondary) "processed" that it would be a rational bit of information devoid of the humanity and subjectivity of the analyst. Even if such a lifeless interpretation could be formulated (which I doubt since such an interpretation would convey something of the lifelessness of the analyst and hence would also be an expression of the analyst's subjectivity), it would be clinically inert. Therefore, Etchegoyen's insistence that the psychoanalytic method is constituted by unilateral data generation obscures the recognition that, at least inadvertently, the analyst's associations are also self-revealing and that therefore data generation is inevitably at least partially a two-way process.

MUTUALITY AND SYMMETRY IN PSYCHOANALYSIS

In the previous chapter's exploration of intersubjectivity, I emphasized, following Gill (1982) and Hoffman (1983), that one aspect of the analysis of transference is that the analyst examine and make explicit a patient's perceptions of the analyst's subjectivity. I wrote that the analyst's establishment of his or her own subjectivity in the analytic situation was essential and yet problematic. Here, I argue that an excellent way (although not the only way) for the analyst to establish himself or herself as a subject is through the use of interpretations, which while explicitly about the patient, carry a great deal of implicit data about the subjectivity of the analyst.

In choosing to emphasize the patient's experience of the analyst's subjectivity, and in implementing this choice technically, the analyst provides the patient with further opportunity to observe, experience, think, fantasize, and make inferences about the person of the analyst. Every intervention (as well as every lack of intervention), reveals something to the patient about the psychology of the analyst, his or her interests, concerns, motivations, blind spots, sensitive points. Since patients seek to connect with their analysts, and also anxiously need to guard against their analysts, they are strongly motivated to observe their analysts and probe beneath their analysts' façades, to learn about their analysts as people. Anonymity is never an option for an analyst. You can sit, but never hide, behind the couch! The patient's perceptions and observations of you are relevant even if you do not recognize yourself in the patient's descriptions. This is to say that analysts are not in an unbiased position to judge the accuracy of their patients' observations, although analysts are indeed in a position to have their own unique points of view about their patients' observations. The analyst's perspective may be asserted for exactly what it is, one point of view, a view different from the patient's and therefore potentially enriching for the patient to consider. It is this intersubjective approach to clinical psychoanalysis that I have been referring to as relational-perspectivism.

While anonymity is never an option for an analyst, neither is full self-disclosure an option. No matter how much we might think that we are being open and honest, we, like our patients, are always both revealing and concealing much of ourselves. I do believe that there are many times when a direct expression of the analyst's experience is useful. To be specific, I believe that it is often useful to share one's associations with a patient when those associations provide data that are absent from and yet directly relevant to the patient's associations; I am arguing for the advantages of a method that permits the mutual generation of data. Often I find that revealing my own associations occurs when I am explaining to a patient how I came to formulate a particular interpretation. What I believe to be particularly problematic are self-revelations in which the analyst states what she or he feels about a patient in a way that closes off further discussion, for example, saying to a patient, "Yes, you are right. I was annoyed when I said that!" or "No, I'm not aware of feeling impatient with you." These types of self-revelation are troublesome, not because they reveal too much of the analyst, but because they imply too much certainty on the analyst's part, minimize the extent to which the analyst too has an unconscious, and hence discourage further exploration by the patient (see Hoffman, 1983, and discussion of Bollas later). Of course, if the analyst is careful to say that there may be more that he or she is feeling that is out of awareness, then this may serve as an invitation to the patient to speculate about the analyst or to come forth with further observations, and in this manner it may prove useful. The critical issue seems to be whether the analyst's interventions invite or discourage further elaboration, correction, observation, and association from the patient.

Burke (1992) places the principle of mutuality in opposition to the principle of asymmetry. He suggests, for example, that the principle of mutuality leads the analyst to more frequent self-revelations and the principle of asymmetry leads the analyst to less frequent self-revelations. The problem with this notion is that it forces analysts to choose between believing in mutuality and therefore advocating self-disclosure or believing in asymmetry and therefore recommending anonymity. I believe that this conceptualization mistakenly collapses too many dimensions of the analytic interaction into one and therefore limits our thinking about some very complicated matters. The meanings of the words mutuality and symmetry remain unclear or are confounded with the question of self-disclosure. I would like to sort out a number of uses of the word mutuality and distinguish these from symmetry and from the question of self-disclosure in order to help clarify some of these controversial issues.

As I noted in the preface, symmetry is defined as a correspondence in form or arrangement on either side of a dividing line or plane. Symmetry implies similarity and quantitative equality between the two sides. How much do we think of the patient and analyst as performing equivalent functions and roles in the analytic process? I think of the psychoanalytic situation as inevitably asymmetrical because of the inherent differences in the patient's and analyst's roles, functions, and responsibilities in the analytic process, such as free associating, interpreting, confronting resistances, establishing ground rules, and setting and paying fees. My own position is that psychoanalysis is inevitably asymmetrical perhaps most importantly because there are differences in power between patient and analyst. While the roles and functions of patient and analyst are asymmetrical they do not need to be defined as rigidly dichotomous. We may think of their functioning as having overlapping qualities, for example, while the patients' function may be to free associate, to communicate as much as possible about their psychic lives, the analyst's function may be thought of as largely to listen and attempt to understand the patients' communications. This division of functions remains asymmetrical even though we recognize that analysts also communicate aspects of their psychic lives and patients also listen and attempt to understand their analysts. Etchegoyen's

(1991) position, which insists on exclusively unilateral data generation may be described as extremely asymmetrical and rigidly dichotomous.

Remember too that the essence of the word mutuality is a sharing in common or a sharing between people. In Chapter 3 I began to sort out two ways of thinking about mutuality in psychoanalysis. There I differentiated mutual recognition from mutual regulation or mutual influence. Here I want to distinguish yet another aspect of mutuality, namely, mutual generation of data. Recall that the classical method advocates unilateral data generation, whereas interpersonal and relational approaches are characterized by mutual data generation. Again, I need to emphasize that mutuality does not mean equality, and I am not implying that the data come from the patient and the analyst in equal measure or that the data generated by the analyst should be seen as having the same priority as data generated by the patient. While both patient and analyst contribute data (and therefore I speak of mutual data generation), nevertheless the patient and analyst have separate roles, functions, and responsibilities and therefore the data that they generate are not equivalent (and therefore I speak of asymmetry).

Using the word mutual alone without specification is problematic because there are so many aspects of mutuality. I conceive of the analytic relationship as fully mutual in the sense that mutual regulation needs to be assumed to be occurring at all times between patient and analyst. I view mutual recognition as one of the goals of analysis, and, in addition, I advocate mutual data generation in contrast to unilateral data generation as a general principle of the psychoanalytic method. Nevertheless, I think of the analytic situation as asymmetrical inasmuch as there are clear differences between patient and analyst regarding the purpose for which they are meeting, in their functions and responsibilities, and in the consequences for the two participants if the goals of the analysis are not met.

The meaning and clinical implications of the term asymmetry are far different from what Greenacre (1954) meant by a "tilted" emotional relationship (p. 630). Greenacre, within the context of the development of ego psychology and in her attempt to preserve and promote the patient's autonomy, suggested that the analyst's nonparticipation with the patient in a personal way should lead to a tilted emotional relationship and thus should promote the transference neurosis. My use of the term asymmetry is meant to preserve a space within relational psychoanalytic theorizing, amidst the various dimensions of mutuality, for acknowledgment of and attention to differences in power and responsibility between patient and analyst.

A discussion of some of the technical developments emerging out of the Winnicottian tradition in the British Independent Group, and particularly as developed in detail by Christopher Bollas, will clarify some of the controversy regarding symmetry and asymmetry, interpretation and self-revelation. I do not intend this to be a systematic or sequential historical review of the literature regarding interpretation. I prefer to move back and forth between a variety of theoretical positions, all of which are active and influential in contemporary psychoanalytic practice. My aim is to allow the positions to talk to each other and inform each other rather than portray psychoanalysis as having moved in a progressive, linear direction.

WINNICOTT ON INTERPRETATION

Winnicott's contributions to the theory of interpretation and analytic process, and especially the way in which his ideas have been developed by analysts within the British Independent Group, provide an alternative to the traditional, unilateral data-generation model presented by Etchegoyen (1991).

Winnicott was highly critical of, as well as very respectful and appreciative of, the two prevailing psychoanalytic methods, the Freudian and the Kleinian, and much of his writing can be read as a critique of these techniques (see Phillips, 1988). Winnicott evolved a point of view that shifted the emphasis of the psychoanalytic process from knowledge and insight to intersubjective recognition and acceptance of spontaneity and play, and therefore of true self. He gradually and subtly transformed the method of psychoanalysis from one that emphasized the patient's internalization of the analyst's reason, rationality, and insight, to one based on the patient's "use of the object" analyst for the expression of true self.

Since Winnicott did not spell out the implications of his contributions for psychoanalytic technique, it is necessary to extract technical suggestions from his more general writings. Drawing on the imaginative and articulate elaboration of his ideas by Christopher Bollas (1987, 1989, 1992, 1995) and the careful biographical exegesis of his writing by Adam Phillips (1988), I will describe three Winnicottian metaphors that shed light on Winnicott's attitude toward interpretation.

Winnicott (1941) described his use of a spatula in evaluating children. He observed a mother–infant pair at his desk where he had left a shiny spoon. He observed how the infant hesitated before reaching for the spatula and noted how the infant first checked back and forth from mother's face to Winnicott's face before picking it up. Gradually the child took the spatula, played with it, held it, bit on it, sucked it, threw it on the floor, and got down on the floor to play with it. Here Winnicott provides us with one metaphor for an interpretation. The analyst needs to provide the patient with an interpretation and observe the way in which this exciting piece of information is accepted by the patient. The interpretation, like the shiny spatula, "is a glittering object which excites the patient's greed," (1941, p. 67) and the patient wants more and more from the analyst. Following this metaphor, we would expect the patient to hesitate, to take time to decide whether it is safe to accept the interpretation. Resistance is not reluctance or a refusal to accept new knowledge but, rather, is "a period of hesitation," a slow coming to realization. Attempting to force a patient to accept an interpretation is like trying to shove the spoon down the infant's mouth. With the metaphor of the spatula, Winnicott shifts the focus from the analyst as the active purveyor of carefully constructed interpretations to the patient as the active participant who takes what the analyst has to offer and reshapes it and recreates it in accord with his or her own needs.

A second metaphor (and the overarching concept) that depicts Winnicott's (1951) take on interpretation is that of the transitional object. A parent may place a variety of items in the infant's crib and hope that the infant will select one particular item or another as a transitional object, but the parent cannot choose which item the infant will select. Winnicott implies that so it is with interpretations. The analyst puts out interpretations but cannot select which of them the patient will accept or cling to. Furthermore, the interpretation may be useful not because of the new information that it provides, but because it represents a link with the analyst. The interpretation can be carried around and sucked on when the analyst is away. The patient can play with the interpretation, cling to it, incorporate it, love it, modify it, attack it, discard it, transform it, or throw it back at the analyst.

It is with the third metaphor that we can see the full development of Winnicott's attitude toward interpretations. The model of the squiggle game, a therapeutic technique that Winnicott developed for use with older children, is relevant as a model of the kind of interaction that Winnicott might have advocated with patients generally. In the squiggle game, Winnicott (1971b) plays with his patients freely and spontaneously. Winnicott draws a line on a piece of paper, and the child has to turn the line into something. Then the child draws a line, and Winnicott has to complete it. Whose squiggle is it? Is it the child's or Winnicott's? Like the transitional object, it does not belong inside or outside, to Winnicott or to the patient. Like an interpretation, in

Winnicott's view, it does not come from the analyst or from the patient; rather, it emerges from the transitional space between them.

When Winnicott squiggles his line he does it spontaneously. He has the patient in mind. But he does not deliberately or intentionally plan his squiggles. On the contrary, they express his spontaneity; they are spontaneous gestures, reflections of true self. He does not necessarily know what will come out when he begins to draw. If he did, it would feel contrived and false. Similarly, by the end of his life, Winnicott advocated that the analytic process be thought of as an expression of play between analyst and patient. Grolnick (1990), in describing the analytic process as a form of squiggling with adults, wrote:

> Squiggling, *bilateral mutual play*, is at another realm of discourse than standard free associative technique [p. 157, italics added]. . . . The radical nature of the squiggling technique is that it involves the sharing of reactive imagery in order to foster the associative and symbol building capacities [p. 163].

Winnicott fundamentally altered our understanding of the meaning and function of interpretation. As one component of the analytic setting, interpretation represents for Winnicott a form of provision analogous to maternal care. Whereas analysts had previously focused on gaining understanding, he, however, saw the need to interpret and understand as frequently rooted in the analyst's anxiety and need to do something for the patient. Winnicott shifted our view of the analyst as active and in control (as the interpreter) to one in which the patient actively takes in from the analyst what is most useful and reshapes it to meet his or her own needs. In Winnicott's view, the analyst is encouraged to tolerate not knowing and, instead, to offer spontaneous and authentic responsiveness, the point of interpreting being to show the patient that the analyst is fully alive and imperfect. Winnicott's conceptualization of transitional phenomena destroys the sharp distinction between interpretation and free association that is central to classical technique. In this respect Winnicott not only makes clear the importance of mutuality of regulation and mutuality of recognition between patient and analyst, but also, in his clinical approach, he advocates the mutual generation of psychoanalytic data.

INTERPRETATION AND SELF-EXPRESSION: THE BRITISH INDEPENDENT GROUP

British Independent Group analysts, following Winnicott as well as Balint (1968), reconceptualized interpretation as a fundamentally relational activity (Mitchell, 1988a). For Klauber (1981), analysts need to be both authentic and spontaneous, not only for their own sake, but also so that their patients can "use" them. In arguing for analysts' spontaneity, Klauber explicitly attacks the notion that an interpretation should always be filtered through the analyst's secondary-process thought. Klauber argues that a patient knows much more about the analyst than has been recognized, and he understands the nature of therapeutic action as emanating from this "mutual participation in analytic understanding" (p. 46) in which interpretation leads to deep emotional contact between the participants, which is healing.

According to Symington (1983), interpretations not only need to be authentic and spontaneous, but also are markers of a change in the relationship between the patient and the analyst. Rather than thinking of the interpretation only as leading to change in the patient, it is, according to Symington, more accurate to view the interpretation as the expression of a change that has already occurred. If an interpretation is thought of as more than just conveying information but, rather, is seen as the carrier of the relationship, then the relationship would have had to change if the analyst is to be able to interpret in a way that he or she could not have interpreted before.

> The inner act of freedom in the analyst causes a therapeutic shift in the patient and new insight, learning and development in the analyst. The interpretation is essential in that it gives expression to the shift that has already occurred and makes it available to consciousness. The point though is that the essential agent of change is the inner act of the analyst and that this inner act is perceived by the patient and causes change [p. 286].

Lomas (1987) points out the limits of interpretation when interpretations are stripped of the analyst's emotional responsiveness. He encourages analysts to "try to reveal their true feelings as far as possible" (p. 132). His rationale is that by disclosing countertransference responses the analyst increases the patient's insight into the ways in which the two of them may unwittingly affect those around them. Lomas is critical of the blank-screen approach, anonymity, and abstinence because they tend to conceal interpersonal reality and lead to "mystification." Instead he recommends revealing oneself openly and honestly so that patients are in a better position to understand where their projections depart from reality. These representatives of the British Independent tradition are giving increased emphasis to mutual processes in psychoanalysis and to varying degrees are advocating that analytic data are generated mutually between patient and analyst.

EXPRESSIVE USES OF COUNTERTRANSFERENCE

Bollas (1987, 1989) has suggested that analysts need to establish themselves as subjects in the analytic field. He cautiously advocates that there are moments in the clinical situation when countertransference disclosure is indicated. By countertransference disclosure, Bollas means a disclosure of mental content, psychic process, emotional reality, or self-state that is congruent with the character of the analyst, that is, that is authentic. Bollas argues that insofar as patients use projective identification, they place into their analysts dissociated aspects of themselves. Analysts also become "mediums for the psychosomatic processing of the patient's psyche-soma" (p. 59). Therefore, much of the data that need to be processed analytically exist within the analyst rather than within the patient, and the analytic work needs to take place predominantly in the analyst. Bollas recommends a method he calls "the dialectics of difference," in which the analyst reveals more of him- or herself than is traditionally sanctioned. The analyst is encouraged to describe to the patient how he or she arrived at a particular interpretation rather than just making the interpretation in the finished form of secondary process. In advocating these procedures, Bollas suggests caution and is careful to clarify that all of this requires discipline.

Bollas, however, like Winnicott before him, underplays the extent to which these technical suggestions mark a fundamental break with the classic analytic method. Bollas's recommendations represent a radical change in technique because, by revealing his inner process, the analyst is sharing with the patient his or her own associations and in doing so is promoting the mutual generation of data between patient and analyst. As we saw in our examination of Etchegoyen (1991), the consensus among mainstream psychoanalysts is that psychoanalysis is defined by a unilateral method of data generation. For Bollas, the analyst is no longer the representative of rationality and reality as in the classical model, but now reveals his own psychic reality. Thus, by actually contributing data and not just explanation of data, the analyst takes on a function that previously was thought to be the prerogative of patients.

Bollas's procedure calls on the analyst to free associate with the patient. The analyst's associations are thought of as "musings," which may be freely shared with the patient; patient and analyst are squiggling together. For example, the analyst may share his or her own associations to a patient's dream as a way of facilitating the associative process in the patient. Interestingly, analysts writing from within a more radical interpersonal tradition, with an emphasis on increased symmetry as well as mutuality, have considered sharing not only associations to a patient's dreams, but even relating one's own dreams to the patient (Tauber, 1954). Here we can see the contrasting technical implications of varying positions along the axis of unilateral versus mutual data generation.

Bollas encourages the analyst to differ with himself. For instance, Bollas may tell a patient that he disagrees with a prior interpretation that he made. In doing this, Bollas not only brings into the analytic situation his own psychic reality, but also introduces attenuated aspects of his own psychic conflict. Bollas highlights those moments in which his patients disagree with him and thus paves the way to disagree with and confront a patient with alternative perspectives. It seems to me that this dialectic of difference makes it easier for patients to acknowledge their own psychic conflict since they are not forced into a position in which they are the only one in the room experiencing conflict.

In introducing the analyst as a subject in the analytic field, with his or her own associations, psychic reality, and conflicts, Bollas has modified the classical method, in which all of the relevant data of study is contributed by the patient, and instead acknowledges that data is contributed for analysis by both participants. While Bollas's contribution is clearly in the Winnicottian tradition, Bollas is more explicit about his recommendations for clinical psychoanalytic technique than Winnicott was. Therefore, although he presents himself as part of the psychoanalytic mainstream, the radical nature of his contributions is more obvious than Winnicott's were. The neat distinction between interpretations and other interventions (such as sharing one's own associations or musings) breaks down. The procedure remains asymmetrical in the sense that emphasis is given to analyst's retaining full responsibility for determining precisely what, when, and how to share selective aspects of their own subjectivity.

MUTUALITY WITH ASYMMETRY

After advocating procedures that emphasize expressive uses of the countertransference and the dialectics of difference, Bollas (1987, 1989) asks how we can share our associations with our patients and not have this process become an intrusion onto what should be the patient's space. How can we avoid "a subtle takeover of the patient's psychic life with the analysts?" (Bollas, 1989, p. 69). Bollas defers a full consideration of the technical issues, but he answers briefly that

> the analyst's reporting of his thoughts and associations must be momentary and set against the background of the patient's discourse and the silence that creates the analytic screen. A continuous, incessant flow of the analyst's thoughts or observations would not be appropriate. . . . So, although there will

be occasions when the analyst will elaborate associations, it is important for the analyst to stop in order to create a boundary around the association [p. 69].

I have argued, along similar lines, that analysts risk abandoning traditional anonymity only to substitute imposing their subjectivity on patients and thus depriving patients of the opportunity to search out, uncover, and find the analyst as a separate subject, in their own ways and at their own rate.

Hoffman (1991) similarly stressed the "importance of the asymmetrical arrangement as a means of insuring that the patient's experience remains at the center of attention" (p. 92). The analytic relationship needs to be mutual and yet asymmetrical. (See Baranger and Baranger, 1966; Wachtel, 1986, and Hoffman, 1991, for similar proposals.) Some degree of asymmetry is a necessary, although certainly insufficient, condition for analysis. The optimal balance or tension between participation and nonintrusiveness cannot be established in advance by a standard set of rules or by a "model technique." Rather it must emerge from the analytic work between a particular patient and a particular analyst and will likely change, even from moment to moment, within a given analysis. Technical recommendations cannot be made independent of a consideration of the individuality of the analyst and of the patient, since the meanings of self-exposure versus anonymity and closeness versus distance will vary from one analyst to another as well as from one patient to another.

RELATIONAL PERSPECTIVES ON THE ANALYST'S SELF-EXPRESSION

Relational theorists have reconceptualized the nature of analytic change and especially the interaction among insight, structural change and the analytic relationship, giving an emphasis to the ways in which interpretations are themselves "complex relational events" (Mitchell, 1988a, p. 295). We saw that Winnicott and British Independent analysts reconsidered the significance of interpretation in psychoanalysis. Similarly, Kohut (1984), shifted the focus of our interpretive efforts from explanation to understanding, proposing that new experience with the analyst as selfobject is as important as explanation.

The interpersonal tradition, with its emphasis on interpretation as an interpersonal participation by the analyst, provides yet a different perspective. The interpersonal approach views the analyst as a "participant-observer" (Sullivan, 1953) or "co-participant" (Wolstein, 1981) functioning within an interpersonal field, and the "detailed inquiry" (Sullivan, 1954) is a "collaborative inquiry" (Chrzanowski,

1980) in which the analyst is as free to provide data as the patient is. Since the analyst is free to provide data and not just interpretation, interpersonal analysts suggest that one may at times share one's own associations and experiences with the patient even before one knows its meaning or significance (Ehrenberg, 1992). This procedure is suggested in the hope that by discussing the analyst's experience with the patient some meaning or significance will be established. Clearly, the American interpersonal tradition has been the most explicit and most radical in advocating mutuality in the generation of psychoanalytic data.

From a contemporary interpersonal perspective (Levenson, 1972) transference-countertransference interactions are mutually constructed, are never simply talked about, but are always enacted as they are being discussed. The analyst must recognize her or his participation in the enactment and work her or his way out of it either through further inquiry or through interpretation. Even in "accurately" interpreting a transference–countertransference enactment, however, and thus in working one's way out of an interaction, the analyst may well be participating in or enacting another interaction. Therefore, what may be an interpretation (a working one's way out) of one transference–countertransference enactment may be a participation in (being pulled into) another enactment (Gill, 1983b). Speech always serves more purposes than simply to communicate; speech always is, in addition, a form of action. When we speak, we act on the person spoken to. The implication here is that interpretation cannot be seen simply as in the service of communicating information or knowledge to the patient; rather, interpretation is itself an interpersonal act. Interpretation is one form—and for some it is the only form—by which analysts participate in the interaction with their patients. (Chapter 7 elaborates in detail on interaction from an interpersonal perspective.)

Another argument, supporting asymmetry while recognizing the subjective dimensions of interpretation, is offered by Smith (1990), who puts forth the thesis that all mutative interpretations are first enacted in the countertransference and that therapists gain awareness of the nature of the transference through these enactments. In other words, often, and perhaps regularly, we do not know the "correct" interpretation until after we make an interpretation. It is only by interpreting, which is our analytic form of participation, that we can recognize the nature of the interaction that we are involved in with the patient. Smith, however, in contrast to the radical interpersonalists, while acknowledging that "actual neutrality is a fiction" (p. 100), does not conclude that neutrality should be abandoned. Instead, he argues that, paradoxically, "the less possible it is to be neutral in fact, the more crucial it is to strive toward it" (p. 101).

To round out this comparison of relational perspectives on the nature of interpretation I would like to highlight the contributions of Baranger and Baranger (1966), who write from within a Latin American, Kleinian metapsychological orientation. They apply to the analytic situation the concept of the *field*, from Gestalt psychology and from the phenomenology of Merleau-Ponty. They view the analytic situation as a "bipersonal field" (p. 384) and highlight mutuality and interactional aspects of the process. The bipersonal field is structured by the interaction and communication arising from both the patient and the analyst. What distinguishes the psychoanalytic field is that it is structured as an unconscious fantasy comprising contributions from both members of the bipersonal field through mutual projective and introjective identifications and counteridentifications. Symptoms, resistances, and insights are all viewed as products of the field and therefore as resulting from joint participation by both members of the field. The Barangers note that both the patient and the analyst tend to repeat past problematic patterns of relations in their contemporary interpersonal life. Therefore, for the Barangers, the analyst's interpretations serve to modify the analyst's relation to the patient as well as the patient's relation to the analyst. Put simply, the interpretation, in reducing the pathology of the bipersonal field, serves to cure both the analyst and the patient. Nevertheless, the Barangers consider the structure of the analytic situation to include a "basic asymmetric functional relationship" (p. 384) between patient and analyst.[2] Etchegoyen (1991) has legitimately questioned in what respects the Barangers' position remains asymmetrical. He disagrees with them in that he insists that what defines the psychoanalytic method is that all of the data be provided by the patient rather than by the analyst, furthermore he argues that they neglect the differences between patient and analyst in the degree and form of their participation.

CASE ILLUSTRATIONS AND CRITIQUES

From Hoffman

Hoffman (1992a) suggests that supervisees may report that they are struggling in their work with patients because, on one hand, they would like to tell the patient X but they are afraid of Y. At these moments,

---

[2] I am indebted to the monumental scholarship of Robert Langs (1976, 1981), which first acquainted me with the controversial ideas of the Barangers and their critics.

Hoffman says, he often suggests to supervisees that they tell the patient just that, that is, that they tell the patient, "I want to tell you X but I am afraid of Y." Hoffman cites a number of examples that take this form. In one, the supervisee is encouraged to say something like the following. "I am pulled to see your point of view or to take your side in this conflict that you describe with your friend; however, I have to admit I also feel some sympathy with this other person because similar things have happened between us and I have felt like I was in their position." Using a similar example, Hoffman suggests an intervention along the following lines: "I am inclined to give you the reassurance that you want because it seems like that is what you need. However, I worry that in doing that I am perpetuating your dependency when it really is not necessary." Without knowing more about these hypothetical cases we are really not in any position to decide how useful we think this intervention would be.

It is clear, however, that, in line with Bollas's suggestions, Hoffman is here revealing his own, or encouraging his supervisee to reveal his or her own, subjectivity. I do not think it is an accident, although Hoffman is not explicit about this, that what is revealed in particular is an aspect of conflict in the analyst. (See, however, Hoffman's [1983, p. 420] discussion of the patient's perception of conflict in the analyst.) As I have said, once analysts take the step of introducing the data of their own experience, then they are revealing aspects of their own psychic reality, and naturally enough that will include a focus on the analyst's conflicts. When Bollas (1987, 1989) disagrees with himself, establishing a dialectic of difference, he is revealing his own conflictedness. I believe that, in moderation, doing so is useful by demonstrating to the patient that his or hers is not the only psychic reality in the room and, further, by educating the patient about the ways in which an analyst thinks about psychic reality, namely, in terms of conflict (see my discussion of Mitchell in Chapter 2, regarding the centrality of conflict in relational theories). Of course, the impact of the analyst's modeling is a form of suggestion that itself needs to be brought into the analysis at appropriate moments.

FROM CASEMENT

This example highlights the therapeutic power of the analyst's interpretation containing aspects of the analyst's subjectivity and, in particular, aspects of the analyst's psychic conflict.

In what has become a well-known and frequently cited teaching case, Casement (1982) presents his dilemma with a patient who was demanding that he allow her to hold his hand during one phase of her analysis. This patient had been scalded when she was an infant, and at 17 months she required surgery, which was performed under local anesthesia. During the surgery, the patient's mother fainted and the patient panicked when her mother's hand slipped away from hers.

At first, Casement offered to consider the patient's request, but, after thinking about it over the weekend, he told her that he thought it would be a mistake because it would side-step her reexperiencing of the childhood trauma; therefore in giving her his hand, he would be failing her as her analyst. The patient's response was to feel that in taking back his original offer, he had repeated the original trauma; that is, he gave her his hand and then withdrew it from her. She inferred that he could not stand to remain in touch with her emotional reliving of the traumatic experience. In reaction to this feeling of abandonment, the patient developed a psychotic transference reaction and expressed that she was fully suicidal.

This case has been discussed by Fox (1984), for whom the principle of abstinence requires that a balance be maintained between frustration and gratification in the form of emotional availability. According to Fox, Casement was correct that if he had held the patient's hand he would have been providing a corrective emotional experience. Fox, however, believes that in initially considering to hold her hand and not immediately refusing, Casement was providing the optimal balance between frustration and emotional availability.

I would like to speak to a different aspect of Casement's technique. Following the development of her psychotic transference, the patient became suicidal and hopeless about the treatment, feeling that she could not go on with the analysis. She lost any sense that her analyst was not really her mother or the surgeon. At this point, Casement (1982) offered the following interpretation:

> You are making me experience in myself the sense of despair, and the impossibility of going on, that you are feeling. I am aware of being in what feels to me like a total paradox. In one sense I am feeling that it is impossible to reach you just now, and yet in another sense I feel that my telling you this may be the only way that I can reach you. . . . Similarly I feel as if it could be impossible to go on, and yet I feel that the only way that I can help you through this is by my being prepared to tolerate what you are making me feel, and going on [p. 283].

It was this interpretation that Casement identifies as the turning point in the patient's recovery from psychosis and suicidal despair. This is similar to the famous case in which Winnicott (1960) tells a depressed patient that he (Winnicott) is hopeless about the treatment and yet willing to continue, and for the first time the patient feels hope.

The interpersonal field between Casement and his patient is likely to have been more complicated than he portrays. His extremely lucid and engaging case presentation raises highly controversial issues concerning psychoanalytic technique. His interpretations contain and convey a great deal of his personal subjectivity and express his own conflict about his relationship with the patient. In my view, it is only when he explicitly conveys to her his own struggle, hope, and despair about ever reaching her, and in so doing shares his psychic reality with her, that she is able to emerge from the psychotic transference. It seems to me that what was therapeutic in this case was not that Casement walked the tightrope of abstinence, as Fox would have it, but rather that he fully engaged the patient by sharing with her his own psychic reality in the form of an interpretation that clarified both his own and the patient's psychic functioning as well as the intersubjective engagement that had developed between them.

From Etchegoyen

Etchegoyen (1991) describes an incident that took place after he had moved his residence into an apartment on the same floor as his consulting room and his wife had moved the doormat from the front of the former office to the front of his home. A female patient of his, whom he describes as coming out of a long period of confusion, told him that she thought that she must be crazy because she had seen the old doormat in front of the other apartment. Etchegoyen interpreted to the patient that she thought that the doormat had come from his former office and that she believed that it was as if he had purposely moved the doormat so as to let her know where he lived. He added that, by telling him that she thought she must be crazy, she was communicating her belief that he had gone crazy. Since she generally saw him as rigid, she knew that it would not be his style to leave the doormat where it would be spotted. So for him to do such a thing he must have gone mad. Etchegoyen observed that, following the interpretation, the patient's anxiety decreased as if by "enchantment," and furthermore the analyst felt calmer. The patient then said that she had noticed the doormat the very first day of the move and now concluded that his wife had probably moved it there without his noticing. Etchegoyen concludes that it is only a short step from this to the primal scene.

Etchegoyen reveals to us, his readers, but not to his patient, that it was in fact his doormat and that his wife had moved it to his home doorway. He tells us that he was actually conflicted about moving the doormat. He first wanted to tell his wife not to move it, because a patient might notice and so find out where he lived; but then he thought that this was taking analytic reserve to the extreme. Etchegoyen deliberately does not reveal any of this to the patient, nor does he confirm or disconfirm that it is in fact his doormat. This is consistent with his belief, learned from Strachey (1934), that the best way to reestablish a patient's contact with reality is not to offer reality to the patient ourselves. Furthermore, it is in accord with his strictly maintained position that the analytic situation must be asymmetrical.

When, however, an analyst says to his patient that she had the thought that he wanted her to know where he lived, and when the analyst tells us that he is aware of being conflicted about putting the mat there because a patient might know where he lives, this raises interesting questions. Is it not possible that he had some conflict about this patient's knowing where he lived? That part of him wanted her to know? When he quickly interprets that she thought that he wanted her to know, and when this interpretation is made so quickly, with relatively little data from the patient (at least little data is provided the reader), is it not possible that the patient would hear this as confirmation that the analyst did have some conflict about her wanting to know? How else would the analyst come to this conclusion so quickly, unless he resonated with the patient's conflict? As Singer (1968) says, "It takes one to know one, and in his correct interpretation the therapist reveals that he is one" (p. 369).

What am I suggesting that the analyst might have done differently? Am I suggesting that he reveal his conflict to the patient? Yes and no! In some ways, I believe that the analyst has already revealed quite a bit through his creative and precipitant interpretation. I believe that subtly he has provided some data that at least make it plausible to the patient to believe that the analyst was conflicted about wanting her to know where he lived. Furthermore, her associations reveal that she believes that she notices things about her analyst that he does not notice; she says that she noticed the doormat but that the analyst probably did not.

The master analyst from Buenos Aires is being consistent with his Kleinian technique when he interprets so quickly and so certainly. I am suggesting that he might have either waited to acquire more information or inquired along the following lines. If the patient thought that she saw the analyst's doormat, what was her idea about how it got there? If she believed that the analyst wanted her to know where he lived, how did she explain that to herself? What had she noticed about him that led her to think he would want her to know where he lives? Why did she wait before mentioning the doormat when she had noticed it right away? Had she noticed anything else about him that she believed he has not noticed? Once the analyst makes the interpretation as Etchegoyen did, there needs to be a follow-up inquiry into how the patient experienced the interpretation. The patient may very well have taken the interpretation as confirmation of her belief that the analyst was conflicted about wanting her to know where he lived.

Etchegoyan concludes that it is only a short step from here to the primal scene, but why jump so quickly to the primal scene? What does the patient imagine about the analyst and his wife to make her believe that the analyst wants her to know where he lives? Or that his wife wants her to know where they live? Rather than move to the primal scene, I would first want to explore thoroughly the patient's beliefs, fantasies, observations, and inferences about the analyst in the here-and-now.

The analyst might tell the patient that she thought that he was conflicted about wanting her to know where he lived. How different is it if the analyst tells the patient that she had the fantasy that the analyst was conflicted about this or that she had noticed that the analyst was conflicted about this? The subtleties matter, and not just in the words but in the tone of voice and attitude. What is critical is not whether or not the analyst acknowledges some subjective state explicitly, but, rather, whether it is done in a way that furthers the analytic inquiry or in a way that shuts it down. If the analyst reveals something about himself with a tone of certainty and authority, then he may close off further inquiry rather than opening it up. On the other hand, the analyst may reveal some aspect of his subjective reality in a way that allows room for the patient to accept it, modify it, challenge it, or move beyond it.

From Aron

A young, attractive, married, female patient told me that it seemed to her that in the past week I had become more aloof than usual. She wondered if anything was wrong or what was going on in me. She did not refer to it, but I remembered that in the prior week there had been some banter between us in the context of highly charged sexual material in her associations. I thought that she was right; it did feel to me as if I had pulled back from her following this exchange in an attempt not to get caught up in a seductive or flirtatious enactment. I did not share my thoughts with the patient but simply listened.

She went on to tell me that a supervisor of hers at work had recently asked if she had any single sisters that she could introduce him to. He knew that she was married, but he had often flirted with her. This was the closest he had ever come to telling her directly that he was interested in someone like her. Following his asking her about her sisters, my patient noticed that he did not speak with her for a few days. I told the patient that she believed that I had become uncomfortable with the intensity of our closeness, particularly when we were talking about such hot sexual material. She must have guessed that I had pulled away because of my own discomfort, that I was conflicted about flirting with her. She agreed and went on to discuss her own conflicts about her temptations to have an affair and her embarrassment about expressing her sexual feelings to me.

This was a "good" patient. She was compliant and protective of me; she did not feel the need to push me further. She could have said, "Well, are you conflicted about your sexual feelings toward me? Have you backed away from me because you were afraid of your own temptations?" It is my belief that it was not necessary to reveal my own thoughts and feelings about this situation any further with this patient at this time. In my interpretation to her I revealed enough, namely, that I was comfortable enough with these sexual feelings to risk talking about them with her. I believe that she knew that I could not have made that interpretation, in the way that I made it, unless I had experienced such feelings to at least some degree. This example illustrates how making the interpretation serves to "cure" the analyst; by making the interpretation, I repositioned myself in relation to the patient. That is, by interpreting, I freed myself so that I did not have to resort to such a distant defensive posture as I had previously maintained.

What if she had not been such a cooperative patient? What if she had pushed me further and asked what I had felt, or might I ever feel such a conflict about her? Rather than resort to silence and evasiveness, I might have said or implied that I would fully expect to have a wide variety of thoughts and feelings toward my patients as well as conflicts about them, just as I would expect that they would have a wide variety of thoughts and feelings and conflicts about me. If she pushed further and asked, "Well, if you have feelings like that toward me will you tell me?" I could say, only, "First of all, I might not have to tell you because you might know. In fact you might notice some of these things about me before I do." And, finally, I might say, "If you are quite sure that you want to know, I will try to describe my experience to you, and if I have reservations about doing so then I will discuss my hesitancy with you."

Here is the asymmetry: it is the patient who must attempt to tell all; the patient has to try to free associate. The analyst may or may not associate on the basis of his or her own clinical judgment of what is in the patient's interests or, more accurately, the interests of the analytic process. Finally, it is legitimate to ask whether or not I should have confronted her with her not asking me directly if I had pulled away from her because of my own anxiety. By not demanding a response, she was being a traditionally "good" or compliant patient and in that way protecting me as well as herself. Should this not be brought to her attention?

FROM ARON

Beginning with Ferenczi (1932) analysts have recognized that patients may serve at least to some extent as their analysts, interpreting the analyst's countertransference (Hoffman, 1983). Searles (1975) has enumerated the ways in which the patient can serve as therapist to the analyst, and in the next chapters we will study this tradition of mutuality in psychoanalytic history.

It is important, however, to recognize that an interpretation, if it is intersubjectively constituted, must have consequences for both partners in the dialogue. That is, an interpretation has an impact on the one giving it as well as on the one receiving it. That is one reason that a patient's interpretation to the analyst may be of benefit not only to the analyst but to the patient as well, and vice versa. Hoffman (1983) writes that "at the very moment that he interprets, the analyst often extricates himself as much as he extricates the patient from transference–countertransference enactment" (p. 415), and interpretations are effective partly because they have a "reflective impact" (p. 415) on the interpreter himself or herself. All interpretations are at least implicitly self-interpretive (Singer, 1968). Thus, interpretation is a complex, intersubjective, and mutual process that benefits both the interpreter and the one to whom it is intended. The following clinical material illustrates these points.

A patient was working for the first few years of his analysis on the issue of his conflicts regarding expressing feelings, both in general and to me specifically. As would be expected, he was much concerned with his bodily orifices and with the dangers of fluids and bodily contents leaking outward. Hence, he was concerned with his bowel movements, constipation and diarrhea, and was self-conscious about sneezing, coughing, crying, sweating, vomiting, and spitting. All this was analyzed and was related to his conflicts regarding holding in his inner thoughts and not letting out any feelings, particularly toward me. This theme emerged repeatedly and was gone over again and again, but it was only with the following incident that it took on new meaning.

At one point while the patient was discussing his fear of letting his anger show, I coughed, but coughed quietly, stifling the full extent of the cough. The patient, who was on the couch, first reacted by saying

that he thought he had heard me laugh. He assumed that I was laugh-
ing at him because of his continued inability to express himself. I
inquired as to why the patient thought that I would be glad to humiliate him. The patient then said that another thought had suddenly
crossed his mind; perhaps I had coughed, but it sounded like a laugh
because I had stifled the cough. But why would I stifle my cough? he
wondered, unless I was just like him, holding in my expressiveness? I
said, "So I would want to laugh at you and humiliate you in order to
distance myself from you and hold myself above you, so that I could
avoid recognizing how similar we are and deny to myself and to you
that I struggle with similar conflicts."

I benefited enormously from this interaction. I stopped inhibiting
myself and felt freer in my own self-expression with this patient. In the
course of the continuing analytic work, the patient noticed the
increased freedom and spontaneity in me, and the patient's contribution to this change was recognized and acknowledged by both of us.
This interaction led to greater insight by the patient into his own
tendency toward inhibition and to increased openness and spontaneity
on his part in relation to me.

INTERPRETATIONS AND OTHER INTERVENTIONS

Often, noninterpretive interventions, and even nonverbal interventions, may have profound therapeutic consequences because of the
ways in which they express aspects of the analyst's subjectivity. While
traditionally one criterion defining psychoanalysis has been that interpretation is the primary, if not the sole therapeutic intervention, this
demand is based on the premise that there is a clear and stable distinction between words and acts. Just as an analysand should limit communication to the verbal arena through the free association method, so
too the analyst should limit intervention to the verbal arena through
the interpretive method. As we have seen, however, contemporary
theorists have deconstructed this neat distinction between words and
acts for both the patient and the analyst.

Just as interpretations are not simply verbal communications but also
are interpersonal acts, so too a patient's associations not only are
verbal communications but have the impact of actions on the analyst.
We know that the adage "sticks and stones may break my bones, but
words will never harm me" is not completely correct. Words can harm;
they can have the impact of action. We also know that actions
can communicate important information. "A picture *is* worth a thou-
sand words," and a patient's or analyst's actions can have a greater

impact than some verbal interpretations. We have come to value patient's "acting out" as an important analytic communication, similarly analysts' actions may at times be more valuable than their interpretations.

Consider one of the best known examples in the analytic literature of a noninterpretive intervention. Balint (1968) reported the case of a young woman whom he was treating in the late 1920s in Budapest. She had finished courses at a university but could not complete the exam for her degree, could not become involved with a man, and generally felt that she could not achieve anything. He had interpreted to her that "apparently the most important thing to her was to keep her head safely up, with both feet planted firmly on the ground" (p. 128). In response, she told Balint that although she had tried, she could never do a somersault. He suggested, "What about it now?" (p. 128). The young woman "got up from the couch and, to her great amazement, did a perfect somersault without any difficulty" (p. 129). Balint reports that this turned out to be a genuine breakthrough in the case. "Many changes followed, in her emotional, social, and professional life, all towards greater freedom and elasticity" (pp. 128–129).

Now, I agree that it stretches the term interpretation too far to refer to this intervention by that name. Nevertheless, Balint's question to his patient, while apparently a suggestion, was also a communication to her, a communication about what could happen in analysis, a communication about his willingness to engage her beyond words; and it was clearly an attempt to move beyond the intellectual/cognitive dimension of analysis to both the experiential and the interactive dimensions. Undoubtedly it conveyed other unconscious communications between the two of them, and in the course of an analysis some of these messages would probably be talked about, and, inevitably, some would not. How much of this intervention's effectiveness came about because it brought a bodily enactment into the analytic situation? How much because she experienced Balint's suggestion as encouragement? How much because of Balint's affective responsiveness and participation when she did the somersault? How much because it was experienced by both Balint and the young woman as an enactment of a loving/playful/ sexual relation between them? How much because it was experienced by both of them as father–daughter play? Undoubtedly, much of what is powerful about psychoanalysis is beyond words, contained in what Ferenczi (1915) called "dialogues of the unconscious" (p. 109). What seems clear, however, is that Balint's intervention communicated something to this young woman about himself, his response to her, his desires, hopes, and expectations for her, as well as his willingness to participate with her. As analysts, we try to explicate, in words, the meanings of these intersubjective dialogues. We succeed at best only to a small degree.

SUMMARY

In this chapter, I have drawn on numerous psychoanalytic theorists to reexamine the nature of interpretation and other interventions from a relational perspective. I am in agreement with Mitchell (1988a) that there is a great deal that unifies the variety of relational approaches, in spite of their widely divergent metapsychologies, in their reconceptualization of the nature of interpretation. I would emphasize that relational analysts have come to pay much more attention to how interpretations are arrived at through mutual processes occurring between patient and analyst and that relational analysts similarly pay increased attention to the ways in which interpretations are needed by and affect both patient and analyst. Furthermore, relational analysts tend to concentrate on the affective aspects of interpretations. This emphasis on affect is clearly apparent in Spezzano's (1993) suggestion that

> interpretation expresses the analyst's thinking about the affects emerging in him and the analysand, about the unconscious processes out of which these affects have emerged, and about the ways in which they have been communicated between them [p. 229].

What relational approaches have in common, then, is an understanding of interpretation as a mutual, intersubjective, affective, and interactive process. An interpretation is an interpersonal participation. It is an observation from within the interaction rather than from outside of it.

> An interpretation is a *complex relational event*, not primarily because it alters something inside the patient, not because it releases a stalled developmental process, but because it says something very important about where the analyst stands vis-a-vis the patient, about what sort of relatedness is possible between the two of them [Mitchell, 1988a, p. 295]

Interpretation is the principal process by which analysts position and reposition themselves interpersonally in relation to their patients, and in this sense interpretations contain aspects of the analyst's subjectivity made available for use by the patient. Insofar as the analyst has captured aspects of the patient's psychic life in a particular interpretation, and the interpretation also expresses aspects of the analyst's subjectivity, interpretation is best thought of as the quintessential container and purveyor of intersubjectivity between patient and analyst.

Viewing interpretation as an intersubjective process, rather than as an act on the part of the analyst, has the advantage of focusing attention both on the interpersonal context in which interpretations are coconstructed and on the patient's and the analyst's mutual responses to interpretations. Furthermore, viewing interpretation as a process, rather than as an act, highlights the way in which interpretation complements, proceeds in tandem with, and is itself one aspect of psychoanalytic inquiry.

The interpretive process, which includes the interventions that prepare for interpretations, as well as the follow-ups to interpretations, and especially the exploration and inquiry that are essential to the interpretive process, is the form by which analysts and patients participate with each other in the analytic endeavor. Inasmuch as they are interpersonal acts of participation, it is through interpretations that the patient, as well as the analyst, comes to know where the analyst stands in relation to the patient, and it is through interpretations that the analyst best conveys his or her interest in, capacity to understand, and respect for the individuality of the patient. Insight may be thought of as a marker of change intrapsychically, and interpretation may be thought of as a signal of change intersubjectively. Interpretations should be thought of both as markers of change and as facilitators of change in the relationship between patient and analyst, which means that they clarify and cumulatively cure the patient, the analyst, and the interactional field that exists between them.

Interpretations, and other interventions, are useful because they contain three dimensions: the affect/experiential dimension, the cognitive/insight dimension, and the relationship/interaction dimension. Classically, the cognitive, insight-oriented dimension has been emphasized in explaining the nature of psychoanalytic change. I believe, however, that the affective component of the analyst's interventions has been systematically downplayed in psychoanalysis even by those who have acknowledged the relational/interactive dimension. In contrast, I believe that all three dimensions are important, but, because it has been so neglected, I want to emphasize the analyst's affective responsiveness, or, to use terms current within post-Kohutian self psychology, "optimal responsiveness" (Bacal, 1985) or "optimal affective engagement" (Tolpin, 1988). One of the things that is reflected in each of the foregoing examples is that the analyst's interpretation (or intervention) conveyed to the patient something of the analyst's affective responsiveness.

In the previous chapter we reviewed a wide variety of formulations stressing intersubjectivity, which includes, as one important component, interaffectivity (Stern, 1985, p. 132). We have talked about people's needs to connect with others, to attach, to know, and to be known by the other. Children and adults, patients and analysts, all need to feel that the affect that they express toward the other reaches the other, finds its target. People need to feel that they are having an impact on others, and patients need to feel that they are having an emotional impact on their analysts. They can know this only if the objects, the targets of their emotional expression—separate subjects—*respond* in some way that demonstrates that they have been *affected*, moved, changed. Maroda (1995) has beautifully described this process. She refers to it as "completing the cycle of affective communication." Stern (1985) discusses the need in infants and children for "affective attunement," and self psychology, more than any other analytic theory, has emphasized the continual need for affective attunement in adults. For relational analysts what is essential is the intersubjective encounter, an affectively and experientially felt meeting of minds. Interpretation and insight are one way to achieve this meeting. I want to place special emphasis on the role of affects and affective experience because one important trend in relational theory has been to place affects at the center of the psychoanalytic theory of motivation and to regard affect and interaffectivity as at the core of human subjectivity and intersubjectivity (see especially Spezzanno, 1993).

But if, as I am arguing, it is the analyst's affective responsiveness that is critical, then why make any attempt to interpret or transform this affective response into a technical intervention? Why not just express your emotional reactions to the patient in as "authentic" a manner as possible? There are a number of reasons why I think this is inadvisable. First, as I have indicated, it is not only the analyst's affective response that is important: affect/experiential factors, cognitive/insight factors, and relationship/interaction factors are each important, and channelling our emotional responses into technical interventions and interpretations best protects an optimal balance among these factors. Second, channeling the analyst's affective response into an interpretation promotes the *modulation* of that response and therefore makes it more likely that it will be experienced by the patient as in the service of the patient's rather than predominantly the analyst's needs. We need to balance the value of emotional spontaneity and the equal value of sustaining our emotional reactions and thus containing, holding, processing, digesting, modulating, and sublimating them. (See Mitchell, 1995, as well as Chapter 8 for further elaboration of these themes.)

I am suggesting that interpretations, at their best, have always been useful because they contain affective, cognitive, and relational components. But the analyst's emotional contribution has been consistently neglected. Analysts' interventions are often useful precisely because they contain aspects of the analysts' subjectivity and particularly affec-tivity. Analysts' interventions are effective to the degree that analysts express their affective responsiveness as a component of these inter-ventions. I support Maroda's (1995) plea that we must "show some emotion." I would emphasize, however, that we must show some emotion in a modulated manner as one aspect of our technical inter-vention, thus maintaining the tension between the personal and the technical aspects of analytic work (Hoffman, 1994). Our interpreta-tions are expressions of our subjectivity (affectivity), and they further the intersubjective and mutual, although asymmetrical, analytic process. An interpretation connects the analyst and analysand; it bridges the transitional space between them, linking them in a meeting of minds.

5 | Aspects of Mutuality in Clinical Psychoanalysis

"Must every case be mutual—and to what extent? (Ferenczi, 1932, p. 213). This was Ferenczi's question, shortly before his death, as he wrote the last entries in his *Clinical Diary*. In this chapter, I explore the question of in what sense and to what extent psychoanalysis can be said to be a *mutual* endeavor. We pick up in the 1990s Ferenczi's question of 1932, a question and a clinical approach with implications so terrifying for psychoanalysis that they have been suppressed and silenced for more than half a century. In the next chapter we explore Ferenczi's most original experiments with "mutual analysis" and have a chance to critique them from the point of view being developed here. "Must every case be mutual—and to what extent?"

What unites the many, so called relational schools of psychoanalysis is not any shared metapsychology, nor is it a shared criticism of classical metapsychology, although certainly this is a common element of many relational contributions. What many relational theorists have in common seems to be an emphasis on the mutuality and reciprocity between patient and analyst in the psychoanalytic process. But as contemporary psychoanalysts have begun to speak about, and even to emphasize, mutuality, we must ask exactly what we mean by this term.

We have seen (in Chapter 3) that it is important to differentiate between mutuality of recognition, in which two individuals are capable of acknowledging each other as separate subjects, and mutuality of regulation, which refers to the reciprical control that two people in a relationship continuously exert on each other. We have also seen (in Chapter 4) that one important axis along which to organize the psychoanalytic method is the unilateral, versus the mutual generation of data, one. Whereas classical analysts have consistently defined the psychoanalytic method in terms of the patient's providing the data predominantly through free associations and the analyst's interpreting this data, relational analysts speak to the mutual generation of data between patient and analyst.

The point that I want to make as we begin to discuss clinical aspects of mutuality is that the term mutuality may be legitimately used to refer to an array of aspects of the psychoanalytic situation. Mutuality of recognition, mutuality of regulation, mutuality in generating data, and Ferenczian mutual analysis, along with a variety of other meanings of mutuality are very different concepts, and the implications of each must be considered separately. Nevertheless, it is fair to generalize and say that relational psychoanalysis incorporates many aspects of mutuality; it concerns itself with what the patient and the analyst have in common rather than with what differentiates them. Even while emphasizing mutuality, however, one must keep in mind the important differences between patient and analyst in their roles, functions, power, and responsibilities; this dimmension of the relationship I refer to as asymmetry.

THE WORKING ALLIANCE AND MUTUALITY

For the traditional model, the concept of the working alliance captures that aspect of personal relatedness between patient and analyst which entails a joint or mutual agreement about the work. Mutuality has a place in classical theory, but it is a relatively narrow one, limited to the shared agreement, contract, or pact. Gill (1994) called the alliance concept "a somewhat grudging concession by classical analysts" (p. 40) to a view of psychoanalysis as a two-person relationship. In the classical model, analyst and patient have mutual goals and established a common communicative field in which to pursue those goals. For relatively healthy, "analyzable" patients (speaking, for a moment, from a classical perspective), the working alliance can almost be taken for granted; it resides as a background phenomenon, only to be attended to when, for one reason or another the common communicative field has been temporarily disrupted. This viewpoint leaves the analyst throughout most of the work to attend to the patient's neurosis, fantasy, and distortion, thus artificially exaggerating the differences between the relatively ill patient and the relatively healthy analyst. Contemporary Freudian authors speak of the psychoanalytic method as a "joint venture" and as a "mutual activity" (Kris, 1982, p. 3). They view psychoanalysis as mutual in that both patient and analyst are working together toward a common goal. Thus, for the classical analyst, psychoanalysis may be described as a mutual process. What is thought to be shared between patient and analyst, however, is limited to the actual work of analysis and the therapeutic pact to do that work. Thus it is the alliance that is mutual. This is a comparatively narrow use of the term mutuality. It is quite clear that from a clasical perspective neurosis, pathology, irrationality, and transferential distortion are not shared or mutual. Nor is there any emphasis placed on the importance of the patient's caring, reaching, penetrating, loving, healing, or analyzing the analyst.

MUTUAL PARTICIPATION

A broader notion of mutuality emerges from the idea that both patient and analyst participate in the analytic process, that they mutually regulate or mutually influence each other both consciously and unconsciously. From a relational perspective, who the analyst is and his or her personal contributions to the analytic process are fundamental to the psychoanalytic investigation. The analytic method cannot be considered as isolated from the personal variables and immediate affective experience of the individual analyst. From this point of view, countertransference is not an occasional lapse that intermittently requires investigation and elimination but rather is a continual and central element of the investigation. The analyst as a person and his or her shifting affective experience is both a major component of the analytic method and a primary variable in what is being investigated.

Harry Stack Sullivan's articulation of the participant-observation model represented a full development of the interpersonal model in theory, even if not in his own practice (see Hirsch and Aron, 1991; Hoffman, 1983). Although Sullivan created the participant-observation model, he personally avoided examination of the transference—countertransference interaction in the here-and-now. It was Ferenczi, among the early psychoanalytic pioneers, who first acknowledged the need for the analyst to invite the patient's observations regarding the analyst's participation in the treatment; the analyst inevitably becomes enmeshed in the interactional world of the patient. In Levenson's (1972) language, the analyst becomes "transformed"; in Sandler's (1976) terms, the analyst has been "nudged into role-responsiveness." Contemporary Kleinian and other object-relationists use the language of projective identification to indicate the many ways in which the patient evokes particular feelings and responses in the analyst. But here I want to emphasize that certainly the analyst also "nudges" the patient into "role-responsiveness" and "transforms" the patient on the basis of the analyst's own past history of relationships. The analyst projectively identifies aspects of him or her own self into the patient. In short, if the patient is influencing the analyst's behavior and role responsiveness, the analyst also is influencing the patient's. While this influence may not be quantitatively equal, it is nevertheless reciprocal. There may, indeed, be times when the analyst's efforts to repeat his or her past history of relationships so dominates the transference–countertransference interaction that we might speak of "counter-transference dominance" (Maroda, 1991, p. 49). Participation and enactment are mutual and reciprocal features of the analytic interaction.

In contrast to classical analysts who may emphasize the shared quality of the working alliance, relational analysts assign to mutuality a much broader place and more profound meanings in the clinical psychoanalytic undertaking. Mutuality includes, of course, mutual agreement to undertake the analytic task, but it goes further, to the heart of the therapeutic relationship. While ultimately aimed to benefit the patient, the analysis is not of the patient by the analyst, and not even of the patient by the analyst with the patient's help, as the working alliance concepts would have it. Rather, analysis is inevitably a joint endeavor, since the object of the investigation is not only an object but a separate subject.

Let me be quick to say that some of the most powerful and most articulate criticism of Freudian theory has come not from outside critics, but from within the ranks of Freudian loyalists. Loewald (1980) has elegantly and persuasively argued that analysts are not extraneous observers, but are part and participant of the field. He raises questions about the usefulness of thinking of the individual human mind as an independent unit of investigation:

> The individual's status in this regard, however, is questionable and cannot be taken for granted. If nothing else, the phenomena of transference and resistance, encountered in both analysand and analyst during the investigation of our object of study, demonstrate the precariousness of that status and show that the individual cannot be studied psychoanalytically as though he were simply a closed system investigated by another closed system. We even have to qualify our speaking of investigator and object, insofar as the object, by the very nature of the psychoanalytic process, becomes an investigator of himself, and the investigator-analyst becomes an object of study to himself. At the same time, the analysand, although not in a scientifically and professionally informed and skilled way, "studies" the analyst in the analytic process, and the analyst must hold himself open as an object of the analysand's search (by this, of course, I do not mean that he must answer questions and tell the analysand about himself) [p. 278].

In this last parenthetical remark, Loewald makes clear that he is not advocating symmetry between patient and analyst. He writes that it is "unquestioned" that "the analytic relationship is an asymmetrical one" (p. 279). His emphasis here is on the mutuality of the analytic function in the clinical situation and on the importance of recognizing both the analyst and the analysand as being both subject and object to themselves and to each other.

Mutuality, in any relational model, including those which may be nominally Freudian, becomes a central principle and a predominant area of investigation precisely because of the recognition of the analyst's participation and the inevitability of mutual influence. Analysis of transference cannot meaningfully occur without at least implicit analysis of countertransference. Neither pathology nor health is thought to reside in either the patient or the analyst exclusively; neither is the analyst thought to have a corner on truth and insight. Resistances do not occur in the patient but, rather, are interactional phenomena that can be metaphorically located only in the space between analyst and patient. To put it differently, the notion of resistance becomes coterminous with transference and countertransference (see Schafer, 1992), or, more simply, we may refer to mutual resistances. As we saw in the previous chapter, interpretations are not given by the analyst to the patient; instead, the interpretive process occurs reciprocally. Thus the questions of who made a particular interpretation, who thought of it (the patient or the analyst), who first suggested an idea cannot be answered unambiguously because a good interpretation occurs in transitional space (Winnicott, 1951) and has an effect on both participants. We may refer to processes of mutual interpretation or at least acknowledge that interpretation is likely to have reverberating effects on both analytic participants. Analysis takes place *between* the patient and analyst as they analyze *each other*, even if often much of this analysis takes place implicitly or unconsciously, and even if the relative contributions of the two participants is not equal.

I believe that what may be the critical difference between most Freudian analysts and most relational analysts is that Freudians assume a relatively well-analyzed, relatively healthy analyst who can monitor intermittent countertransference disruptions through continual self-analysis. Even those Freudian analysts who acknowledge the ubiquitous occurrence of enactments continue to assume that the analyst will maintain enough relatively autonomous observing ego capacity to monitor and analyze these enactments. Relational analysts, by contrast, assume, first, that in spite of having undergone an intensive analysis of his or her own, the analyst nevertheless is inevitably drawn into ongoing enactments with the patient (mutual participation or mutual enactment), and they further assume that analysts will not be detached enough (if working properly) to observe and work through these unconscious participations on their own. Relational analysts assume that, in one way or another, the analysis of these enactments will occur mutually, with patient and analyst both interpreting as well as resisting the interpersonal meanings of their interactions and engagements.

INTERPRETING IN TRANSITIONAL SPACE: CASE ILLUSTRATION

A patient has been associating for some time about sadomasochistic interactions, sexual fantasies of anal penetration, and feelings of abuse, dominance, and submission. I interpret the patient's idea that I am dominating him, controlling him, and expecting him to submit to me. The patient expresses his belief that I want him to submit and that he always feels that this is what I expect from him. After hearing further associations in which the patient reveals anal sadistic masturbation fantasies, I say, in a tone that I hope conveys that I am musing or thinking out loud, "The entire analysis is a sexual conquest for me, in which I become excited by your submission." I leave ambiguous whether I mean that this is his belief or fantasy or my own experience. As I say this to the patient, I may very well be unclear in whose voice I am speaking. The interpretation is not necessarily directed at him or at me; it is not clear whose idea it is, and it may just as well lead to insight in me as to insight in him. If I do not dismiss all my patient's thoughts as projections or displacements from past objects, but instead consider that they may have some basis in my interaction with the patient, then, in the very act of interpreting to the patient, I may learn something about myself and the analytic interaction. For example, as I tell the patient that I derive sexual excitement from dominating him, I may recognize some excitement in my tone of voice, excitement that I perhaps had not been aware of. Or I may realize that my interpretation has a more aggressive or penetrating quality than I previously realized. I may, for example, have the thought that I am being a pain in the ass, and this may lead to further associations from each of us. Optimally, this transaction leads to joint insight and mutual change.

It is not uncommon for me to phrase interpretations in an ambiguous manner, leaving open whose idea it is. I may say, "It is as if I am trying to dominate you" or, as in this example, simply, "I am trying to dominate you." I speak in a way that communicates that I am just thinking out loud, rather than saying, "You believe that. . . ." or "You have the idea that . . ." or "You have the fantasy that . . ." I have found it comfortable and useful to phrase these comments in the form of "Perhaps I am . . ." or "Could it be that I am . . . ?" or "I wonder if I might be . . ." I believe that this "subjunctive" wording[1] of my interpretation can feel like less of a challenge to the patient's perspective, but, more important, it can have a greater emotional impact on me, at least at times when I am not overly defensive. Of course, the wording is not nearly as important as the tone of voice, the emotional conviction, and my genuine receptiveness to shifting perspectives. Nevertheless, the words matter as well.

It is not that I expect that my patient will regularly interpret something dramatically new to me. After all, if I had no idea that I was susceptible to issues of dominance and control, I believe it would be quite unlikely that I could hear my patient's associations as interpretations and make good use of them. What occurs more commonly is that the patient will cue me in to some conflictual area that I do know about but was not sufficiently aware of at the moment, in the present analytic context. The patient serves as my analyst by helping me to work through a conflict that was previously worked on in my own personal analysis. There are risks and complications in this approach, but the fact that thinking in terms of mutuality is complicated and hazardous does not mean that it is to be avoided.

MUTUAL EMPATHY AND MUTUAL ANALYSIS

It seems obvious that analysts need to empathize with patients. One of the earliest and most consistent findings in the psychotherapy research literature is the importance of the therapist's empathy for the patient. What may be less immediately apparent is that the patient must mutually empathize with the therapist if the therapy is to move forward. The contributions of a group of theorists associated with The Stone Center at Wellesley College have highlighted the value of thinking about empathy as a mutual process. On the basis of their collective research and thinking about women's psychological development, they have argued that empathy needs to be seen as a mutual, active, and interactive process and have suggested the term mutual empathy to emphasize their point (Surrey, Kaplan, and Jordan, 1990). They argue that there is a developmental need not only to be understood, a need for empathy, but also a need to be empathic with others. Therefore, the concept of mutual empathy suggests that one goal of development is toward mutually empathic, two-directional relationships. In their discussion of mutual empathy, they put forth the idea that psychotherapy should be thought of as a mutual process in which each participant, patient and

---

[1] I owe to Stuart Pizer (in press) the idea of phrasing certain interpretations in the subjunctive mood.

analyst, must experience the other's empathy in order for the experience to be growth promoting for both. Empathy exists not only in the
mind of the analyst and not only in the patient's mind. Rather, in the
therapeutic process, empathy may be best thought of as "a quality of
relationality, a movement or dynamic of relationship" (p. 2).

Within psychoanalysis proper, however, the analyst's need for the
patient and the patient's impact on the analyst has traditionally been
underplayed. Freud (1905), however, did acknowledge that his patients
could have a personal effect on him: "No one who, like me, conjures
up the most evil of those half-tamed demons that inhabit the human
breast, and seeks to wrestle with them, can expect to come through the
struggle unscathed" (p. 109). Freud acknowledged the tremendous
personal and emotional toll that psychoanalytic work takes on the
analyst. In that passage we can see that Freud was aware of a mutual
influence that occurs in psychoanalysis. If things go well, then the
analyst certainly has an impact on the patient; but here Freud declared
that the patient inevitably had an impact on him. Freud's emphasis,
however, was on the damage caused to the analyst in his struggle with
the demon that is the patient's neurosis. Compare, however, Freud's
statement with Sándor Ferenczi's (1932):

> A last, not unimportant, factor is the humble admission, in front of the patient,
> of one's own weaknesses and traumatic experiences and disillusionments, which
> abolishes completely that distancing by inferiority which would otherwise be
> maintained. Indeed, we gladly allow the patients to have the pleasure of being
> able to help us, to become for a brief period our analyst, as it were, something
> that justifiably raises their self-esteem [p. 65].

In these quotations we see both Freud and Ferenczi acknowledging
that it is *not* just the analyst who has an impact on the patient, but the
patient who has a reciprocal impact on the analyst. Freud, perhaps
characteristically, referred to the harmful consequences of the psychoanalytic process for the analyst; Ferenczi, as was typical for him,
asserted the patient's curative impact on the analyst as a person. For
Freud, psychoanalysis is a struggle, a metaphorical combat; for Ferenczi
psychoanalysis is an act of mutual "maternal" kindness, a collaboration.
We need to bring together these two viewpoints and recognize both
the collaborative and the combative aspects of clinical psychoanalytic
work.

We analysts intuitively know the dangers that Freud refers to. We
are intimately involved in our patients' struggles, and we inevitably
emerge from the analytic experience as changed people. As Freud
cautioned us, we can not "hope to come through the struggle
unscathed." Perhaps it is for this reason, more than any other, that we

crave the certainty that comes from knowing. Perhaps it is because those dangers arouse such intense anxieties that we long for the security that comes from a good theory, particularly, from an unambiguous theory of technique, a theory that guides our behavior with patients and seems to eliminate or minimize our individual subjectivities. If only we can know about the patient, know about the analytic process, know about patients' conflicts, know about the meaning of our interventions, then we can remain at some distance from patients and their affective experience. We can use our knowledge as a barrier to keep patients from touching us, wrestling with us, harming us, changing us, making us feel. From a Ferenczian perspective, we might say that we resist our patients' therapeutic strivings.

To remain unscathed, we keep our distance. To remain unscathed, we think of psychoanalysis as a unilateral, unidirectional process, a one-way street. We are there to help the patient. We are there to analyze the patient's conflicts, the patient's mind, the patient's psychopathology. We are there to change the patient. We remain neutral, anonymous, abstinent; we stay outside of the mine field (mind field) of the patient's psychic conflicts, equidistant from the forces that so shake and disturb the patient. We seek to remain unscathed.

There have always been some voices within the psychoanalytic community, however, who have argued that this attitude limits our work. Some have dared to suggest that the psychoanalytic process works best when the analyst is affected by the patient, and some even rarer voices have been heard to advise that psychoanalysis has its most profound impact when the analyst lets the patient know that the analyst has felt emotionally moved and may have even changed or been helped by the patient.

This subversive line of thought, emphasizing the mutuality inherent in the psychoanalytic situation can be traced back, to Sándor Ferenczi (1932), who went on to write:

> Should it even occur, and it does occasionally to me, that experiencing another's and my own suffering brings a tear to my eye (and one should not conceal this emotion from the patient), then the tears of doctor and of patient mingle in a sublimated communion, which perhaps finds its analogy only in the mother-child relationship. And this is the healing agent, which like a kind of glue, binds together permanently the intellectually assembled fragments, surrounding even the personality thus repaired with a new aura of vitality and optimism [p. 65].

Ferenczi was influenced by his close friend and colleague, the "wild analyst" Georg Groddeck, who in 1923 wrote, "And now I was confronted by the strange fact that I was not treating the patient, but that the patient was treating me. Even to get this much insight was difficult, for you will understand that it absolutely reversed my position in regard to the patient" (quoted in Searles, 1979, pp. 262–263).[2] One can clearly hear the reciprocal influence of Ferenczi and Groddeck on each other, each advocating the recognition of mutuality. Ferenczi's work on mutuality culminated in the finding that patient and analyst ultimately care for each other and cure each other through mutual participation, mutual establishment of relatedness, mutual failures in empathy, and mutual forgiveness.

Ferenczi was not the only one of the early analytic pioneers to attempt mutual analysis, and neither was he the first. Jung attempted some mutual analysis as early as 1908 with Otto Gross. Jung wrote to Freud regarding his analysis of Gross, "Whenever I got stuck, he analyzed me. In this way my own psychic health has benefited" (May 25, 1908, in McGuire, 1974, p. 153). Jung was intensely involved in this brief analysis and reported that he was working on the Gross analysis "day and night." He came to feel that Gross and he had much in common and compared him to a twin brother, except that after a few days of this mutual analysis he decided that Gross was incurable, suffering not only from drug addiction but from dementia praecox. It is ironic indeed that Sándor Ferenczi wrote to Freud in regard to Jung's work with Gross, "*Mutual analysis* is nonsense, also an impossibility" (December 26, 1912, in Brabant, Falzeder, and Giampieri-Deutsch, 1993, p. 449).

In later years Jung developed a model for psychotherapy that did include the recognition of mutuality far more than mainstream Freudian psychoanalysis did. He wrote in 1929:

> By no device can the treatment be anything but the product of mutual influence, in which the whole being of the doctor as well as that of the patient plays its part. . . . For two personalities to meet is like mixing two chemical

---

[2] Georg Groddeck (1866–1934) was the Medical Director of a sanitarium in Baden-Baden who in 1912 published a novel attacking psychoanalysis and deploring its emphasis on sexuality. In 1917 he wrote his first letter to Freud in which he admitted that he had never thoroughly read Freud's works and had attacked him out of envy. In the letter he asked Freud if he could call himself an analyst. Freud replied that he considered Groddeck an analyst of the first order. In 1920 at the International Conference at The Hague, Groddeck shocked his audience by declaring himself a "wild analyst." Groddeck is known for having had an intuitive appreciation of the unconscious (he coined the term *Das Es*, later adopted by Freud and translated as the Id), for his contributions to psychosomatic theory, for his early appreciation of the mother transference, and for his recognition of mutuality between patient and analyst (see Grotjahn, 1966).

substances; if there is any combination at all both are transformed [cited in Fordham, 1969, p. 264].

Contemporary Jungians have continued this tradition of viewing psychoanalysis as a mutual and dialectical procedure in the archetype of the "wounded healer" and in their extension of Jung's metaphor of the analytic situation as a chemical (or alchemical) process in which mutual transformation among the individual elements takes place (Samuels, 1985). Some contemporary Jungians have followed Jung in recognizing mutual transformation as the goal of analysis. Drawing on Jung's analogy of alchemical processes in which individual base elements are mutually transformed into gold, Jungians see the therapeutic relationship as a process of mutual and reciprocal transformation in which patient and analyst must be equally transformed. Commenting on the implication of "equality" between patient and analyst, Samuels makes the same distinction that I have made here regarding mutuality and symmetry:

> Jung's word *equality* represents difficulties then. A better word, and one which finds a wide currant, is 'mutuality.' The possibility of this term's becoming idealized, with a connotation of coziness or even exclusiveness, is countered by referring to *asymmetrical mutuality*, suggesting the differing roles of patient and analyst. Other asymmetrical but mutual relationships would be those of mother and child and teacher and student [p. 175].

One of Winnicott's greatest achievements, according to Phillips (1988), was to evolve a genuinely collaborative model of psychoanalytic practice: "Though obviously prone to sentimental mystification, the idea of the reciprocity of the professional relationship was a new note in psychoanalysis" (p. 13). For Winnicott, psychological health was defined by one's ability to engage in the mutuality of relations.

With a few notable exceptions, direct acknowledgment of the patient's contributions to the analyst appears to be relatively rare in the mainstream psychoanalytic literature (Bass, 1993). One exception is Winnicott's acknowledgment to Guntrip that his analysis of Guntrip was good for him, the analyst, as well:

> You, too, have a good breast. You've always been able to give more than you can take. Doing your analysis is almost the most reassuring thing that happens to me. The chap before you makes me feel I'm no good at all. You don't have to be good for me. I don't need it and can cope without it, but in fact you are good for me [quoted in Guntrip, 1975, p. 62].

From a classical perspective, Winnicott's statement to Guntrip has all sorts of technical problems. It violates anonymity; the analyst is no longer a blank screen. It gratifies the patient, and likely gratifies infantile and omnipotent fantasies, and libidinal fantasies at that. It fosters competitive devaluation of others. If it is acknowledged, however, that patients do observe their analysts and make inferences about their observations, and if much of this observation goes on unconsciously, then part of the analyst's work is to help bring these observations and inferences to consciousness. Among the patient's observations may be that the analyst has been aided, influenced, or moved by the patient. How can patients' therapeutic efforts on behalf of their analysts be recognized by analysts who attempt to maintain conditions of abstinence and anonymity?

Winnicott's focus on mutuality may have been a "new note" for mainstream psychoanalysis, but it has always been an essential element of the interpersonal tradition. Clara Thompson, Ferenczi's patient and supervisee, in discussing the role of the analyst's personality in therapy, described how she, Sullivan, and Fromm-Reichman, following Ferenczi, had moved in the direction of greater participation in the analysis. She wrote that encouraging patients to tell all that they have observed or thought about the analyst "may actually increase the analyst's insight into himself to the benefit of both" (Thompson, 1956 p. 170).

Consider the following remark by Erich Fromm (1960), another of the originators of the interpersonal school. In the paragraph preceding the one I am about to quote, Fromm traced the origin of this line of thinking back to Ferenczi and Sullivan.

> The analyst analyzes the patient, but the patient also analyzes the analyst, because the analyst, by sharing the unconscious of his patient, cannot help clarifying his own unconscious. Hence the analyst not only cures the patient, but is also cured by him. He not only understands the patient, but eventually the patient understands him. When this stage is reached solidarity and communion are reached [p. 112].

Following the Frommian tradition, Edward Tauber (1952) wrote:

> The therapist cannot validly learn all about his own counter-transference difficulties through supervision or personal analysis but must establish an atmosphere where he can learn something about himself from his patients. One does not show all of one's personality to any one person and *one has to solve each so-called me-you relationship within its own domain* [p. 228, italics added].

Later, Lucia Tower (1956), a classical analyst who cited the work of Tauber and who was much cited by interpersonalists, wrote:

> I simply do not believe that any two people, regardless of circumstance, may closet themselves in a room, day after day, month after month, and year after

year, without something happening to each of them in respect to the other. Perhaps the development of a major change in the one, which is, after all, the purpose of the therapy, would be impossible without at least some minor change in the other, and it is probably relatively unimportant whether that minor change in the other is a rational one. It is probably far more important that the minor change in the other, namely, the therapist, be that which is specifically important and necessary to the one for whom we hope to achieve the major change. [p. 139]

Further in the line of this interpersonal tradition is Singer (1971), who suggests not only that patients may be genuinely helpful to their analysts, but also that analysts may express gratitude for this help. Perhaps this tradition culminates in the famous paper by Searles (1979), "The Patient as Therapist to the Analyst." In his descriptions of "a mutually growth-enhancing [therapeutic] symbiosis," Searles suggests that patients are ill because, and to the degree that, their own psychotherapeutic strivings toward their parents have been frustrated and left unacknowledged. In the transference, these psychotherapeutic strivings are remobilized to aid the analyst, and patients monitor their analysts to see if they are benefiting from these therapeutic efforts. It is only insofar as patients can now succeed in equivalent therapeutic strivings directed toward their analysts that they can make reparation, lessen their guilt, become sure of their "symbiotic worth" (p. 385), and therefore feel fully human. Searles points out that in his view the patient's therapeutic strivings are not secondary to unconscious hostile strivings; that is, they are not only reparative but also derive from a primary human need to give love and have it accepted. In addition, Searles suggests that

> The more I have come to accept comfortably this dimension as inherent to the treatment process, the more, I feel sure, does my whole demeanor in the work with the patient come to include an implicit acknowledgement that the therapeutic process at work between us is a mutual, two-way one [p. 428].

One can follow this line of thought directly into the most recent interpersonal literature. Levenson (1993) has written that "cure becomes a mutual process, and the patient is not only the interpreter of the analyst's experience, but a collaborator in the therapist's cure" (pp. 393–394). Similarly, Wolstein (1964, 1975, 1981, 1983, 1994) has articulated an interpersonal view in which the mutual coparticipant inquiry into transference–countertransference interlocks is curative to patient and analyst, both of whom must change for an analysis to progress.

The line of thinking that I have just traced has never received mainstream acceptance by the psychoanalytic community. It has always met with a response that acknowledges that mutuality between analyst and analysand may happen sometimes, and may be powerful when it does happen, but it should not occur too often if the analyst is well-enough analyzed to begin with. After all, the obvious argument goes, the analysis is supposed to be for the patient's benefit, rather than for the analyst's. How unethical and unprofessional it is to put the analyst's needs ahead of the patient's.

The tradition that runs from Groddeck and Ferenczi through Fromm, Searles, Winnicott, Levenson, and Wolstein turns this argument on its head. Their legacy paradoxically suggests that the patient may well need to put the therapist's needs first at least in some respects. Unless patients can feel that they have reached their analysts, moved them, changed them, discomforted them, angered them, hurt them, healed them, known them in some profound way, they themselves may not be able to benefit from their analyses. From this perspective, psychoanalysis is a profound emotional encounter, an interpersonal engagement, an intersubjective dialogue, a relational integration, a meeting of minds.

Empathy, or analytic love, must be mutually given and mutually accepted. Psychoanalytic thought holds that children need to be loved by their parents; analysts, however, have by and large not addressed the inverse, namely, that children also have a great need to love their parents and have their parents accept this love. Most exceptional are the assertions regarding the importance of mutual give-and-take by two pioneer object relations theorists, Suttie and Fairbairn.

Ian Suttie (1935), influenced by Ferenczi, developed an early object relations theory that identified the craving for sociability and companionship and the need to love and to be loved as fundamental human motives. In striking contrast to the classical tradition that preceded him, he wrote:

> The baby then not only starts life with a benevolent attitude, but the Need-to-Give continues as a dominant motive throughout life ... the *need to give* is as vital, therefore, as the *need to get*. The feeling that our gifts (love) are not acceptable is as intolerable as the feeling that other's gifts are no longer obtainable [p. 53].

Fairbairn (1952), in an approach that has certain affinities to Suttie's, showed his appreciation of the need for mutual empathy in his assertion that "the greatest need of a child is to obtain conclusive assurance (a) that he is genuinely loved as a person by his parents, (b) that his parents genuinely accept his love" (p. 39).

No psychoanalytic school of thought has stressed the role of empathy as much as self psychology has, and, in recent writings, self psychologists have begun to underscore the importance of mutual empathy between patient and analyst. In describing the way in which patients use their analysts to perform *selfobject* functions—that is, where the analysts are used to evoke, maintain, or enhance the patients' sense of self—Bacal (1995a) writes that

> The analyst, in effect, also experiences a *selfobject relationship* with the patient in which he comes to expect that certain of his selfobject needs will be met by the patient's ongoing responses, and his analytic function may be substantially interfered with when these responses are not forthcoming [p. 363].

He suggests that we have been so intent on the experience of needing and *receiving* selfobject experiences that we have not paid enough attention to the experience of *providing* selfobject experiences. There may be benefits to giving as well as to receiving empathy. "To the extent that one experiences oneself as providing it," Bacal (1995b) writes, "this may also evoke and vitalize the sense of self of both analyst and analysand. In this sense as well, the selfobject concept is truly relational" (p. 403).

In a related statement, Stolorow (1995) suggests, "An intersubjective field is a *system of reciprocal mutual influence* (Beebe and Lachmann, 1988). Not only does the patient turn to the analyst for selfobject experiences, but the analyst also turns to the patient for such experiences" (p. 396). As I pointed out in Chapter 2, Bacal and Stolorow are among the leading self psychologists who are building bridges with relational theory more widely, and, therefore, it is in keeping with my thesis that mutuality is a central principle within relational theory that these self psychologists too are paying increased attention to mutual empathy and mutual selfobject experiences.

The empirical findings of psychotherapy outcome research may be interpreted to support the spirit of these hypotheses about mutuality (for a review, see Whiston and Sexton, 1993). It has been shown that not only are the therapist's warmth and acceptance of the patient predictive of good outcome, but the patient's warmth and acceptance of the therapist are significant factors. An effective therapeutic relationship or working alliance seems to be associated with mutual and reciprocal affirmation, understanding, affiliation, empathy, and respect. The analytic relationship, however, perhaps unlike some of the short-term therapies on which these research findings were based, must include a wide range of mutual feelings, not limited to the positively toned feelings of warmth and love, but also including such feelings as mutual mistrust and fear, mutual competitiveness, mutual envy, and mutual hate. I would hypothesize, that in long-term, intensive psychotherapy and psychoanalysis it is not just mutual empathy that is predictive of therapeutic outcome, also that it is the capacity of both participants to feel a wide range of feelings toward each other, perhaps under the dominance of mutual warmth and empathy, that predicts positive outcome.[3] Since the outcome research also shows that therapist variables are most predictive when measured from the patient's perspective, rather than either from the therapist's perspective or from some objective observer's or global rating, there is good reason for therapists to pay particular attention to their patients' experience of the analysts' subjectivity.

NEGOTIATION

We generally speak of cognitions and affects as residing within individual selves. We speak of my feelings of fear, or your feelings of hope, or what he thinks about her. Individuals are considered the autonomous agents, and we view relationships as secondary and as derivative byproducts of individual units. Gergen (1991) writes that we have an "impoverished language of relatedness" (p. 160), that we do not speak of relationships' wishing, hoping, or fearing. We speak only of individuals' determining relationships rather than of relationships' determining individuals. It is out of this habit of language that we speak of the analyst's interpretation or the patient's resistance leading to a particular therapeutic relationship. With the postmodern turn, it might be better said that the relationship interprets, or that the relationship resists, or even that it is the relationship that is unconscious. Perhaps we should speak of a relational unconscious, of mutual unconsciousness, mutual resistance, and mutual interpretation. The contemporary relational perspective maintains a dialectical approach by considering both that individuals determine relationships and that relationships determine individuals.

The language of contemporary psychoanalysis is replete with words with the prefixes co, inter, and bi. Thus one finds terms like coparticipant, coconstruction, coinvestigator, interactional, intersubjective, interpersonal, interrelational, interaffectivity, bipersonal, bidirectional. These terms highlight the emphasis being placed on mutuality and

---

[3] At times, these feelings may be experienced as concordant and at times as complementary (Racker, 1968), but over the course of the analysis they should encompass a full range of affects for both participants.

reciprocal processes. The word "negotiation" has been used to make a similar point. We might say that not only do patient and analyst negotiate fees, schedules, and cancellation policies, but also, more fundamentally, patient and analyst negotiate the meanings that are cocreated between them. It could be said, too, that interpretations are negotiated between patient and analyst, that we negotiate the location of the resistances, that we negotiate the quality of our relationships with patients, and that we negotiate the construction of a psychoanalytic narrative. Similarly, we might think of the affective climate in the consulting room, the relative amount of talk or silence, and the psychological distance between patient and analyst all as products of interactional, conscious, and unconscious negotiation, a meeting of minds.

Mitchell (1991) has drawn attention to the usefulness of negotiation as a metaphor for many aspects of the analytic process. Mitchell argues that the attempt to distinguish patient's "needs" and "wishes" retains the purely intrapsychic framework of classical theory. "Needs and wishes are considered different motivational states *in the patient*, which the analyst is supposed to be able to discern" (p. 152). In contrast, for Mitchell, the analyst's experience of the patient's desire is reflective of the nature of that desire, but is codetermined by the analyst's own character. Therefore, whether a particular desire feels like a wish or a need will depend on the relational context.

> What may be most crucial is the process of negotiation itself, in which the analyst finds his own way to confirm and participate in the patient's subjective experience, yet over time establishes his own presence and perspective in a way that the patient can find enriching rather than demolishing [p. 164].

To return to the impoverishment of relational language, we might be better off if our language permitted us to say "the relationship needs" or "the relationship wishes" rather than imply through our language that wishes and needs exist only in individual selves.

Pizer (1992) has eloquently described how the therapeutic action of psychoanalysis is constituted by the engagement of two persons in the process of negotiation. Patient and analyst say to each other, "You can make this of me, but not that of me"; "I will be this for you, but not that for you." Pizer writes, "The very substance and nature of truth and reality—as embodied both in transference–countertransference constructions and in narrative reconstructions—are being negotiated toward consensus in the analytic dyad" (p. 218). Loewald (1988) introduced the concept of invention to make a similar point about the origins of subjectivity, "Mother and infant may be said to invent each other in the mouth-breast encounter. . . . I introduce the concept of invention, as distinguished from discovery and creation, in order to highlight the reciprocal complementary tension and readiness of agent and 'material.'" (p. 76). Speaking in a thoroughly relational language, Loewald emphasizes the mouth-breast as an invented "combination" (p. 76). Similarly, we might think of the patient–analyst dyad as a continually invented, destructed, and reinvented combination.

If we negotiate who we will be for the patients, and who they will be for us, we also negotiate how we view the goals of each analysis. The patient presents one set of problems, and we hear a different set of problems. We hope that over the course of the analysis, the patient will come to see the problems more as we do. And yet, as the analysis progresses, we may also let go of some our preconceptions and recognize that there was more in the patient's perspective than we at first could see. This capacity to negotiate with the patient recalls Ferenczi's (1928) adopting a term suggested by a patient, "the elasticity of technique," in which "the analyst, like an elastic band, must yield to the patient's pull, but without ceasing to pull in his own direction" (p. 95).

Negotiation is an inherent feature of the relational model because the theory takes for granted that the analyst influences the patient and the patient influences the analyst. Since interpersonal influence is assumed, it is clear that the analyst is moved, influenced, and transformed by the patient; and so who the analyst is and how the analyst acts are not givens based on the rules of analytic technique or based on the character structure of the analyst, although these are factors. Rather, it is presumed that the analyst is different with different people and in different relationships. Therefore, who the analyst is, is to some degree determined by who the patient is. Since this interpersonal process is mutual and reciprocal, the patient continually influenced by the analyst and vice versa, one can legitimately claim that the very essence of who the patient and analyst are with each other is negotiated.

Relationships are made up of individuals, and individuals are constituted by their relationships. Following Beebe, Jaffe, and Lachmann (1992), I believe it is useful to think of the dyadic system as organized by an integration of stable, individual characteristics and by emergent dyadic properties: one- and two-person psychologies. One of the clinical consequences of this theoretical position has to do with thinking diagnostically about patients. If analysts are viewed as "coparticipants" (Wolstein, 1975) who became caught up inside the analytic system, then they too must be the objects of study, for they inevitably influence the data being investigated. From a relational or interpersonal viewpoint, rather than diagnose the patient as an individual, the analyst attempts to evaluate the state of the relationship evolving between the patient and the analyst. In this way, analysts recognize their own embeddedness as participants in the very field that they are simultane-ously observing. Participant-observation, the study of transference and countertransference, is inherent in this model. Traditional psychiatric, and even traditional psychoanalytic, diagnostic thinking has conceptu-alized disorders as diagnosed in individuals. Only recently has serious consideration been given to developing classifications of relationships and their disorders (Sameroff and Emde, 1989), that is, to thinking in terms of relational disorders and diagnosis.

From the point of view being developed here, relational psychoanal-ysis attempts to maintain some balance between thinking in terms of one- and two-person psychologies. The individuals determine the rela-tionship and the relationship determines the individuals. Therefore, analysts would need to think diagnostically both in terms of the patient's relatively stable characteristics as they seem to transcend the unique therapeutic relationship and in terms of a relational diagnosis of the emergent dyadic properties organizing the analytic interaction. Analysts would further need to acknowledge that *both* types of diag-noses are made by them from within a dyadic system and not from outside of it. Thus diagnoses made by the analyst are reflections of the analyst's subjectivity as much as they may also be reflections of the patient's inherent characteristics. Analysts become genuinely inter-ested in their patients' diagnoses of their analysts as well as in the patients' relational diagnoses of the therapeutic system.

NEGOTIATION AND CLINICAL PRACTICE

The topic of negotiation raises some of the issues that are inevitably involved in initiating a treatment process and negotiating the "therapeutic contract." In recent years, I have come to share much more with my patients, especially about my motives and my rationale for various technical procedures and decisions, than I would have done previously and certainly much more than I was encouraged to do in my own training as a Freudian analyst. The following are illustrations of a way of working that involves some increased self-disclosure for the purpose of facilitating negotiation and maximizing mutuality.

In his recommendations on psychoanalytic technique, Freud (1913) wrote that he required analytic patients to recline on a sofa while he sat out of sight. He noted the historical origins of this procedure but added that there were personal and technical reasons for it as well. He explained that he did not like to be looked at all day and added that he wanted to feel free to give reign to his unconscious reactions and not have his expressions give the patient any indications of his reactions that might influence their associations.

I believe that Freud was on the right track in explaining to his readers his personal reasons for the use of the couch rather than only
explaining the technical and historical rationale. I have found it useful
to explain to patients my personal preferences as well. My experience
has been that the more I explain to patients my personal reasons and
preferences for doing any technical procedure, the less difficulty I have
in examining and interpreting whatever reactions patients have to
these procedures and whatever meanings they have for patients. So,
with the couch, I might very well tell patients that, in addition to finding that patients often feel it beneficial, in that it helps them to let their
minds go, I have personal reasons for using it too. I might say something
like this:

> I have a personal preference for the couch because it is easier for me to listen to
> you and to let myself relax and try to tune into what you are saying when I
> don't have the pressure of being looked at. In not being observed, I can be less
> self-conscious. I can join you in a state of mind in which we both may hear and
> see things differently than we usually do.

There have been times when patients have told me how isolated they
have felt on the couch, and I told them that I found the couch to be a
deprivation as well, since I missed not seeing them in the usual manner
and had given up a more social position in relation to them. Patients
have been quite surprised to learn not only that I might miss them, but
that I have mixed reactions to the couch. Patients often assume that
the analyst is free of conflict and ambivalence, and, while this fantasy
needs to be analyzed rather than corrected by introducing reality in the
form of the analyst's confessions of conflict, I believe that the usual
anonymity and lack of personal reactions lend themselves to a notion
that it is only the patient who has conflict. I do not see how this denial
can be analyzed effectively if analysts collude with patients in conveying that they are conflict free. Some self-disclosure by the analyst
(mutual disclosure) may heighten mutual recognition.

It may seem that some patients would not be able to recognize the
individuality of the analyst to the degree that this approach would
require. It may be argued that some patients need the freedom to not
consider the analyst as an individual with his or her own needs. This
line of thinking brings us back to the analyst as outside of the system,
diagnosing "the need" that is thought to reside in the patient. Is it the
patient's need? The analyst's? The relationship's? Should we say that
the patient cannot tolerate this, or that the relationship, at this point,
cannot tolerate it or contain this mode of interaction?

It should be kept in mind, however, that analysts who have worked,
in the tradition of Ferenczi and Searles, with the most severely dis-

turbed or "primitive" patients (those whom one might have expected to be least developmentally capable of tolerating the independent subjectivity and autonomy of the analyst) have found these patients quite responsive to an approach that includes a certain degree of self-disclosure from the analyst. In my own clinical work, I have not found any consistent relation between patients' diagnoses or levels of psychopathology and their capacity to work in the way that I am describing here.

Consider the following, less routine example. A supervisee consulted me regarding a suicidal patient. She had told the patient that she was concerned about him and felt that it was necessary for him to get a psychiatric consultation. Furthermore, she told him that she felt it would be in his best interest for her to let one of his close relatives know that he was suicidal and needed support. The therapist and patient had spent some time discussing this and arguing about it. The patient accused the therapist of not acting in his best interests but, rather, in her own interest. In response to this accusation, the therapist became more defensive, more concerned, and more insistent.

I suggested that the therapist explain to the patient that he was absolutely right in certain respects. As the therapist, I would say that indeed I was anxious, that I felt that I had certain responsibilities regarding the patient's life, and that I felt that I had a responsibility to the patient as well as a need of my own to cover myself legally, ethically, and professionally. I would explain that I simply could not work well, which means that I could not listen carefully to my patient and think clearly about what I was doing when I was too anxious. I would add, "Right now, given that you are telling me that you may kill yourself while under my professional care, I am indeed also anxious." Therefore, I would insist on taking whatever steps I felt necessary, including a psychiatric consultation or informing relatives, in order to take care of my own anxiety. Furthermore, I would put it to the patient that this was something that I expected him to do both for his own good and for my good. "I need you to take care of me and help me keep my anxiety level at a manageable level so that I can be free to work at my best with you." None of this precludes the need to interpret to the patient the attempt to rid himself of any sense of urgency or panic by placing that feeling into the analyst.

This is not just an exercise in reframing or reverse psychology. I believe that it is exceptionally therapeutic for the patient to know that, indeed, the analyst feels anxious and needs help from the patient, and that the patient can actually help the therapist. Further, I think it is important to communicate to a patient that I am determined to protect myself and can put my own needs first when necessary.

When I make recommendations to patients about beginning treatment, I encourage them to come as frequently as possible. Once again, I explain to them some of the reasons why I believe this to be in their best interest. I may say that greater frequency gives us more time to understand them and the way their minds work, that it allows us greater continuity from one session to the next, and that it allows us the luxury of focusing on their inner worlds rather than on just what events happened or what problems came up from one week to the next. I try to be clear, however, that I prefer to work with patients more frequently also because it is more interesting to me to be able to work with each person in depth and that it is frankly easier for me to understand patients and become involved in their world when I can see them more frequently. Of course, patients may then feel that they are disappointing me personally if they choose not to come more frequently. I try to be open about the fact that a good deal of what goes on between us is negotiable, not everything, but much is. The parties to any negotiation generally each gain something and give something up. One works out the best compromises one can: "I may be disappointed in you at times, as I am sure you will be with me. If things go well here, we are bound to feel a wide variety of feelings toward each other."

MUTUAL REGRESSION

Using the idea that patient and analyst always mutually regulate each other in various ways, Annabella Bushra and I (Aron and Bushra, 1995) have suggested that one psychic function that is mutually regulated between patient and analyst is the quality of their states of consciousness, or what in psychoanalytic parlance is generally referred to as their states of regression. "From a relational position," we argue, "the patient and analyst each mutually regulate (regressive) states in each other, and that this process is an important aspect of the analytic process" (p. 3). We have traced the resurgence of interest among psychoanalysts in the phenomena of (altered) states of consciousness (see, for two excellent examples, the work of Bromberg, 1994, from an interpersonal/relational perspective and Bach, 1994, from a contemporary Freudian perspective). We attribute this revival of interest to such factors as the renewed interest in trauma, multiple personality disorder, and dissociative disorder, as well as to postmodern thought more generally and its focus on the deconstruction of the self and the critique of the subject.

> Relational theorists, because of their focus on two- person events, may have a
> tendency to pay inadequate attention to those phenomena that are typically

thought of as existing intrapsychically within the individual. By reconceptualizing regression as a two person process, we hope to place it as a central area of
investigation within a relational approach [Aron and Bushra, p. 19].

Regression is an example of a concept that is thought of by classical
analysts as a phenomenon that occurs (most regularly and most
predominantly) in the minds of individual patients. But with the
growing awareness of the analyst's participation has come an increased
attention to his or her psychic participation in altered, dissociated, and
regressed states of mind. By focusing on the ways in which patient and
analyst mutually regulate each other's state of consciousness, we
attempt to move regression out of the individual's mind and into the
space between the participants. Thus we speak of mutual regression or
of mutual regulation of regression.

CASE ILLUSTRATION

The case of Mr. P, presented by Wolfenstein (1993), lends itself nicely
to my purpose of illustrating the mutual regulation of regressive states.
Mr. P, a successful academician in his late 20s, came to analysis complaining that he felt damaged and expressing the idea that, although he
believed he could accomplish great things in his life, the thought of
realizing his potential was accompanied in his mind with images of
disaster. Mr. P was the only child of parents who had divorced when he
was six years old. Following the divorce, he lived with his mother, with
whom he had little emotional contact. He described having had a
lonely and isolated childhood. A significant feature of his relationship
to his mother as he remembered it was that, after a long and lonely day,
he would try to talk to his mother and she would fall asleep.

Not surprisingly, the first thing that Wolfenstein tells us about his
reactions to Mr. P is that, when Mr. P first began telling him his life
story, he put his analyst to sleep. Wolfenstein writes that he found Mr.
P "mildly agreeable. . . . He did not evoke strong feelings in me one
way or the other. He did make me sleepy" (p. 357). The analyst's
sleepiness was from the very beginning of the analysis to play a significant role in the treatment.

Wolfenstein relates a typical instance in which he would begin a
session feeling well rested and alert. Mr. P would be talking in an
orderly, logical, somewhat repetitious way, seeming to be intensely
involved in the content of his communications, which might be about
an event in his present life, a previous analytic session, or a dream. He
would be lying motionless, and his tone of voice would be well modulated within a narrow range. Wolfenstein describes how he would be

following Mr. P's associations with relaxed attention, when, "quite suddenly, I would feel as if I had been injected with a sleep-making drug. I would find myself trapped between antithetical imperatives: I must go to sleep! I must stay awake!" (p. 358). When the session ended the analyst would feel groggy but within a few minutes would return to himself with perhaps some lingering weariness. Wolfenstein reports that his sleepiness was limited to his sessions with Mr. P and that he did not feel this way with patients he saw just before or after Mr. P. This experience of "antithetical imperatives" experienced by Wolfenstein is precisely the kind of paradoxical suggestion designed to produce confusion and to result in an escape into trance, much like the "psychological effectiveness of opposites" described by Ferenczi (1913, p. 340) as a method of inducing trance states.

Wolfenstein (1993) explores a few possibilities to determine the meaning of his sleepiness with Mr. P. These include the obvious reenactment of Mr. P's experience with his mother, who would fall asleep as he told her his stories of the day. Wolfenstein also considers that his sleepiness might be a form of withdrawal from Mr. P, that he might be expressing his resentment at the emotional barrenness of Mr. P's communications. Mr. P may have been emotionally withdrawn, rendering the analyst's efforts futile, and the analyst may have withdrawn in hostile retaliation. A further possibility is that Mr. P's conflicts and defenses were too similar to his own in certain respects and that his own sleepiness was a defensive response in an effort to avoid contact with problems that were hitting too close to home.

Wolfenstein moves from contemplating each of these possibilities to the broader one that his sleepiness might be more than just a countertransference response in the narrow sense of the term. He considers that perhaps his sleepiness itself is an integral part of the analysis. Perhaps, he wonders, Mr. P is disconnected with himself and the analyst is connecting with Mr. P's very disconnectedness. If the sleepiness originates in Mr. P and yet it is the analyst who is feeling sleepy, than the sleepiness itself may be understood as a form of connection to the patient. Patient and analyst are always mutually involved in regulating each other's states of consciousness. Usually this aspect of mutual regulation is a background phenomenon not requiring attention and explication, but under certain circumstances it may come, or need to come, to the foreground, to become a focus of the analytic exploration. When an analyst finds him- or herself experiencing difficulty in the smooth and automatic regulation of their states of consciousness, it is likely that the patient is using the analyst's mind excessively as a regulator, relying on mutual regulation of ego states, instead of relying predominantly on self-regulation. I hypothesize that a patient does this because of some difficulty with self-regulation of behavioral states, that is, some difficulty in state constancy that needs to be addressed within the analysis.

Wolfenstein suggests, much along the lines that I have just drawn, that Mr. P might have been traumatized as a child, when he might have relied on a hypnoid state as a defense. Mr. P

> might now be putting me into a hypnoid state, not only to avoid a repetition of the trauma but also to communicate to me the nature of the catastrophe that had occurred. There might also be a dream or a fantasy within the hypnoid condition, which might only be accessible through my own reverie. If this were true, attempting to dispel the sleepiness would be the real countertransference response [p. 359].

Wolfenstein recognizes that the alteration in his state of consciousness is the very means by which he can come to enter Mr. P's inner world.

Wolfenstein, attempting to account for further experiences of sleepiness with Mr. P, proposes that Mr. P was unconsciously engaged in autohypnotic activity: "His absolute physical immobility and the modulated, subtly rhythmic quality of his voice suggested as much" (p. 364). Wolfenstein concludes that his own sleepy reaction was not simply a byproduct of his patient's autohypnotic activity, but was more directly a result of Mr. P's unconscious efforts to put his analyst to sleep as he had done to his mother. In experiencing the sleepy state, the analyst was holding Mr. P's projected image of himself and his mother, a relational experience that the patient could not bear to experience on his own.

Following a great deal of work in the analysis, and in particular much attention to Mr. P's tendency to split his object world into good and bad, Mr. P, feeling somewhat less paranoid, asked his mother what it had been like when he was a nursling. His mother told him that she had been very happy with him and loved nursing him. She added that he would fall asleep at the breast, and she would fall asleep too.

Bromberg (1994) notes that "dissociated domains of self can achieve symbolization only through enactment in a relational context" (p. 535), and therefore analysts must have a special attunement to the impact that the patient is having on their own self-states at any given moment. Bromberg's point is that these dissociated self-states cannot be put directly into words and can therefore be known by the analyst only through their relational enactment. The impact of this enactment may be known by the analyst only as it is experienced as an alteration in the analyst's states of consciousness. How analysts manage these alterations in consciousness, how comfortable they are entering, sustaining, and allowing these states to deepen instead of snapping themselves out of these altered (regressed) states, how they intervene or interpret on the basis of these self-states, all these factors, in turn, regulate the patient's states of consciousness. Wolfenstein's case presentation is evocative of the ways in which patient and analyst mutually regulate each other's self-states throughout an analysis.

MUTUAL REGULATION AND MUTUAL RECOGNITION

There is a convergence taking place among thinkers in a number of related disciplines regarding the theoretical importance of mutuality. In an elegant overview of the theoretical conclusions that have emerged out of infancy research, Beebe, Jaffe, and Lachmann (1992) describe a dyadic systems view of communication. They define communication "the mutual modification of two ongoing streams of behavior of two persons. . . . Communication occurs when each person affects the probability distribution of the other's behavior" (p. 62). Using such terms as a system of mutuality, a system of reciprocal relations, mutual obligations, and mutual recognition, a wide variety of philosophers and scientists studying interaction have converged in a dyadic-systems view of communication. Beebe and her colleagues report that, in research on mother–infant interaction, bidirectional influence has been systematically documented, and a systems model of the dyad has been established.

Whereas, in earlier work, researchers emphasized the parental influence on children to the relative exclusion of the child's influence on the parents, contemporary researchers, with increasing recognition of infants' competencies, have become more interested in a bidirectional, or mutual model of influence. Mutuality does not, of course, imply equality. Beebe and her coworkers acknowledge that there are, though, some infant researchers whose conclusions romantically verge on a notion of adult–infant symmetry. Beebe and her colleagues, however, emphasize the distinction between mutuality and symmetry: "The mother obviously has a greater range, control, and flexibility of behavior than the infant" (p. 65).

The work of Beebe, Jaffe, and Lachmann attempts to balance the importance of self-regulation and mutual or interactive regulation of behavior. Psychic structure formation is based not on dyadic interaction alone, but on the organism's own self-regulatory capacities. Similarly, individual stability of responsivity must be balanced with the emergent properties of the dyad. They write, "an integration of these factors provides a view of the dyadic system as organized *both* by stable characteristics of the participants (a one-person psychology model) and by emergent dyadic properties (a two-person psychology model)" (p. 67).

Beebe and her colleagues emphasize that mutual regulation continues to operate even under relational conditions of misattunement. For example, even in an interaction of "chase and dodge," the mother's chase behaviors influence the child's dodge behaviors. Therefore, while the interaction may be misattuned or unpleasant, it is nevertheless still mutually regulated. Furthermore, Lachmann and Beebe (1992) have suggested, mother–infant relatedness is not characterized by continuous harmony and synchrony, but, rather, by disruption and repair. Intersubjectivity may be best conceptualized as existing only in dialectic tension with a subject–object relationship, a position compatible with Ogden's (1986, 1989) notion of a dialectic relation between the paranoid-schizoid and depressive positions. This dialectical conceptualization has direct relevance for Benjamin's (1988) conceptualization of intersubjectivity.

The question of whether and how psychoanalysis is mutual is actually very complex. When I say that psychoanalysis is a mutual endeavor, I mean, more precisely, that patient and analyst create a unique system in which, from their very first encounter, there is reciprocal influence and mutual regulation; this is consistent with Stolorow, Atwood, and Brandschaft's (1994) idea of intersubjectivity and with Beebe, Jaffe, and Lachmann's (1992) use of the term mutual regulation. Mutual recognition, as discussed by Benjamin (1988) and Stern (1985), is a more difficult matter and cannot simply be assumed. It may take very long, indeed, before patient and analyst recognize each other as separate people, each with his or her own subjectivity, and even when intersubjectivity is achieved it is not a stable, final achievement. Rather, the experience of self and other as separate subjects always exists in dynamic tension with the experience of self and other as objects. We each operate simultaneously in the paranoid-schizoid and depressive modes, always experiencing ourselves and each other paradoxically as both subject and object (Ogden, 1986, 1989, 1994). Whereas mutual regulation is a conceptual assumption of relational theory, mutual recognition may be thought of as one of its primary goals. Intersubjectivity, however, is not a final replacement for the subject–object relation. Rather, they coexist in mutual relation to each other.

Perhaps this is a good place to repeat that it is not particularly meaningful simply to say that psychoanalysis is a mutual process. One needs to be specific —mutual how? If one means by mutual that there is a bidirectional influence between patient and analyst, then it is certainly mutual. But one cannot assume that at any given moment there is mutual recognition between patient and analyst. This is a developmental achievement that may not have been reached by the patient and that may very well be lost during moments of regression by either the patient or the analyst. This distinction is important because the term intersubjectivity is used confusingly to refer to both of these very different meanings.

MUTUALITY AND INTIMACY

Intimacy involves both similarity and difference, mutuality and autonomy. When two people have only commonality and similarity, they are lost in each other; this is not intimacy, but merger. Intimacy consists of similarity, commonality, united interests, sharing, and mutual recognition of each other as *separate* subjectivities, separate individuals. Bach (1994) writes that "for mutuality to exist we must have two participants who feel themselves to be autonomous people, capable of saying 'yes' and 'no' to each other while maintaining respect for each other's point of view" (p. 43).

Furthermore, intimacy requires not only the capacity to see the other as a separate subject, to engage in a subject-to-subject relation, center-to-center or core-to-core relatedness (Fromm, 1960), an I–Thou relation (Buber, 1923), but also the capacity to use the other as an object of desire and to be used by the other as the object of desire. We do not give up objectifying the other with whom we are intimate; rather, mutuality of recognition of separate subjectivities coexists in a dialectic with the subject–object, I–it, relation. When Bach (1994) says that "it is the treatment of another person as a thing rather than as a human being that I see as a perversion of object relationships" (p. xv), I believe he means that perversion is based on treating the other essentially or exclusively as a thing. As Bader (1995), following Winnicott, has suggested healthy sexual excitement requires an element of ruthlessness to be successful. What is lost in character perversions is the ability to maintain the dialectic tension between viewing the other as a separate autonomous person and as an object of one's own desire, between egoism and empathy, ruthlessness and concern.

Where mutuality and intimacy are lacking, the only alternative is sadomasochism. If two people do not acknowledge each other as separate autonomous subjects, then in one way or another they are dominating and submitting to each other (see Frankel, 1993). Even a sadomasochistic relationship requires mutuality of regulation, but not the recognition of each other's subjectivities, and thus there is no mutuality of recognition or intersubjectivity. The sadist's behaviors predict and control the masochist's. The masochist, however, simultaneously and paradoxically controls and invites the sadistic attack. The difference between mutuality of regulation and mutuality of recognition is critical because, when analyst and patient participate in relations of dominance and submission, they are still mutually regulating this interaction. Thus, the very capacity or incapacity for mutual recognition is itself mutually regulated. Intimacy and collaboration are not easily achieved, because patient and analyst will enact power struggles between them that must be continually examined, articulated, and worked through. Mutuality is achieved not through intellectual or ideological indoctrination but through the analyst's sustained empathic immersion in and subjective attunement to the patient's subjective world. Intersubjectivity is gradually negotiated in the direction of true collaboration and mutual trust.

The word autonomy, so prominent in classical theory and so important a value for psychoanalysts, means self-governing or self-regulating. Thus, if psychoanalysis is to promote the capacity for intimacy, it must function with principles of mutuality and autonomy, of interaction and self-regulation. In this sense, it is best to think of autonomy and mutuality, self- and mutual regulation, as dialectic principles. Mutuality of recognition is really recognition of each other's autonomy. A person's sense of autonomy in a relationship is itself a mutually regulated state. For mutuality of recognition to exist in a relationship, there must be two participants who feel themselves to be autonomous people capable of agreement and disagreement. Here, the postmodern emphasis on deconstructing dichotomous terms (Derrida, 1978, 1981) can be used in reconceptualizing mutuality and autonomy as paradoxical and dialectical principles rather than as dichotomous ideas. Keller (1985) introduced the notion of "dynamic autonomy" (p. 95) as a way of dealing with the problem that autonomy so often connotes a radical separation and independence from others. By contrast, dynamic autonomy is seen as a product of relatedness with others as well as of separation from them. Dynamic autonomy develops not only from a sense of competence and effectance, but also out of a sense of continuity and reciprocity of feeling in formative interpersonal experience. The notion of dynamic autonomy is an attempt to deconstruct the misleading opposition between autonomy and connection to others that so pervades our culture. From this perspective, analysts continue to value preserving the patient's autonomy, but maintaining autonomy is always seen as in tension with the need to preserve connection and attachment.

Drawing on Beebe's observations that intimate relationships build on cycles of disruption and repair, Benjamin (1992) has linked Winnicott's (1971a) notions about destruction and survival to disruption and repair sequences. Pizer (1992), also elaborating on Winnicott, addressed this same issue in his discussion of the negotiation of ruthlessness and concern. In accord with them I am suggesting that the intersubjective relation is continually disrupted between people— including between patient and analyst—exchanged for a subject– object relation, and then the intersubjective relation is restored. I believe that intimacy is not coterminous with the intersubjective but, rather, transcends this dialectic relation. Intimacy involves the survival and sustenance of a relation through the ongoing creation and destruction of intersubjectivity. The vision being proposed here is of psychoanalysis as a creative process, in which people expand their awareness and develop their most personal, unique individuality in intimate relation to another (Wilner, 1975; Ehrenberg, 1992; Wolstein, 1994). Intimacy requires mutual openness, mutual directness, interaffectivity, and personal exposure and risk. Patient and analyst must remain open to mutual and reciprocal affective engagement, each by the other, and to the expansion of their own personal, unique experiences. In balancing mutuality and the unique experience of the self, we may promote the patient's capacity for dynamic autonomy.

While psychoanalysis takes place in a two-person, intersubjective field, it requires conditions, for at least certain phases of the process, that permit an experience of essential solitude. What I mean, following Winnicott (1958), is solitude in the presence of the analyst. Once again, to illustrate the poverty of our everyday language to express relational ideas, I have not been successful in finding a word that captures this experience. Benjamin (1988) uses the word disengagement (p. 42) to capture this state; but while this word connotes a sense of freedom, it also connotes withdrawal and separateness. It might be better to describe this solitude as solitude-in-relation, or perhaps, following Keller's (1985) term, "dynamic autonomy," we might speak of "dynamic solitude." Phillips (1993) has described a similar state as a "solitude a deux" (p. 29). Once again, we are discussing the dialectics of autonomy and mutuality, one- and two-person psychologies.

The patient's observations of the analyst, inferences about the analyst, and analysis of the analyst go on all the time. These activities, however, usually occur unconsciously, as background phenomena, with the analysis of the patient taking center stage. I believe that it is occasionally very useful to take the focus off of the patient, reverse figure and ground, and make the analysis of the analyst central, as, for example, in what Steiner (1993) has called "analyst centered interpreta-tions" (p. 131) or in the analytic procedure that Blechner (1992) has referred to as "working in the countertransference" (p. 164). If the balance shifts too much in the direction of the analysis of the analyst, however, if the analyst takes up too much room at center stage, than the patient may rightly feel sacrificed to the analyst's needs. An essen-tial aspect of being in analysis is the experience of solitude-in-relation, of being left alone in the presence of the analyst. Lasky (1993) distin-guishes between talking to the analyst and talking in the presence of the analyst. One of the drawbacks of psychoanalytic approaches that are overly interactional is that all the patient's associations may be heard only as if they were directed *to* the analyst, rather than as associ-ations in the analyst's presence, thus depriving the patient of an expe-rience that permits therapeutic regression to an altered state of consciousness in which perception is aimed inward and away from interpersonal interaction (Aron, 1990a, b, 1991a).

Solitude, however, is not the opposite of mutuality, and I do not want to set up a false dichotomy between them. Solitude is necessary at certain moments for both the patient and the analyst, and so solitude itself may be mutually desired and must be mutually regulated between the two participants. I believe that a balance is needed in psychoanaly-sis between one- and two-person psychologies because it permits the recognition of sameness and difference, relatedness and detachment, interactive states and meditative states, mutual regulation and auton-omy, mutuality and asymmetry.

It is precisely the capacity to form relationships that entail mutuality of recognition (recognition, that is, of the autonomy of self and other) that is lacking in many patients seeking psychoanalysis. Thus, achiev-ing this capability becomes a goal of psychoanalytic work. This goal includes being able 1) to view oneself as an autonomous agent, as the center of one's own experience, as having a core and cohesive self, as a center of subjectivity, and 2) to recognize oneself as an object among other objects in the world, including the object of the other's desire. Bach (1994) refers to these two separate achievements as "subjective awareness" and "objective self-awareness." The goal also includes the ability to view the other as both an autonomous subject and the object of one's own desires. Achieving these capabilities and maintaining the tension between them may be viewed as a principal goal of psychoanalysis.

If one problem that brings patients to analysis is that they lack cohe-sion and integration, another is that some people are overly unified; their identity is too fixed, too rigidly set. Hence, if one goal is to help patients achieve a cohesive self, a solid identity, then another goal is to give them access to their multiplicities (see Aron, 1995a). The clinical paradox is that, to participate adequately in the psychoanalytic process, it is precisely these capacities that are needed to begin with. To begin the analytic process, the patient must have at least some rudimentary capacities along these lines, some sense of the stability of self and other and some sense of self and other as fluid and capable of change and process. As Bach (1994) suggests,

> it is precisely this capacity to form a mature object relationship, a working alliance, or a transference neurosis that is lacking in narcissistic patients to a greater or lesser degree. . . . A mature relationship and a true transference neurosis require both a self and other who are whole, vital, and unfragmented [p. 43].

Thus one of the key paradoxes of psychoanalysis is that the process depends to a great degree on the very qualities that the patient is in analysis to acquire. It is for this reason that all the criteria that have been described in delineating the good-enough patient, "the criteria for analyzability," look so much like the goals of analysis. Winnicott (1971a) wrote that the patient needs to be able to play if analysis is to work, and yet, when the patient is not able to play, then the goal of analysis becomes to help the patient learn to play. Similarly, mutuality is necessary for participation in analysis, and, when the patient is not capable of mutuality, then it is precisely mutuality that the patient needs to achieve.

There is a danger, however, that psychoanalysts will attempt to impose covert norms of intimacy and mutuality onto their patients (Barratt, 1994), just as analysts may seek to push other values, such as autonomy. While I do value both intimacy and autonomy, it should not be either that is the immediate goal of the psychoanalytic process (Levenson, 1983). Rather, the analyst seeks to promote intrapsychic and intersubjective dialogue, and both intimacy and autonomy emerge as by-products of this psychoanalytic dialogue.

MARTIN BUBER, THE INTERHUMAN DIALOGUE, AND EXISTENTIAL MUTUALITY

Among all 20th-century philosophers, Martin Buber elaborated a philosophy of dialogue that most closely resonates with the relational psychoanalytic approach and its emphasis on mutuality. Following World War I, Buber was troubled by the social conditions of modern society and especially by the alienation that he believed characterized modern life.[4] Our ordinary way of experiencing the world is by observation, examination, quantitative measurement, analysis, and synthesis. This involves manipulation of the object to achieve understanding of it and requires us to distance ourselves from the object under study so as not to contaminate our investigation with our own involvement. This mode, the paradigm of which is objectivist scientific thought, Buber referred to as the realm of the I–It. Buber recognized an alternative mode, which he designated the realm of the I–You or I–Thou. Within the realm of the I–You, relation is nonpurposeful and nonutilitarian; the I–You relation is immediate and direct.

> Rejecting the prevailing views of persons as individual entities essentially concerned with satisfying basic needs and gratifying instincts, Buber conceived of human life as grounded in relation. . . . In contrast to the individualistic, atomistic conception of person that prevails in Western thought, Buber advocated a relational view of the human being; a person exists not in isolation from others, but only through relationships [Siberstein, 1989, p. 127].

Buber's relational view of human existence looked not to the individual or to the social group primarily to explain the human condition of alienation, but instead addressed what he called the interhuman. He thought that genuine dialogue occurred when two people could be fully present with each other, withholding nothing, and confronting each other as whole people. Within the I–You mode of being whole persons relate to whole other persons, rather than as subjects to objects. In contrast, in the I–It mode, the ego experiences the object, uses it or manipulates it as a thing.[5] In the language of psychoanalytic object relations theory, Buber was distinguishing between instrumental part–object relations (which take place in the paranoid-schizoid mode) and whole object relations (which take place in the depressive mode). Like object relations theorists, Buber assumed an innate and primary longing for relation. As we discussed in Chapter 2, Ghent (1992a) has used Buber's (1947) proposal of the "originator instinct" (the need to make things) and the "instinct for communion" (the need to enter into mutuality) in his own efforts to elaborate a relational theory of motivation.

---

[4] A discussion of alienation in Buber's work is to be found in the work of Silberstein (1989), who also provides a useful introduction to Buber's impact on existential psychotherapists. Farber (1967) provides a very interesting comparison of Buber and Sullivan. Friedman (1994) examines many schools of psychotherapy from Buber's dialogical perspective.

[5] Interestingly, as Kaufman (1970) points out, Buber's *Ich und Du* [I and Thou] appeared in the same year as Freud's *Das Es und Das Ich* [The Ego and the Id]—1923. Literally, Freud's title would be translated *The It and the I.*

In the decades following publication of *I and Thou* (Buber, 1923), Buber refined his categories pertaining to the interhuman. Whereas in *I and Thou* he presented these two realms as dichotomous, in later years he introduced the notion that relationships could exist in gradations between the two extremes. Buber suggested that, for understanding dialogue between people, our customary categories are insuffient. He was led to postulate "the category of the between" (Buber, 1967, p. 707). Buber's "category of the between" is strikingly similar to Gergen's (1994) "realm of the between" (p. 217) both in meaning and in emphasis, and both bear comparison with Winnicott's (1951) concept of transitional space. Similarly, Buber's emphasis on the interhuman, on dialogue, and on the I–You mode of relating bears comparison to contemporary intersubjective conceptualizations.

In Buber's writing such terms as dialogue, the essential relation, the between, and mutuality, while they shift slightly in meaning from place to place, are each attempts to capture the essence of the interhuman. For Buber, the fulfillment of human existence is to be found in the mutuality of human dialogic relations (Rotenstreich, 1967). Buber (1923) distinguished between reciprocity and mutuality. Reciprocity refers to any situation in which each being acts on the other; mutuality, in contrast, refers to a situation in which one experiences an event both from one's own and from the other's perspective. Reciprocity seems closer to what I have called mutuality of regulation or mutuality of influence, whereas what Buber terms mutuality I have referred to as mutuality of recognition. Buber suggested that genuine relation is mutual. I–You relations, however, could exist that were not fully mutual, such as when a person relates to an object or art of an animal in an I–You mode. Only in the interhuman realm can two beings enter into a fully mutual relation with each other.

Throughout his life, Buber had an interest in psychotherapy, and in the 1950s he spoke on several occasions to groups of psychotherapists. Buber, like relationalists, believed that psychopathology results not from within the individual, but from impaired relationships, and he consequently saw the psychotherapeutic relationship as modeled on dialogue. Buber (1965) suggested that what differentiates humans from animals is the mutual need to confirm and be confirmed by the other in relationships. Further, in an argument reminiscent of Loewald's (1960), Buber suggested that we need to confirm and be confirmed not only in who we are but in who we may potentially become. Surprisingly, Buber believed that the relation between therapist and patient, like that between teacher and student, could not be fully mutual. He viewed each of these relationships as instrumental, in that one person acts upon the other to accomplish a specific goal. Mutuality requires

authenticity and genuineness, an absence of pretense. Since the therapist is trying to achieve specific goals, and since the therapist assumes a
greater responsibility than the patient does, full mutuality cannot be
achieved. Genuine dialogue is required for psychotherapy, but he did
not conceive of it as mutual.

While Buber's approach to philosophy is quite compatible with relational theorizing, particularly in his emphasis on the interhuman, on
the category of the between, on dialogue, and on mutuality, I suggest
that my attempt to distinguish many dimensions of mutuality in the
therapeutic relationship is useful in utilizing Buber's work. Like many
analysts who have loosely used the word mutuality, Buber did not
consider its diverse meanings and implications. On one hand, Buber
suggested that teachers help students, and therapists help patients, to
become whole persons by engaging them in I–You relations. On the
other hand, he suggested that therapists and teachers maintain their
distance and not make themselves fully present to their pupils and
patients. In my view, what Buber was objecting to in arguing that psychotherapy could not be fully mutual is more clearly stated by noting
the inevitable asymmetry in the relationship, the differences in roles
and responsibilities between patient and therapist. There are many
respects in which psychoanalysis and psychotherapy are indeed mutual,
but not in all respects, and our emphasis on mutuality should not
neglect the implications of asymmetry. When Buber discussed full
mutuality, he meant a relation that goes beyond even mutuality of
recognition, because mutuality of recognition (intersubjectivity) does
not require that both persons fully disclose themselves to each other.
Buber's mutuality (perhaps we might refer to it as "existential mutuality") is yet another dimension of mutuality to be distinguished from
those I have previously described.

An emphasis on mutuality and intersubjective negotiation should
not be taken to imply a conception of the psychoanalytic relationship
in which discord is minimized between patient and analyst. Mutuality
does not mean agreement or premature consensus. Buber emphasized
that a genuine disagreement with the other could be quite affirming,
and genuine dialogue between people may include a conflict in
viewpoints.

MUTUAL CONTRIBUTIONS TO PSYCHOANALYSIS

Before bringing this chapter to an end, I want to suggest one further
dimension of mutuality in psychoanalysis that has generally gone unnoticed, namely, the ways in which both patient and analyst mutually

contribute to the development of psychoanalytic theory and practice. It was the first psychoanalytic patient, Anna O (Berth Pappenheim) who in a very real way developed the "talking cure." It was she, at least as much as Breuer, who generated the cathartic method of "chimney sweeping" by which she traced her symptoms back to past emotional experiences. It was she herself who went into spontaneous, self-induced trance states before Breuer learned to induce hypnosis in her. Similarly, Emmy von N (Fanny Moser) encouraged Freud to abandon his use of hypnosis, and it was largely from his treatment of Cacilie M (Anna von Lieben), whom Freud repeatedly called his "teacher" (see, Swales, 1986), that he moved toward the free association method. Ferenczi repeatedly quoted his patients in his scholarly articles, some-times (as in the case of Elizabeth Severin, whom we discuss in the next chapter) he went so far as to cite them by name for their contributions as colleagues. Regarding the invention of psychoanalysis, Ferenczi (1929) wrote that it was "the shared discovery of an ingenious neurotic and a clever doctor" (cited by Micale, 1995, p. 142n). Micale, a lead-ing scholar of the history of psychiatry, points out that the major break-throughs in psychiatric history have come about with the patient's often playing a highly active and creative role. Micale writes, "In fact, considered cumulatively, Freud's intellectual debt to the 'sick' women in the *Studies on Hysteria* is staggering" (p. 142).

Mutuality plays an important role in training and supervision as well as in analysis. The most significant training experiences that I have had occurred in those marvelous situations when my supervisors felt and acknowledged my contributions to their thinking or to their own growth. I consistently find that I do my best work with supervisees whom I feel are enriching and teaching me, and the supervisory rela-tionship is greatly enhanced when each of us can appreciate and acknowledge this mutual impact. I also believe that some of the most creative thinking in psychoanalysis emanates not from the solitary, isolated, heroic figure, but from groups of colleagues, mutually influ-encing and facilitating each other's growth, so that the precise origin of any particular new idea emerges from the group, rather than from any individual. But just as the group context should not be minimized, neither need the individual get lost in the group. It is only by thinking in terms of both autonomy and mutuality, both the individual and the social, both independence and dependence on others that we can best understand creativity. Relational theory does not embrace the radical and cynical postmodern rejection of the subject; rather, it draws on an affirmative postmodern sensibility and maintains *both* that relationships determine individuals *and* that individuals determine relationships.

6 | The Dialectics of Mutuality and Autonomy
The Origins of Relational Theory in the
Contributions of Sándor Ferenczi and Otto Rank

My focus throughout this book has been on the many ways in which contemporary relational approaches have viewed mutuality and inter-subjectivity as central to both the theory and the practice of psychoanalysis. I have stressed mutuality and relationship (supposedly "feminine" values) because psychoanalysis and our culture at large have so consistently privileged individuality and autonomy (which our culture marks as "masculine" attributes). Nevertheless, I have continually argued that the conceptualization of the analytic situation that emphasizes mutuality needs to be balanced in practice by a recognition of the inevitability of asymmetry, and that the principle of mutual regulation must be held in tension with self-regulation or autonomy. In the discussion of one- and two-person psychologies (in Chapter 2) we reviewed Bakan's (1966) distinction between "communion" and "agency" as well as Buber's (1947) differentiation between the "originator instinct" and the "instinct for communion" and suggested that relational theory attempts to maintain the pull between these two forces.

In this chapter, I trace the origins of contemporary relational theory back to the early contributions of two psychoanalytic pioneers, Sándor Ferenczi and Otto Rank, whose clinical ideas balanced each other in terms of two complementary postulates of autonomy and mutuality, agency and communion. I am highlighting these two creative trailblazers because I believe that together their contributions represent the nucleus of relational theory. A comprehensive history of the development of relational ideas would, however, not only have to look at how these were embedded in aspects of Freud's own work, but also would have to take into account the important contributions of Adler, Jung, Abraham, Reich, and others. Needless to say, a study such as this would represent a book in itself. Here I will limit my review only to those aspects of Ferenczi's and Rank's work that is directly relevant to the dialectical principles of mutuality and autonomy.

While both Ferenczi and Rank proposed fundamentally relational theories, Ferenczi's work leaned in the direction of mutuality, relationship, and communion whereas Rank's theory was more heavily weighted toward autonomy, individuation, and agency. Ferenczi focused on the reciprocal processes operating between self and other; Rank's theory had to do with the emergence of the self within a relational context. (Keep in mind the development of relational theory that was reviewed in Chapters 1 and 2.)

Recall that one of the unique features of Mitchell's (1988a) relational approach is his effort to bring together the contributions of a variety of relational theorists that heretofore were independent and isolated. Some of these theorists, like Fairbairn, tended to focus on the object; others, like Winnicott and Kohut, on the self; and still others like Sullivan, on the interactions between self and object. One can describe each of their contributions as broadly relational. As Bacal (1995b) has pointed out, "Object relations theory and self psychology are both misnomers—misnomers of omission" (p. 406). Object relations theories, while placing the object at the center of investigation, are also implicitly psychologies of the self as constituted by these internal objects; whereas self psychology, while highlighting the psychology of the self, is also implicitly a theory of the object relationship that affirms, sustains, disrupts, and repairs the self. Similarly, Ferenczi's theory of the mutuality of relationship is also implicitly a psychology of the self, a self that may be split, fragmented, or dissociated owing to trauma and that can be healed, ultimately, only through love. Rank's theory of the birth of the self is also a psychology of relationship, one that provides the necessary affirmation for the strengthening of the individual's will. The two emphases need, balance, and compensate for each other.

SÁNDOR FERENCZI AND MUTUAL ANALYSIS

> The sudden emergence in modern psychoanalysis of portions of an earlier technique and theory should not dismay us; it merely reminds us that, so far, no single advance has been made in analysis which has had to be entirely discarded as useless, and that we must constantly be prepared to find new veins of gold in temporarily abandoned workings [Ferenczi, 1929, p. 120].

As he wrote these words, Sándor Ferenczi could have had no idea how prophetic they would be with respect to his own work! Sixty years after his clinical experiments with countertransference disclosures, we return to his work "to find new veins of gold in temporarily abandoned workings." Ferenczi's clinical experiments with mutuality, as well as his theoretical revisions regarding trauma, are among the most controversial innovations in the history of psychoanalysis. His therapeutic investigations led to theoretical, clinical, and technical discoveries concerning trauma, dissociation, the use of countertransference, and enactment within the transference–countertransference matrix. These still controversial ideas continue to occupy center stage in contemporary debates about psychoanalysis and psychoanalytic technique. Ferenczi's work with countertransference disclosure, which culminated in "mutual analysis," remains to this day unparalleled in its boldness.[1]

In the writings of recent scholars, Ferenczi emerges as a complex figure, hero, flawed hero, man of excesses, courageous innovator, "enfant terrible," dissident, madman, passionate follower, and friend to classical analysis and to Freud. In some lights he is the prescient innovator of all modern trends, champion of egalitarianism and mutuality, as well as crusader for the recognition of child abuse and trauma. For others, he is the precursor; he sowed the fascinating seeds that have flourished and evolved within the main body of psychoanalytic thought. Ferenczi's contributions to the early history of the psychoanalytic movement were second only to Freud's. He was a central organizer of the movement, a leading spokesperson and lecturer, and a theoretical and clinical contributor of the first rank. He was the founder of the International Psychoanalytical Association, founder of the Budapest Psychoanalytic Association, the first Professor of Psychoanalysis at a university (The University of Budapest), and organizer of the *International Journal of PsychoAnalysis*. Above all else, Ferenczi was widely regarded as the leading psychoanalytic clinician of his day, "the specialist in peculiarly difficult cases" who had a "kind of fanatical belief in the efficacy of depth-psychology" (Ferenczi, 1931, p. 128). Freud (1937) himself memorialized Ferenczi as a "master of analysis" (p. 230) who "made all analysts into his pupils" (Freud, 1933, p. 228).

---

[1] For an excellent chronological review of Ferenczi's contributions to psychoanalysis, see Lum (1988a, b). For a broad introduction to the range of his contributions as they anticipated current controversies in psychoanalysis, see Aron and Harris (1993) and Stanton (1991). For a detailed discussion of the origins of Ferenczi's experiments with mutuality in terms of his own character and personality, see Aron, (1995b). For an earlier study of Ferenczi, Harold Searles, and relational theory, see Aron (1992a). For more on mutual analysis, see Ragen and Aron (1993). For a discussion of Ferenczi's contributions in the light of the accusations of his mental disturbance, see Dupont (1988) and the exchange of views between Tabin (1993, 1995) and Aron and Frankel (1994, 1995). For a discussion of Ferenczi as a precursor to postmodernism, see Harris and Aron (in press).

For decades much of Ferenczi's work was suppressed, and he was dismissed by mainstream psychoanalysts, disregarded because of his radical clinical experiments, because of his revival of interest in the etiological importance of external trauma, and because he was perceived as encouraging dangerous regressions in his patients and was attempting to cure them with love. All these criticisms were reinforced with personal aspersions on his character and accusations that he had mentally deteriorated and even gone mad in the final years of his life, at the height of his clinical experimentation and disputes with Freud. Balint (1968) argued that "the historic event of the disagreement between Freud and Ferenczi acted as a trauma on the analytical world" (p. 152). One of the great tragedies in the history of psychoanalysis was the suppression for more than half a century of Ferenczi's clinical experiments, his *Clinical Diary*, (Ferenczi, 1932) as well as of the Freud-Ferenczi correspondence (Brabant et al., 1993). These have been translated into English and published only in the past few years.

Ferenczi's work is largely concerned with the heart of the analytic situation, the relationship between patient and analyst. His discoveries were precisely in those areas that are receiving the most lively attention among current psychoanalytic theorists and practitioners. In many respects, in his disagreements and debates with Freud, Ferenczi set the agenda for almost all the current controversies on the psychoanalytic scene: emphasis on technique versus metapsychology; experience versus insight; subjectivity versus theory; empathy versus interpretation; a "two-person psychology" versus a "one-person psychology."

While Ferenczi's clinical experiments with "mutual analysis" did not actually begin until the late 1920s, Ferenczi had been championing principles of interpersonal engagement and mutuality for decades. He argued idealistically that, once people really understood the workings of their unconscious minds, their world views would undergo significant modifications in the direction of increased openness, honesty, and directness.

> The final consequence of such insight—when it is present in two people—is that they are not ashamed in front of each other, keep nothing secret, tell each other the truth without risk of insult or in the certain hope that within the truth there can be no lasting insult [Freud to Ferenczi, October 3, 1910, Brabant et al., 1993, p. 220].

Ferenczi's enthusiasm about the role of mutuality in psychoanalysis was not simply the product of his later technical experiments with a certain type of difficult case. Nor were they simply the remnants of unresolved transference feelings derived from his brief analysis with Freud. Rather, Ferenczi's romantic longing for mutuality, his thirst for truth, his idealized search for openness, emotional exchange, closeness, and intimacy, all were part of his character structure and became incorporated into his psychoanalytic world view.

A number of clinical pathways converged in Ferenczi's work to lead him toward the end of his life to increasing experimentation with countertransference disclosure as a facilitating clinical technique. One of these pathways was his work exploring the traumatic factors in the pathogenesis of neurosis and character disorders. He discovered that the typical "anonymous" and "neutral" posture of analysts toward their patients repeated elements of the parent–child relationship that had led to the patients' illnesses. Ferenczi saw the polite aloofness of the analyst as a form of professional hypocrisy that kept both the patient's criticism of the analyst repressed and the analyst's true feelings toward the patient masked, although nevertheless felt by the patient. The analyst's emotional inaccessibility and insincerity repeated that of the traumatized patients' parents. The trauma could not be worked through unless the patients reworked it in relationships in which they were confident of the other's emotional honesty, sincerity and accessibility. In Ferenczi's (1933) view, it was the confidence in the fundamental honesty of the relationship that constituted the curative difference between the present and the traumatic past.

Along with his work on trauma, experimentation with the principle of relaxation or passivity was another route by which Ferenczi arrived at what he saw to be the need for countertransference disclosure or countertransference interpretations. He found that patients reacted to his passive permissiveness with increasing demands on, and abuse of, his tolerance and patience. Ferenczi eventually discerned that the patients' escalation was an artifact created by the unnaturalness of his passivity. The escalation abated when Ferenczi expressed opposition, bringing patients into a more beneficial, real relationship in which they had to take into account the needs and sensitivities of the other.

Ferenczi's experimentation with "mutual analysis" emerged from a fundamental conviction, which progressively developed over the course of his work, about the centrality of experience in relationship. For Ferenczi, the roots of pathology lay in early relationships, and new experience in relationship was essential for healing. This idea was later to become the very basis for all interpersonal approaches to psychoanalysis. Ferenczi and Rank (1924) challenged the prevailing notion that remembering was the chief aim of analytic work, whereas repetition was a sign of resistance. In contrast, they maintained, repetition was essential. They proposed that, for cure to occur, what they called a "phase of experience" had to precede the customary "phase of understanding." In this expanded conceptualization of treatment, it is the task of the analyst directly to provoke a reexperiencing of early conflict and trauma, an actual reliving, in the relationship with the analyst. In their view, the analyst's knowledge of universal fundamental early experiences enables him or her "to intervene at the right place, and in the requisite degree (p. 56) so as to provoke this essential reliving. It is only after reliving is accomplished that the phase of understanding can occur.

Then the analyst's task becomes one of interpretation and reconstruction, fostering memory and insight on the part of the patient. The efficacy of interpretation and the healing power of remembering and insight were thought to rest on the ability of the analyst and the patient together to engage in the reliving of the patient's early relationships. Ferenczi and Rank believed that it was the affective relation between analyst and patient that allowed the reliving to unfold and that the reliving further forged the affective bond. In consequence, they concluded that "this kind of therapy consists. . . . far more in experience than in the factor of enlightenment" (p. 56).

This conviction about the essential role of experience for the patient inevitably led Ferenczi to rethink the nature of the analyst's position and activity in the analytic relationship. In his eyes, analysis was first and foremost a relationship. In the experiential reliving of the past, a new present is both found and created—a new self, a new other, and new possibilities for what can occur internally and externally between self and other.

Pursuing this avenue of thought, Ferenczi became increasingly convinced that the reality of the person of the analyst had a decisive impact on the patient and thus had to be reckoned with in the relationship. To ignore it was a pretense and to try to structure the relationship to eliminate it was a contrivance that patients might overtly go along with even though they were nevertheless affected by it. Ferenczi grew to have a sense of conviction about the importance of bringing the analyst's own reactions to the patient into the work. He contended that not doing so repeated the repression, denial, and inaccessibility of the parent, which had been crucial elements in the originally pathogenic situation. He stated that keeping one's reactions secret "makes the patient distrustful" as he or she "detects from the little gestures (forms of greeting, handshake, tone of voice, degree of animation, etc.) the presence of affects, but cannot gauge their quality or importance" (Ferenczi, 1932, p. 11). Secrecy leaves the patient mystified, whereas disclosure allows the patient to know where he or she stands in the relationship and, on the basis of the trust which that generates, to enter into new considerations of self and other.

Inevitably, the growing openness and naturalness that Ferenczi's approach evoked created an atmosphere in which patients felt free to see and speak about his limitations. Patients began to challenge him on what they saw to be countertransference obstacles in his treatment with them. One patient, Elizabeth Severn, identified in the *Clinical Diary* (Ferenczi, 1932) as RN, insisted that she should have the right to analyze Ferenczi because his unresolved conflicts impeded her treatment. And so, in his inimitable spirit of openness, Ferenczi began the experiment of "mutual analysis." I will soon examine the case of RN to determine what was learned from this clinical experiment, what was useful, and what went wrong.

In his *Clinical Diary*, Ferenczi (1932) provides fragments about the specific reasons for which mutual analysis was proposed. He states that the first patient who wanted to analyze him (RN) wished to do so because she "did not have the impression of me that I was completely harmless, that is to say, full of understanding. The patient sensed unconscious resistance and obstacles in me" (p. 73). In a more dramatic entry, Ferenczi states that RN insisted on mutual analysis "as the only protective measure against the inclination, perceived in me, to kill or torture patients" (p. 11). In yet another note, Ferenczi reveals that mutual analysis was initially undertaken in response to the patient's complaints that he lacked "any real empathy or compassion," that he was "emotionally dead." Ferenczi believed that his countertransference did, in fact, confirm the truth of these criticisms. The analysis revealed to Ferenczi that "in my case infantile aggressiveness and a refusal of love toward my mother became displaced onto the patients. . . . Instead of feeling with the heart, I feel with my head. Head and thought replace heart and libido" (p. 86).

Ferenczi considered his "own analysis a resource for the analysand. The analysand was to remain the main subject" (p. 71). With that guiding principle in mind, the question of mutual analysis occupied Ferenczi's thinking until the end. His initial fears of it gave way to much enthusiasm. He entertained doubts and questions. He expanded the scope of mutual analysis to exclude nothing and then drew back to a more limited expanse.

Throughout his experimentation with mutual analysis, he was aware of its inherent difficulties. He was concerned that patients would turn their focus away from themselves and search for complexes in the analyst as a way of avoiding their own problems. He also worried that his own tendency to find fault with himself would divert attention from the patient and would enact a masochistic submission. He raised questions about the problems of confidentiality and discretion as well as the impossibility of being analyzed by every patient. Aware that patients' tolerance for disclosure would grow over time, he wondered about issues of timing.

Although Ferenczi was quite open to his own as well as others' evaluations of his explorations, he also initiated his experiments without much critical reserve. He frequently reversed stands and often took extreme positions throughout his work. He characterized himself as having a "tendency to risk even what is most difficult, and then to find motives for having done so" (p. 73). At the time of these experiments with mutual analysis (on September 15, 1931) Ferenczi wrote to Freud regarding his own tendency to go to the extremes:

> In my usual manner, I do not shy away from drawing out their conclusions to the furthest extent possible—often to the point where I lead myself "ad absurdum." But this doesn't discourage me. I seek advances by new routes, often radically opposed, and I still hope that one day I shall end up finding the true path.
> All this sounds very mystical: please don't be alarmed by this. As far as I can judge myself, I do not overstep (or only seldom) the limits of normality. It's true that I'm often wrong, but I'm not rigid in my prejudices. [Ferenczi, 1932, pp. xiv–xv).

One can see in his *Clinical Diary* how he wrestled with ideas about mutual analysis to the very end of his life. Ferenczi's ambivalence and vacillation concerning mutual analysis are highlighted by three late entries in his diary. On June 3, 1932, he wrote, Mutual analysis: only a last resort! Proper analysis by a stranger, without any obligation, would be better (p. 115). Only two weeks later, on June 18, he stated:

> It is true that as a doctor one is tired, irritable, somewhat patronizing, and now and then one sacrifices the patient's interests to one's own curiosity, or even half-unconsciously makes covert use of the opportunity to give vent to purely personal aggression and cruelty. Such mistakes cannot be avoided by anyone and in any of the cases, but one must (a) be aware of it, (b) taking hints from the patients, admit these errors to oneself and to the patients.
> But such confessions, however often they may be repeated, will not get us any further if we (a) do not resolve to come to a radical understanding through mutual analysis, (b) as a consequence of this, we do not successfully change our attitude toward the patient . . . [p. 130].

Finally, four months later, on the last day he wrote in his *Diary*, Ferenczi noted that, when he attempted to switch from mutual back to unilateral analysis with patients, the "emotionality disappeared" and the analysis became "insipid" and the relationship "distant." He concluded that "once mutuality has been attempted, one-sided analysis then is no longer possible—not productive." Exploring to the very end he asked, "Must every case be mutual—and to what extent?" (p. 213). Ferenczi, who died in 1933, never settled within himself the question of exactly what the extent and nature of his openness and counteranalysis needed to be. But he never gave the question up. It compelled him. It was central to his work.

"Must every case be mutual?" Ferenczi asked in 1932. Can a case incorporate elements of mutual analysis? In what respect is psychoanalysis inevitably a mutual process? are questions that I have been exploring in this book. I want to explore what Ferenczi thought that he was doing in his attempts at mutual analysis, what he learned from these experiments, and what we may learn from them regarding our own affective involvement and openness with patients. Let us look at the "temporarily abandoned workings" of Ferenczi's clinical thought and practice to see if we might find "new veins of gold."

One of the most important discoveries Ferenczi made about the emotional openness of the analyst was that it allowed patients to come to a sense of conviction about the reality of repressed childhood traumas. As Ferenczi moved from a more reserved to a more open stance, he became convinced that it was only through the very natural emotional response of the analyst that patients could come to believe that the traumas that they were remembering were in fact real. The response the patients had originally received from their parents was being repeated in the largely silent, cool, reserved response of the analyst. As Ferenczi (1932) stated, "In most cases of infantile trauma the parents' cure is repression—'it's nothing at all'; 'nothing has happened'; 'don't think about it.' . . . The trauma is hidden in a deadly silence. First references are ignored or rejected . . . and the child cannot maintain it's judgement" (p. 25).

Ferenczi's beliefs about the importance of the analyst's emotional responsiveness to the patient's reliving of childhood trauma are beautifully stated in a *Diary* entry of January 31, 1932:

> Patients cannot believe that an event really took place, or cannot fully believe it, if the analyst, as the sole witness of the events, persists in his cool, unemotional, and, as patients are fond of stating, purely intellectual attitude, while the events are of a kind that must evoke, in anyone present, emotions of revulsion, anxiety, terror, vengeance, grief and the urge to render immediate help; to remove or destroy the cause or the person responsible; and since it is usually a child, an injured child, who is involved (but even leaving that aside), feelings of wanting to comfort it with love, etc., etc. [p. 24].

Moreover, it is the unguarded communication of the deepest empathy inherent in the analyst's responses that Ferenczi sees to be affectively engaging and healing. Ferenczi suggests that the depth of his empathy results from his experience of the patient's suffering coming together with the experience of his own suffering. In his experiments with mutual analysis, Ferenczi permitted this commingling of experiences to occur in a highly radical way. For example, in one session, RN's counteranalysis of Ferenczi led him to explore with her an episode from his own infancy. For the first time, he felt emotion about it and had the feeling that it had been a real experience. This insight, in turn, led RN to gain deeper insight into the reality of events in her own life that previously she had grasped only on an intellectual level.

The radical nature of mutual analysis was seen by Ferenczi (1992) to remove fear of the analyst, which removal Ferenczi thought was essential for the lifting of an infantile amnesia. He wrote:

> Certain phases of mutual analysis give the impression of two equally terrified children who compare their experiences, and because of their common fate, understand each other completely and instinctively try to comfort each other. Awareness of the shared fate allows the partner to appear as completely harmless, therefore as someone whom one can trust with confidence [p. 56].

Ferenczi identified the freedom from fear of the analyst as "the psychological basis for mutuality in analysis" as it was on this that resolution of the infantile amnesia depended (p. 57). More generally, mutual analysis was found to be effective in loosening repression. With mutual analysis, material that had been censored was disclosed. Feelings and impulses that had been unconscious emerged into consciousness. It was Ferenczi's opinion that the destruction of illusion about the analyst that occurred through mutual analysis made this possible (p. 14).

Ferenczi began to recognize the inevitability of the analyst's participation in the patient's transference. He was the first analyst to consider that the patient's resistance needed to be understood as a function of the analyst's countertransference. He began thinking in terms of what I have been calling mutual participation and mutual enactment. Consider Ferenzci's profound observations regarding patients whom we would today refer to, using Shengold's (1989) term, as "soul murdered."

> I have finally come to realize that it is an unavoidable task of the analyst: although he may behave as he will, he may take kindness and relaxation as far as he possibly can, the time will come when he will have to repeat with his own hands the act of murder previously perpetrated against the patient [Ferenczi, 1932, p. 52].

Ferenczi is here proposing a model of the analytic process that is far beyond the simplistic notion that the analyst needs to be a "good object" or better parent to the patient. Here, Ferenczi acknowledges that it is inevitable that the analyst will "repeat with his own hands," will actively participate in recreating the trauma. The analyst has to be a better parent in that, unlike the original, traumatizing parent, the analyst can recognize his or her own participation and can discuss it directly with the patient and, on this basis, change his or her participation. It is in this recognition of the analyst as a participant, pulled into the patient's transference and then observing and interpreting from the countertransference response, that Ferenczi anticipated and led the way for such notions as participant-observation, projective identification, and the usefulness of countertransference.

Ferenczi went even further; not only did he anticipate our contemporary views, but we may still have to catch up with his insights. Not only did he recognize that the analyst is pulled in as a participant in the reenactment of the trauma, that the analyst himself must become the patient's abuser, but Ferenczi also realized that the patient observes this and reacts to it. It is not just that the patient misperceives the analyst as being the abuser in a "transference distortion," but that the patient gets the analyst actually to play that role; the transference is "actualized," in contemporary terms (Sandler, 1976), and the patient then observes the analyst's participation. Unlike some theoreticians who are tempted to use the notion of enactment or induced countertransference as a way of shifting responsibility from the analyst to the patient, Ferenczi insisted that the analyst's own character traits inevitably play a part in the transference and countertransference. Thus, for Ferenczi, transference and countertransference involve mutual participation. Furthermore, the patient can observe the analyst's countertransference responses and character traits and, in turn, react to them. Ferenczi was the first to point out the ways in which the patient becomes the "interpreter" of the analyst's countertransference experience (Hoffman, 1983; Aron, 1991a).

Ferenczi (1931) saw that the patient's transference is not a distortion to be corrected by the analyst. Rather the patient's observations of and reactions to the analyst as a person are to be taken seriously:

> It is advantageous to consider for a time *every one*, even the most improbable, of the communications as in some way possible, even to accept an obvious delusion. . . . thus by leaving aside the "reality" question, one can feel one's way more completely into the patient's mental life. (Here something should be said about the disadvantages of contrasting "reality" and "unreality." The latter must in any case be taken equally seriously as a *psychic* reality; hence above all one must become fully absorbed in all that the patient says and feels.) [p. 235]

Finally, for Ferenczi, it is the analyst's emotional honesty, combined with goodwill, that establishes the bedrock of trust that is essential to the analytic relationship. These two qualities enable the patient to accept, perhaps even embrace, the reality of the limited and faulted analyst and the relationship between the two of them. As Ferenczi (1932) stated toward the end of his life,

> [the analyst] is not allowed to deny his guilt; analytic guilt consists of the doctor not being able to offer full maternal care, goodness, self-sacrifice; and consequently he exposes the people under his care, who just barely managed to save themselves before, to the same danger, by not providing adequate help . . . there is nevertheless a difference between our honesty and the hypocritical silence of parents. This and our goodwill must be counted in our favor. This is why I do not give up hope and why I count on the return of trust in spite of all disillusionment [1932, pp. 52–53].

In his description of analysts failing their patients and then honestly acknowledging their mistakes and limitations until the patients and their analysts come to mutual forgiveness, Ferenczi provides us with a preview of the contemporary self-psychological idea that relationships progress through sequences of disruption and repair (Lachmann and Beebe, 1992). We saw in the previous chapter how contemporary intersubjectivity theory has extended this idea from the realm of mother–infant research to the psychoanalytic context.

Emotional honesty, accessibility, directness, openness, spontaneity, disclosure of the person of the analyst—these create in the patient heightened naturalness, forthrightness, access to the repressed, recognition of and sensitivity to the other, increased self-esteem, and greater realism about, and hence depth, in relationship. This is Ferenczi's legacy. The essence of his contribution is that it opens up the person of the analyst as a domain in which important analytic work occurs. The analyst becomes a distinct and real person whom the patient genuinely affects and is affected by.

Ferenczi's experimentation with "mutual analysis" is an inspiring source of reflection for contemporary psychoanalysis. It is a radical clinical technique accompanied by bold and open thinking that leads us to reexamine the very nature of the analytic relationship. Although in the pages to come, I criticize Ferenczi's experiments with mutual analysis and argue that it is not viable in its extremes, it nevertheless contains rich and vital elements. The legacy that he left psychoanalysis is valuable independent of the specifics of his technical approach. I believe that Ferenczi's spirit of empirical experimentation must remain alive. Psychoanalysis is no closer now than it was in Ferenczi's day to a definitive or final technique. We need to acknowledge, as Ferenczi (1931) did more than 60 years ago, that "analytical technique has never been, nor is it now, something finally settled" (p. 235). At the center of the temporarily abandoned workings of Ferenczi's mutual analysis lie new veins of gold.

HISTORICAL INVESTIGATION OF ELIZABETH SEVERN (RN)

Having examined Ferenczi's ideas on mutuality gleaned from his own writings, let us take a closer look at his most important case of mutual analysis, his work with Elizabeth Severn (RN). But this time we will examine the treatment as it revealed not only in Ferenczi's *Diary*, but also in the most recent biographical and historical scholarship regarding Severn. The following description is based almost exclusively on Fortune's (1993a, b, 1994) exciting historical research.

Severn's (RN) eight-year-long analysis began in 1924 and lasted until shortly before Ferenczi's death. It coincided with the end of Ferenczi's experiments with his active technique; proceeded through his period of elasticity of technique, relaxation, and indulgence; and concluded with his experiments with mutual analysis. It was this analytic experience, more than any other, that led to Ferenczi's recognition of the prevalence and pathogenic significance of childhood sexual abuse, which he simply and directly referred to as rape. Furthermore, it was in this analysis that Ferenczi learned of the reciprocal action of transference and countertransference and of the value and significance of countertransference interpretation. Furthermore, Severn assisted Ferenczi in his experimentation with relaxation and trance states, and she taught Ferenczi about the importance of splitting and dissociative phenomena in persons with severe pathology and in victims of childhood abuse.

From historical research we now know that Severn, born Leota Brown, had been a sickly child, plagued with fears and anxieties. She suffered from an eating disorder, headaches, fatigue, and frequent nervous breakdowns. When she reached adulthood, her symptoms included hallucinations, nightmares, and depression, which often left her suicidal. She repeatedly spent time in mental sanitariums and was treated by numerous therapists. At age 27, she felt the calling to become a healer and changed her name to Elizabeth Severn to begin a new life. While traveling as a door-to-door salesperson she found that people valued her advice, so she set up an office and handed out business cards that read "Elizabeth Severn, Metaphysician." She referred to herself as a Ph.D., although she had no credentials or formal education, and was elected honorary vice-president of the Alchemical Society in London. In 1914, after a brief stay in London, Severn moved to New York where she spent the next 10 years practicing and writing about psychotherapy. Her therapeutic practice consisted in promoting the power of positive thinking, visualization, telepathic communication, and the "healing touch," with which she claimed to have cured someone of a brain tumor. By 1924, after many attempts at psychotherapy

for herself, including a period with Otto Rank, Severn, considered a
hopeless case, decided to try analysis with the analyst of last resort,
Sándor Ferenczi. She moved to Budapest, taking four or five of her
own devoted and financially well-off patients with her. Reading
Fortune (1993a, b, 1994), one gets a sense of just how disturbed and
yet how resourceful and powerful Severn was. She became Ferenczi's
analysand and coanalyst. Freud was to call her "Ferenczi's evil genius."
(Fortune, 1993a).

At first, Ferenczi was intimidated by and disliked Severn. Looking
back some years later, Ferenczi wrote, "Instead of making myself aware
of these impressions, I appear to proceed on the principle that as the
doctor I must be in a position of superiority in every case" (p. 97).
Ferenczi disguised his antipathy for the patient and went out of his way
to indulge her. By 1928, Ferenczi who was then experimenting with
indulgence and driven by what Freud called his *furor sanandi,* the rage
to cure, was seeing Severn twice daily in her hotel room for a period of
four or five hours, plus weekends and at night. She was too sick to get
out of bed, except, of course, to see her own patients. Ferenczi even
allowed Severn to accompany him and his wife on their vacation to
Spain. Later, in 1930, concerned about Severn's deteriorating state, he
waived his fees so that her daughter could afford to come and look after
her for a few months. Ferenczi would come to refer to Severn as "the
Queen."

Severn interpreted all of this as a sign that Ferenczi had become her
"perfect lover" (Ferenczi, 1932, p. 98). Ferenczi protested that this was
"all an intellectual process, and that the genital processes of which we
were speaking had nothing to do with my wishes" (p. 98). Ferenczi
then pulled back from his involvement with the patient and reduced
the number of her sessions. At this point Severn accused Ferenczi of
hating her. She insisted that she be allowed to analyze him, so that
ultimately her own analysis could progress. Ferenczi resisted this
suggestion for over a year but ultimately was forced by the logic of his
own views to admit that she was right. He did have resentments against
her that needed analysis, and who better than she to help him overcome his resistances?

The mutual analysis was literally a dual analysis. They tried a variety
of procedures, including alternate sessions and alternate days of analysis, and, for a while, Ferenczi submitted to being exclusively the
analysand. Recent historical research described by Fortune (1994)
suggests that in the last year of his life, as Ferenczi's terminal illness was
progressively worsening, Severn's own analysis stopped and for some
time (probably in the late fall of 1932) she analyzed him exclusively.
On the basis of letters that Severn wrote to her daughter at the time of

the analysis, Fortune (1994) has suggested that Ferenczi probably paid Severn for this analysis. He also suggests that Ferenczi insisted that she keep her analysis of him a secret and that she proclaim herself cured by him. (It should be kept in mind that Ferenczi was dying of pernicious anemia and by the fall of 1932 was quite sick and was in and out of sanatoriums for cures.) The analysis finally ended in February 1933, when Severn left Budapest for Paris. At that time her daughter wrote Ferenczi a letter of protest because she found her mother in a state of mental and physical collapse. Ferenczi was too ill to reply to the letter, and he died in May 1933. By June 1933, Severn resumed her own practice of therapy in London and, soon after published her third book on psychotherapy (Severn, 1933). The book makes little mention of Ferenczi or mutual analysis. Years later, Severn's daughter acknowledged that she had no doubt that Ferenczi's analysis of her mother had "ultimately saved my mother's life" (cited in Fortune, 1994, p. 222).

CRITIQUE

I have attempted to elucidate in some detail the many rich contributions that emerged from Ferenczi's clinical experiments with mutuality and self-disclosure. His work has been continually inspiring as a model of openness and directness, for dedication to patients' welfare, for continual self-reflection on the nature of analysts' participation with patients, for taking patients seriously, and for not blaming patients for treatment failures. We can continue to learn a great deal from Ferenczi's efforts. Nevertheless, we also need to face straightforwardly the limitations and excesses of his clinical approach. I believe that the distinctions that I have been making in this book between mutuality and symmetry are helpful in our reexamination of Ferenczi's project.

In my view, Ferenczi mistook symmetry for mutuality and, therefore, in his clinical experiments abandoned the essential asymmetry required for psychoanalysis. Ferenczi was aware that he was enacting a masochistic submission to his patient's demands, but in his attempt to avoid being the bad object, to avoid repeating the patient's trauma, he was unable to find a way both to enter the patient's system and to interpret his way out of it. To be a part of the system and yet remain out of it requires both mutuality and asymmetry. Using the terms mutuality and symmetry in the way that I have in this book, I would describe what Ferenczi and Severn did together as an experiment in "symmetrical analysis" rather than in "mutual analysis," in that the roles and functions, and ultimately even the professional responsibility and financial remuneration became blurred, if not completely reversed.

Ferenczi repeatedly claimed that his own analysis was to serve as a resource for his patient's analysis. But for how long could Severn analyze Ferenczi unilaterally, with Ferenczi continuing to believe sincerely that this was ultimately for her good more than for his?

Part of the difficulty for Ferenczi, we see in retrospect, was that inasmuch as he decided to enter into a mutual analysis he took his obligation to free associate seriously, and, understanding this to be the fundamental rule of analysis, he did not leave himself the right as the "analyst" to withhold anything from his patient. This is one way in which the necessary asymmetry broke down between him and Severn. Under these conditions, Ferenczi could not maintain the distance necessary to preserve analytic space between himself and his patient. Furthermore, I would judge that Ferenczi and Severn did not actually engage in a mutual analysis, but rather that they engaged intermit-tently in two separate, parallel, unilateral analyses. He interpreted her transferences and she interpreted his, but Ferenczi did not consolidate his faint recognition that his transference and hers mutually consti-tuted each other. Analyzing his transference to her and separately analyzing her transference to him, Ferenczi and Severn conducted two independent but overlapping analyses. Mutual analysis would entail their joint recognition that both of their transferences were mutually constituted, and each could be understood only in the context of the other. In addition to his character disturbances, his idealization of "truth," his exorbitant need for love, his longing for further analysis, his isolation from Freud (his friend, hero, and analyst), and the effect of his illness in the last year of his life, Ferenczi just did *not* yet have the conceptual tools necessary to understand the interweaving of their two transferences.

Ferenczi became overly identified with his traumatized patients and in his state of identification he sought to provide them with the love and reparative experience that he wished for himself. Ferenczi described his mother as "harsh" and unable to supply him with the nurturance he needed (letter from Ferenczi to Freud, 13 October 1912, quoted in Grubich-Simitis, 1986). He identified with his patients' sense of entitlement and masochistically submitted to their demands. In his brief "analysis" with Freud (seven weeks of analysis spread out over a few years) it could hardly be expected that Ferenczi could have resolved these problems. With Ferenczi blurring the boundaries between his own traumatization and that of his patients, it is not surprising that he would develop a technique of mutual analysis in which the very functions of patient and analyst would become blurred. In the reversal of roles in which Ferenczi became the patient and the patient became the analyst, Ferenczi masochistically submitted to patients' sadistic reenactments of their own childhood abuse. Ferenczi's extraordinary efforts to repair his patients through love was an effort to provide the love that he himself wished for, as well as an attempt, through reaction formation, to disguise his resentment for not having received enough love.

Once again, I believe that, in addition to his personal problems, Ferenczi just did not have the conceptual understanding of the analyst's participation fully worked out. He often wrote as if it were just the analyst's love and empathy that was curative. This is, I believe, only a partial truth. At times, as I have indicated, Ferenczi recognized that the analyst had to be available to the patient to participate in a much fuller way; for example, the analyst had to feel pulled into repeating the patient's childhood trauma. So, certainly, at those moments when the analyst had to enact the role of the "bad parent" the analyst was not being loving and empathic in any simple way (of course, one could say that at those moments the analyst is empathizing with the patient's bad internal object). But Ferenczi resisted the full recognition that he had to allow himself to be the patient's "bad" object, not just the "good," "empathic," loving one. It was in getting caught up in the compulsion to be the "good" object that Ferenczi lost the ability to see the ways in which he, in fact, was failing his patients.

Clearly Ferenczi had a number of characterological difficulties that led him to his technical experiments. He was known for his extreme zeal and particularly for his therapeutic enthusiasm, the *furor sanandi*, that swept him away in one passion after another. He was often described as childlike in his wild enthusiasms and his capacity to let himself go. This trait led him temporarily to go to extremes and to neglect the balanced view one would expect of a more mature thinker. Nevertheless, Ferenczi's enthusiasm served him well in that he pushed things to their extremes and in so doing discovered more clearly than anyone before the underlying assumptions and limitations of certain psychoanalytic ideas.

In this critical scrutiny of Ferenczi's personality and how his personal difficulties led him to the excesses of mutual analysis, it is important that we recognize that this retrospective attack on a theorist's character is an ad hominum argument of the worst sort! Is there any analyst, from Freud onward, who could stand up to biographical scrutiny and emerge unscathed? If we invalidated theorists' contributions because of their personal foibles, there would not be much left of psychoanalytic theory. Indeed, we might ask why, in every discussion of Ferenczi's technical experiments there needs to be reference to his psychopathology? I cannot emphasize enough the incredible damage that has been done in the history of psychoanalysis by casting aspersions of poor mental health on a theoretical opponent. Elsewhere Frankel and I (Aron and Frankel, 1995) wrote:

> In our view, subjective factors can provide the basis for a heightened alertness to various psychological phenomena, leading to discoveries that have broad application. Freud's own personal oedipal struggles are an excellent example of this. A person's contributions should be evaluated on their merits. The presence of subjective factors in the contributor—including psychopathology—does not diminish their value [p. 318].

Thus, while I am very interested in the relationship between analysts' theoretical contributions and their personal background, it is one thing to examine this relationship to gain a better understanding and another thing to use these findings to invalidate theoretical formulations or to discredit clinical innovations.

With this word of caution, we may return to our critique. There are entries in the *Clinical Diary* indicating that Ferenczi himself may have been the victim of sexual abuse (see, for example, Ferenczi, 1932, p. 61). It is hard to know, however, how much credence we should put in these "memories" of Ferenczi since they emerged in the course of his mutual analysis with Severn. One problem is that Ferenczi and Severn were experimenting together with "trance states" and "relaxation" procedures (Ferenczi had a very rich background and had written a good deal on clinical hypnosis), and they were encouraging each other to remember early childhood events. We now know that working in trance states frequently leads individuals to generate and report more material as memory than they would without the use of these procedures. More importantly, however, hypnotic procedures may lead individuals to be inappropriately confident of the accuracy of their memory reports. We now know that it is prudent to be extremely cautious about the effects of hypnotic procedures on remembering (McConkey, 1992). Furthermore, in the context of Ferenczi's and Severn's joint theoretical interests in trauma, the likelihood is enormous that mutual suggestion effects would come into play. I must conclude that any inferences regarding childhood abuse that are based solely on the mutual analysis as reported in the *Clinical Diary* should not be relied on as biographically true for either Severn or Ferenczi unless they are substantiated by confirming historical evidence. (In fact, Severn, with Ferenczi's encouragement, did hire an investigator to try to establish the historical accuracy of her traumatic memories.)

Ferenczi evidently believed that he and his patients were uncovering the "truth" about his patients' childhoods. Similarly, as Ferenczi recovered childhood memories of his own, he tended to assume that they were veridical portrayals of his childhood experience. Ferenczi came to the conclusion that one of the most deleterious aspects of trauma was the confusion that is engendered by parents' attempts to deny and cover up abusive incidents. He directly related this parentally evoked confusion to the etiology of splitting and fragmentation of the self. Hence, in more contemporary language, it is the mystification of experience that traumatized the patient and led to the shattering of the self. Like contemporary theorists (such as R. D. Laing and E. Levenson) who attribute an etiological role to the mystification of experience, Ferenczi considered the cure to consist of demystifying experience, finding out what "really" happened, uncovering the "truth." Here, however, Ferenczi fell into the trap of polarizing the distinctions between reality and fantasy, truth and mystification, and therefore he maintained a simplified and idealized notion of the truth. As a result, he seems at times to have accepted his patient's (as well as his own) recovered memories of abuse as veridical, literally true; while at other moments he seemed to recognize that these truths were "valid" only perspectivally, that is, that they expressed the truth of the patient's experience. The question of the veracity of recovered traumatic memories in psychoanalysis continues to be highly controversial. (For a fuller discussion of this issue, see Harris, 1996; Davies, 1996; and Crews, 1996). While most analysts agree that whether traumatic abuse really occurred or was fantasized to have occurred does indeed matter, knowing whether a memory is of a real or fantastical event is highly problematic, and the belief on the part of most clinicians that this difference between fantasy and reality is significant is a serious challenge to those (generally academics, not clinicians) who advocate radical constructivism.

Wolstein (1991) has persuasively argued that the case of RN belongs to the line of historically significant cases for psychoanalytic discoveries that leads from Anna O to Dora to RN. Ferenczi was

> the controversial, even vilified master during the 1920s and early 1930s of fresh experiment and radical innovation, the likes of which were not seen undertaken with such clinical freedom and far-reaching therapeutic influence since Breuer and Freud wrote up their landmark findings in 1895. . . . That is, from the first study of hypnoid states in Breuer's case of Anna O (1880–1882), to the first awareness of transference in Freud's case of Dora (1900/1905), to the first exploration of countertransference in Ferenczi's case of RN [pp. 168–169].

Now that we have seen how Ferenczi conducted mutual analysis with his patients, it should not be surprising to learn that he also wished to engage in a mutual analysis with his analyst, and indeed he did attempt this. Ferenczi was the only one of Freud's disciples to suggest seriously to the master, who was also his analyst, that he (Ferenczi)

would travel to Vienna in order to analyze him (Freud); Freud appre-
ciatively declined Ferenczi's offer (see Jones, 1957, p. 120). In
attempting to analyze Freud's countertransferential and characterological limitations, Ferenczi was anticipating the role that he would
come to outline for the patient, that of therapist to the analyst, given
that the analyst can tolerate and encourage this function in the
patient.

Listen to the plea as well as the concern in a letter in which Ferenczi
offers to analyze Freud. Remember that, by this time, they had been
best friends and colleagues for 18 years:

> Perhaps this is the occasion on which I can say to you that I actually find it to be
> tragic that you, who gave psychoanalysis to the world, [find it] so difficult—
> indeed are not in a position—to entrust yourself to someone. If your heart
> complaints continue and if medications and diet don't help, I will come to you
> for several months and will place myself at your disposal as analyst—naturally:
> if you don't throw me out [letter from Ferenczi to Freud, February 26, 1926,
> quoted by Hoffer, 1994, p. 201].

In response to Freud's warm, gracious, and moving decline, Ferenczi
persists, confronting Freud, the master himself, with his resistance to
analysis. Ferenczi writes on March 1, 1926,

> Naturally neither can nor should [one] be pressured into analysis, but please
> keep in your [mind's] eye that as soon as your disinclination (should I say resis-
> tance?) is halfway overcome, I can immediately come to Vienna. . . . I thought
> of a stay of a few months [p. 202].

As Hoffer points out, Ferenczi's offer to analyze Freud should be
seen, and indeed was seen by Freud, as the offer of a loving gift.
Throughout their relationship, from beginning to end, Ferenczi's longing for mutuality included *both* the desire for greater intimacy between
himself and Freud as peers and the continued mutual need to be cared
for by Freud and to care for him in turn. The theme of mutuality runs
through Ferenczi's life, whether as patient, as analyst or as friend. He
knew that his idealization of mutual honesty had neurotic origins, but
as to that he wrote, "There is certainly much that is infantile in my
yearning for honesty—but it certainly also has a healthy core—Not
everything that is infantile should be abhorred" (p. 224). (For a more
detailed study of Ferenczi's lifelong yearning for mutuality, see Aron,
1995b.)

We have seen that mutuality does not imply equality and needs to
be differentiated from symmetry. And we have seen how Ferenczi's
attempts at mutuality became confused with symmetry and ultimately

broke down. The question to be considered is, can there be some increase in mutual disclosure without necessarily compromising the necessary differences between patient and analyst? This is a modification and extension of Ferenczi's question, "Must every case be mutual—and to what extent?" Let us first turn to the contributions of Ferenczi's friend, colleague, and collaborator, Otto Rank, and see the ways in which his work converges with and yet departs from and complements Ferenczi's innovations.

OTTO RANK AND THE BIRTH OF INDIVIDUALITY

Otto Rank and Sándor Ferenczi not only were collaborators on an important treatise on psychoanalytic technique, they also shared a common fate; to different degrees, both men were ostracized and their writings suppressed or dismissed. Aspects of Ferenczi's work were sequestered from psychoanalytic study by Jones, who kept Ferenczi's final paper from being translated into English for some 16 years; for a variety of reasons (see Aron and Harris, 1993), Ferenczi's *Clinical Diary* was not published for over half a century. Similarly, nothing that Rank wrote after his break with Freud was read or cited by classical analysts, and much of it was never even translated into English. None of Rank's work is ever assigned as reading in classical institutes, while Ferenczi's work has only recently begun to receive renewed attention. Jones (1957) forever linked the two men when he wrote that

> Rank and Ferenczi, were not able to hold out to the end. Rank in a dramatic fashion . . . and Ferenczi more gradually toward the end of his life, developed psychotic manifestations that revealed themselves in, among other ways, a turning away from Freud and his doctrines. The seeds of a destructive psychosis, invisible for so long, at last germinated [p. 45].

This was only one of the more dramatic ways in which Ferenczi and Rank were marginalized by the analytic establishment. Jones's comment not only maligns them as people, but leads to a dismissal of their contributions as manifestations of their psychoses.

Whereas Ferenczi was able to stay within the psychoanalytic movement (although only because his final experiments were not made public), Rank lived from 1926 to 1939 in exile, excommunicated from the psychoanalytic world. Rank belatedly found some historical luck, however, in a way that Ferenczi did not. Specifically, Rank is the subject of an appreciative intellectual biography by E. James Lieberman (1985); there is as yet no comprehensive biography of Ferenczi.

Lieberman's biography, together with the extensive rediscovery of Rank by Esther Menaker (1982), has led to the recent reemergence of interest in his work.

Rank, like Ferenczi, was a pupil and close associate of Freud. Rank's role within Freud's inner circle, was as Freud's adopted son. Lieberman (1985) reports that Rank, alone among the close associates, regularly edited and contributed to Freud's writings, and Freud even went so far as to include chapters written by Rank in several editions of *The Interpretation of Dreams*. From 1912 to 1914, Rank was the editor of the first two psychoanalytic journals: *Imago* and *Internationale Zeitschrift fur Psychoanalyse*. From 1919 to 1924 he directed Freud's psychoanalytic publishing house, *Der Internationale Psychoanalytische Verlag*. Rank's collaboration with Ferenczi occurred around 1923, the same year that he wrote *The Trauma of Birth* (Rank, 1929). It and *The Development of Psychoanalysis* (Ferenczi and Rank, 1924) initiated a brief transitional period before Rank was tragically to part company with Freud and Ferenczi. (The break among these men was tragic for all of them.)

The Development of Psychoanalysis is best remembered for the stress that Ferenczi and Rank placed on the mutative primacy of *experience* in the here-and-now of the transference. At the time of its writing, Freud's emphasis was on intellectual insight as the agent of change. This focus was even more true of the Berlin school, as the approach of Karl Abraham and Hanns Sachs was known, which was devoted to theory and intellectual understanding in the attention that it did pay to therapeutic considerations. In striking contrast to this concentration on the intellect, Ferenczi and Rank championed the living and reliving of affective experience. Ferenczi and Rank, along with stressing the experiential, also valued the importance of action and repetition over verbal memory. "Thus we finally come to the point of attributing *the chief role of analytic technique to repetition instead of to remembering*" (Ferenczi and Rank, 1924, p. 4). Their recommendations for the analyst's active therapeutic interventions were linked to what they believed was the necessity for the patient's active reliving and reenacting of experience. Ferenczi and Rank did not advocate the elimination of insight, understanding, or memory; rather, they believed that these needed to follow after enactment and experience.

Rank's (1929) *The Trauma of Birth* was not intended by him as a heresy, but it soon was viewed as one. It is best known for its assertion that the origin of anxiety lies in the act of birth, an idea that Rank attributed to Freud and that Freud, in turn, attributed to Rank. Rank initially thought of the trauma of birth as, quite literally, a physical trauma that left its mark in the form of psychic anxiety. But soon after the book's publication, Rank made it clear that he was advocating the importance of psychological separation experiences, particularly the child's initial separation from the mother of infancy. The trauma of birth came to mean the trauma of psychological birth, human separation and individuation. Rank's early study of separation-individuation certainly stands as an important precursor to much of the relational tradition and especially to the contributions of Mahler, Winnicott, and Kohut. (This theme is traced by Rudnytsky, 1991 as well as in Menaker, 1982.)

In shifting his understanding of the origins of anxiety from castration anxiety to the birth trauma, Rank was not only moving the origins of anxiety back in time, from the oedipal to the preoedipal, he was also shifting focus from the father as the important object to the mother. For Freud, the important figure was the patriarchal father who threatened the son with castration anxiety, and the central drama of childhood, the nucleus of neurosis, was the Oedipus complex. Psychoanalysis, until the early 1920s, paid relatively little attention to the relationship to the mother. Rank was not alone in challenging this neglect of the mother. Groddeck (1923) and Ferenczi (1932, 1933) also gave consideration to the mother, but they did not give the mother the centrality in theory that Rank did. Melanie Klein (1932) would soon come to give the preoedipal mother due importance, but she did not cite Rank following his *Trauma of Birth* because he represented her worst nightmare—a heretic who was excommunicated (Grosskurth, 1986).

Rank argued that the central drama of life begins with the vicissitudes of human separation and individuation in relation to the preoedipal mother. Rank's great discovery, however, was in linking this idea with the analysis of transference. For Rank, the most fundamental transference to the analyst was as the mother from whom one had to separate and establish one's own individuality. Rank (1929) came to view the psychoanalytic process as an act of psychological birth in which patients create themselves anew with the help of the analyst, who serves as midwife.

The image of the analyst as a (presumably female) midwife is telling, particularly in contrast with Freud's portrayal of the analyst as a (presumably male) surgeon. We might speculate regarding the impact of Rank's ideas on the male analysts of the 1920s. We know that Freud himself acknowledged that he was uncomfortable being placed in the role of mother in his patient's transferences. He wrote to the poet HD (1933), "I do not like to be the mother in the transference, it always surprises and shocks me a little. I feel so very masculine" (pp. 146-147). Undoubtedly, other analysts had reactions similar to Freud's; they may have been more comfortable viewing themselves as distant and detached male authorities than as women, who have to participate in the birth process. In any event, it was just these ideas that would be at the heart of the dispute that led to Rank's rejection. Jones (cited in Lieberman, 1985, p. 223) reported that when James and Edward Glover criticized Rank's birth trauma theory, it was precisely these two points that they attacked, the rejection of the centrality of the father and the displacement of primary importance away from the Oedipus complex.

As Rank took leave of Freud and the psychoanalytic establishment, Freud interpreted to him that his theory was a way for him to defend against his own oedipal conflicts, particularly in regard to his wish to disregard the father. Rank countered that the personal experiences that lead to insights and theoretical formulations are not relevant to evaluating their worth. In addition, Rank countered with an interpretation of his own. From his point of view, Freud's interpretation of the Oedipus myth ignores the fact that the father Laius set out to kill his son because of his own fears of being displaced by him. Now, he insinuated, Freud, the patriarchal father, was afraid that he would be displaced by the elevation of the mother in Rank's theory and by his adopted son, Rank, in intellectual life. From Rank's perspective, Freud, like Laius, would renounce his son rather than face his own inevitable mortality.

As Rank developed his ideas in the years following his separation and individuation from Freud (his own psychological birth), he elaborated a unique vision of psychological development and constructed what amounts to a "psychology of the self." His focus became the development of personal autonomy and the existential creation of meaning. Individuation begins with the early psychological separation from the mother, proceeds through the development of the will, and culminates in the creative act of generating a unique personality, a distinct self. Rank defined the will as "an autonomous organizing force in the individual which does not represent any particular biological impulse or social drive, but constitutes the creative expression of the total personality and distinguishes one individual from another" (cited in Lieberman, p. 404). For Rank, the will is active rather than reactive; it implicates that force in people which leads them to experience themselves as active agents of their own lives, authors of their own texts, forgers of their own destinies.

Rank (1945) appropriately entitled a chapter in his book *Truth and Reality*, "The Birth of Individuality." He explained that will always develops in relation to others. Originally, will develops in opposition to the mother, as one aspect of the child's separation from her. Will begins as counterwill, and since the expression of will always takes place in relation to and at the expense of the other, the exertion of one's will inevitably leads to feelings of anxiety and guilt. Neurosis comes about when the person has achieved individuality too much through negative or counterwill and is therefore trapped in conflict between autonomy based on opposition and the wish for love and connection. The most fundamental conflict that we struggle with is between birth, life, separation, and individuality on one side and dependency, merger, loss of self, the symbolic return to the womb, and death on the other.

Will therapy, as Rank came to call his approach, has to do not with intellectual understanding and cognitive insight, but with the affirmation of the patient's will in relation to the therapist. Calling for an active, flexible, and creative approach on the part of the therapist, Rank suggests that the therapist accept the patient as a person and encourage his or her psychological birth through acts of will. The restoration of confidence that is brought about through the therapeutic interaction liberates the patient's will and ushers in the birth of individuality. We will see in the next section of this chapter how this therapeutic perspective leads to a significant transformation in the meaning and clinical approach to resistance.

Clearly, Rank's approach emphasizes the centrality of relationship. More specifically, he anticipated many of the distinguishing marks of contemporary relational theories. Indeed, in 1929 Rank defined psychology as a "science of relations and interrelations" (Lieberman, 1985, p. 283). He speaks of the early relationship to the preoedipal mother and how this early relationship is reenacted in the transference. He focused clinically on the here-and-now and on the experiential reality of the immediate therapeutic interaction. He advocated an active and flexible therapeutic approach and he took an affirmative approach to resistance. His overall approach, however, represents a psychology of the self in that he (much like Mahler, Pine, and Bergman, 1975) sees the direction of growth from merger toward separation and individuation as culminating in the independence of self, rather than as movement from nonattachment to attachment (more in keeping with such thinkers as Bowlby, 1988, and Ainsworth, 1982). Of course, all these theorists would recognize that attachment needs to be balanced with exploratory behavior, connection with separation. Nevertheless, the direction of their approaches remains important. Rank privileges the move away from the other, toward autonomous self-functioning. This is true notwithstanding that he also came to see certain acts of merger as steps in the direction of creativity. The thrust of his theory is in the direction of autonomy, individuality, and the self.

RELATIONAL PERSPECTIVES ON RESISTANCE

Resistance is one example of the ways in which Ferenczi's and Rank's contributions can be seen to anticipate contemporary relational developments in psychoanalysis. Ferenczi's and Rank's ideas complement each other, and taken together they constitute the heart of contemporary relational thinking. Contemporary analysts have approached the concept of resistance quite differently from the way in which it has been treated by classical analysts. Classical analysis views resistance as *opposition to* the analytic work. In early Freudian thinking, resistance was viewed as opposition to remembering traumatic events. Later, its connotation shifted to opposition to the uncovering of repressed infantile wishes. Greenson (1967) writes, "Resistance means opposition . . . operating against the progress of the analysis, the analyst, and the analyst's procedures and processes" (pp. 59-60). Sandler, Dare, and Holder (1973), in their review of the classical approach to the concept of resistance, describe resistance as concerned "with elements and forces *in the patient* which *oppose the treatment process*" (p. 71, italics added). I suggest that relational revisions have occurred along two related lines corresponding to the two phrases that I highlighted in the foregoing definition of resistance. First, there has been an attempt to reconsider the location of resistances, by reconsidering whether they are best thought of as "in the patient." Second, there has been an effort to remove the pejorative connotations of the word resistance by questioning whether these behaviors really "oppose the treatment process."

British object relations theorists have approached resistance along more affirmative lines than did classical theorists. Fairbairn (1952) conceptualized resistance as based on the fear of retraumatization. He conceptualized the antilibidinal ego as a source of resistance to the emergence of dependency needs on the part of the needy libidinal ego, and he spoke to patients' fears of relinquishing their ties to internal bad objects. Guntrip (1969), following Fairbairn (1952), viewed resistance as due to fears of feeling or appearing weak or inadequate and therefore experiencing shame and humiliation. Patients were therefore motivated to keep their self-experience of being weak and needy out of awareness and to keep their therapists at a safe distance. This object relations approach to resistance was an improvement on the classical approach in giving priority to the patient's needs for safety. It therefore may be seen as representing an affirmative approach to resistance. Unfortunately, however, this aspect of the theory alone continues to lend itself to the analyst's interpreting resistance in a critical manner, for the analyst may imply that patients should not be so afraid of taking risks or exposing their vulnerabilities. The analyst may interpret the

experience of lack of safety as an intrapsychic one and not connect it
to his or her own behavior in the present clinical encounter. In other
words, the patient's sense that the analyst is dangerous may be interpreted as a transference distortion rather than accepted as a plausible
view of the analyst. In addition, however, to viewing resistance more
affirmatively, some British Independent analysts have also shifted to a
view of the analytic process in which both patient and analyst are
locked into mutually constituted resistances (Kohon, 1986).

Kohut (1971, 1977), more than any other psychoanalytic theorist,
led the way in revolutionizing our understanding of resistance. Self
psychology views resistance as the self's attempt to protect itself *not*
against drive derivatives, but against the repetition of traumatic experience. People live with the dread of being retraumatized by bad objects.
From this point of view, resistances are healthy and necessary functions
of the self. Self psychology has taken the affirmative approach even
further by suggesting that patients' resistances must be taken to mean
that patients experience their analyses as dangerous; and rather than
blame patients for not feeling safe, analysts must consider what they
are doing that continues to keep the patients from feeling secure.
Analysts must consider that what seems like resistance in patients is
actually a response to an interpersonal event, a failure of empathy on
the part of the analyst.

Schafer (1983, 1992) is a leader in the reconceptualization of resistance within post-ego psychological psychoanalysis. First, Schafer
(1983) has encouraged analysts to remove the pejorative connotations
of the concept resistance by taking "an affirmative theoretical and
clinical approach to resisting. This affirmative approach focuses largely
on what resisting is *for* rather than simply what it is *against*" (p. 162).
Schafer suggests that the classical tradition encourages an adversarial
conception of resistance that leads away from an analytic attitude and
potentially represents a significant interference with the analyst's
empathy. Rather than view resistance as opposition, Schafer suggests
that resistance is the patient's "next significant step in the analytic
process" (p. 171). His critique clearly challenges the accepted idea that
resistances "oppose the treatment process."

More recently, Schafer (1992) has gone even further in his critique
of the classical approach to resistance. Schafer now makes the more
radical suggestion that we eliminate resistance as a central factor in the
analytic process, and in its place he suggests that we substitute the
analysis of countertransference: "*In place of the analysis of resistance, we
may install the analysis of countertransference alongside the analysis of
transference and defensive operations as one of the three emphases that
define a therapy as psychoanalytic*" (p. 230). Schafer's point is that much

of what we have traditionally thought of as resistance is behavior on
the patient's part that has elicited negative countertransference. He
acknowledges that these ideas about resistance are not completely new
or original but, rather, derive from a variety of theoretical frameworks,
including that of self psychology. Nevertheless, Schafer is entitled to
much credit for systematically rethinking these ideas.

Let us return now to Ferenczi's and Rank's ideas about resistance.
As our review of Ferenczi's clinical contributions would lead us to
expect, in his reconceptualization of the psychoanalytic endeavor,
Ferenczi challenged the classical approach to resistance. Rather then
view resistance as due to defense against instinctual drives, Ferenczi
began to view it as an expression of the patient's developmental needs
and as a specific response to the analyst's countertransference.

Ferenczi (1931) attributed occasional failures not to the patients'
unconquerable resistances or impenetrable narcissism or to "incur-
ability" or "unanalyzability" but rather to his own lack of skill (p. 128).
One of Ferenczi's important clinical contributions was his critique of
the idea of analyzability and his refusal to blame the patient for a failed
treatment. While forthrightly acknowledging his own limitations, he
persisted in experimenting with technique in the hope that a new
approach might ultimately be of benefit to even the most hopeless of
cases.

Ferenczi recognized that resistance not only was determined by
internal defenses of the patient but also was provoked by the analyst.
Rather than interpret the patient's resistance, which could amount to
blaming the patient, Ferenczi advocated that the analyst listen differently, modify his or her technique, and respond more naturally and
lovingly. He recognized the reasonable act of self-protection contained
in the patient's resistance. Ferenczi (1928) suggested that the analyst's
lack of empathy stimulates the patient's resistance. With these recommendations, Ferenczi anticipated some of Kohut's (1971, 1977) most
salient technical contributions to the understanding and management
of resistance, especially in identifying the mutuality inherent in what
until then had been seen as resistance in the patient. He began to
listen to patients as they interpreted to him what they observed of his
own resistances. Ferenczi's contribution, then, was to reconceptualize
resistance as something that existed between the patient and the
analyst, in the relationship rather than in the patient's mind.

Rank (1945) too, in his own way, reformulated the classical notion
of resistance. For Rank, the need for self-definition is universal. The
striving for individuation finds expression in the manifestations of the
individual will, which always begins as counterwill, opposition to the
will of the other, such as the familiar negativism of the small child. The

ability to will depends on obtaining the affirmation of the other. One thinks here of Rene Spitz's (1959) idea that, for the child, learning to say no is an important developmental organizer of the psyche. Like Rank, Spitz linked this developmental achievement with the early development of object relations and with the "emergence of the self and the beginnings of social relations on the human level" (p. 97). It is critical that parents not squelch their children's early efforts at individuation through the exercise of their will. Rather, parents need to understand that their children's negativity and oppositionalism represent fledgling efforts to separate and exercise autonomy and that these efforts need to be met with parental affirmation (which is not to say that parents need to submit to the whims of their children). Rank (1945) implies that this parent–child situation is analogous to the therapy situation where what looks like negativity and opposition (the resistance) needs to be seen as the patient's efforts to exercise autonomy and self-definition, efforts that need to be met with recognition and affirmation by the therapist (although, once again, this does not mean that the therapist needs to comply with the patient's will).

Bromberg (1995) has elegantly written about resistance and human relatedness in a way that is strikingly reminiscent of Rank's thinking:

> I would argue that the human personality, in order to grow, needs to encounter another personality as a separate center of subjective reality, so that its own subjectivity can oppose, be opposed, confirm, and be confirmed in an intersubjective context. "Resistance-as-obstacle" functions inherently as a necessary guardian of self-continuity during this process and, in that sense, an obstacle, as opposition, is an intrinsic aspect of the growth dialectic that makes clinical psychoanalysis possible [p. 176].

Together, Ferenczi and Rank have provided the conceptual tools necessary to rethink resistance. From Ferenczi we take the idea that resistances are to be seen as existing in the communion between patient and analyst, that they are mutually constituted as part of the two-person relational system. Resistances in the patient may well arise in reaction to the analyst's countertransference instead of vice versa. From Rank we learn that resistances are to be viewed affirmatively as important steps in the patient's development of will, which, if these resistances are met by the therapist's affirmative response, will lead to individuation, autonomy, and agency. Both Ferenczi and Rank saw resistance in the context of the relational system. From Ferenczi, we take a focus on mutuality; from Rank, a focus on autonomy. Together they anticipated the dialectical approach that constitutes contemporary relational thinking, balancing agency and communion, one-person and two-person psychologies.

7 | Enactment, Interaction, and Projective Identification

The Interpersonalization of Psychoanalysis

Classical psychoanalytic theory has little room for the concept of interaction because the analyst historically has been viewed as a blank screen or mirror, functioning to observe and interpret the contents of the patient's mind. Only recently has the term interaction, which was not used by Freud, been conceptualized as a technical term within mainstream psychoanalysis, and even now it remains an ambiguous and controversial term. Analysts of all persuasions have become increasingly likely to speak of the psychoanalytic process not in terms of one person projecting internal impulses onto a blank screen, but of two separate personalities in interaction. Whatever the individual analyst's technical approach and personal style, whether more or less active or passive, talkative or silent, questioning or interpretive, anonymous or self-revealing, authoritarian or egalitarian, all analysts today acknowledge that their behavior in relation to a patient constitutes a particular type of interaction. There is, however, a great deal of disagreement about how to think about interaction in a way that remains psychoanalytic. The critical issue for classical analysts seems to be how to acknowledge the place of interaction without abandoning the centrality of the investigation of intrapsychic experience. In other words, how can classical analysts fully acknowledge the centrality of interaction without becoming "interpersonal"?

As traditional analysts have attempted to make room within their theories for interaction, they have coined yet another new technical term, enactment, which has been widely written about in recent years and has become central in the reconceptualization of Freudian clinical theory, (see, e.g., Jacobs, 1986; McLaughlin, 1991; Smith, 1993). The term actualization has also been introduced as a technical term in an attempt to think about interactive elements of the psychoanalytic process. The three terms—interaction, enactment, and actualization—

each contain the word *act*. Their introduction into the lexicon of psychoanalysis as technical terms points to a major shift in theory that moves psychoanalysis from a treatment that relies on associations and interpretations, words and understanding alone, to the recognition that the psychoanalytic process involves verbal and nonverbal action and interaction.

Yet another technical term, projective identification, is related to the others in that it too has come to take on significance as an interactional term. While the terms interaction, enactment, and actualization have become popular among classical and postclassical Freudian analysts, the term projective identification emerged largely from within the Kleinian and post-Kleinian theoretical tradition although it has become popular across all schools of psychoanalytic thought. Like the other terms, projective identification has been used to create a space within psychoanalysis for an interactional dimension that previously was undertheorized and unconscious.

Technical terms have been used, on one hand, to create a conceptual space within which to house interactional concepts, that is, to make room for them within psychoanalytic theory. In this respect, they represent the expansion of psychoanalysis. On the other hand, these terms have been used precisely to contain and constrain the interactional dimension of psychoanalysis. By giving interactional concepts a limited place under the rubric of enactments or projective identification, these traditional theories have sealed off interaction, limiting the recognition of the centrality of the interactional dimension and obscuring the continual and unending role of interaction, in effect, keeping it in its place and hence setting limits on the interpersonalization of psychoanalysis.

Within the culture of classical psychoanalysis, countertransference was, until quite recently, viewed largely as an obstacle to be overcome. Jacobs (1991) states that when he was an analyst in training very little attention was paid to the psychic experience of the analyst. Countertransference, while recognized as important, was still used in its pejorative sense and was given little attention in case seminars or case conferences. The contributions of Annie Reich (1973) were used to highlight the ways in which countertransference could distort the analyst's view, and the emphasis was placed on analyzing, and thus eliminating or minimizing, countertransference. The goal for classical analysts was to eliminate as much as possible of the analyst's subjectivity so that the analyst could function as an objective observer of the patient's psyche. Because the model called on the analyst to remain objective and detached, concepts implicating interaction were excluded from the theory. Analysts were invested in remaining in control of their behavior. Furthermore, it was expected that an analyst who had been well-enough analyzed could meet this expectation. Thus to question this requirement would be to confess that one had not been well-enough analyzed.

In addition to the danger of introducing the analyst's subjectivity and thus abandoning the image of the analyst as an objective scientist, there was another reason for repudiating interactional elements within psychoanalysis. Analysts have always been concerned about using their personalities to effect change in their patients. Even when Freud was employing hypnosis in his work with patients, he differentiated cure based on hypnotic suggestion from cure based on the memories uncovered during the hypnotic trance. This concern with eliminating the influence of suggestion was very important because it protected the patient's autonomy. From the very beginnings of psychoanalytic history, then, analysts were concerned with avoiding cure by suggestion, that is, cure based on the persuasiveness or personality of the analyst rather than cure through insight. Analysts felt that, if they could cure their patients through insight or recovery of memories, the patients were being changed from within, on their own, rather than as a result of having borrowed strength from their analysts. It was to protect the patients' autonomy that analysts' attempted to eliminate cure through the analytic relationship. In pursuing these legitimate concerns, however, analysts neglected to attend to interactive features of the analytic process. Not only did they place insight over relationship as the basis for change, but they also neglected the analyst's unique individual identity and character. The value of countertransference, the positive contributions of the analyst's subjective responses, and the role of the analyst's psychology were generally not recognized or acknowledged.

For all these reasons, classical theory encouraged analysts to rely on interpretation as the exclusive vehicle of psychoanalytic change. Classical analysts were to view themselves as providers of insight through the transmission of verbal interpretations and were not to act on patients in any other way. Neither the patient nor the analyst acts upon the other; rather the patient was to associate, communicating as much as possible through words alone; the analyst, likewise, was supposed to communicate with the patient exclusively (or nearly so) through verbal interpretations.

The classical model made a sharp distinction between words and acts. Renik (1993b) has traced this dichotomy back to some early ideas of Freud, (1900), who developed a model of mind based on the reflex-arc as it was then understood. According to that model, impulses could be channeled along one of two paths: efferent, leading to motor activity; or afferent, leading to stimulation of the sensory apparatus. One path led to action; the other, to thought, fantasy, and ideation. This conceptualization led to the dichotomization of action and ideation: one either thinks or one acts. If in sleep, for example, action is blocked, then one's impulses are expressed ideationally in dreams. If people act out their impulses then they do not have to think about them; consequently, to get people to analyze their impulses the analyst first has to get them to stop acting on those impulses. These assumptions led to the clinical view that patient's impulses had to be frustrated in order for analysis to be successful. Renik asserts that, as far as he knows there has never been any empirical research to support these assumptions and that there is no reason to believe that thought and action were mutually exclusive. Renik goes on to raise serious questions about the Freudian view of interaction and challenges, as well, the accepted wisdom about self-disclosure. (We will return to Renik's contributions later in this and in the next chapter.)

As we saw in Chapter 6, Sándor Ferenczi did challenge many of the fundamental assumptions of Freudian theory and technique. Ferenczi devoted a good part of his analytic career to the investigation of the role of activity in analysis by both the patient and the analyst. He subtly attacked the distinction between words and deeds (Harris and Aron, in press). Ferenczi recognized that the patient is always communicating, both verbally and nonverbally, and he also saw that communication is itself a form of action. It was not until considerably later in the century that this approach was clarified philosophically. Wittgenstein (1953) argued that language is best conceived of as an activity involving the use of words as tools. Words are not simply labels for things but gain their meaning through their use in social interchange, language games. If words are acts, and if acts are communications, then psychoanalysis can no longer be thought of as only a talking cure; psychoanalysis must involve action and interaction.

The talking cure is transformed into a cure through action, interaction, and enactment, in which what is talked about is enacted and what is enacted must be talked about. Interpersonal theory is essentially a field theory that conceptualizes psychoanalysis as an interpersonal process. Sullivan (1953, 1954) implied that we are what we do, rather than what we say. In interpersonal psychoanalytic work, the focus is on what the patient does with the analyst, how the patient is being with the analyst, rather than predominantly on what the patient is saying to the analyst. The sharp dichotomization of words and deeds has never been as sharp for interpersonalists as for mainstream analysts. Sullivan's (1953, 1954) principle of participant-observation was defined within the framework of this interpersonal field theory. It was a revolutionary contribution to psychoanalysis and one that the psycho-analytic mainstream has only begun to rediscover (for an exceptionally good description of this "rediscovery of the advantages of the partici-pant-observation model," see Hirsch, 1985; Hirsch and Aron, 1991).

Contemporary interpersonalists have further developed Sullivan's concept of the interpersonal field. For example, Levenson (1983) has enriched the idea of the interpersonal field by suggesting that what is central to psychoanalysis is the detailed inquiry or deconstruction of the here-and-now transference–countertransference interaction as a cocreation of patient and analyst. Levenson suggests that "*the language of speech and the language of action will be transforms of each other*; that is, they will be, in musical terms, harmonic variations on the same theme" (p. 81). Levenson (1972) was among the first analysts following Ferenczi, but now with the benefit of semiotics, structuralism, and post-structuralism, to deconstruct the distinction between words and acts more precisely: "Psychoanalysis had originally postulated a serious antinomy between word and deed. It was the 'talking cure,' and what was acted upon could not be spoken about, or analyzed" (Levenson, 1983, p. 87). Ferenczi could not have articulated this insight in these terms, but his clinical thinking anticipated much of it. The talking therapy is an active and interactive technique. For Ferenczi, and later for interpersonalists, psychoanalysis is where the action is!

That the participant-observation model takes into account ongoing mutual influence or coparticipation should not necessarily be taken to imply that the analyst makes active or artificial attempts to participate or to influence the patient through the self-conscious or purposeful adoption of a role. The analyst using participant-observation is primar-ily an observer, but one who recognizes that the observer inevitably becomes part of the observed. Analysts must become skillful at partici-pating with patients in an interpersonal interaction, while maintaining some perspective on the analytic field, including their own participa-tion in that field, and while continuing to recognize how limited their own reflexive observational perspective is. A balance needs to be main-tained between participation and observation, with the recognition that the act of observation is itself a form of participation and that the effects of participation must be subject to ongoing examination. Hirsch (1987) has referred to analysts' working in this way as "observing-participants," borrowing the term from Fromm (1964) and Wolstein (1964). Hirsch's emphasis is on *participation*, with *observing* as the mod-ifying adjective. As Bromberg (1984) has argued, the implications of participant-observation are not that the analyst needs to be more active or more "interactional" than in the classical stance. Participant-observation is not a "prescription" for a certain type of behavior on the analyst's part (Greenberg, 1986); it is, rather, a description or recognition of the inevitability of participation and of the need to observe the effects of this participation on the analytic process. Greenberg (1991) writes:

> The relational model postulates an analyst who is, in Sullivan's phrase, a "participant-observer," or in Fairbairn's, an "interventionist." These concepts are not themselves technical prescriptions (suggestions that one *ought* to participate or intervene); they are statements of fact from a particular philosophical perspective [p. 214].

I want to emphasize this point because I find it to be among the most frequently misunderstood aspects of relational theory: relational theory does not dictate a particular form of analytic activity so much as it insists on the recognition of inevitable and continuous participation.

Under the widespread influence of postmodernism, the deconstruction of the distinction between speech and action that was anticipated by Ferenczi and that was always an aspect of the interpersonal approach has become part of contemporary Freudian writings. Levine (1994), for example, has argued that the analyst's interpretations always contain a performative or action-oriented sense. Levine states that he does not simply mean that the patient hears the analyst's interpretations as if they were actions, but that the analyst's words actually are a form of unintended action. Levine adds that Freud was well aware of these considerations but that, in his effort to eliminate suggestion in psychoanalysis, he repeatedly asserted that the analyst's interpretations are informative rather than performative and that analytic change comes about through the impact of the analyst's words rather than through the analyst's actions. Levine argues that eliminating the impact of suggestion would be possible if we could distinguish between words and actions; but, since no such easy distinctions can be drawn, it is not possible to distinguish between interpretation as a source of information from its impact as a source of suggestion.

INTERACTION

For decades classical analysts considered any talk of interaction to be outside of the range of psychoanalysis proper. The only interaction that they were interested in was that among intrapsychic structures, but not interaction between people. This focus has changed dramatically in recent years—witness the American Psychoanalytic Association-sponsored panels at their fall meetings in 1991 and 1992 that attempted to define the concept of interaction and to address interpretive perspectives on interaction (Panel, 1995a, b).

I want to introduce the term *Freudian interactionists* to refer to a broad range of contemporary writers who are identified with the Freudian tradition and who also focus on various aspects of interaction and enactment. I use the term to point out a trend found within the "left wing" (Druck, 1989) of the Freudian community, which pays serious attention to interactional aspects of psychoanalysis. It will become clear as we proceed, however, that this is a widely divergent group of writers who vary a great deal in how they conceptualize interaction. The consequences of their formulations for clinical technique would also vary greatly. Nevertheless, I believe that grouping them together serves a heuristic purpose in highlighting this trend in contemporary Freudian writing, and it will be useful to us later in attempting to look at the similarities and differences between this group and contemporary relational and interpersonal contributors.[1]

Dale Boesky, who participated on both American Psychoanalytic Association panels, has made important contributions to the Freudian view of interaction. In his review of the concept "acting out" Boesky (1982) uses the term actualization to describe the subtle, nonmotoric, and undramatic behaviors of patients that are often neglected in consideration of acting out. Boesky's point is that the term acting out has unfortunately become associated only with more significant impulsive, gross motor behaviors and that another term is needed to describe the subtle actions that occur more frequently.

In a frequently cited article on the psychoanalytic process, Boesky (1990) struggles with the pull to bring interactional components into psychoanalysis without abandoning an intrapsychic focus. Boesky acknowledges that the analyst's unconscious has always manifested itself into the analytic work in the form of minor intrusions in the process. Since these intrusions are ubiquitous and inevitable, Boesky suggests, they must be understood as more than just lapses of proper technique. Rather, these intrusions must be studied for the light they shed on "the psychoanalytic process as the expression of an interactional experience" (p. 574).

On one hand, Boesky views his own position as strongly interactional. He sees resistance as occurring in interaction with the

---

[1] Mainstream Freudian authors continue to caution that "an interactive technical emphasis has the potential for and sometimes serves defensive purposes in its focus on the reality of the analytic relationship" (Inderbitzin and Levy, 1994, p. 776). While this point has merit, relational analysts would counter that an intrapsychic technical emphasis has the potential for, and sometimes serves, defensive purposes in its avoidance of the interactional. Any technical focus must narrow the analyst's vision and may be used defensively.

analyst's counterresistance and countertransference. He writes, "If the analyst does not get emotionally involved sooner or later in a manner that he had not intended, the analysis will not proceed to a successful conclusion" (p. 571), a statement that sounds remarkably like relational and interpersonal formulations.[2] On the other hand, Boesky is quick to distinguish his point of view from that of relational authors. He continues to place interpretive factors over relational ones in his theory of therapeutic action; he continues to view the psychoanalytic situation as the domain of a one-person psychology; and he continues to believe that it is possible to distinguish between countertransference and the rest of an analyst's subjectivity.

In the 1991 panel on interaction, Boesky, (Panel, 1995a),[3] further differentiating his position from a more relational one, suggested that a major disadvantage of the term interaction is that it invites a blurring of the distinction between the intrapsychic and the interpersonal (as if without the term interaction these two spheres would be clearly distinct). For Boesky, only in a stalemated analysis would patient and analyst be collusively joined in mutual enactments and unrecognized transference and countertransference wishes, a statement that seems much more conservative than his earlier assertion that intrusions from the analyst are universal and inevitable. According to Boesky, interaction serves resistance. Arnold Richards, the discussant for this panel, has rightly pointed out that Boesky does *not* embrace a view of interaction that takes into account the behavior of the analyst. Boesky says that he is strongly interactional, but, as in the traditional model, all the interaction seems to take place in the mind of the patient. Boesky is one of the more conservative analysts writing in the Freudian interactionist group.

In many important respects, Boesky's Freudian position is similar to the self-psychologically inspired position of Evelyn Schwaber (discussed in Chapter 2), who also appeared on both panels. Schwaber also suggests that psychoanalysis remain a one-person psychology inasmuch as it is interested in interaction only from the point of view of the patient. Schwaber suggests that we think of interaction psychoanalytically as

---

[2] Compare Boesky's to Mitchell's 1988a statement: "Unless the analyst affectively enters the patient's relational matrix or, rather, discovers himself within it—unless the analyst is in some sense charmed by the patient's entreaties, shaped by the patient's projections, antagonized and frustrated by the patient's defenses—the treatment is never fully engaged, and a certain depth within the analytic experience is lost" (p. 293).

[3] Note that the 1991 panel presentations were published as Panel (1995a, b).

the patient's experience of the two-person analytic interaction. She views countertransference as any move by the analyst away from the patient's experience. Commenting on Schwaber's paper in the 1991 panel, Richards (Panel, 1995a) pointed out that Schwaber claims to interpret interaction as it is experienced by the patient, but she clearly uses her own subjectivity in attempting to reach the patient's perspective. How, he asked, can she claim that this represents a one-person psychology?

Also present on the 1991 panel was Joseph Sandler. In an earlier article that has become a classic in psychoanalysis, Sandler (1976) used the term actualization (p. 45) to describe the patient's efforts to impose on the analyst an intrapsychic object relationship. Sandler made the valuable point that transference is not just a misperception of the analyst in which the analyst is a blank screen. Rather, transference involves not just perception but activity. The patient actively attempts to get the analyst to play out a particular role; the transference is actualized through the analyst's "role-responsiveness" (p. 45). Sandler repeatedly emphasized patients' active efforts to "provoke," "prod," "manipulate," and "impose an interaction, an interrelationship" between themselves and their analysts as well as their tendency to unconsciously scan and adapt to the analyst's reaction to this provocation (p. 44). This important contribution by a respected classical analyst implicates analysts as participants rather than as neutral observers. In the 1991 panel, Sandler, rejecting the role of the analyst as a mirror or blank screen, suggested that, inescapably, there is interaction between two parties to the analytic engagement. Sandler argued for the need to oscillate between one-person and two-person psychologies.

A sign of how dramatically things are changing on the psychoanalytic landscape is evident by looking at who else was invited to speak at these panels. The 1991 panel included a paper by Jay Greenberg, and the 1992 panel included one by Edgar Levenson. It is remarkable that at the classical American Psychoanalytic Association papers are being invited from interpersonal and relational authors. Indeed, at the close of the 1992 panel, Owen Renik, who had presented a paper at the panel, remarked that, listening to Levenson's presentation, he had found himself thinking how much of it he agreed with, and he noted that Levenson had been saying much the same thing for the past 20 years. Renik called on classical analysts to abandon their narrow parochialism. Renik (1993a, b, 1995) followed up with papers that more directly acknowledge interpersonal contributors, and, as editor of the *Psychoanalytic Quarterly*, he has begun to invite relational and interpersonal contributions.

ENACTMENT: FREUDIAN INTERACTIONISTS AND THE INTERPERSONAL TRADITION

The analyst who is perhaps most responsible for the introduction and acceptance of the term enactment within the mainstream psychoanalytic community is Theodore Jacobs. Following Jacobs's (1986) seminal article, the technical term enactment became a central notion in the reconceptualization of Freudian clinical theory. The term enactment has now been used by many classical analysts in papers devoted to the subject. A 1988 panel of the American Psychoanalytic Association dealt with this theme (Johan, 1992), as does Jacobs's (1991) book throughout. What is meant by the term enactment, and what does it contribute to psychoanalysis that is new or different? Why has psychoanalysis adopted terms that refer to various aspects of interaction when it never acknowledged a need for such terms before?

When Freud (1914) first talked about "acting out," he had in mind that the transference itself was an acting out, a repetition with the analyst, instead of an act of remembering (Freud, 1914). Analysts, however, came to think of acting out as being in opposition to transference. Acting out occurred outside of the analysis, with other objects, in contrast to repeating with the analyst in the transference. Alternatively, acting out occurred with the analyst or in relation to the analyst, but its very purpose was to oppose communication and to disrupt the analytic task (Etchegoyen, 1991). Therefore, to address the potentially constructive role of action with the analyst, another term was needed.

The term acting in was coined by Zeligs (1957), who was referring to the patient's postural attitudes displayed in the analytic situation. "Acting in," however, was never widely adopted by analysts. It referred to body movements, postures, and nonverbal activity that occurred inside the analysis rather than outside of it. No convincing metapsychological or clinical distinction, however, seemed to be gained by the use of the term acting in. Both acting out and acting in were used to refer to aspects of patients' behavior, rather than to an interactional process that occurred between patient and analyst.

The term enactment, as it is used by Jacobs (1986, 1991), was meant to describe the ways in which patient and analyst act upon one another verbally and nonverbally. Drawing on the earlier work of Boesky (1982), Jacobs notes that one difference between the term enactment and the term acting out is that enactment refers to subtle interpersonal activity and not just to gross or impulsive behavior. Another difference is that enactments may refer to activity that takes place even in the course of doing a technically correct analytic function. For example, an enactment may take place not through any action by the analyst but in the course of making an analytic interpretation.

By attending to nonverbal material, as well as on his own physical and emotional responses in the course of doing analysis, Jacobs (1991) has attempted to explore in great depth and detail the nature of conscious and unconscious communication between patient and analyst. Jacobs articulates an interactional view of the psychoanalytic process. He acknowledges the mutual and reciprocal contributions of patient and analyst to transference, and he views unconscious communication and interpersonal influence between patient and analyst as continually operating in both directions. Jacobs suggests that both patient and analyst unconsciously "enact" certain subtle transference—countertransference interactions. Enactments, for Jacobs, are a two-way street; they are initiated by both patient and analyst. Jacobs speaks of the "interplay" and the "interweaving" of enactments as essential, and often overlooked, aspects of the analytic process (p. 32). Thus, a key difference between the older term acting out and the newer term enactment is that acting out was conceptualized within the context of a one-person psychology. The patient acted out or, more rarely, an analyst acted out; there might even have been times where they acted out with each other. Nevertheless, acting out was essentially viewed as an individual activity. In contrast, in Jacobs's work, enactment is viewed within the context of a two-person interactional psychology: enactments require mutual participation.

McLaughlin (1981) is among the most articulate of the Freudian interactionists. He has demonstrated that the classical tradition conceives of the patient's contributions as having an infantile origin while stressing the mature wisdom and scientific objectivity of the analyst. By declaring that the patient is not the only one in the consultation room with a psychic reality, infantile wishes, and transferences, McLaughlin was illustrating the mutuality of the psychoanalytic situation and moving analytic theory away from and beyond the vision of the analyst as a detached and objectifying scientist-observer. McLaughlin persuasively argued for an increasingly mutual view of analysis "which places the psychic reality of patient and analyst in an ambiguous and relativistic opposition, far from the early claims of the latter to a secured and superior reality-view" (p. 658).

McLaughlin has attempted to clarify the meaning and significance of the term enactment. He begins with a very broad definition of enactment as including all types of interaction between patient and analyst, particularly on the nonverbal gestural and postural components of the patient's communications. Since this definition is quite broad and would have to include all the behaviors of both patient and analyst,

McLaughlin narrows it down. The narrow version refers to events occurring between patient and analyst that each experiences as being the consequences of behavior by the other. His perspective on interaction implies that close scrutiny of the interpersonal behaviors of both participants will lead to a better understanding of the patient's intrapsychic conflicts as well as to a clearer understanding of the object relations that have been actualized in the analytic relationship.

Using the concept of enactments, McLaughlin has demonstrated the ongoing interpersonal and interactional nature of the analytic process. The words enactment, interaction, reenact, actualization, acting out, and acting in each connote activity, participation. The patient's words and associations are no longer seen as simply communicative, intended to convey meaning. McLaughlin argues that the patient's words themselves are loaded with affective appeal and coercion; words themselves are actions or incitements to action. Thus, while enactments may refer to the nonverbal, they do not have to be limited to that, for patients and analysts words themselves are enactments.

McLaughlin's tracing of the word enactment both historically and etymologically led him to understand it as an action intended to influence, persuade, or force the implied other in the interactive field. McLaughlin insists that the term enactment implies mutual influence within a two-person model of the analytic situation. Unlike such terms as acting out, projective identification, and countertransference, which, according to McLaughlin, reflect only the unilateral perspective of the analyst and his or her determination of meaning from an assumed position of objectivity and uninvolvement, the term enactment denotes a "cojoint process of attempted mutual influence and persuasion" (p. 605). Furthermore, McLaughlin does not construe enactments as occasional lapses or discrete phenomena; rather enactments in the broad sense are contained in all of the behaviors of both patient and analyst.

Jacobs's and McLaughlin's points of view are much more radical than those of some of their colleagues in that both theorists conceptualize enactment in terms of mutual participation and bidirectional influence. For these reasons I would place them toward the more radical pole of the Freudian interactionists. Consider, by way of contrast, the more conservative view of Chused (1991). Chused defines an enactment as "a nonverbal communication (often cloaked in words) so subtly presented and so attuned to the receiver that it leads to his responding inadvertently in a manner that is experienced *by the patient* as an *actualization* of a transference perception, a *realization* of his fantasies" (p. 638, italics added). Notice that the definition takes it for granted that the receiver of the enactment is the analyst and that the communication is initiated by the patient. This very definition of enactment presumes a one-way influence, in contrast to Jacobs's and McLaughlin's espousal of the two-way directional influence of enactment. Chused continues in the same vein. Throughout an analysis, she suggests, *patients* engage in symbolic actions that generate corresponding impulses for action in the analyst. But this conceptualization obscures the recognition that analysts also engage in symbolic actions that generate corresponding impulses for action in their patients.

Chused supports the ideal of analysts's containing their impulses, examining them, and using the information gained to enrich their interpretive work. Yet she recognizes the trouble that maintaining this ideal can lead to: when actions are forbidden, she notes, often the experiencing of the impulse also feels forbidden. Chused therefore encourages a certain degree of spontaneity on the part of the analyst. Chused is clear that she does not believe the analyst should "confess" his participations in enactments. (If enactments are *not* viewed pejoratively, as lapses or as due to the analyst's faults, why the use of the word confess? Indeed, elsewhere, she refers to enactments as "the analyst's mistakes" [Chused and Raphling, 1992, p. 89].) Chused advises that, when the patient points out to the analyst his or her awareness that the analyst is participating in an enactment, then the analyst should not deny it or obscure it by interpreting the observation as a transference reaction. Rather, Chused accepts the observation and explores its implications and ramifications.

In my view, Chused's portrayal of the analyst's handling of enactments without self-revelation is a simplification because she begins with the assumption that the patient is straightforwardly telling the analyst that he or she has observed the analyst's participation. Of course, when this happens, it is relatively easy for the analyst to accept the observation without further comment. What about the patient who the analyst suspects has noticed something and who does not comment on it or associates to it only through disguised derivatives in the associations? How can the analyst in this case interpret this to the patient without at least some implicit acknowledgment that the observation is plausible? Perhaps it is possible, but it gets trickier, and in many cases, to many analysts, it feels disingenuous.

Schafer (1992) has also begun to employ the concept of enactment, although, once again, unlike Jacobs and McLaughlin, Schafer, rather than adopting a view of enactment as a two-person interactional phenomenon, asserts that it is the patient who enacts. In reexamining the idea of resistance from a contemporary Freudian approach, Schafer suggests that analysts should give hardly any weight to the idea of resistance. He recommends instead that analysts think in terms of the patient's transference and defensive operations, and the continual analysis of countertransference becomes central to the analytic process. Instead of thinking of certain of the patient's behaviors as resistances, he recommends that we think in terms of enactments. A focus on enactment destabilizes psychoanalysis as purely a "talking cure" and places more attention on action and interaction. Schafer sees enactment as a concept that can free analysts and analysands from the tyranny of verbalization, specifically, from the limited role of the spoken word as merely a conveyor of content. Furthermore, Schafer points out, the term enactment does not have the same pejorative connotation as do terms like acting out and resistance. Enactments, for Schafer, are unconsciously devised communications that convey the fantasies that dominate the analysand's conscious and unconscious experience of the conduct of both parties to the analytic relationship. For him, enactments are expressions of the *patient's* experience. Enactments are viewed not as resulting from the mutual influence of both patient and analyst or as two-way communications between patient and analyst, but as having a unidirectionality from patient to analyst.

Of all the Freudian interactionists that we have discussed, Owen Renik has in recent years taken the most radical position, one that in many respects can be described as interpersonal.[4] I will briefly examine Renik's recent contributions before returning to the question of the relationship between Freudian authors and the interpersonal tradition. Renik (1993a, b) argues that even the most subtle countertransference behaviors, such as subtle kinesthetic tensions or other "microactivity" on the analyst's part, often have an impact on the patient. Renik concludes that countertransference enactments precede countertransference awareness. Just as we expect patients to act out their transferences before becoming aware of the meanings of their actions and their motivations, so too should we expect that analysts will enact their countertransferences before they become aware of their meanings and motivations. For Renik, countertransference awareness always emerges after an enactment. The clinical implication of this for Renik is to encourage a technique that leaves more room for the analyst's spontaneity. Acceptance of his theoretical conclusions would result in a clinical atmosphere that lends itself to analysts' expecting themselves

---

[4] A legitimate question may be raised as to why I have chosen to consider Renik a Freudian. Are we bound to accept a theorist's self-description, or must we spell out other criteria? In this case, I have designated Renik as a Freudian interactionist because of his long history of affiliation with the American Psychoanalytic Association and the *Psychoanalytic Quarterly*, as well as on the basis of his written work, which was until recently quite classical. I recognize that categorizing theorists in this manner is highly arbitrary, but I believe it is sometimes useful for didactic purposes.

to "enact," to "act out their countertransferences," and to analyze their participation rather than to attempt to eliminate their participation. Like Hoffman, Mitchell, Greenberg, me, and other relational analysts who espouse the inevitability of analysts' using and communicating their own subjectivities, Renik has concluded that the analyst's subjectivity is irreducible.

Renik is critical of the principle of analytic anonymity and believes that analysts have endorsed this precept largely because it protects them and contributes to their idealization and authority. Renik takes the radical position that we should not merely discard the principle of analytic anonymity, we should actively contradict it. In its place he suggests an ethic of self-disclosure and authentic candor. (More about his controversial views on self-disclosure in the next chapter.) Renik (1995) has become the only major representative of the psychoanalytic establishment to cite interpersonal and relational contributions as direct influences on his own thinking. The last Freudian analyst to do this explicitly was Merton Gill, who encountered tremendous criticism and even hostility as a result.

Having described the contributions of a wide variety of Freudian interactionists, and having seen that mainstream psychoanalysis has moved increasingly in the direction of acknowledging interaction, we may ask how does the work of these theorists differ from that of contemporary relational and interpersonal analysts. Before turning to this theoretical question, however, I must first address what seems like a less significant and largely political issue. First we must ask why it is that, with very few exceptions (Renik being notable), none of these Freudian interactionists have cited the interpersonal literature or have recognized the interpersonal approach as an important influence in their thinking at all! The only "interpersonalist" generally referred to by Freudian analysts is Merton Gill. While Gill is cited by Freudian authors, and while it is true that Gill (1983b) adopted an interpersonal perspective in the latter part of his career, he was not truly a representative of the interpersonal tradition. Where are the references to the interpersonal literature as it is represented in interpersonal journals and by authors identified with the interpersonal approach? We must deal with this political question before turning to an examination of the similarities and differences between these theorists. By not citing interpersonal writers, these Freudian authors have made it more difficult to compare and contrast their respective traditions.

Hans Loewald was among the first analysts working in the Freudian tradition to emphasize the inevitability of the analyst's participation within an interactive field. He was a forerunner of contemporary Freudian interactionists, just as, in a wider sense, he was viewed by

Druck (1989) as the model for the "Freudian left." Loewald (1970) wrote of the analyst as a participant in a field. Like almost all the Freudian interactionists to follow him, Loewald felt obliged to differentiate his position from that of the interpersonalists. Loewald was careful to caution:

> Far from doing away with intrapsychic structure and conflict (a tendency inherent, for instance, in Sullivan's interpersonal theory), such a theoretical formulation is based on the reconstruction of the individual psyche from its component elements and takes into account the organizing currents which shape the individual psychic structure and its internal conflicts [p. 293].

But I would certainly question whether interpersonal theory (even Sullivan's original view) would not take into account "the organizing currents which shape individual psychic structure and its internal conflicts," or whether Sullivan's theory was not precisely an attempt to account for these organizing currents on the basis of interpersonal experience. Sullivan would have objected to an overly concretized notion of psychic "structure," and he would indeed have objected to "conflicts" only if the word referred narrowly to conflicts between drive and defense inasmuch as he certainly acknowledged that people were conflicted. But, Loewald had so modified the notion of drives, seeing them as fundamentally "relational phenomena," that even this formulation might not differentiate him from interpersonalism.

Poland (cited in Jacobs, 1991) acknowledges that progress in shifting from a one-person view to a two-participant view has been slow for classical analysts who have resisted this paradigm shift. He writes, "The resistance to new attention to 'the interpersonal' arose not only from unyielding conservatism, but also from a valid perception that 'interpersonal' was often used as a sophisticated defense against crediting the power of active unconscious forces" (p. xii). Poland's claim is that classical analysts need to dissociate themselves from the interpersonalists because, while the interpersonalists may have made valuable contributions to recognizing the analyst as a participant in the interaction, they nevertheless have used these insights to "screen out unconscious forces" (p. xii). Poland claims that a contemporary view of the analytic process no longer consists of the analyst's studying the patient's mind from a detached impersonal distance, as if in a test tube. Nor, he says, does it consist of "merely the dynamics of a private two-person small group therapy, the interaction always relatively close to the surface" (p. xiii). This is the only hint that Poland gives of how he views the interpersonal way of working.

Gill (1994) observed that the dismissal of the interpersonal perspective by classical analysts is often based on the mistaken idea that interpersonalists and relationists are most concerned with studying "external" interpersonal relations, that is, relations in the sociological rather than in a psychoanalytic sense. Gill argued, however, that a study of their contributions demonstrates that interpersonal and relational analysts understand interpersonal relations not only in this sociological sense (as they would be viewed from the perspective of an outside observer) but particularly as they are experienced in psychic reality by the participants. It is remarkable that, in differentiating themselves from the interpersonal school, not Poland, McLaughlin, or Jacobs refers to any specific interpersonalists. I believe that this scholarly omission further obscures any similarities or differences between the approaches. Furthermore, it leads me to wonder how well acquainted these Freudian writers are with the interpersonal tradition and whether it is still forbidden to cite by name various interpersonalists in Freudian writings. Of course, as I noted earlier with regard to Renik's recent work, there is some evidence that this situation is beginning to change.

As we have noted, McLaughlin (1981) views the analyst as a participant, caught up in a two-person communicative field with transference–countertransference constantly at play and with neutrality and nonparticipation not viable options. McLaughlin feels the need to dissociate his position from the interpersonal view, much as Loewald had done earlier. McLaughlin (1981) writes, "I am not referring to the ever-present alternative of interpersonal psychology" (p. 652). Nowhere, however, does McLaughlin go on to say how his position is different from the interpersonal position. I can only conclude that he was not so much differentiating his viewpoint from an interpersonal one as he was being politically correct and dissociating himself from unacceptable company.

Jacobs (1991) addresses the relationship between his ideas on interaction and enactment and the views of interpersonal psychoanalysis by acknowledging that the interpersonal school developed similar ideas much earlier. Classical analysts, however, were unable to use these ideas at that time for a number of reasons. Jacobs argues that classical analysis was still new in this country and was under siege from many quarters, and, in his view, it is understandable that they regarded the interpersonalists as their adversaries. The interpersonalists, according to Jacobs, neglected the unconscious and denied infantile sexuality. Furthermore, they emphasized the role of the object to the neglect of the drives. From the perspective of classically trained psychoanalysts, in their mode of practice, interpersonal practitioners seemed to omit the very essence of psychoanalysis. Jacobs (1991) admits that, in this atmosphere, appreciation and exploration of the interactional elements of psychoanalysis was slow to develop.

> The antagonism that developed toward the interpersonalists, with its accompanying tendency to regard material on the transactional level as superficial and not worthy of serious study, slowed recognition of the importance of the analyst's contribution to the development of the transference and to the character and fate of the analytic process [p. 221].

Jacobs goes on to discuss how Freudian analysts have gradually begun to pay increasing attention to interpersonal ideas. He believes that British object relations and the Kleinian school played a historical role in paving the way for this development in classical analysis. These schools emphasize the importance both of early object relations and of the interaction between patient and analyst. As I read Jacobs, his point is that early classical American analysts were not able to benefit from the interpersonal schools emphasis on interactional dimensions of treatment because they were too embattled with that school and simply dismissed their contributions as nonanalytic. Because they had less of an adversarial history with the British analysts, who were members of the International Psychoanalytic Association, classical analysts were able to absorb some of their contributions more readily.

Let us examine Jacobs' (1991) portrayal of the interpersonalists. I read him as saying that the classical school dismissed interpersonalism as not really being analysis. Why was it not analysis? Because interpersonalists denied the unconscious, he says. In focusing on the interpersonal, they were being superficial. But is it true that any of the interpersonalists denied the unconscious (as Jacobs repeatedly claims without citing a single source)? Not really. Sullivan did object to speaking of the unconscious, in a reified sense, as if it were a place in the head. Sullivan, however, paid a great deal of attention to what was avoided, selectively attended, or dissociated. (For a detailed discussion of Sullivan's position on the unconscious and the relationship between the intrapsychic and the interpersonal, see Mitchell, 1988b.) Certainly, any reading of the contemporary interpersonal literature—even a cursory reading of any issue of *Contemporary Psychoanalysis*, the leading interpersonal journal—would convince a reader that interpersonalists are interested in unconscious processes. There are arguments and disagreements about how unconscious processes should be thought of and conceptualized (for an elegant discussion of this topic see, D. B.

Stern, 1983, 1990), but interpersonal analysts certainly work with a sense of unconscious processes.

The more legitimate issue has to do with the content of the uncon-scious (see Greenberg's, 1991, excellent discussion of this issue). Jacobs (1991) is on more solid ground when he argues that early interperson-alists denied infantile sexuality and the drives. Even here, however, the argument is slippery. Sullivan, Fromm, and other early contributors to the interpersonal tradition recognized that biological drives are relevant. The real question concerned whether the edifice of psycho-analytic theory was best built with biological drives as the central foun-dation. Interpersonalists were reluctant to accept the universality of the Oedipus complex or the assumed importance of the biological unfolding of erogenous zones as central to development. In this, they were ahead of their day; most analysts today think of patients' pre-oedipal and postoedipal issues as equally important in psychic development and in psychopathology. Many contemporary Freudians now pay relatively less attention to libidinal phase issues and relatively more to ego functions and deficits and to the vicissitudes of object relations.

The early interpersonalists were clear that they did not accept libido theory and the centrality of the Oedipus complex. In their attempt to differentiate themselves from the Freudians, however, they may have thrown out the baby with the bath water, for they seemed not only to dismiss the sexual drive but also to minimize the clinical importance of sexual conflicts. Similarly, while objecting to the centrality and univer-sality of the Oedipus as based on drives, the interpersonalists may have underemphasized the value of thinking about oedipal dynamics in less reductionistic terms. As we saw in Chapters 1 and 2, the contemporary relational approach came about precisely to correct these excesses. Thus, the development of relational theory has begun to allow increased dialogue between the Freudian and interpersonal groups.

I believe that there is some truth in Jacobs's (1991) claims that clas-sical analysts had substantive reasons to dismiss the contributions of the early interpersonalists. It should be clear, however, that these reasons also were rationalizations that covered up largely political differences. Furthermore, whatever reasons there may have been to dismiss inter-personal contributions in the past, these reasons would not hold today. In my view, given the similarity of interpersonal ideas, even in only certain respects, to the writings of the Freudian interactionists, it is inexcusable, on the grounds of respectable scholarship, that these Freudian writers have not referred to the numerous relevant interper-sonal contributions.

In what is otherwise a most admirable, scholarly, and comprehensive article suggesting that our understanding of countertransference has emerged as the common ground for psychoanalysts of diverse theoretical perspectives, Glen Gabbard (1995) has, in a subtle way, continued the long tradition of excluding interpersonal contributions. He compares the two key concepts, projective identification and countertransference enactment, as well as the notion of role-responsiveness, to show that we have come to think of countertransference as a mutual construction. He concludes that the belief that the countertransference represents a joint creation involving contributions from both analyst and analysand is now endorsed by classical analysts, modern Kleinians, relational theorists, and social constructivists. What makes this inclusive list so striking is the absence of interpersonalists, particularly in a discussion of this topic, which has been central for interpersonalists for more than half a century. I applaud Gabbard for his inclusion of such relational and constructivist authors as Mitchell, Hirsch, Gill, Hoffman, Tansey, and me. But why is there not a single reference to so major a concept as participant-observation? Why is there no hint that Levenson, Wolstein, Ehrenberg, Stern and many other interpersonalists have been dealing with this topic for decades, not to mention the lack of reference to such historical figures as Fromm, Sullivan, Fromm-Reichman, and Thompson or to such second-generation interpersonalists as Singer and Tauber, all of whom dealt with the issue of countertransference and the analyst's participation?

As the terms interaction, enactment, and actualization have become accepted and even celebrated, the Freudian community has undergone a conceptual and technical revolution. They have moved from the intrapsychic to the interpersonal: not that they have abandoned the intrapsychic, but, rather, they understand it differently. From this contemporary perspective—and this was, indeed, Sullivan's perspective (see Mitchell, 1988b and Ghent 1992a)—rather than contrast the interpersonal and the intrapsychic, it makes more sense to think of *the intrapsychic as interpersonal*. From words, associations, and meanings, the Freudian interactionists have shifted to activity and subtle interactional behaviors on the part of patient and analyst. The sharp distinction between words and acts has been challenged. From the patient's mind, they have shifted to the patient–analyst, two-person, transference–countertransference field as the scene of the action to be investigated analytically. For many of these theorists, mind itself is now seen as inherently relational and interpersonal. Psychoanalysis has gone interpersonal! It has done so, however, without acknowledging and embracing all of the history of psychoanalysis.

PROJECTIVE IDENTIFICATION AND
INTERACTIONAL CONCEPTS

The positive reception given to the term enactment in Freudian circles is similar in some respects to the way in which the term projective identification was received within post-Kleinian and relational circles. Klein (1946) originally coined the phrase to depict an intrapsychic phantasy in which some content from inside of the infant (or patient) was put *into* the mother (or analyst). Projective identification referred to a phantasy in the mind of the infant (or the patient), and so it was an intrapsychic phantasy of interaction that was being described, a formulation within a one-person psychology.

To whatever extent an analyst was actually influenced and effected by the patient's behavior, Klein understood this to reflect counter-transference, in the narrow (and pejorative) sense of this term (Spillius, 1992). Klein and her close collaborator Paula Heimann ran into serious interpersonal conflict over Heimann's (1950) wish to extend the concept of countertransference to include all the analyst's emotional responses to the patient. Klein was worried that such a usage of these concepts would lead analysts to blame patients for their own difficulties. While, for Klein, projective identification was strictly a phantasy, for today's British Kleinians it is generally accepted that patients can behave in ways that arouse within their analysts feelings that the patients cannot contain within themselves. If a patient can not find any other way to communicate a feeling, then one option is to act in such a way so as to provoke that feeling in the analyst.

Spillius (1992) traces the history of the concept as it developed in the work of Bion, Rosenfeld, Money-Kyrle, and Joseph. Bion in partic-ular had the greatest influence on the notion of projective identifica-tion, transforming it into an interactional construct. Bion (1959) suggested that the analyst would actually feel manipulated by the patient into playing a role in the patient's phantasy. For Bion, the phantasy of projective identification is accompanied by unconscious efforts to coerce the analyst into playing a role. Joseph (1989) suggests that patients "nudge" their analysts, unconsciously pushing and pulling them, to adopt positions that correspond to their projections. She further believes that it is necessary for the analyst to respond to these pressures in an attenuated way in order to become aware of the nature of the patient's projections. Joseph believes that the analyst should allow him- or herself to become aware of these attenuated feelings before they are grossly acted out, but she recognizes that some degree of action is likely to occur. This idea is remarkably similar to Renik's (1993a) proposal that analysts must inevitably act on their countertransference before they become aware of it. The difference, however, is that, whereas Joseph maintains the ideal of not acting on these feelings or doing so only in a very attenuated way, Renik believes that maintaining this ideal hinders the analyst's responsiveness.

Thomas Ogden (1979), a post-Kleinian analyst, contributed to the acceptance of projective identification in America. For Ogden, projective identification refers to the fantasies of ridding the self of unwanted aspects, along with the enactment of object relations that accompany these fantasies. In addition, it refers to the depositing of these aspects of the self into another person, and, finally, it includes the recovery of these parts of the self in modified form. Extending this line of thinking, Tansey and Burke (1989) speak of empathy and projective identification as radically mutual and interactive processes.

Gabbard (1995) does a superb job of linking the Kleinian writings on projective identification with Freudian writings on interaction, enactment, role-responsiveness, and actualization. He concludes that there is now broad agreement that projective identification is not a mystical exchange of psychic content but, rather, that it is an interactional process that relies on interpersonal pressure being put on one person by another. Symington (1990) speaks of this process as the patient bullying the analyst into thinking the patient's thoughts. Gabbard suggests that the recipient of this interpersonal pressure would not be moved unless the projection connected with some psychic element in him- or herself. Therefore, he suggests, projective identification requires a "hook" (p. 477) in the recipient of the projection to make it stick. From this perspective, even if an analyst feels that he or she is being manipulated into feeling something that is not his or her own, as Bion described, what is actually happening is that a repressed or dissociated aspect of the analyst's self has been activated by the interpersonal pressure put on him or her by the patient. This leads the analyst to feel that he is not quite him or herself.

For some years, interpersonalists were quite critical of the notion of projective identification for a number of reasons. First, it seemed to be a description of something that went on between people. Interpersonalists believed, however, that by attributing the process to an internal phantasy in the mind of one person the concept of projective identification obscured the behavioral and interactional components that would be most useful in explaining the phenomenon. If the analyst began to feel hopeless, it would be too easy, just as Klein feared, to blame the patient for the analyst's hopelessness by attributing it to projective identification; the patient put his hopelessness into me! Interpersonalists were more interested in examining the interactions that go on between the two people. What did the patient do, in what way did the patient act that would lead me to feel hopeless? Further-more, what is there in me that would respond to whatever it is that the patient did? In what way am I, as a person, vulnerable to hopelessness? Whose hopelessness is it, anyway—mine? the patient's? Is it the patient's mother's hopelessness that I am feeling? My mother's?

The standard interpersonal response to the concept of projective identification was that it maintained the image of the analyst as a blank screen, but now, using Bion's image of the container and the contained, interpersonalists were suggesting that Kleinians were promoting the image of the analyst as an empty container (Hoffman, 1983; Levenson, 1983; Hirsch, 1987). I believe, however, that as Kleinians have gained experience with the use of this concept, they too have attended to these concerns and the concept of projective identifi-cation has increasingly been assigned to the interaction between two individual people. Kleinians have become intensely concerned with the actual interactions between the participants, especially the way in which interpretations are experienced as interactions (Joseph, 1989).

In my view, the terms interaction, enactment, and projective identi-fication have served very similar theoretical purposes. While the terms are not equivalent, each has defined a certain area of investigation, a certain space within psychoanalytic theory, that permits analysts to consider the interactional behavior of patient and analyst. Projective identification has become an important and popular clinical concept precisely because it fills a void in the theoretical structure of psycho-analysis; namely, it allows analysts to focus on interaction by disguising interaction as fantasy. Projective identification thus serves as a bridge between the intrapsychic and the interpersonal (Ogden, 1979), but it does so by obscuring that this shift is indeed taking place. Mitchell (1995) has described the transformation of this concept as "the inter-personalization of the concept of projective identification" (p. 79). Mitchell's phrase may correctly be applied to so many of today's psychoanalytic concepts that it is legitimate to speak of the interper-sonalization of psychoanalysis.

I have serious reservations about the terms enactment and projec-tive identification. Precisely because they isolate a certain aspect of the analytic process that is marked off as interactional, they may inadver-tently cover up the interactional dimension of other aspects of the analytic process. In other words, one may acknowledge facets of the analytic process to be enactments or projective identifications and therefore recognize that those phenomena are interactional; but by labeling those isolated processes as enactments, one is then permitted to view other aspects as *not* being enactments and therefore *not* to be viewed interactionally. The positive contribution of the terms enactment and projective identification is that they draw psychoanalysts to the interactional dimensions at some moments, but this advantage is simultaneously its major drawback because it may obscure the great extent to which the entire psychoanalytic process is in some respects interactional.

Essentially, I view the current usage of the concepts enactment and projective identification to be a rhetorical strategy that permits the recognition of interactive elements within orthodox (Freudian and Kleinian) psychoanalytic theory. To speak of enactments suggests that these "events" happen from time to time, maybe even with some frequency, but it denies that the patient and analyst are always enacting, that analysis is interactional from beginning to end. Just as the acceptance of the ubiquity of countertransference began with the recognition that countertransference was inevitable *on occasion*, and particularly with very disturbed patients or at times of serious stalemate, so too we begin with the recognition that patient and analyst interact or enact on occasion, once again particularly with very disturbed patients or in the midst of chronic impasse.

Projective identification is a concept that brings us back once again to the distinction between words and deeds. Analysts who use this term distinguish between those patients, presumably more primitive than others, who use projective identification because they are not psychologically and emotionally sophisticated enough to communicate these particular feelings through more mature forms of communication, namely, through words. Since they are not capable of symbolization, they resort to subtle forms of action. Words are privileged over actions, viewed as more mature and healthy than actions. But as we pay increasing attention to projective identification, as we become better able to identify the use of projective identification, as we identify its more subtle forms, we come to the realization that projective identification is more widespread than we thought. Just as we gradually came to speak of countertransference as tied to transference and as equally constant and universal, we need to recognize enactment as a continual process, rather than as a discrete event. Likewise for projective identification.

We began by describing enactment as a fairly infrequent event that occurs only with very disturbed patients who need to use primitive forms of communication. Before long we realized that healthier patients too use this mechanism, and later we realized that analysts do too. And now we may begin to wonder whether speech is ever used only to communicate and not also as a form of action. Then we realize that if the patient's associations are actions then so too are our interpretations. Before long the very distinction between words and acts breaks down. Which is not to say that there is no meaningful difference between words and acts; after all, just because they are not sharply distinguishable does not mean that there is no difference between them. Some words may be more like actions than others and some actions may be more communicative than others. Analysts must recognize, however, that both dimensions occur continually in the psychoanalytic process. No one uses words only to communicate; nor does anyone communicate only through words.

To my mind, the word interaction conveys this sense of continuity and process, whereas the term enactment too easily implies a discrete event (see also Smith, 1993). Smith claims that he can not picture a completely enactment-free exchange. Similarly, Boesky notes that "It is a bit hard to say what is *not* an enactment" (cited in Smith, 1993, p. 96). Unfortunately, though Smith writes convincingly and eloquently about the ubiquity of enactment as an interactive component of transference, he, like all the other classical analysts that we have reviewed, fails to make any reference to interpersonal theory and fails to cite any of the numerous interpersonal authors who have long championed a similar point of view.

A COMPARISON OF THE APPROACHES

We are now in a position to ask how contemporary mainstream analysts, both Freudian interactionists and the post-Kleinians, are similar to or different from contemporary relational and interpersonal analysts. There are many similarities and some subtle distinctions. To begin with the similarities, I agree with Gabbard (1995) that psychoanalysts of all persuasions have increasingly recognized countertransference as a joint creation of patient and analyst. I prefer to say that patient and analyst mutually construct their relationship and mutually regulate their interaction as well as their experience of the interaction. They have begun to pay attention to the subtle interactions that go on between patient and analyst. Psychoanalysts of all persuasions have begun to acknowledge that even their most pure interpretations also are based on aspects of their own subjectivities and express aspects of themselves. In short, we are witnessing the interpersonalization of psychoanalysis.

I believe that, as a group, relational analysts are more likely than other analysts to advocate a high degree of freedom of expression and spontaneity on the part of the analyst. They tend to give themselves more latitude to respond in what feels like a personally expressive way. If what is thought to be transformative is not only insight but new forms of engagement, if relationship is privileged along with interpretation, if what matters most is the patient's meeting with an authentic response from the analyst, if what is most vital about an interpretation is the way in which it expresses something essential about the analyst's subjectivity, then why limit our interventions only to formal interpretations?

While insight and interpretation (verbal symbolization) continue to be valuable to relational analysts, they do not retain the centrality that they have for classical Freudian and Kleinian authors. Interaction itself is viewed as a factor that may legitimately lead to analytic change. We generally do not know what helps people get better, but, when asked, even people who seem to have had relatively successful analyses often point to noninterpretive factors as beneficial. Relational analysts generally believe that what is most important is that the patient have a new experience rooted in a new relationship. Old patterns are inevitably repeated, but, it is hoped, the patient and the analyst find ways to move beyond these repetitions, to free up their relationship and construct new ways of being with each other. This is what is critical and ultimately what leads to change. Sometimes interpretation and insight may be the optimal way to move the relationship forward; sometimes changing our ways of interacting more directly may accomplish the same thing. Relational analysts are more likely than more traditional theorists to credit interaction as directly leading to change. Optimally, for all analysts, the combination of insight and new forms of interpersonal engagement works synergistically to produce change.[5]

An even stronger point is that, within the context of the psychoanalytic situation, interpretation and verbally achieved insight *are* relational experiences, and interaction *is* itself interpretive, which is to say that it conveys meaning. I have repeatedly emphasized that interpretations are "complex relational events," as Mitchell (1988a, p. 295) says, or suggestions, as Gill (1993) suggested. Protter (1985) made the point that every interaction is also an interpretation. Ogden (1994) has noted that frequently analysts express their understanding to patients through nonverbal actions, and he refers to this as "interpretive action" (p. 108). The point that I want to make here is that the very dichotomy of (verbal) insight and (interactional) experience, in which for traditional psychoanalysis the first is valued over the second, needs to be deconstructed. Insight is an experience, and experience is simultaneously an insight (Gill, 1993). It is not that they are two separate

---

[5] For an illustration of symptom relief brought about without verbal interpretation, and discussions of this phenomenon by a variety of relationally minded analysts, see Eagle, 1993.

events that work together; rather, they are always two aspects of the same phenomenon.

Inevitably, since we are all more simply human then otherwise (Sullivan, 1953), analysts will have some characteristics that are similar to the original objects and some characteristics that are different, at least in intensity. These qualities will optimally allow patients to organize their experience of the analyst along the lines of their significant childhood others (repetition), but also be able to view the analyst as unique and new, not exactly like their parents (new experience). The relational model, unlike the classical one, acknowledges that the analyst is indeed going to be like the old objects in some respects and that the patient's perceptions of these similarities will not be viewed as distortions needing correction by the authority of the analyst. From within this model, enactments and reenactments are crucial therapeutic events that constitute the very essence of the treatment. Davies and Frawley's (1994) description the psychoanalytic treatment of adult survivors of childhood sexual abuse is largely based on this way of conceptualizing the function of enactments as a means of unconsciously expressing in action dissociated aspects of self- and object representations. Neutrality, from this perspective, refers to "the clinicians' capacity to keep such reenactments fluid and ever changing" (p. 3) rather than allowing themselves to get stuck in the perseverative reenactment of any single relational pattern. Interpretation is one vehicle to keep the flow of interaction from stagnating, but the enactments themselves may serve a therapeutic purpose.

Hoffman (1992b) points out that what seems to be part of something old (repetition) may turn out to be part of something new, and that what seems like something new (new experience) may turn out to be a repetition of something old. Even when the analyst is reenacting with the patient an aspect of an old object relation, the repetition is unlikely to be an exact equivalent to the old experience; rather, it is likely to be analogous to it. Similarly, when the analyst is a new object, even providing a "corrective emotional experience" for the patient, it is unlikely that the analyst is literally the opposite of the old object; rather the analyst is likely to provide a relatively healthy variation of the old experience.[6]

---

[6] Hoffman (1995) is critical of Greenberg (1991) for suggesting that the analyst maintain a position of neutrality by sustaining the tension between being an old object and being a new object. He views this recommendation as a form of "technical rationality" and believes that Greenberg takes for granted that the analyst can know in advance just what would be taken by the patient to be old or new object experience. My own reading of Greenberg has never given me the impression that he intends to convey that the analyst can predict the patient's response with any certainty in

MUTUAL ENACTMENT AND MUTUAL PARTICIPATION

Many of the Freudian interactionists continue to believe that counter-transference can be differentiated from the rest of the analyst's subjectivity. They continue to assume that the monitoring of countertransference by a well-analyzed and well-trained analyst can eliminate this source of interference and keep the analyst's behavior on track. Similarly, contemporary Kleinians suggest that analysts should be able to differentiate the feelings that result from projective identification from what is part of their own psychic content. I believe that this expectation is the single most important difference between the Freudians and the Kleinians, on one side, and the interpersonalists and relationalists on the other. From a relational-perspectivist position, there is no way to sort out which element in the analysis belongs to the patient and which belongs to the analyst. This is another way of saying that, since interaction is mutual and continual, it is never possible to say who initiated a particular sequence of interaction. Traditional analysts believe that, having been well-enough analyzed and well-enough trained, they should be able to function with a fair amount of autonomous and conflict-free ego functioning. They assume a greater degree of "objectivity" than that which relational analysts would be willing to grant. Every interpretation, and for that matter every intervention, by the analyst reveals a great deal about the analyst's subjectivity, and patients continually observe the nature of our participation with them; they often notice aspects of our participation that we have not yet noticed ourselves. If we agree that mutual enactment and mutual participation are inevitable, then we must pay serious attention to our patients' perceptions of our participation.

Since relational analysts view interaction and enactment as inevitable, continuous, and useful, and since they therefore allow themselves some leeway in responding freely and spontaneously, and since they also assume that their patients notice their participation and make inferences based on their observations, relational analysts are also more likely than other analysts to talk with their patients about what they have observed and inferred. This form of participant-observation leads relational analysts to be more likely than others to use purposeful self-disclosure as a legitimate intervention.

---

advance, but, rather, that like Hoffman, Greenberg is attempting to convey that the analyst needs to aim to keep some balance between being too much like the original objects and being too radically different from them.

A CLINICAL ILLUSTRATION

The following clinical material, taken from Goldstein (1994), illustrates some of the questions that have been raised about interaction, enactment, and the analyst's spontaneity. Goldstein describes a 33-year-old woman, the daughter of two psychiatrists, who began treatment with her one year after terminating a 10-year analysis with a male analyst. Although the patient reported that the analysis had been helpful in improving her relationships with men, she continued to suffer from work-related and self-esteem problems. She had begun to form an idealizing transference when one day, upon leaving Goldstein's office (which was in her apartment), the patient acknowledged the baby grand piano that could be seen in the living room and asked whether Goldstein played. In a light and offhanded way, Goldstein replied, "Well I play but not very well" (p. 423). Goldstein reports that at first she was concerned that her "self-disparaging" comment might interfere with the developing idealizing transference.

Self psychology suggests that a common form of countertransference is to feel uncomfortable with the intense idealization of a narcissistic transference. Goldstein, who uses a self-psychological approach, was quick to think that she may have been responding to this countertransferential discomfort by putting herself down and so setting limits on the idealization. Presumably her patient would object to her refusal to play the part of the idealized object in the transference.

Her patient did not respond as predicted. Instead, she wanted Goldstein to know how much she appreciated her analyst's honesty and humility.

> While I'm sure you play better than you said you did, it made me feel good that you don't feel you have to be perfect at what you do or portray yourself as if you can do everything well. . . . I always thought that my parents were perfect and that I had to be. My analyst acted like he was perfect and I never felt that I was good enough. When I left here I suddenly realized that maybe I don't have to be a star or do everything just right [p. 424].

Goldstein reports that this self-disclosure was accompanied by significant change in the patient's ability to take more risks in her own life. Goldstein says, "I do believe that her experience of me spoke louder to her at this particular time than any interpretation I could have made since she was so distrustful of her parents' and former analyst's interpretive stance toward her and their always being 'right'" (p. 424).

Goldstein's spontaneous self-disclosure, which went beyond what the patient had directly asked her, was a therapeutic enactment that seems to have forwarded the analytic work without involving an explicit interpretation. Of course, one way of viewing this incident is that her patient continued to idealize her by incorporating the analyst's self-disclosure into the fabric of her idealizations. Now the analyst would be idealized precisely because she could be so modest. From this point of view, further analysis is necessary; for example, at some point the analyst might wish to interpret the ongoing idealization and confront the patient's reluctance to accept her perception of the analyst's self-disparagement and insecurities. But perhaps not. Perhaps by the time the patient was ready to hear such a confrontation, she might not need to keep idealizing the analyst in that way and the interpretation would prove unnecessary.

What if the analyst had told the patient that she was concerned that she had made a mistake by telling the patient what she told her? She could have said to the patient that she was worried that the patient might not take it well that her analyst was so insecure, and she was concerned that she had said something that would interfere in their relationship. Of course, this might have proved to be a terrible mistake, compounding the original error by exposing even more of the analyst's insecurity. If the patient "needed" to idealize the analyst, then would this not have interfered? Perhaps, but, as we have seen, if a patient "needs" to idealize the analyst then there are many ways to do it. The patient could just as easily insist that this new "confession" revealed the analyst's ideal qualities. Opening up this subject to further mutual analysis by both the patient and the analyst might have led to some interesting questions about the need for idealization. Did this need exist only in the patient, or was there some need on the analyst's part to be idealized and yet some simultaneous conflict about this need. Not all the need for idealization was in the patient, and neither was all the conflict. The patient may have known more about the analyst's conflict than she was able to verbalize at the moment.

At what point in this illustration would we want to say that they were "enacting" something between them? When and where was the enactment? When did the enactment begin? When did they stop enacting? Who was "nudging" whom in this example? Who was evoking a role in whom? Who was being asked to play a part in whose script? Who was projectively identifying what into whom? Did the enactment begin when the analyst made the "mistake" of saying that she didn't play the piano that well? Did it begin when the analyst chose to set up a practice in her home? Did it begin when the patient asked for the first time about the piano? Or did the enactment begin the first time that the patient came to the office and did not notice the piano or did not let herself mention it? Did the enactment begin the first time that some reference to music or performance was made in the analysis and when no one connected this to the visible piano?

Are not patient and analyst always enacting their internal sets of self- and object relations? Are we not each always enacting our intrapsychic worlds, using each other as characters in the scripts that we are playing out and acting out? Is not that interaction continuous between us whether we are associating, interpreting, questioning, or remaining silent? And is it not a remarkable analytic accomplishment when we can help our patients get to the point where they can help us notice ways that we are interacting with them that we did not consciously know? Not only is enactment a mutual process, but so too is the analysis of "the interplay of enactments" that goes on continuously.

What if we had been told by Goldstein that this incident was not as spontaneous as it seemed. What if Goldstein had said that, in fact, at the moment that the patient asked her about the piano it had occurred to her that it would be good for the patient to know that she, the analyst, was not so great at everything? What if the thought had crossed her mind that everyone else in the patient's life had tried to be perfect and here was an opportunity to let her know that she was not like that? That would make this a "witting" or deliberate intervention, an attempt by the analyst to be the "good" object. Would it therefore be a manipulation? According to Gill (1994), it would qualify as a manipulation only if the analyst did not intend to analyze it. But what would it mean to analyze it? Would that mean simply to ask the patient what it had meant to her that her analyst told her what she did? That would not really analyze the interaction at all. Would analyzing the interaction mean Goldstein's telling the patient that she had told her that she was not that good a piano player because Goldstein felt that the patient was idealizing her too much? This is closer to Renik's (1995) suggestion that analysts attempt to communicate as much as possible about the reasons for their analytic activity. Of course, to do this well, the analyst might have to free associate for some time with the patient, which would lead to something like a mutual analysis. Perhaps what is most important is that the analyst share her immediate reaction with the patient. In this case, that reaction would be the analyst's worry that she had disturbed their relationship because of some discomfort on her own part about being idealized.

Clearly, our conventional ways of thinking about these matters do not work very well. Once we recognize the continual nature of enactment and interaction, once we recognize that our words are actions and our interpretations are suggestions, the standard rules of analysis do not hold up. The analytic situation consists of two people, each of whom brings the fullness of his or her personality to the encounter, each of whom acts upon the other and in response to the other, and each of whom notices some things (and does not notice other things) about his or her own and the others' actions. This study of enactment and interaction has led us, inevitably I believe, to the controversial topic of the next chapter: self-disclosure.

8 | On Knowing and Being Known

Theoretical and Technical Considerations Regarding Self-Disclosure

A study of the accumulating analytic literature on self-disclosure should lead us to marvel at the incredible transformation that has taken place in the world of psychoanalysis in just a few short years. It is, indeed, only recently that the analyst's self-disclosure has appeared on the psychoanalytic scene as a topic of panels and symposia in our meetings and as a subject worthy of investigation in our journals. In the near future, textbooks on psychoanalysis will undoubtedly contain chapters on self-disclosure, and institutes will have courses and clinical case seminars devoted to this subject.

The topic of the analyst's direct and purposeful self-disclosure is certainly one of the most controversial topics in contemporary psycho-analysis. The question of self-disclosure logically follows, however, from the recent acknowledgment of the importance of interaction and enactment in psychoanalysis. As long as it was taken for granted that analysts were to maintain a baseline of anonymity, abstinence, and neutrality there was no point in asking such questions as, What do patients learn about their analysts as people? What, if anything, should patients be told about the analyst's subjective experience or personal reactions to them as patients? Is the analyst's self-disclosure ever a useful and constructive aspect of psychoanalytic technique? As Green-berg (1995) asked in the title of a recent symposium regarding the topic of self-disclosure, "Is it psychoanalytic?"

Historically, the answer to Greenberg's question has been decisively that self-disclosure is not psychoanalytic. Freud said so himself, emphatically! While personally quite open and spontaneous with patients, Freud forcefully and decisively established the rules of psychoanalytic anonymity and abstinence.

Consider the following passage from Freud's (1912) paper on tech-nique. It includes his well-known and often criticized analogy of the analyst's remaining opaque and mirrorlike. I believe that Freud's thinking about technique developed very much in reaction to his early dealings with his friend and colleague Sándor Ferenczi, who during the years 1911 and 1912, prior to embarking on his brief formal analysis with Freud, incessantly pushed Freud for mutual openness, personal candor, and disclosure. Consider the following of Freud's recommendations on technique while keeping in mind our review in Chapter 6 of Ferenczi's advocacy of an affective technique employing mutuality and openness.

> Young and eager psycho-analysts will no doubt be tempted to bring their own individuality freely into the discussion, in order to carry the patient along with them and lift him over the barriers of his own narrow personality. It might be expected that it would be quite allowable and indeed useful, with a view to overcoming the patient's existing resistances, for the doctor to afford him a glimpse of his own mental defects and conflicts and, by giving him intimate information about his own life, enable him to put himself on an equal footing. One confidence deserves another, and anyone who demands intimacy from someone else must be prepared to give it in return.
>
> But in psycho-analytic relations things often happen differently from what the psychology of consciousness might lead us to expect. Experience does not speak in favour of an affective technique of this kind. Nor is it hard to see that it involves a departure from psycho-analytic principles and verges upon treatment by suggestion. It may induce the patient to bring forward sooner and with less difficulty things he already knows but would otherwise have kept back for a time through conventional resistances. But this technique achieves nothing toward the uncovering of what is unconscious to the patient. It makes him even more incapable of overcoming his deeper resistances, and in severe cases it invariably fails by encouraging the patient to be insatiable: he would like to reverse the situation, and finds the analysis of the doctor more interesting than his own. The resolution of the transference, too—one of the main tasks of the treatment—is made more difficult by an intimate attitude on the doctor's part, so that any gain there may be at the beginning is more than outweighed at the end. I have no hesitation, therefore, in condemning this kind of technique as incorrect. The doctor should be opaque to his patients and, like a mirror, show them nothing but what is shown to him [pp. 117–118].

That passage may be read as Freud's response to Ferenczi's personal (analytic) longings for personal openness and candor between himself and Freud. Freud condemns "an affective technique" that privileges mutuality and intimate self-disclosure. He warns of the dangers of the defensive use of mutuality as a resistance to intrapsychic exploration and of what many years later came to be called "malignant regression" (Balint, 1968, p. 149). Freud recommends an approach that is considerably more detached and removed, ultimately, like a mirror. It was precisely this approach that Ferenczi was later to challenge. Each of these pioneer analysts developed an approach to psychoanalytic tech-nique that suited his character and temperament. Can analysts today suspend Freud's recommendations long enough to discover for them-selves the advantages and disadvantages of self-disclosure?

Consequent to Ferenczi's radical experiments with mutual analysis, a great taboo restrained the analytic community from exploring the technical use of self-disclosure. Nonetheless, in Britain, following some hints by Winnicott (1949) concerning his conservative use of counter-transference disclosure, Little (1951, 1957) advocated a much freer use of self-disclosure. In America, the interpersonal tradition provided some encouragement for the use of self-disclosure (see especially Tauber, 1954; Singer 1968, 1977; and Searles, 1979), but even in the interpersonal literature little was written that systematically explored technical considerations of the principles of self-disclosure. More recently, this issue has become increasingly discussed. Some excellent examples of the reconsideration of self-disclosure in the current litera-ture include Bollas (1987, 1989), Gorkin (1987), Ehrenberg (1992, 1995), Maroda (1991, 1995), Davies (1994), Mitchell (1995), and Renik (1995).[1]

When is it useful for an analyst deliberately to self-disclose? (I am emphasizing purposeful and deliberate self-disclosure because I take it for granted that we are always revealing aspects of ourselves whether we intend to or not.) For which patients is self-disclosure useful? At what point in analysis? For what purpose? About what topics? Under which conditions? In what sequence? What conditions should be met first? How is the patient to be prepared for the analyst's self-disclosure? In what way do these self-disclosures interact with interpretations? What clues does the patient provide about the appropriateness of self-disclosure? How spontaneous should the analyst's self-disclosures be? Are there certain self-disclosures that should be attempted only after careful reflection; and, if there are, how is one to make room for spon-taneity and affective immediacy? How much affect is it appropriate for the analyst to express directly? Are there certain topics that should never be disclosed—sexual desire or murderous impulses toward a patient, for example? What precautions need to be considered to protect the patient from being intruded on by the analyst's self-disclo-sures? How does the analyst evaluate the impact of a self-disclosure? How should the analyst manage the anxiety stirred up in him- or

---

[1] The controversy around self-disclosure has been surveyed elsewhere, and I refer the interested reader to these literature reviews for further details (see Burke and Tansey, 1991; Gorkin, 1987; Greenberg, 1995).

herself following self-disclosure? What are the ethical considerations that need to be considered regarding self-disclosure?

What is truly wonderful about opening up this subject is that, for the first time, we as psychoanalysts may begin to think together about self-disclosure in a more refined, differentiated, and systematic way. From my reading of the current debate about self-disclosure, I am impressed by the wide range of activities that fit into the category of self-disclosure and by the diversity of personal styles and technical approaches that can be developed as analysts with different personalities and theoretical commitments, working in a variety of settings and with different patient populations, experiment with self-disclosure and report on their findings.

CLINICAL ILLUSTRATION

The following is an anecdote, a clinical moment from my work with a young man, that illustrates the use of self-disclosure in the service of "interpretation." To put it in somewhat less technical language, the following vignette depicts one way I think of myself as working analytically, namely, that, at times, I think out loud with my patients, not knowing exactly where my thoughts are going, selectively associating. Because self-disclosures come in so many varieties and forms, I am aware that this anecdote is only an illustration; it is not representative of self-disclosures in general, nor does it have probative or scientific value. I offer it as a talking point, a way of getting us started on a conversation about self-disclosure.

This patient knows that I am married, but in the years that we have worked together in analysis he has very rarely asked me anything directly about my wife or my marriage. In a recent session, he was describing his fears that his own relationship with his girlfriend, which had become quite serious, would not survive his recently recognized ambivalent feelings toward her. He was unusually emotional, tearfully expressing his concern about how he could possibly continue his involvement with his girlfriend now that he knew that there were important things about her that he did not like. I made some challenging comments, asking him why he could not continue to get close with her just because there were some things about her that he did not like. We had many times discussed the reverse situation, namely, his expectations that someone would have to like everything about him or else the person would abandon him. If she "didn't love his shit" then she wouldn't love him.

But now we were talking about the reverse: could he continue to love someone if there were things about her that he did not like? He suddenly asked me, in a challenging and provocative, but also pleading, tone. "Are there important things about your wife that you don't like?" I was taken aback, but after a moment of hesitation I responded, "Yes, there are important things about my wife that I don't like." After another brief, thoughtful pause I added, "More significant, perhaps, there are important things about me, that my wife doesn't like." And after yet another silent, thoughtful moment, I continued, "You know, there are important things about myself that I don't like—why should she have to like them?"

Without going into any detailed follow-up on this incident (which in any event would *not* prove conclusive regarding the efficacy of my intervention), I will say that I felt then, and I believe now, that my patient had experienced it, as quite useful. The episode certainly led us to explore the issue directly in the transference. How much could he acknowledge things about me, important things, that he disliked and continue to feel that I was good for him as his analyst? How much could I dislike important things about him and still genuinely like him and want to help him? My response, no doubt, tended to obscure other dimensions of what he was trying to communicate. For example, it may have delayed, for at least a little while, his coming to terms with the horrible thought that he would really decide to give up on this relationship and face the inevitable loss of his girlfriend as well as his own guilt about abandoning her. Perhaps I was communicating to him my (unconscious) preference that he remain in the relationship with this woman for a while more before deciding to give up on it and move on. And perhaps, I was also suggesting (again unconsciously) that he do the same in regard to me and the analysis.

How are we to think about this type of intervention? Is it a self-revelation? Yes, in the strict sense of the term; of course, it is. Instead of "analyzing" his question, I answered him directly and even volunteered further information. Furthermore, it was personal information in the sense that I revealed some thoughts and feelings that concern my wife and me and our relationship. I had, in a symbolic way, given my patient a glimpse of the primal scene, some of the dynamics between my wife and me. Should I have been concerned that this would gratify or over-stimulate him?

On the other hand, did I really reveal anything personal at all? Perhaps not. All human relationships are ambivalent; no one likes anyone else completely, nor does anyone like himself or herself completely, nor should one feel one has to. My remarks, then, could have been an interpretation to the patient, an interpretation in the manifest form of a self-disclosure. Without being explicit, I have said to the patient something like the following:

"It is expectable that people feel ambivalently toward those that they love and are closest to. You seem to have the mistaken belief that, if you have any negative thoughts or feelings toward someone, then that means you don't really love them. By these standards you will certainly never be able to love anyone or feel that you are loved by them. And, because you feel this way, you cannot stand looking at any things about yourself that you don't like, because if you did you would have to conclude that you don't like yourself at all. Therefore, you deny these negative feelings and avoid recognizing any flaws in yourself, just as you have been doing in relation to your girlfriend."

If my patient could hear in my response this implied interpretation, he also would have understood, because we had been over this subject repeatedly, that his conflict was related to his family's inability to acknowledge and discuss any conflict or disagreement among themselves. And he would understand that his conflict gets in the way of his having critical thoughts about me and affects how he perceives any criticism that I express toward him. Also, clearly implied in my "interpretation" is the idea that he is not alone in feeling ambivalently toward those he loves, that to feel ambivalent is usual and even inevitable. Indeed, given the progress of the treatment beyond this point, I am quite sure that my patient did hear what I said to him very much along these lines, but because it was personal, spontaneous, mildly humorous, affectively alive, and more about myself than about him, it seems to have reached him in a way that previous interpretations had not.

My patient had, though, been feeling intensely sad and frightened and was showing me the intensity of his feelings, and perhaps with my attempt at lightheartedness I had simply distracted him from these painful feelings. Also implied in my response was the idea that, unlike my patient, I had no trouble acknowledging that my relationships were imperfect and that I had some sense of humor about myself. Perhaps I was showing off to my patient that I was less defensive than he. I was being competitive, saying not only that yes, I am in a relationship, but also that I don't take myself as seriously as he does. My patient was ultimately able to hint at his realization that this had been quite a power play, a way of my outdoing and even intimidating him. To make matters even more complicated, it was particularly difficult for the patient to confront me with this aspect of my character precisely because he experienced me as being sincere and well intentioned.

Like any intervention, what I said to the patient revealed more than what I consciously intended and thus expressed an aspect of my subjectivity that my patient and I may or may not have come to know. That an intervention may need to be pursued because it directly reveals something about the analyst's subjectivity does not distinguish it from any other interpretation that may do the same, albeit more subtly. Perhaps we might think of certain self-disclosures as being "implicit interpretations" or "self-disclosures in the service of interpretation." Following Ogden's (1994) recent proposal, we might think of self-disclosure as a variety of "interpretive action," although I recognize that Ogden does not intend to condone or promote self-disclosure. Nevertheless, his point is that often interpretations are conveyed in ways other than direct verbal symbolization.

An objection that has been raised to this type of intervention (Rothstein, 1995) is that I capitalized on a permissive parental transference instead of analyzing the transference, and in doing so I encouraged the patient's dependence and interfered with the development of his autonomous capacity for self-analysis. I was essentially saying to the patient, "Come on, we're all ambivalent about relationships. You are and I am too, and that's O.K." This reassurance would be expected to result in a transference cure or a cure based on interpersonal suggestion, but not based on "internal structural change."

Rothstein raises an important point, but in my view not a decisive objection to this type of intervention. First of all, the objection is rooted in a theory of mind to which I do not subscribe. That is, it is based on a model of the person as an "individual" and the mind as "autonomous." As I have suggested throughout this book, I prefer a model of mind that is less individualistic, more relational, and in which mind exists only in relation to others, always dependent to a degree and never fully autonomous. While promoting the patient's autonomy is an extremely important value, it is not, to my way of thinking, the ultimate goal. It is just as important to value connection and relatedness as it is to value autonomy and independence. The important thing about any intervention, including self-disclosure, is not whether it promotes autonomy or connection, but whether or not it opens up or forecloses analytic inquiry.

Second, I am sure that Rothstein is correct that there was a paternal transference operating here. He seems to imply, however, that had I not answered the patient's question, had I not self-disclosed, there might have been some way for me to avoid entering into an enactment of the transference. But, if I had not answered the patient's question, would I not then have enacted some other version of the patient's father transference? Who is to say which behavior the patient would have experienced as more power wielding and paternal? No matter how the analyst responds, a certain element of suggestion is always present in our work. Once again, I do not accept the absolute distinction between a "transference cure" and a cure based on suggestion. Insight and interpretation always have a suggestive dimension, and interaction may well convey insight. Analytic "structural" change is achieved through some synergistic working of both insight and relationship. The implication of Rothstein's position is that he knows a way (classical technique) to avoid the use of suggestion. This is where we disagree.

Third, we must consider what my intervention means to the individual patient. For instance, this young man's father would not have been likely to share this kind of impression with him. He would never have acknowledged an aspect of himself that his wife did not like or an aspect of his wife that he did not like. So, in answering as I did, I was being explicitly different from his father. I was not consciously adopting an artificial role; rather, I was attempting to express what I had experienced as a surprising and spontaneous association. When the patient later told me that this was something his father would never have said, I told him that perhaps I was trying to show him that I was not exactly like his father.

Rather than avoid an enactment such as this, my preference is to create an analytic climate where I tolerate a greater range of behaviors in myself than is traditionally acceptable and I try to analyze them to as great a degree as possible, yet I know that I will not be able to analyze all of them completely. By participating more spontaneously and personally, one risks having a good deal of oneself exposed and open to the patient's scrutiny. But if the analyst can remain open to this feedback from the patient, then the patient's participation in the treatment in this way may lead not only to greater relatedness but to greater analytic autonomy as well. My intervention, afterall, took place after many years of working on this problem and in the context of our having interpreted these dynamics traditionally many times. Under these conditions, it may be useful to balance the anonymity and distance of traditional interpretation with the impact of increased personal and spontaneous participation.

THE INEVITABILITY OF SELF-REVELATION

I cannot emphasize too strongly that *self-revelation is not an option for the analyst; it is an inevitability!* In this chapter we are concerned with those interventions that purposely and deliberately disclose aspects of the analyst's subjectivity. But our discussion here of this type of deliberate self-disclosure should not obscure the inevitability of ongoing verbal and nonverbal self-revelation. Communication about the therapist's internal states are continuously conveyed to the patient. All our interventions are behaviors, including our decisions not to intervene; our silences, too, are behaviors, and all behaviors are communications.

Watzlawick, Bavelas, and Jackson (1967) state the first axiom of communication theory as follows:

> First of all, there is a property of behavior that could hardly be more basic and is, therefore, often overlooked: behavior has no opposite. In other words, there is no such thing as nonbehavior or, to put it even more simply: one cannot *not* behave. Now, if it is accepted that all behavior in an interactional situation has message value, i. e., is communication, it follows that no matter how one may try, one cannot *not* communicate. Activity or inactivity, words or silence all have message value: they influence others and these others, in turn, cannot *not* respond to these communications and are thus themselves communicating [p. 49].

To repeat, the first axiom of communication theory is that "*one cannot not communicate* (p. 51). The second axiom of communication theory, derived from the work of Bateson (1972), is that all communication involves metacommunication. All communications have report, or content, aspects and command, or relational, aspects. Thus every communication defines the relationship and conveys content. Defining the relationship implies how one sees one's self and how one sees the other. On the metacommunicative level, communications convey such information as, "This is how I see you," "This is how I see you seeing me," "This is how I see you seeing me seeing you," and so forth.

By directly extending these principles of communication theory to the psychoanalytic situation, (as was first done by Levenson, 1983), we can say that the analyst is always behaving in one way or another and is, therefore, always communicating and therefore always defining and redefining his or her relationship with the patient. Given these basic axioms of communication theory, we postulate that the analyst is never neutral or anonymous but is always self-disclosing and indeed *suggesting* something about and coconstructing his or her relationship with the patient. In Pizer's (1992) words, patient and analyst are always "negotiating" with each other who and what they will be for each other. Patient and analyst, in every communication to each other, are saying something like "No, you can't make this of me, but you can make that of me" (p. 218). In our consideration of deliberate self-disclosure by the analyst, we should not lose sight of the inevitability of continuous, inadvertent self-revelation. The line between deliberate and inadvertent (conscious and unconscious) self-disclosure is highly ambiguous.

ADVANTAGES AND DISADVANTAGES OF SELF-DISCLOSURE

There are some very good reasons for the analyst not to self-disclose to a patient. The reasons that are generally given include that it complicates the treatment unnecessarily; it burdens the patient with the analyst's problems; it deflects attention from the patient's concerns; and it reflects the analyst's needs and not the patient's. Classically, it is not in keeping with being a "blank screen." It may be too gratifying to the patient; it is a form of "acting out" on the part of the analyst; and, perhaps most important, it obscures the nature of the patient's transference. Since, in the classical model, transference is viewed as a distortion that is thought to unfold from within the patient, based on displacements from old objects, anything that analysts communicate about themselves will either interfere with this spontaneous emergence from patients or may make it more difficult to sort out where distortion ends and interpersonal reality begins. Too much information about the analyst may inhibit or restrict the patient's fantasies and reactions. While clearly I do not think of transference as operating in this way, I do believe that there are reasons to be cautious about self-disclosure. The disclosure of countertransference, like any other technical intervention or any other type of participation on the part of the analyst, may, indeed, be countertherapeutic.

Another objection to the analyst's self-disclosure (voiced even by contemporary relational analysts) is that it tends to disrupt the transitional space of psychoanalysis because it concretizes what ought to remain in the symbolic realm (for an interesting dialogue about this issue, see Benjamin, 1994; Davies, 1994; Gabbard, 1994). If a patient suspects that an analyst wants to kill him, for example, this fantasy remains in the symbolic realm; but if the analyst tells the patient that she wants to kill him, this confession concretizes the fantasy and potential space closes rather than opens. Closing the analytic space means that the freedom of the patient to create what she or he needs to create in the analytic situation is limited. We must remember, however, that this analytic creation by the patient is always illusory. The patient never really has this freedom because the analyst always plays a role in shaping the analytic space, and the "potential space" that is the essence of psychoanalysis is a space created by both the patient and the analyst through their mutual participation. The analyst always cocreates the analytic space with the patient, and to speak of the analyst's closing off this space or opening it up is problematic; it is a mutual creation. The analyst's revealing what he or she is feeling does shape the analytic situation in one way rather than in another; but the analyst's feeling something that is not discussed with the patient also shapes the analytic space. The analytic interaction opens up some possibilities and forecloses others. The analyst cannot help but participate in the shaping of analytic space; in this sense, analysts are always limiting their patient's analytic freedom.

But are there any benefits to be gained by self-disclosure that would make it worth risking the disadvantages? Gorkin (1987) suggests that disclosures of countertransference made sparingly and selectively can provide therapeutic traction. He lists the following arguments in favor of selective self-disclosure: (1) Self-disclosures may confirm the patient's sense of reality. (2) They may help to establish the therapist's honesty and genuineness. (3) They show that the therapist is not so different from the patient, that the therapist too is human and has transferences. (4) Self-disclosures clarify the nature of the patient's impact on the therapist and on people in general. (5) Self-disclosures may help to break through treatment impasses and deeply entrenched resistances.

Some analysts, especially those influenced by interpersonal theory, suggest that the judicial disclosure of the analyst's subjective experience (in which ideas, impressions, observations, and, perhaps most important, affective responses are shared and commented on by both patient and analyst) leads to the creation of a "collaborative inquiry" (Chrzanowski, 1980) in which the analysis is enriched by encompassing "data" contributed by both the patient and the analyst. Chrzanowski writes that "a major therapeutic instrument [of interpersonal psychoanalysis] lies in the judicious sharing with the patient of countertransferential experiences" (p. 141).

In addition to expanding the analytic data base, the selective sharing of countertransference more readily lends itself to affective interpersonal encounter and engagement. Goldstein (1994), writing about self-disclosure from a self-psychological perspective (and whose case vignette we discussed in the previous chapter) has similarly reported that the use of self-disclosure can be considered a form of empathic attunement and selfobject responsiveness. Ehrenberg (1995) writing from a contemporary interpersonal perspective suggests that judicious countertransference disclosure encourages patients to collaborate more fully in the investigation of the immediate analytic interaction. She expresses the radical position that countertransference disclosure, used judiciously, may facilitate the analytic engagement in *all* patients.

Jacobs (1995), whose work on enactment was considered extensively in the previous chapter, like many authors who have argued in favor of restrained and cautious self-disclosure, states that sometimes conveying something to the patient in the form of a self-disclosure allows the patient to experience the analyst's message as more authentic and more personal and thus has a greater impact on the patient. But are these not precisely the arguments that Freud (1912) suggested reflect "the psychology of consciousness" and that he warned are not borne out by the psychoanalytic method? Should we abandon Freud's advice and align ourselves instead with an affective approach like Ferenczi's mutual analysis?

Greenberg (1995), who is *not* against self-disclosure in principle and has elsewhere (Greenberg, 1991) given examples of its usefulness, has presented the case of a patient who asked him for a relatively simple piece of information about whether he (Greenberg) had received a message from the patient that was left on his answering machine. Greenberg's illustration notes that withholding this simple piece of information (*not* disclosing) initiated a powerful and ultimately constructive and transformative interaction with the patient. In this instance, the analyst's refusal to self-disclose expressed and established his independent subjectivity better than disclosing would have.

Thus, I argue that analysts' freedom to use themselves fully, which includes both the option for increased self-disclosure and the choice not to disclose, provides the optimal conditions for both cognitive, interpretive understanding and affective, interpersonal engagement. To get along well in life, it is important to have flexibility, to keep one's options open. So too, for analysts, it is useful to have a flexible repertoire of interventions. Our theory should not constrain our analytic behavior so tightly that we eliminate self-disclosure from our repertoire, as Freud would have us do, for at times it can be a powerful therapeutic intervention. Neither, however, should our theory lead us to feel obliged to self-disclose compulsively, as Ferenczi did, in the mistaken belief that this is the only "honest" and "authentic" form of participation. As discussed in Chapter 5, intimacy requires both autonomy and connection. Theory should *not* restrict our choices; it should help us, at least retrospectively, to understand how and why we choose one option over another.

ON KNOWING AND BEING KNOWN

The psychoanalytic relationship is fundamentally paradoxical: at one and the same time it involves the patient and analyst in both a most personal, intimate, and spontaneous relation and a professional, reserved, and technical relation. It requires an honest and authentic engagement between two people, but, at the same time, as a fiduciary relationship, it demands a focus on the patient's experience that is different from the attention paid to the analyst's experience; and it requires the continual recognition that there is an imbalance of power and responsibility between patient and analyst. I have tried to capture this dialectic tension by balancing my exploration of mutuality with a recognition of the inevitability of asymmetry.

Hoffman (1994) describes the therapeutic process in terms of dialectical thinking. He focuses on movement between the analyst's more detached, reflective, and interpretive stance and more personal engagement with the patient. He characterizes the process as one of dialectical movement or tension between psychoanalytic discipline and reflective participation. The very dichotomy, however, between the personal and the technical, if drawn too far, is problematic. It is not so easy to decide when something is being done for personal or for professional reasons; indeed, the trend in contemporary psychoanalytic thought is more in the direction of claiming that the technical is always influenced by the personal. Psychoanalytic technique, as Renik (1993a) suggests is always irreducibly subjective.

When, for example, an analyst feels some hesitation in saying something to a patient, is this a personal reaction or a professional response? Is it an aspect of psychoanalytic technique that comes under the category of tact and timing, or is it a spontaneous, personally engaged, empathic response to the sensitivities of the other. Of course, it is all of these. Feminism has taught us that the personal is political; and, I would say, for psychoanalysts *the personal is technical and the technical is personal.* Our theory of technique cannot determine when, where, how, or what an analyst should disclose without taking into account the meaning of self-disclosure to the individual analyst. Self-disclosure is bound to have different meanings and different outcomes for analysts, depending on how personally comfortable they are with being seen and being known. As discussed in Chapter 6, Freud's rules of technique could never work for an analyst with Ferenczi's temperament, just as Ferenczi's affective approach, with its emphasis on mutuality, would never have suited an analyst with Freud's personality.

Just as children observe and study their parents' personalities, our analysands study ours. Children attempt to make contact with parents, and analysands with analysts, by reaching into the inner world of the other. They are powerfully motivated to penetrate into the center of their parents' and the analysts' selves. One state of mind inevitably seeks another state of mind; this is one aspect of what has been described as intersubjectivity (see Chapter 3). We also know, however, that people are rightfully reluctant to be so penetrated to the very center of their selves. Adults, children, analysands, parents, and analysts, all have a strong need to protect some aspects of themselves that need to remain private and reserved. We each have an essential, built-in desire for contact with the other (an object-seeking drive, for those who like that language), which includes two distinct aspects: the desire to know the other and the desire to be known by the other. In classical terms, these desires are often expressed by, but also reduced to, the component drives of scoptophilia and exhibitionism. I would emphasize the wish to reveal oneself to the other as well as the longing to find the essence of the other. In some families, this wish may be expressed concretely, through sexually exhibitionistic and scoptophilic fantasies or behaviors (Mitchell, 1988a).

In addition to these two complementary wishes—to know and be known—there is a contrasting set of wishes and needs. There is a strong desire to avoid contact with the other, to be hidden, protected, left alone. If infants can be shown to move toward objects in the earliest days of life, they can also be shown to move away from objects in the earliest days of life. Winnicott (1963) developed the theme of this conflict and distinguished between "pathological withdrawal and healthy central self-communication." He wrote, "Although healthy persons communicate and enjoy communicating, the other fact is equally true, that *each individual is an isolate, permanently non-communicating, permanently unknown, in fact unfound*" (p. 187, emphasis in original). Winnicott noted two trends: the need to communicate and the still more urgent need not to be found. Winnicott implied that the self plays a continual game of hide and seek with the other. Seen from this perspective, not only is resistance the negative side of the wish to express something, but also it becomes the positive side of the self's wish to remain elusive, to protect its autonomy (a conceptualization that in Chapter 6 we traced back to the work of Otto Rank). There seem to be natural pulls in both directions, toward and away from others. Here, too, we can break this tendency down into two parts: the wish to hide, to protect oneself by not being revealed to the other, and the complementary wish to avoid knowledge of the other, to avoid contact with the inner world of the other. A sexual analogy or metaphor might be the wish to penetrate the other and the wish to be penetrated by the other, versus the wish to avoid being penetrated and the fear or avoidance of penetrating the other.

Now, by extension to the analytic process, we have two people, analyst and analysand, each with both sets of these complementary and contradictory desires. The patient and the analyst each want to be known and to hide, and each also wants to know the other and to avoid knowledge of the other. Both the patient and the analyst are motivated toward isolation and toward relationship, toward autonomy and toward mutuality, toward agency and toward communion. But the traditional analytic situation splits up these pairs asymmetrically. The analyst is supposed to know the other but not be known by the other, and the analysand is supposed to be known by the other but not know the other. The patient on the couch is to be seen but not see, to be penetrated but not penetrate; the analyst is out of sight, seeing and knowing in the patient what the patient can not see and know, but the analyst remains unseen, unknown, anonymous, and impenetrable.

From a relational perspective, however, every aspect of the patient's and the analyst's behavior may be seen as a compromise among the conflicting motives that I have just described. (This is an important way in which relational theory is a theory of conflict, as was discussed in Chapter 2.) Patient and analyst are viewed as continually negotiating their mutually conflicted needs for intimacy and isolation (Pizer, 1992). Every association and every interpretation both reveals and conceals; each is an attempt to make contact and to avoid contact, to know the other and to avoid knowledge of the other. Greenberg (1995), making a similar observation, suggests that "if it is true that everything we do reveals something, it is equally true that everything we do conceals something else (p. 195). In the light of these observations, I should make clear that, when I wrote earlier that "self-revelation is *not* an option; it is an inevitability," I was speaking descriptively *not* prescriptively. Relative anonymity is also *not* an option, but an inevitability, since we are always concealing even while we are revealing! If it is inevitable that we will reveal aspects of ourselves, it is equally inevitable that we will conceal aspects of ourselves.

I propose that this constellation of complementary and contradictory desires may be useful in our consideration of the dilemmas posed by the analyst's purposeful or deliberate self-revelations. In these multilayered conflicts, we would notice that the analyst's purposely revealing something to the patient would activate complementary conflicts in both patient and analyst, since each is struggling to be known and not to be known and with desires to know the other and not to know the other. Psychoanalytic technique cannot be prescribed independent of the individual analyst's personality. There are analysts whose characters and dynamic conflicts around these issues of knowing and being known may encourage them to be less purposefully revealing, that is, to work in a more traditionally anonymous way, even while recognizing that self-revelations occur unconsciously and inadvertently all the time. There are other analysts whose character types make them more comfortable with a freer use of themselves and with more active use of self-disclosures. Add to this diversity among analysts that patients vary in regard to these conflicts as well, and the situation becomes enormously complex. The very expression, self-disclosure, is misleading in that it implies a cohesive self choosing to disclose the inner center of its being. In my discussion of intersubjectivity (Chapter 3), however, I suggested that intersubjectivity inevitably refers to the interplay of multiple selves and multiple others. From this perspective, when an analyst self-discloses, the question becomes which of the analyst's many selves is disclosing and to whom of the patient's multiple selves is it being disclosed?

SELF-DISCLOSURE AND THE ANALYST'S AUTHORITY

Purposeful self-disclosure by the analyst, just like an association by the patient, needs to be considered for what it expresses and for what it obscures. This is a point that is easy to overlook. Greenberg (1995) states that "both patient and analyst believe that when the analyst shares a personal thought or a feeling something has been given, and they collusively ignore what has been withheld" (p. 196). Because analysts are always viewed as carrying a certain measure of authority in the clinical situation, when they reveal something about themselves to patients there is an expectation that it will be accepted as the truth (Hoffman, 1983). For this reason, a potential danger of the analyst's self-disclosure is that it may foreclose further investigation because the disclosure is taken at face value as the analyst's authoritative truth.

In a radical move away from traditional Freudian technique and extending the early interpersonal position of Irwin Singer, Renik (1995) argues that not only should we disregard the principle of analytic anonymity, but we must actively and forcefully contradict it. He argues that by not self-disclosing, by maintaining the classical position of anonymity, we solicit and accept our patients' idealizations of us, even though we claim that we are committed to analyzing this idealization. Renik suggests that rather than aim at anonymity and personal ambiguity, analysts make their thinking about the nature of their participation with patients as available to their patients as they can. He believes that we have avoided doing this because we are motivated to maintaining our position as authorities even as we claim that psychoanalysis eschews such a suggestive influence on patients.

In striking contrast, however, is Lawrence Epstein's (1995) interpersonal position that we should not "demystify" ourselves for our patients, rather that we should establish the optimal conditions for the patient to demystify us themselves. Epstein's concern is that, under the rubric of establishing our own subjectivity, we may instead impose our subjectivity on the patient, rather than allow patients to discover and uncover our subjectivity as and when they are ready. The implication of Epstein's remarks is that the analyst's ambiguity may serve a useful purpose. The imposition of the analyst's subjectivity too quickly in the analysis may limit patients' attempts to experiment with the full range of their perceptions of the analyst. It is a sign of the times that here we have a well-known Freudian analyst arguing *for* self-disclosure and a highly respected interpersonalist suggesting caution.

Consider an illustration provided by Renik (1995):

> A patient had the idea that I was being extremely gentle and careful with him the prior hour because I was afraid of hurting him. I responded that I was not aware of any particular concern on my part, and that, therefore, from my point of view at least, the patient has his own reasons for imagining that I consider him so fragile. I feel it is useful to make explicit my own perception of my emotional state during the hour in question, since it is partly upon that perception that I base my hypothesis that the patient has an ulterior motive for experiencing me as gentle and cautious [p. 485].

While I am sympathetic to Renik's desire to establish self-disclosure as a legitimate analytic intervention, I see this example as highly problematic. Unfortunately, this case illustrates the danger that the analyst's view of his or her own participation with the patient will be taken by both analyst and patient as the authoritative truth about the nature of their interaction. Renik asserts that he presents his idea to the patient only as his own perception of his own emotional experience. Nevertheless, on the basis of Renik's self-perception the patient is encouraged to turn his attention back upon himself and his own "ulterior motives" for distorting his perception of the analyst. This has the potential to *stop* further inquiry by the patient into the analyst's subjectivity. In his very effort to demystify and deidealize the analyst, Renik ends up asserting his own authority as the judge of the quality of his participation with the patient, even while officially disclaiming that he is acting as the arbiter of truth.

Rather than saying to a patient, "I'm not aware of feeling overly concerned about your fragility and therefore you must have other reasons for thinking that I am so concerned," I suggest saying, "I'm not aware of feeling overly concerned about your fragility, but you seem to think that I am. What am I doing that is giving you that impression? Perhaps you are picking up on something that I haven't noticed."

Analyzing the impact of any self-revelation, deliberate or not, becomes complicated because the patient's perceptions of the analyst are likely to be unconscious. As part of our traditional job description —to make the unconscious conscious—we have some responsibility to help patients know consciously whatever it is about us that they may have noticed unconsciously. Helping the patient become aware of unconscious perceptions of the analyst is complicated because whatever it is that a patient has learned about us, we may or may not be conscious of ourselves. In fact, one reason a patient may keep it unconscious is out of fear that acknowledging it would create anxiety in the analyst. Therefore, as they may well have done in childhood with parents, and as they may well do in other areas of their life, patients do not let themselves know what they know about us, because to know about us would make us too anxious. This is essentially Sullivan's (1953) view of the origins of selective inattention.

But how can I, the analyst, help the patient become conscious of something about me when I myself am still not conscious of whatever it is that my patient knows? In Chapter 3, I suggested that the analyst develop the technique of pursuing the patient's perceptions of the analytic relationship, or what I called the patient's experience of the analyst's subjectivity. This was an extension of Racker's (1968) suggestion that, among the best avenues to the investigation of the patient's transference is the pursuit of the patient's fantasies about the analyst's countertransference. If you keep searching for the patient's experience of your own subjectivity, however, the patient may soon demand to know more about your subjectivity directly from you. By focusing on the patient's experience of the analyst's subjectivity, you are likely to stir up conflicts in both the patient and yourself about knowing and being known. It is one thing to not reveal much to your patient when you have not focused the analytic lens on this area of inquiry, but, once you do, the patient may be unable to tolerate not receiving any response, and it may feel tortorous to you to not provide some response. Furthermore, the very act of inquiring into a patient's perceptions of your subjectivity is likely to reveal a good deal about you. Included in what patients know about their analysts, but that they may not know that they know, is their recognition of the analyst's conflicts about being known.

Self-revelation is not a technique. It is not a new relational gimmick. It is simply one among many ways of being with a patient, no longer taboo, but a technical and personal option—an option that always reveals and conceals, making the analyst and the patient both more and less accessible and, therefore, an option that always must be scrutinized and reflected upon by both participants. We must not simply contradict standard technique, as Renik (1995) proposes, and substitute the principle of self-disclosure for the principle of anonymity. This kind of simple reversal of principles does not leave us enough technical flexibility. We should not replicate Ferenczi's mistake of reacting against Freudian anonymity by going to the opposite extreme of self-disclosure as a standard technique. Self-disclosure should, instead, be viewed as one technical and personal option to be used with clinical discretion and mutual reflection.

To whatever degree self-revelation is done in the deliberate attempt to be the good object, to that degree it becomes too much a technique and loses some of the benefit that resides in its spontaneity and authenticity. As Bromberg (1994) has written regarding self-disclosure:

> Its usefulness to the analytic process is organized by the quality of its genuineness as a human act, particularly the degree to which the analyst is free of internal pressure (conscious or unconscious) to prove his honesty or trustworthiness as a technical maneuver designed to counter the patient's mistrust. The analyst's self-disclosure must be what Symington (1983) calls an "act of freedom" in which the analyst comfortably retains his right to not disclose or, if he does choose to disclose, to claim his own privacy and set his own boundaries [p. 540].

It is this technical and personal freedom for the analyst that, I think, is the most advantageous position to work from, and, in preserving our options deliberately to share or withhold our experiences, we maintain the optimal degree of asymmetry. As we saw in Chapter 6, it was precisely this freedom that Ferenczi lost in his clinical experiments with mutual analysis.

VARIETIES OF SELF-DISCLOSURE

One reason it is so difficult to generalize about self-disclosure is that the term refers to so many different activities. The following is hardly an exhaustive list, but it portrays just how great is the range of activities that fall under the heading self-disclosure:

(1) There can be self-disclosures about what the analyst is thinking while with the patient. A simple example would be telling the patient about the analyst's associations to a particular dream image that the patient has reported.

(2) There can be self-disclosure of the analyst's immediate affective response while he or she is with the patient; for example, telling or showing a patient that one is feeling sad or annoyed.

(3) Some self-disclosures involve sharing with the patient more of one's thinking and one's affective reactions regarding the interaction between the patient and analyst; for example, telling a

patient who has noticed that the analyst is acting more distant and removed in the past week some thoughts about what has occurred between them as well as what the analyst is consciously aware of feeling and discussing what the analyst suspects may have led to this behavior on his or her own part. Another example would be telling a patient about the way in which the analyst is conflicted about how to approach a particular issue in the analysis.

(4) Some self-disclosures concern the analyst's thoughts about the patient that occur outside of the treatment setting altogether; for example, telling a patient that you thought of him or her when you read an article in that morning's newspaper. A more extreme instance of this type of self-disclosure would be the analyst's sharing a dream that he or she had about the patient. I call this extreme because the material being disclosed may be much more complex and ambiguous than sharing other information.

(5) There can be self-disclosures of why the analyst feels as he or she does, incorporating genetic or characterological determinants that stand outside the current analytic interaction.

(6) There can be self-disclosures in response to simple objective questions, such as a patient's questioning the analyst's age or marital status, or whether the analyst has children, or what kind of car the analyst drives.

(7) Each of these categories refers to direct and purposeful self-disclosures that we must, in turn, distinguish from all the implicit or less directly expressed self-revelations that occur all the time in analysis.

(8) Yet another distinction that transcends all these others is the difference between sharing a thought, feeling, or experience that the analyst has already thought about and processed versus sharing any of these things more spontaneously before the analyst has had a chance to process them. (See Burke and Tansey, 1991, for a discussion about this in relation to the work of Ehrenberg, 1992.)

(9) Another distinction has to do with whether the analyst volunteers a piece of self-disclosure or reveals something only after the patient has brought the topic up and directly asked the analyst for the information. (Maroda, 1991, uses this as the single most important criterion for determining when to disclose countertransference.)

(10) One can also distinguish between types of self-disclosure on the basis of the content of the analyst's experience. For example, we might choose to make distinctions between self-disclosures with

aggressive content versus disclosures with sexual content versus disclosures about other affects.

In regard to the last distinction, Davies (1994) discusses an incident in which she told a male patient that she had sexual fantasies about him. The report of this controversial intervention provoked a very heated exchange in which Gabbard (1994) suggested that the disclo-sure of the analyst's sexual feelings should be considered in a class by itself and should not be revealed to patients under any, or almost any, circumstances. Both Gorkin (1987) and Maroda (1991), who take liberal positions regarding revealing feelings to patients, are quite cautious about revealing sexual countertransference. Barratt (1994), in his discussion of Ehrenberg's (1992) *The Intimate Edge*, points out that, in spite of her frequent illustrations of sharing her emotional responses to patients with them, she never gives any example of disclosing to a patient that she was sexually aroused by them. He concludes from this observation that "there are assumptions and limits to this sort of clini-cal method but that the character of the method requires that they go uninterrogated" (p. 279). It is just this sort of interrogation of the assumptions and limits inherent in the clinical method that is being undertaken in this chapter, as well as in Davies's (1994) paper, and in the discussions that followed by Benjamin (1994) and Gabbard (1994).

Another characteristic that distinguishes between types of self-disclosure has less to do with the content of the disclosure and more to do with the manner in which the disclosure is made. Some disclosures (or interpretations or other interventions) are made in such a way that they close off a topic, whereas other disclosures are made in such a way that they open up further dialogue. It seems to me that the difference here may lie in whether whatever is said is said with an air of certainty and authority or whether it is said in the spirit of exploration and play. Winnicott (1954), for example, was known to urge caution regarding the analyst's intrusiveness into the psychoanalytic environment. Bollas (1987) points out nevertheless, that as a clinician, Winnicott worked in a highly idiomatic way, verbally squiggling with his patients back and forth. Bollas asks how it is possible to reconcile Winnicott the clinical theorist advocating unobtrusiveness and Winnicott the clinical analyst who is so much himself as a presence in the analysis. Bollas suggests that the answer lies in Winnicott's attitude toward the thoughts he was sharing with patients. He treated his own thoughts and interpretations as

"subjective objects . . . rather than as official psychoanalytic decodings of the person's unconscious life. The effect of his attitude is crucial, as his interpreta-

tions were meant to be played with—kicked around, mulled over, torn to pieces
—rather than regarded as the official version of the truth [p. 206].

One's attitude toward one's own thoughts, feelings, associations and
interpretations is likely to be more important than the content. Whatever the analyst discloses, it is the analyst's attitude toward the disclosure that determines whether the intervention leads the patient to feel
increasingly safe or increasingly in danger.

Among the previous attempts to distinguish a variety of categories of
self-disclosure, perhaps the most persuasive suggestion was put forth by
Searles (1975) in his disagreement with those interpersonal analysts,
like Singer (1968), who argued in favor of a marked reduction of the
analyst's anonymity. Searles wrote that in his practice "while being
relatively freely revealing of feelings and fantasies I experience during
the analytic session itself, I tell patients very little of my life outside the
office" (p. 458). This distinction between disclosures about what is
transpiring *in the session* and those about the therapist's life *outside* of
the treatment has become one of the key distinctions in pursuing the
question of whether or not to self-disclose.

Basescu (1987, 1990) asserts that disclosing one's personal reactions
to what is occurring in the treatment situation is the most relevant,
the most important, and the least controversial area of self-disclosure. Wachtel (1993) cites a number of reasons why this type of
revelation is beneficial for the analytic process, particularly that
to share one's own reactions to the patient and to what the patient
has said demonstrates that one has been listening and that one
is emotionally present and responding to the patient. Wachtel argues
that, by sharing one's emotional response with the patient, one
demonstrates that the patient has had an emotional impact on one,
which may be precisely what the patient needs to realize. Most
important, Wachtel argues that sharing one's emotional reactions with
the patient may promote a greater understanding of the patient's experience. The analyst's self-revelations may contribute to the patient's
gaining a better understanding of the interpersonal context of the
transference.

While Wachtel (1993) agrees with others who have promoted the
use of self-disclosure when the content of the disclosure seems directly
tied to the immediacy of the analytic process, he also suggests that the
very distinction between "inside" and "outside" easily breaks down. He
suggests that, even if the analyst reveals something to the patient that
does not seem to be about what is happening in the immediacy of the
therapeutic interaction, still, on reflection, it is likely that what was
revealed relates in some meaningful way to what is going on in the

moment. Thus, even material external to the analysis may be usefully utilized.

Consider, for example, the recommendations made by Karen Maroda (1991) in her book *The Power of Countertransference*. This is a marvelous and in certain respects groundbreaking work in which the author argues forcefully for modifying clinical practice in the direction of the analyst's freer use of immediate affective responsiveness. Maroda's call for the clinical use of self-disclosure is the most thoughtful, systematic, and thoroughgoing of any analytic theorist's to date. She suggests that analysts first share only their immediate affective experience and only later in the analysis reveal the origins of these feelings in their own personal life. In other words, she advocates, first, the disclosure of the analyst's countertransference; second, the analysis of the impact of this disclosure on the transference–countertransference matrix; and finally, usually only in the termination phase of analysis, the analyst's deliberate analysis of the countertransference in terms of its genetic and characterological origins. Her overarching guideline is that the analyst should disclose countertransference only at the patient's request or following careful consultation with and approval by the patient. I think that these guidelines are extremely useful clinically.

Nevertheless, I am concerned that what are meant as guidelines may be taken as rules, and that this mistaken use may prevent further useful clinical exploration. For example, I have worked with patients who I feel benefited greatly from my willingness to reveal something private about myself, including the origins in my personal life of a particular reaction, very early in their analysis. Furthermore, Maroda's distinctions imply a patient who will wait until the termination stage of an analysis before probing the analyst about a countertransference difficulty. My experience, perhaps because of my focus on the patient's experience of the analyst's subjectivity, is that some patients will push me to uncover this with them much earlier on in the analytic work. Also, Maroda indicates that in the late stages of the analysis the analyst may reveal more of his or her countertransference to the patient, but my attention is, following Ferenczi, more to the patient's implicit interpretations to me about aspects of the countertransference that I may not be conscious of. In other words, Maroda seems more concerned with analysts' disclosure of what they know about their own countertransference, whereas my own emphasis is more on patient's helping their analysts come to recognize aspects of their own participation that they were not aware of. Of course, both processes operate in tandem.

Maroda also suggests that self-revelations be made only after the analyst has figured out and processed the disclosure's likely implications on the patient. I think that, once again, this may be a good guide-line, especially for teaching student analysts, but my inclination is to agree with Ehrenberg (1992) that sometimes it is best to respond more immediately and spontaneously, without first processing one's reac-tions, and then to analyze with the patient what the impact on the analytic process has been.

As can be seen from just these few questions that I am raising regarding Maroda's guidelines, perhaps the most important thing that can be said about the subject of self-disclosure is that, once it is opened up for discussion as an important clinical question, it becomes obvious that there is indeed a good deal to be discussed. When self-disclosure is dismissed from consideration as blurring professional boundaries, or when it is considered a violation of the analytic frame, then it becomes impossible to think through any of these distinctions or technical ques-tions. Although I have some reservations, for example, about some of Maroda's clinical guidelines, nevertheless, I believe that I have a good deal in common with her; both of us believe in the inherent mutuality of the psychoanalytic process; both of us value the analyst's affective responsiveness, and both of us advocate the utility of at least some forms of self-disclosure. More important, Maroda, Gorkin, Ehrenberg, Tansey and Burke, Goldstein, Bollas, Greenberg, Mitchell, Renik, and Wachtel, while each approaching the topic somewhat differently, are all struggling with how to approach self-disclosure in a way that promotes the analytic process, protects patients from abuse, and preserves the analytic space as a place that predominantly serves the patient's therapeutic needs. I believe that deciding what to select to share with patients from the endless stream of associations and feelings is an individual decision, one that varies from analyst to analyst, from patient to patient, and from moment to moment in any analysis. I think that these attempts at categorization are a useful first step in promoting clinical research and investigation.

OBJECTIONS TO SELF-REVELATION ON THE GROUND THAT IT DISTRACTS FROM THE FOCUS ON THE PATIENT'S EXPERIENCE

One of the most frequently raised objections to self-revelation by analysts is that any expression of the analyst's subjectivity is a distrac-tion from what should be an exclusive focus on the patient's experi-ence. Colleagues point out that not maintaining this attention on the patient likely stems from the analyst's own needs for attention and that its occurrence in the analytic situation is a reenactment of the very problem that many patients suffered as children, their parents, too, having forced them to adapt to their (the parents') needs. Thus, for the analyst to shift the focus of attention from the patient's experience to the analyst's is to intrude or impinge on what should be the patient's potential space; the result is, at best, false self-compliance. This argument is strengthened even further when analysts point out that often our patients are narcissistically vulnerable, do not have sufficiently developed object relations, and are not yet capable of the sophisticated level of relating necessary for true mutuality or intersubjectivity. On this basis, the argument is made for extreme caution with regard to self-revelation.

Of course, we would all agree, on professional and ethical grounds, that in doing analysis we must aim to work in the long-range interests of our patients. That said, there is room for legitimate difference about the extent to which the analyst's personal exposure and involvement can be in the patient's long-term interest. Patients need to be given space to make use of the analysis in the ways they need, but the most important issue is the ambiguity surrounding what constitutes giving patients as much space as possible. First, even if one accepts that too much self-exposure by the analyst may be destructive, there is still considerable room for some self-disclosure to be constructively utilized. Second, there are limitations to the developmental argument just put forth, which emphasizes the destructiveness that ensues when parents demand that their children meet the parents needs. Wachtel (1993) argues that

> totally selfless child rearing, in which the parent's own needs and feelings are kept out of the picture, is not only impossible but undesirable. Children need to *know* their parents, even as they need to be known by them. The foundation of the capacity both for intimacy and for personal identity require a sense of the parent as another experiencing being and as an active agent with wishes of his or her own [p. 213].

I would quickly add, however, that children also need *not* to know aspects of their parents lives and also need to have aspects of themselves that remain unknown to their parents. We may extrapolate from this developmental model that, similarly, patients not only need to be understood and known by their analysts but also need to know and understand a good deal about the character and interpersonal relations of their analysts. In turn, patients also need to be given room *not* to know aspects of their analysts and also need room for private space where their analysts may not know them. Maroda's (1991) technical recommendation that, before self-disclosing, analysts always follow the patients' lead by directly asking patients if they want to know the analysts' reactions is an attempt to deal with this concern. While I generally agree with this suggestion, as with all guidelines, there may be exceptions; even Maroda suggests that a patient's use of projective identification may be an implicit call for the analyst to self-disclose. For example, there are times when an analyst may well decide that a patient should be confronted with the analyst's reactions even when the patient would prefer to be "left alone." This clinical judgment can be a difficult, but important, clinical decision and the "right choice" may be different, depending on factors in the patient or stage of treatment and varying from one analyst to another. Furthermore, patients' statements that they either do or do not want to know something about their analysts are likely, upon examination, to turn out not to fully reflect their desires.

Consider the following example provided by Gabbard and Wilkinson (1994) in their discussion of the use of countertransference with borderline patients. Ms. N is agitated and has been intimidating her therapist, Dr. M, with threats of destroying his office alternating with threats of suicide. She is raging that therapy is useless and her therapist worthless. Ultimately, Dr. M tells her, "Now I feel like hell, I'm concerned. I think you're making me feel the hell in you" (p. 147). Following this self-disclosure, the patient is reported to calm down and for the first time to feel genuine sadness. According to the authors, by sharing his emotional response with Ms. N, Dr. M identified and modified the transference–countertransference interaction that had been cocreated between them. Through the use of what Gabbard and Wilkinson call "clinical honesty" (p. 143), by disclosing his own tortuous impotence and rage, Dr. M reclaimed his self as distinct from Ms. N and thus furthered the clinical work. Sometimes analysts should not wait for patients to ask for their reactions or feelings. There are times when analysts need to confront patients directly with their own affective reactions, whether or not patients are asking for this feedback.

SELF-DISCLOSURE AND THE ANXIETY OF THE ANALYST

This brings me to a further argument against self-disclosure that I would like to address. Gill (1983b) suggested that when analysts do reveal things about themselves they need to analyze the patient's experience of such a report. He said that it is best to be conservative about self-revelations because they may tend to shut off further inquiry into the patient's experience, not least because such inquiry might lead to the exposure of something in the analyst that he would rather not know about (Gill, 1983b, p. 228).

Wachtel (1993) elaborates on this point and suggests that the asymmetry of the analytic situation, and the analyst's freedom not to reveal his or her own associations, serves as a protective measure allowing the analyst to work in an atmosphere of relatively less anxiety because there is less of a personal threat about his or her own exposure. He argues that ultimately preserving the analyst's right to privacy serves the patient, since every time we expose something shameful or anxiety laden in a patient, if we felt the need to expose something similar in ourselves, then we would have to be paragons of strength and virtue to do this work. Because we are not such paragons, he argues, we need the protection of the asymmetric structure to protect us from our own anxiety so that we can pursue matters wherever they lead knowing that we will not be personally exposed. Hoffman too (1994) elaborates on this point. He suggests that

> regard for the *analyst* is fostered partly by the fact that the patient knows so much *less* about him or her than the analyst knows about the patient. The factor of relative anonymity contributes not only to the irrational aspect of the analyst's power but also to a more rational aspect. The analyst is in a relatively protected position, after all, one that is likely to promote the most tolerant, understanding, and generous aspects of his or her personality [p. 199].

The point being made by these writers is that it is precisely the protection offered the analyst by the asymmetric position of relative anonymity that allows the analyst to function at his or her best as an analyst, thus providing an interactional basis for the patient's idealization of the analyst (Hoffman, 1994).

A major source of conceptual and semantic confusion has been the equating of the analyst's subjectivity with self-revelation. *It seems to me that sometimes the very act of choosing not to disclose may be the best way to assert and express one's own subjectivity.* We should not assume that purposely to reveal some content about oneself is more self-revealing than to not reveal that very content. Not revealing one aspect of ourselves may be a forceful revelation of another aspect of ourselves. For example, answering a patient's question directly, while seeming to be an act of self-disclosure, may very well be an effort (conscious or unconscious) to conceal one's anxieties or to conceal one's hostility. Honesty, truth, openness, and genuineness are always highly ambiguous. Subjectivity is not a simple or singular essence like "true self" (Mitchell, 1993a).

Consider, for example, a patient who asks why the analyst began a session a few minutes late. The analyst, consciously trying to be open and honest with the patient, answers him, saying that she was sorry for the lateness but she was with another patient who was in a crisis. The patient immediately responds by feeling hurt and depressed. He tells the analyst that she must be "really angry" with him. At first the analyst is surprised and confused. Her self-experience was that she was trying to be direct and open with the patient, and she was not at all aware of feeling angry. The patient, however, points out that his perception is that the analyst told him about her involvement with the other patient in order to convey that the other patient's problems were more urgent and important than his own. He feels that the analyst told him this so quickly, without the usual inquiry into what meaning the question had for him, because she wanted to rub his face in the fact that she was so busy with other patients. On reflection, the analyst considered that there might well be some truth to what the patient said and together they were able to move forward.

Consider, however, that the patient might not have been able to confront the analyst with this observation. What of the patient who quickly suppressed this thought and accepted the analyst's self-perception as kind, caring, and well meaning? These kinds of interactions can sometimes be resolved and prove productive; they also may be unnecessarily hurtful to patients, and, perhaps most dangerously, they may lend themselves to imposing the analyst's conscious self-portrayal on the patient. The point is that self-disclosures, even those made with the analyst's immediate sense of being open, honest, and direct, express a great deal that is not intended by the analyst and always both obscure and reveal the analyst's subjectivity, which is always more complex than the analyst can convey through a specific self-disclosure. This complexity should not lead to the conclusion that one should not self-disclose, but rather to the understanding that the meanings of self-disclosures should not be taken as any more simple and self-evident than the patient's associations.

It seems clear to me that one aspect of maturity as an analyst is the recognition that much that we might prefer to keep hidden is indeed exposed and that our patients, if we are working well, may come to see sides of us that we have still not admitted to ourselves. While I do not want to idealize our personal qualities or self-analytical capacities as analysts, it does seem to me that to do this work well analysts must have some fair capacity and willingness to expose aspects of themselves that make them anxious and to contain this anxiety sufficiently to work with this material in the long-term interest of their patients and themselves. *I am suggesting that one way of thinking about the quality of our "expertise" is that it is part of our function as analysts to allow ourselves to be and (through our own "training analysis") to prepare ourselves to be emotionally vulnerable with our patients.* I agree with Levenson, who said that we analysts are paid to be vulnerable (cited by Hirsch, 1992).

It is not that I think analysts can reveal themselves and not get lost in the transference—countertransference tangle; it is just that I think being lost in that tangle is valuable and that patient and analyst may together be able to work their way out of it. Part of our analytic exper-tise lies in our disciplined skill at listening to patients' associations for feedback about their perceptions of our own participation. At times, our patients may be better able to help us understand how we have been participating with them when we are willing to share with them some of our thoughts, feelings, and reactions. That our capacities have limits is clear, but anonymity provides no safe escape from participa-tion. *If in the classical model the idea is to be analyzed well enough to keep one's own problems out of the way, in a relational model, I suggest, the analyst needs to be analyzed well enough to tolerate some degree of anxiety about having a good deal of his or her character exposed and scrutinized by patients.* We need to become comfortable with our conflicted desires to know and not to know the other, to be known and to avoid being known by the other.

Our understanding of insight has changed radically over the years. What we think of as insight now is not limited to an understanding of what things mean to us, what our associations mean, what our dreams mean, or what our symptoms mean, as if that meaning existed in our minds alone. Now we focus more of our attention on understanding the interpersonal impact that we have on others and the impact of others on us. Levenson (1983) has characterized this as a shift from asking the patient "What does it mean?" to asking "What's going on around here?" (p. ix). What is the patient doing to me now, and how am I participating in what is going on? I may be able to figure out what a dream symbol means to me, intrapsychically, but I cannot gain insight into how another person has a particular impact on me without know-ing something about that other person, and, similarly, I cannot gain insight into how I affect other people if I am not able to observe a good deal about them. This type of insight is contextual and interpersonal. It requires that two people know important things about each other. It is inevitably two-directional and mutual.

Patients gain insight into their analysts as an essential aspect of acquiring knowledge of themselves. Since the self exists in relation to others, insight into oneself must include insight into others. My insight into myself must include an awareness of my impact on others and of their impact on me. In facilitating my patients' awareness of their impact on me and of my impact on them, I must be prepared to be studied, affected, and analyzed by them in the service of *their* analytic needs. Self-revelation, as one form of technical and personal participa-tion, may both clarify and obscure the nature of the analytic interaction. No technical formula—neither the rule of anonymity nor the compulsion to self-disclose—can eliminate the need for the analyst to make a personal and professional decision, in each instance, on a moment-to-moment basis about what course of action is most compatible with the balance of forces between the patient and the analyst regarding knowing and being known, hiding and avoiding contact with the other, danger and safety, and in maintaining the optimal tension between a personal and technical relationship. It is the resultant of these forces in both participants that will determine whether and how any intervention will further the analytic process.

CONCLUSION: SELF-DISCLOSURE, AND AUTHENTICITY

Once upon a time, many decades ago, psychoanalysts had certain commonly accepted fundamental beliefs about doing analysis. They knew that analysts should be anonymous, a blank screen; that analysts should refrain from being too gratifying, and that analysts should remain neutral, that they should not respond contingently to the patient's transference. As analysts have questioned some of the assumptions underlying these technical recommendations, and especially as they have downplayed the importance of insight alone and instead highlighted the importance of the relationship, they have been tempted to abandon these rules and guidelines. To some, it seems that what really matters is connecting with the patient in an intense, personal engagement, an affectively responsive relationship, an existential encounter.

There is a strong tendency to move from one extreme to another, to shift between a view of analysis as a personal encounter in which rules and guidelines are obstacles and hindrances and a view of analysis as a technical and somewhat impersonal, codified and more restricted procedure that includes a narrowly defined therapeutic alliance. My task in this chapter has been to think through the question of self-disclosure without falling into either of these two traps for too long. I do not agree with the more conservative position that analysts should practically never reveal anything about themselves. Nor am I altogether comfortable with the "anything goes" mentality implying that analysts can say or do anything as long as it is "analyzed" or talked about. As Inderbitzen and Levy (1994) have noted, not everything is "grist for the mill." While analysts may try to analyze everything, not everything is analyzable (p. 764).

Mitchell (1995) takes a similar position in contrasting the interpersonal and the Kleinian positions on interaction in psychoanalysis.

Mitchell views the Kleinians as emphasizing the analyst's restraint and silent processing of affective responses, containing the countertransference, and using it to form an appropriate interpretation. By contrast, Mitchell depicts interpersonal analysts as more likely to express their immediate affective reactions directly in the form of self-disclosures. Mitchell attempts some reconciliation between these two extremes by suggesting that there are advantages and disadvantages to each. He likes the elements of spontaneity, freedom, and emotional honesty offered by the interpersonal school, but values the countertransference containment and restrained affective processing of the Kleinians. In thinking through the advantages of the Kleinian method, Mitchell points out that, when an analyst discloses a particular feeling to a patient, the feeling may represent a dissociated aspect of the patient (put into the analyst through projective identification). By disclosing the feeling to the patient, the analyst may be reinforcing the patient's dissociation of the feeling in himself or herself. Mitchell suggests that, by containing the feeling rather then by expressing it directly, the analyst may encourage patients to own the feeling as their own.

The implication of Mitchell's argument is that, by containing, holding, processing, and digesting their immediate affective experiences, analysts transcend these momentary individual reactions and gain a better understanding of the place of these feelings in the wider context of their long-term interaction with patients. He writes, "Analytic reflection forces an attention on other features of the analyst's feelings about the patient than may be in the immediate forefront at any particular moment" (Mitchell, 1993a, p. 146). An impulsive reaction is not necessarily more *authentic* than a restrained and considered response: "Authenticity in the analyst has less to do with saying everything than in the genuineness of what actually is said" (p. 146).

While I am in complete agreement with Mitchell that authenticity should not be equated with the compulsive need to speak impulsively to one's patients, the problem of authenticity is enormously complex. After all, is it really any easier to determine whether what is said is "genuine" than it is to determine what is "authentic?" One analyst's authenticity and spontaneity is another analyst's impulsiveness and self-indulgence. What feels to one analyst like disciplined restraint and the holding and processing of feelings may feel to another analyst like "sitting on one's feelings," being overly constrained, emotionally withholding, or personally unengaged, or falling back on authority. Mitchell wisely suggests a combination of the two approaches to balance thoughtful restraint and discipline with the vitality of spontaneity and free emotional expressiveness.

While traditionally an analyst was expected to maintain a baseline of relative (if not extreme) anonymity, more recently suggestions have been made that doing so may be a hinderance to effective analytic work. Lehrer (1994), for example, has suggested that "humane responsiveness and self-disclosure regarding the therapeutic interaction may prove to be a more constructive baseline" for conducting an analysis (p. 514). I do not believe that there is any single right way to conduct an analysis, nor do I think that there is a "correct" amount of self-disclosure that is optimal. Lehrer's phrase "humane responsiveness and self-disclosure," by tying together these two terms, may suggest that it is inhumane *not* to respond or self-disclose, and I certainly do *not* believe that this is always the case. It may be that for some analysts a baseline of relative anonymity is most comfortable, but it is important that even these analysts be flexible enough to deviate from this baseline sometimes, with some patients. There may be some analysts for whom it is more comfortable, and more effective, to maintain a baseline of relative responsiveness and self-disclosure regarding the therapeutic interaction. But for these analysts too it is important to be flexible to deviate from this baseline and to maintain some private space.

Whatever decision is made in a given case, and whatever style is most compatible with a given analyst's personality, it needs to remain open to reflection and analysis by both participants. Neither technical style is more humane or more clinically effective than the other. There are too many variables to consider to reach a definite solution that works well for everyone. I believe that this is one aspect of what Ferenczi (1928) had in mind when describing "the elasticity of psychoanalytic technique." Among the factors to consider in the analyst's decision regarding when and how much to self-disclose are the relative balance of conflicts about knowing and being known, in both the patient and the analyst.

What is most exciting about contemporary developments in theoretical and clinical psychoanalysis is the new openness to pluralism and diversity. There are many effective ways to do psychoanalysis, not just one. There are many technical choices that analysts make, and each of us may choose differently and still be able to conduct analysis effectively, if our theoretical and technical approach is compatible with or complementary to who we are. I do not believe that we have arrived at a final unified approach to psychoanalytic technique, and I hope we never do! A theory of technique that *requires* self-disclosure (that is, disclosure beyond the inevitable) is just as limiting as a theory that bans it. There are no right answers about what an analyst should self-disclose, what should be disclosed, or when to disclose. There are no answers that are independent of the individual patient, nor, more importantly, of the analyst's character. It is for this reason that my technical suggestion is openended and nonspecific. I believe that the question of the degree and nature of the analyst's deliberate self-revelation is open to resolution within the context of each unique psychoanalytic situation. No theory of technique can transcend the analyst's unique character. I think that there are very fine analysts who seldom use self-disclosure purposefully and very fine analysts who frequently use it. A theory of technique cannot dictate self-disclosure without considering what it means to the individual analyst, let alone, what it means to the patient and to the unique analytic dyad.

| Coda

Heinrich Racker (1968) wrote what may be described as the "anthem" of contemporary relational psychoanalysis:

> The first distortion of truth in "the myth of the analytic situation" is that analysis is an interaction between a sick person and a healthy one. The truth is that it is an interaction between two personalities, . . . each personality has its internal and external dependencies, anxieties, and pathological defenses; each is also a child with his internal parents; and each of these whole personalities—that of the analysand and that of the analyst—responds to every event of the analytic situation [p. 132].

This is, for very good reason, an often cited quotation, for it sums up much of the essence of the principle of mutuality that is fundamental to the relational model in psychoanalysis. Racker drew our attention to a number of principles here, including that psychoanalysis is an interaction between two people, who each respond to every event in the analytic situation. That is to say, Racker viewed both members of the analytic couple as being participants in the interaction. Furthermore, Racker refers to the mutuality of neurotic interaction between patient and analyst in his insistence that neither is fully healthy, rational, or adult in his or her functioning.

In a less well-known footnote to this famous passage Racker noted:

> It is important to be aware of this "equality" because there is otherwise great danger that certain remnants of the "patriarchal order" will contaminate the analytic situation. The dearth of scientific study of countertransference is an expression of a "social inequality" in the analyst-analysand society and points to the need for "social reform"; . . . [p. 132n].

In Racker's prose we can hear the reverberations of the democratization of society and of the emergent feminist critique that has come to play an important role in the development of relational theories. Racker recognized and warned us of the dangers of polarizing the analyst and analysand with respect to their health and their capacities to judge reality. He recognized the issues of power, dominance, and authority that are at play between them. When Racker wrote of "equality" between patient and analyst, I believe that he used quotation marks because he did not really mean equality but, rather, the mutual containment of health and neurosis by both the analyst and the patient. Edgar Levenson, the best known contemporary interpersonal analyst, has stated that Racker's object-relational position and Sullivan's (1953) interpersonal dictum that "we are all more simply human than otherwise" (p. 32) "converge in a concept of psychoanalysis as a mutual, respectful exploration of a joint reality" (Levenson, 1987a, p. 214).

Similarly, McLaughlin (1981), a well-respected and senior Freudian analyst, wrote that the traditional view of transference reinforces a model of psychoanalysis that differentiates sharply between a "patient with psychopathology and a physician with a cure" (p. 642). Psychic reality and objective reality become split; transference, psychic reality, and the infantile are attributed to the patient, and objectivity, external reality, maturity, and health are assigned to the analyst. One can see in this brief sampling of Freudian, interpersonal, and Kleinian thinking how a relational position that emphasizes mutuality can transcend narrow political and theoretical affiliations.

Both the shift from drive theory to relational theory (Greenberg and Mitchell, 1983) and the movement from an epistemology of objectivism to constructivism (Hoffman, 1991) have taken place in the wider context of social, political, and economic changes in our larger society. PreWorld War I, Europe, where psychoanalysis was born, was a far more authoritarian time and place than are the societies in which psychoanalysis is now practiced. Social changes in the past century have increased the likelihood that such authority will be challenged and scrutinized. The notion of an objective, "neutral" observer has been called into question on epistemological grounds. Even in such a hard and exact science as physics, Heisenberg and Einstein demonstrated that the position of the observer and the acts of observation influence the nature of the data gathered.

In the postmodern world, conceptions of truth are under attack everywhere. Poststructuralists, such as Derrida (1978, 1981), see meaning as multiple, unstable, and open to interpretation, relative to particular social, political, and historical contexts, and they thus move away from Grand Theory, which purports to assert universal Truth. Philosophers allied with postmodernism, such as Rorty (1979), criticize their predecessors as "essentialists" who assumed that there were innate essential meanings rather than historically contingent or local meanings. Postmodern psychologists, or social-constructionists, have begun to deconstruct such concepts as personal autonomy and the self

(Cushman, 1991; Gergen, 1991, 1994). Deconstructionists decenter the biases and assumptions of texts and move peripheral and marginalized perspectives to the center. Foucault (1984) reveals that multiple perspectives are erased from texts and suppressed and that those voices which are heard are connected to power and with strategies to maintain power. Feminists, particularly postmodern feminists, have alerted us to how fundamental conceptions such as gender, sexuality, and race are cultural and linguistic conventions that, when deconstructed, reveal hidden relations of authority and power. The presumed fixity of the existing social order is destabilized, and prominence is given to suppressed voices; in the mental health field, for instance, to the cries of women, children, minorities, gays, and patients.

Where does all of this leave analysts in their attempts to be the relatively neutral interpreters of patients' psychic reality? The classical conception of the analytic process is based first and foremost on the historical understanding of transference as a distortion of reality. The analyst is in the position of having to interpret to the patient where, when, and how the patient has distorted or misperceived the analyst, who is, after all, a relatively blank screen. Analysts, protected from emotional overinvolvement by their relative silence, distance, anonymity, and containment, as well as by a presumed thorough training analysis and a capacity for ongoing meticulous self-analysis, are thought to be in a good position to sort out what in patients' perceptions is real and what is error or distortion. The analyst must be in a position to judge what is real and what is not; hence, the distinction between transference and reality, transference and alliance, transference and relationship. But when authority is questioned in all areas of life, when interpretation itself is seen as an operation of power, when truth is seen as relative and context bound, when the dominant perspective is decentered and marginalized voices are moved to the foreground, when meanings are seen as socially constructed, and universal laws are devalued, when the very notions of objectivity, reality, and truth are challenged, when every Grand Theory is attacked— where does that leave the psychoanalyst? How can analysts interpret the transference, perform that fundamental psychoanalytic act, when that act, as it has been traditionally conceptualized, implies that analysts have the authority to distinguish truth from distortion and to assign meaning as if they were not involved in a relationship of power over analysands in and through that very interpretive act?

Our most cherished and fundamental beliefs about psychoanalytic technique are all being questioned. With the abandonment of drive theory, the dimension of frustration and gratification that for so long was the single best guide to the role of the object has been decentered.

Consequently, the rules of abstinence, anonymity, and neutrality have had to be forsaken. We do not take for granted the absolute truths of our metapsychologies; how could we when we have so many of them to choose from? So our interpretations must be based on something other than these foundations. It was inevitable that the postmodern condition would affect psychoanalysis, and it has under a variety of rubrics and schools including social-constructivism, hermeneuticism, narrative approaches, and what I have called relational-perspectivism.

Relational-perspectivism eschews the role of the authoritative analyst, who knows truth and represents reality and therefore health, in favor of a view of the analyst as a coparticipant involved in a mutual if asymmetrical endeavor. The tendency to polarize into dichotomous categories such concepts as analyst–analysand, therapist–patient, observer–observed, health–neurosis, scientist–data, experimenter–subject, follows from an acceptance of the traditional dichotomy of subject–object that, in turn, has been intricately connected to the dichotomy male–female. Ideas of male–female opposition have been present in both Eastern and Western cultures throughout history. In the West women have been regarded as the repository of all that is not male; women are assigned the role of "other" to men. The objectivist and positivist experimental model of scientific research that we are so painstakingly taught in graduate school is based on these distinctions. In Francis Bacon's scientific model, nature was depicted as female, to be subdued and conquered by the penetrating male gaze (Keller, 1985). Throughout Western history and culture women have been associated with passion and emotion, and men to reason, technology, and civilization.

In Freud's effort to constitute psychoanalysis as a positive science, he portrayed the analyst's functioning in the image of the phallus. The analyst was thought of as the fearless and adventurous male who seeks to uncover, expose, and penetrate the feminine "unconscious." The analyst needs to be sharp and insightful, brave and intrepid, fearless in "his pursuit" of the feminine unconscious. The analyst is to be "objective," and therefore "the subjective factor"—emotion, passion, subjectivity—has to be eliminated. With the shift in emphasis from a one-person to a two-person psychology, with the rise of a relational and intersubjective psychoanalytic theory, with the acknowledgment of the subjectivity of the analyst comes a shift in our view of psychoanalysis from a relatively detached to a personally and emotionally engaged activity. The subjectivity of the analyst, countertransference in its broadest sense, is not to be eliminated, but used, and the patient's experience of the analyst's subjectivity is to be articulated. The distinctions heretofore accepted between observer and observed, analyst and

analysand, rational and irrational, male objectivity and female subjectivity, all collapse, and ambiguity, multiplicity, and paradox take over
the center where clarity and identity have prevailed.

Does contemporary psychoanalysis advocate that we abandon objectivity? Postmodern theories push in the direction of relativism, and for
this and for other reasons postmodern thinking generates intense
controversy. At stake are fundamental questions about how we know
what we know and whether meaningful progress in knowledge can ever
be made. The older, classical, positivist or objectivist model may have
had the disadvantages of being somewhat authoritarian and even patri-
archical. But at least in that model the analyst had to accept some
responsibility! The analyst may have maintained the myth that "he"
was healthier, wiser, more rational, and more mature than the patient,
at least while he was being the analyst. But with all of this, "he" had to
assume the ethical and moral responsibility to conduct the analysis
appropriately, maintain appropriate boundaries, secure the analytic
frame, interpret correctly and in a timely fashion, distinguish between
what was real and what was distortion and what was progressive from
what was regressive, and differentiate meaningful and authentic
emotional expression from defense and resistance. Once we remove
this striking asymmetry from the analysis, what is left to authorize the
analyst to make these distinctions and thus guide the process as we
would expect any expert to guide a professional undertaking? In short,
with the postmodern collapse of the analyst's authority and power,
what happens to professional expertise, professional responsibility, and
professional ethics?

I want to assert in the strongest possible terms that the abandonment of metapsychological truths and theoretical foundations does not
necessitate the surrender of ethical standards, professional responsibility, or clinical judgment. Quite the contrary, in line with what I
described in Chapter 1 as an affirmative postmodern sensibility, I
believe that an acceptance of the relational-perspectivist approach that
has guided my thinking throughout this book leads to the recognition
that analysts must accept responsibility for the fact that it is their own
personality, their own subjectivity, that underlies their values and
beliefs, that infuses their theoretical convictions, and that forms the
basis for their technical interventions and clinical judgements. There
can be no technical choice or clinical decision that is not imbued with
the analyst's subjectivity. I agree with and wish to emphasize Hoffman's
(1995) forceful statement that, instead of regarding the countertransference as one factor among many that is to be considered by the
analyst in making any intervention, we must recognize "the analyst's
subjective, personal, countertransferential experience as the superordi-

nate context in which everything else, including theory, is embedded" (p. 108). Therefore, instead of disclaiming personal responsibility and attributing their understandings to an abstract metapsychology or universal theory, analysts must accept personal responsibility for their interpretive understandings and clinical interventions. Our understanding is always value laden, and, our values are always personal. There can be no neutral understanding or interpretation.

Bernstein (1983) has described how, having been stripped of the possibility for secure knowledge, we have come to suffer from "Cartesian anxiety," the fear that we will be left with nothing but radical relativism. It is because of our Cartesian anxiety that we long for foundational knowledge. Bion (1990) wrote:

> When approaching the unconscious—that is, what we do *not* know, not what we *do* know—we, patient and analyst alike, are certain to be disturbed. Anyone who is going to see a patient tomorrow should, at some point, experience fear. In every consulting room there ought to be two rather frightened people: the patient and the psychoanalyst. If they are not, one wonders why they are bothering to find out what everyone knows [pp. 4–5].

Being a psychoanalyst, like being an analysand, is no easy matter. It is, and as Bion says, it ought to be, frightening. As analysts, we long for indubitable, foundational knowledge. We want a solid and reliable theory to guide us and relieve our anxieties. But we, like our patients, must struggle without easy solutions. We must continue to make technical choices, to practice in one way rather than in another, to create certain ground rules for ourselves and our patients, to believe in some things and not in others. But we must accept that these choices reflect our own subjectivities; they are personal, and not only technical or theoretical choices. We must choose, but we cannot disclaim our choices as the inevitable outcomes of abstract and universal principles. Rather, we must accept our choices as based on our values, which, in turn, are reflections of who we are.

We might question how we can speak to patients with any sense of conviction if we abandon our beliefs in fundamental truths. Hoffman (1992a, b), Mitchell (1993a), and Stern (1992) have suggested that, paradoxically, within a constructivist approach analysts are freer to speak their minds, because with the elimination of external standards of truth there is more room for spontaneous self-expression and personal conviction. Emphasizing how this approach leads to dialogue rather than to dogmatism, Spezzanno (1993) writes, "To say this is not to give up truth. It is to give up certainty about truth. By giving up certainty we accept endlessness as the most certain thing about our discussions" (p. 29). Since there are no foundations on which to rest, conversation is endless. The analyst cannot end discussion simply by asserting authority; rather, all truths are partial, perspectival, and momentary and need to be questioned and further analyzed.

Advocating that we acknowledge the profound mutuality in clinical psychoanalysis and a greater egalitarianism in our practice as well as in our epistemology does not entail an abandonment of professional expertise or discipline, nor does it require an abandonment of the essential asymmetry between patient and analyst. There is a critical difference between authority and authoritarianism, between conviction and expertise based on experience and training, on one hand, and inflexible certainty on the other. Those psychoanalytic authors (Hoffman, 1991, 1992a, b, c, 1993; Stern, 1992, Mitchell, 1993a) who have most persuasively advocated constructivist approaches have repeatedly pointed out that those approaches do not reduce the need for intellectual and professional discipline and a certain kind of analytic objectivity. But, here again, how can I speak of objectivity? From a perspectivist position, what is meant by analytic objectivity?

In many respects, I have argued in this book that relational psycho-analysis adopts a dialectical approach, attempting to maintain tension between seemingly opposed principles, balancing the intrapsychic and the interpersonal, the intrasubjective and the intersubjective, the indi-vidual and the social, autonomy and mutuality. Rather than maintain the polarization of objectivism versus relativism, the philosophical view that has guided my thinking in this book may be referred to as "the dialectical sense of objectivity" (Megill, 1994, p. 7). Positivist principles of absolute objectivity exclude subjectivity, as Freud did, leading to an aperspectival objectivity or a "view from nowhere," a "God's eye view." Objectivity, in the modernist age, was viewed as an unproblematic quality of knowledge. Megill, surveying the current interdisciplinary debate about objectivity, views it as a contingent, varying, and deeply problematic product of cultural practice. He develops the notion of "dialectical objectivity," which "involves a positive attitude toward subjectivity. The defining feature of dialectical objectivity is the claim that subjectivity is indispensable to the constituting of objects" (p. 8). We do not gain anything if our critique of traditional thinking leads us to engage in a simple reversal of classical values. Traditionally, objec-tivity was prized and subjectivity was disdained. A simple reversal would disparage any attempt at objectivity on the grounds that it was impossible to achieve and would celebrate radical relativity and undis-ciplined subjectivity. The dialectical sense of objectivity, in contrast, recognizes that the extreme polarization of these concepts is itself an aspect of the problem. Dialectical objectivity is informed by subjectivity and includes within itself reflection on the subjective.

To return to the famous statement with which I began this Coda, Racker (1968) went on to say:

> The analyst's objectivity consists mainly in a certain attitude towards his own subjectivity and countertransference. . . . True objectivity is based upon a form of internal division that enables the analyst to make himself (his own countertransference and subjectivity) the object of his continuous observation and analysis. This position also enables him to be relatively "objective" towards the analysand [p. 132].

Racker's description of relative objectivity, like the rest of his contributions, was well ahead of its time and anticipated the notion of a dialectical sense of objectivity as I have just described it, an objectivity dialectically achieved only by reflexive inclusion, rather than elimination, of one's own subjectivity.

Traditionally, the rationale for analysts to have their own training analyses was so that they would gain "control" of their countertransferences, to know their own "personal equation" well enough so that it could be *eliminated* from consideration, to be analyzed well enough so as *not* to act out or participate interactionally with the patient. From the relational point of view being developed here, there is nothing in our training more important than the depth of our own analyses. Since, from the perspective being elaborated here, our subjectivity underlies everything that we do as analysts, and since, within the relational framework that I have described, access to the analyst's affective reactions is critical for his or her effective functioning (whether the analyst chooses to sustain and contain these affects or to express or act on them), the analyst's own analysis remains the most important element of our professional training.

Our analytic expertise does *not* reside in our being "thoroughly analyzed" and therefore immune to neurosis, healthier than our patients and therefore better able to judge reality. Rather, our expertise resides in our acquiring and honing certain personal, interpersonal, and professional skills. These include the ability to reflect on our own participation in interpersonal relationships while recognizing just how limited that reflectiveness is at any moment; the ability to attend to our own affective experience and to reflect on this experience and symbolize it, along with the recognition that at any moment there is always a great deal that we are not attending to in our own experience; a facility in using an analytic theory or model with enough dexterity, or the capacity to move back and forth between a wide variety of analytic models (Mitchell, 1993a), so as to help patients construct pragmatically useful narratives of their own lives; a proficiency in deconstructing whatever storylines our patients present to us or that we have constructed with them so that we and they do not become rigidly fixated to any one narrative construction; the capacity to tolerate a certain level of anxiety and depression as our patients observe and scrutinize our participation with them and explicitly or implicitly comment to us on the nature of our participation with them, and the capacity to enjoy, celebrate, and take pride in the shared growth, intimacy, and mutual satisfactions inherent in the psychoanalytic process. This is a very short list of some of the numerous skills that are necessary for the clinical practice of psychoanalysis; none of them requires the adoption of fundamentalist notions of truth and reality, and all of them testify to the enormous degree of discipline required for the competent practice of psychoanalysis.

Relational psychoanalysis suggests that it is not truth that patient and analyst pursue, so much as it is meaning that they attempt to construct (Mitchell, 1993a). Meaning is generated relationally and interpersonally, which is to say that meaning is negotiated and coconstructed. Analysts cannot simply construct psychoanalytic narratives or interpret patients' associations any way they please; constraints imposed by the structure of reality limit the possibilities of our plausible constructions. Analytic objectivity is dialectical and dialogical; we rely on our subjectivity, but our subjectivity is shaped and constrained by input from the object of our investigation, who is, after all, a separate subject. A dialectical sense of objectivity includes our subjectivity but does not ignore these constraints. Analytic objectivity is negotiated, relational, and intersubjective. Meaning is arrived at through a meeting of minds.

I want to bring this book to a close by repeating Ferenczi's (1931) statement, for it is as true now as it was then: "Analytical technique has never been, nor is it now, something finally settled" (p. 235). There is no single correct way to do psychoanalysis, although there are many ways that do not work very well for far too many patients. Analysts should not be taught technical prescriptions, although they can be taught ways to think about the process of making informed clinical decisions; and they can be instructed in clinical theory, which will serve them well as a compass with which to navigate the deep and troubled waters of clinical psychoanalysis. Rather than viewing the psychoanalytic theory of technique as a manual dictating certain types of behavior, I prefer to view our theory of technique as a system of signposts that encourage reflection-in-action. Analysts have no choice but to experiment; to innovate; through trial and error to learn what seems to deepen the analytic work for themselves and for their patients; and to interpret and intervene, guided by their own moral and professional convictions and by the ethical standards of their professional community. This view of clinical practice leads to intervening not on the basis of a Grand Theory, a prescriptive theory of technique or a "technical rationality" (Schon, 1983), but on the basis of the analyst's own subjectivity (which includes his or her personal history and professional experience, a knowledge of theory, and clinical wisdom) as it has been shaped in dialogue with the subjectivity of the other, the individual patient. Since communal dialogue and endless conversation is the very basis of this meaning system, one caveat for analysts in their explorations is that they should do nothing with patients that they would not in principle be willing to discuss with colleagues, with the professional community, and with the public.

Bion (1990) taught:

> There is a thing known as "classical psycho-analysis": the analyst has an analytic situation in which he practices analysis; he has patients who are suitable patients and gives them suitable, certified-correct interpretations. I have never known that state. The analytic situation is the situation which the particular practitioner finds is adequate for himself [p. 139].

Far from eliminating "the subjective factor," relational psychoanalysis asserts that analytic objectivity is constituted dialectically, rooted in the intersubjective relationship. Psychoanalytic findings may be said to be objective to the extent that they emerge intersubjectively, mutually constructed between analyst and analysand. Psychoanalytic theory, as well as our codes of ethics, may similarly be termed objective in the sense that psychoanalytic knowledge is communal or relational knowledge, socially derived, and based on the negotiated consensus of the psychoanalytic community of practitioners and theorists. That is, it is based on a meeting of minds.

References

Ainsworth, M. D. S. (1982), Attachment: Retrospect and prospect. In: *The Place of Attachment in Human Behavior*, ed. C. M. Parkes & J. Stevenson-Hinde. New York: Basic Books, pp. 3–30.

Altman, N. (1995), *The Analyst in the Inner City*. Hillsdale, NJ: The Analytic Press.

Angyal, A. (1965), *Neurosis and Treatment*. New York: Da Capo Press, 1982.

Arlow, J. A. (1980), The genesis of interpretation. In: *Psychoanalytic Explorations of Technique*, ed. H. P. Blum. New York: International Universities Press, pp. 193–206.

———— (1987), The dynamics of interpretation. *Psychoanal. Quart.*, 56:68–87.

Aron, L. (1989), Dreams, narrative, and the psychoanalytic method. *Contemp. Psychoanal.*, 25:108–127.

———— (1990a), Free association and changing models of mind. *J. Amer. Acad. Psychoanal.*, 18:439–459.

———— (1990b), One-person and two-person psychologies and the method of psychoanalysis. *Psychoanal. Psychol.*, 7:475–485.

———— (1991a), The patient's experience of the analyst's subjectivity. *Psychoanal. Dial.*, 1:29–51.

———— (1991b), Working through the past—working toward the future. *Contemp. Psychoanal.*, 27:81–109.

———— (1992a), From Ferenczi to Searles and contemporary relational approaches: Commentary on Mark Blechner's "Working in the Countertransference." *Psychoanal. Dial.*, 2:181–190.

———— (1992b), Interpretation as expression of the analyst's subjectivity. *Psychoanal. Dial.*, 2:475–507.

———— (1993a), Working toward operational thought: Piagetian theory and psychoanalytic method. *Contemp. Psychoanal.*, 29:289–313.

———— (1993b), Discussion of P. J. Pantone's "Transference: Solutions to integrate the past with the present." *Contemp. Psychother. Rev.*, 8:68–76.

———— (1995a), The internalized primal scene. *Psychoanal. Dial.*, 5:195–238.

———— (1995b), "Yours, thirsty for honesty, Ferenczi": Some background to Sándor Ferenczi's pursuit of mutuality. Presented at the International Psychoanalytical Congress of the International Psychoanalytic Association, San Francisco, CA.

———— & Bushra, A. (1995), The mutual regulation of regression in psychoanalysis. Presented at the spring meeting of the Division of Psychoanalysis (39), Santa Monica, CA.

———— & Frankel, J. (1994), Who is overlooking whose reality? Commentary on Tabin's "Freud's Shift from the Seduction Theory: Some Overlooked Reality Factors." *Psychoanal. Psychol.*, 11:291–301.

———— & ———— (1995), Response to Tabin. *Psychoanal. Psychol.*, 12:317–319.

————— & Harris, A. (1993), Sándor Ferenczi: Discovery and rediscovery. In: *The Legacy of Sándor Ferenczi*, ed. L. Aron & A. Harris. Hillsdale, NJ: The Analytic Press, pp. 1–36.

————— & Hirsch, I. (1992), Money matters in psychoanalysis. In: *Relational Perspectives in Psychoanalysis*. Hillsdale, NJ: The Analytic Press, pp. 239–256.

Atwood, G. & Stolorow, R. (1984), *Structures of Subjectivity*. Hillsdale, NJ: The Analytic Press.

Bacal, H. A. (1985), Optimal responsiveness and the therapeutic process. In: *Progress in Self Psychology, Vol. 1*, ed. A. Goldberg. Hillsdale, NJ: The Analytic Press, 1995, pp. 202–226.

————— (1995a), The essence of Kohut's work and the progress of self psychology. *Psychoanal. Dial.*, 5:353–366.

————— (1995b), The centrality of selfobject experience in psychological relatedness. *Psychoanal. Dial.*, 5:403–410.

————— & Newman, K. M., ed. (1990), *Theories of Object Relations*. New York: Columbia University Press.

Bach, S. (1985), *Narcissistic States and the Therapeutic Process*. New York: Aronson.

————— (1994), *The Language of Perversion and the Language of Love*. Northvale, NJ: Aronson.

Bachant, J. L., Lynch, A. A. & Richards, A. D. (1995), Relational models in psychoanalytic theory. *Psychoanal. Psychol.*, 12:71–88.

Bader, M. J. (1995), Can we still be selfish after the revolution? *Tikkun*, 10:25–27.

Bakan, D. (1966), *The Duality of Human Existence*. Boston, MA: Beacon Press.

Balbus, I. D. (1982), *Marxism and Domination*. Princeton, NJ: Princeton University Press.

Balint, M. (1950). Changing therapeutic aims and techniques in psychoanalysis. *Internat. J. Psycho-Anal.*, 31:117–124.

————— (1968), *The Basic Fault*. London: Tavistock.

Baranger, M. & Baranger, W. (1966), Insight in the analytic situation. In: *Psychoanalysis in the Americas*, ed. R. E. Litman. New York: International Universities Press, pp. 56–72.

Barratt, B. B. (1993), *Psychoanalysis and the Postmodern Impulse*. Baltimore, MD: Johns Hopkins University Press.

————— (1994), Review essay: *The Intimate Edge* by D. Bregman Ehrenberg. *Psychoanal. Dial.*, 4:275–282.

Basescu, S. (1987), Behind the "scenes": The inner experience of at least one psychoanalyst. *Psychoanal. Psychol.*, 4:255–266.

————— (1990), Show and tell: Reflections on the analyst's self-disclosure. In: *Self-disclosure in the Therapeutic Relationship*, ed. G. Stricker & M. Fisher. New York: Plenum, pp. 47–59.

Bass, A. (1993), Review essay: *Learning from the Patient* by P. Casement. *Psychoanal. Dial.*, 3:151–167.

Bateson, G. (1972), *Steps to an Ecology of Mind*. New York: Ballantine.

Beebe, B. & Lachmann, F. M. (1988a), The contribution of mother–infant mutual influence to the origins of self and object representations. *Psychoanal. Psychol.*, 5:305–337.

————— & ————— (1988b), Mother–infant mutual influence and precursors of psychic structure. In: *Frontiers in Self Psychology: Progress in Self Psychology, Vol. 3*, ed. A. Goldberg. Hillsdale, NJ: The Analytic Press, pp. 3–25.

——— Jaffe, J. & Lachmann, F. M. (1992), A dyadic systems view of communication. In: *Relational Perspectives in Psychoanalysis*, ed. N. J. Skolnick & S. C. Warshaw. Hillsdale, NJ: The Analytic Press, pp. 61–82.

Benjamin, J. (1988), *The Bonds of Love*. New York: Pantheon Books.

——— (1990), An outline of intersubjectivity: The development of recognition. *Psychoanal. Psychol.*, 7:33–46.

——— (1992), Recognition & destruction: An outline of intersubjectivity. In: *Relational Perspectives in Psychoanalysis*, ed. N. J. Skolnick & S. C. Warshaw. Hillsdale, NJ: The Analytic Press, pp. 43–60.

——— (1994), Commentary on papers by Tansey, Davies, and Hirsch. *Psychoanal. Dial.*, 4:193–201.

Berger, P. & Luckmann, T. (1966), *The Social Construction of Reality*. New York: Doubleday/Anchor.

Bergmann, M. S. (1993), Reflections on the history of psychoanalysis. *J. Amer. Psychoanal. Assn.*, 41:929–956.

Bernstein, R. J. (1983), *Beyond Objectivism and Relativism*. Philadelphia: University of Philadelphia Press.

Best, S. & Kellner, D. (1991), *Postmodern Theory*. New York: Guilford Press.

Bion, W. (1959), Attacks on linking. *Internat. J. Psycho-Anal.*, 40:308–315.

——— (1970), *Attention and Interpretation*. London: Heinemann.

——— (1990), *Brazilian Lectures*. London: Karnac Books.

Bird, B. (1972), Notes on transference: Universal phenomenon and hardest part of analysis. *J. Amer. Psychoanal. Assn.*, 20:267–301.

Blatt, S. J. & Blass, R. B. (1992), Relatedness and self-definition: Two primary dimensions in personality development, psychopathology, and psychotherapy. In: *Interface of Psychoanalysis and Psychology*, ed. J. Barron, M. Eagle & D. Wolitsky. Washington, DC: American Psychological Association, pp. 399–428.

Blechner, M. (1992), Working in the countertransference. *Psychoanal. Dial.*, 2:161–180.

Boesky, D. (1982), Acting out: A reconsideration of the concept. *Internat. J. Psycho-Anal.*, 63:39–55.

——— (1990), The psychoanalytic process and its components. *Psychoanal. Quart.*, 59:550–584.

Bollas, C. (1987) *The Shadow of the Object*. London: Free Association Books.

——— (1989), *Forces of Destiny*. London: Free Association Books.

——— (1992), *Being a Character*. New York: Hill & Wang.

——— (1995), *Cracking Up*. New York: Hill & Wang.

Bowlby, J. (1988), *A Secure Base*. New York: Basic Books.

Brabant, E., Falzeder, E. & Giampieri-Deutsch, P., ed. (1993), *The Correspondence of Sigmund Freud and Sándor Ferenczi, Vol. I, 1908–1914*, trans. P. T. Hoffer. Cambridge, MA: Harvard University Press.

Britton, R. (1989), The missing link: Parental sexuality in the Oedipus complex. In: *The Oedipus Complex Today*, ed. J. Steiner. London: Karnac Books, pp. 83–102.

Bromberg, P. M. (1984), Getting into oneself and out of one's self: On schizoid processes. *Contemp. Psychoanal.*, 20:439–448.

——— (1985), The politics of analytic treatment. *Contemp. Psychol.*, 30:893–894.

——— (1989), Interpersonal psychoanalysis and self psychology: A clinical comparison. In: *Self Psychology*, ed. D. W. Detrick & S. P. Detrick. Hillsdale, NJ: The Analytic Press, pp. 275–292.

———— (1994), "Speak! that I may see you": Some reflections on dissociation, reality, and psychoanalytic listening. *Psychoanal. Dial.*, 4:517–548.

———— (1995), Resistance, object-usage, and human relatedness. *Contemp. Psychoanal.*, 31:173–191.

Bruner, J. (1993), Loyal opposition and the clarity of dissent. *Psychoanal. Dial.*, 3:11–20.

Buber, M. (1923), *I and Thou*, trans. W. Kaufman. New York: Charles Scribner's Sons, 1970.

———— (1947), *Between Man and Man*, trans. R. G. Smith. London: Routledge & Kegan Paul.

———— (1965), *The Knowledge of Man—Selected Essays*, ed. M. Friedman (trans. M. Friedman & R. G. Smith). New York: Harper & Row.

———— (1967), The philosopher replies. In: *The Philosophy of Martin Buber*, ed. P. A. Schilpp & M. Friedman. La Salle, IL: Open Court, pp. 689–746.

Burke, W. F. (1992), Countertransference disclosure and the asymmetry/mutuality dilemma. *Psychoanal. Dial.*, 2:241–271.

———— & Tansey, M. J. (1991), Countertransference disclosure and models of therapeutic action. *Contemp. Psychoanal.*, 27:351–384.

Casement, P. J. (1982), Some pressures on the analyst for physical contact during the re-living of an early trauma. *Internat. Rev. Psycho-Anal.*, 9:279–286.

Chessick, R. D. (1995), Poststructural psychoanalysis or wild analysis? *J. Amer. Acad. Psychoanal.*, 23:47–62.

Chodorow, N. (1978), *The Reproduction of Mothering*. Berkeley: University of California Press.

———— (1989), *Feminism and Psychoanalytic Theory*. New Haven, CT: Yale University Press.

Chomsky, N. (1957), *Syntactic Structures*. The Hague: Mouton.

———— (1968), *Language and Mind*. New York: Harcourt, Brace & World.

Chrzanowski, G. (1977), *Interpersonal Approach to Psychoanalysis*. New York: Gardner Press.

———— (1980), Collaborative inquiry, affirmation and neutrality in the psychoanalytic situation. *Contemp. Psychoanal.*, 16:348–366.

Chused, J. F. (1991), The evocative power of enactments. *J. Amer. Psychoanal. Assn.*, 39:615–640.

———— & Raphling, D. L. (1992), The analyst's mistakes. *J. Amer. Psychoanal. Assn.*, 40:89–116.

Crews, F. (1996), Forward to 1896? A critique of Harris and Davies. *Psychoanal. Dial.*, 6:231–250.

Cushman, P. (1991), Ideology obscured: Political uses of the self in Daniel Stern's infant. *Amer. Psychol.*, 46:206–219.

Davies, J. M. (1994), Love in the afternoon: A relational reconsideration of desire and dread in the countertransference. *Psychoanal. Dial.*, 4:153–170.

———— (1996), Dissociation, repression and reality testing in the countertransference: The controversy over memory and false memory in the psychoanalytic treatment of adult survivors of childhood sexual abuse. *Psychoanal. Dial.*, 6:189–218.

———— & Frawley, M. G. (1994), *Treating the Adult Survivor of Childhood Sexual Abuse*. New York: Basic Books.

de Beauvoir, S. (1949), *The Second Sex*. Harmondsworth, UK: Penguin, 1972.

Derrida, J. (1978), *Writing and Difference*, trans. A. Bass. Chicago: University of Chicago Press.

———— (1981), *Positions*, trans. A. Bass. Chicago: University of Chicago Press.

Detrick, D. W. & Detrick, S. P. ed. (1989), *Self Psychology*. Hillsdale, NJ: The Analytic Press.

Dimen, M. (1991), Deconstructing difference: Gender, splitting, and transitional space. *Psychoanal. Dial.*, 1:335–352.

Dinnerstein, D. (1976), *The Mermaid and the Minotaur*. New York: Harper and Row.

Druck, A. (1989), *Four Therapeutic Approaches to the Borderline Patient*. Northvale, NJ: Aronson.

Dupont, J. (1988), Ferenczi's madness. *Contemp. Psychoanal.*, 24:250–261.

Eagle, M. (1984), *Recent Developments in Psychoanalysis*. New York: McGraw Hill.

———— (1993), Enactments, transference, and symptomatic cure: A case history. *Psychoanal. Dial.*, 3:93–110.

Ehrenberg, D. B. (1992), *The Intimate Edge*. New York: Norton.

———— (1995), Self-disclosure: Therapeutic tool or indulgence? *Contemp. Psychoanal.*, 31:213–228.

Epstein, L. (1995), Self-disclosure and analytic space. *Contemp. Psychoanal.*, 31:229–236.

Etchegoyen, R. H. (1991), *The Fundamentals of Psychoanalytic Technique*. London: Karnac Books.

Fairbairn, W. R. D. (1952), *Psychoanalytic Studies of the Personality*. London: Routledge, 1981.

Farber, L. H. (1967), Martin Buber and psychotherapy. In: *The Philosophy of Martin Buber*, ed. P. A. Schilpp & M. Friedman. La Salle, IL: Open Court, pp. 577–602.

Ferenczi, S. (1913), Taming of a wild horse. In: *Final Contributions to the Problems and Methods of Psycho-Analysis*, ed. M. Balint (trans. E. Mosbacher). London: Karnac Books, 1980, pp. 336–340.

———— (1915), Psychogenic anomalies of voice production. In: *Further Contributions to the Theory and Technique of Psycho-Analysis*, ed. J. Richman (trans. J. Suttie). London: Rarnac Books, 1980, pp. 105–109.

———— (1928), The elasticity of psychoanalytic technique. In: *Final Contributions to the Problems and Methods of Psycho-Analysis*, ed. M. Balint (trans. E. Mosbacher). London: Karnac Books, 1980, pp. 87–101.

———— (1929), The principle of relaxation and neocatharsis. In: *Final Contributions to the Problems and Methods of Psycho-Analysis*, ed. M. Balint (trans. E. Mosbacher). London: Karnac Books, 1980, pp. 108–125.

———— (1931), Child analysis in the analysis of adults. In: *Final Contributions to the Problems and Methods of Psycho-Analysis*, ed. M. Balint (trans. E. Mosbacher). London: Karnac Books, 1980, pp. 126–142

———— (1932), *The Clinical Diary of Sándor Ferenczi*, ed. J. Dupont (trans. M. Balint & N. Z. Jackson). Cambridge, MA: Harvard University Press, 1988.

———— (1933), Confusion of tongues between adults and the child. In: *Final Contributions to the Problems and Methods of Psycho-Analysis*. London: Karnac Books, 1980, pp. 156–167.

———— & Rank, O. (1924), *The Development of Psychoanalysis*. New York: Dover Publications, 1956.

Fiscalini, J. (1994), The uniquely interpersonal and the interpersonally unique. *Contemp. Psychoanal.*, 30:114–134.

Flavell, J. H. (1963), *The Developmental Psychology of Jean Piaget*. Princeton, NJ: D. Van Nostrand.

Flax, J. (1990), *Thinking Fragments*. Berkeley: University of California Press.

Fordham, M. (1969), Technique and countertransference. In: *Technique in Jungian Analysis*, ed. M. Fordham, R. Gordon, J. Hubback & K. Lambert. London: William Heinemann Medical Books.

Fortune, C. (1993a), The case of "RN": Sándor Ferenczi's radical experiments in Psychoanalysis. In: *The Legacy of Sándor Ferenczi*, ed. L. Aron & A. Harris. Hillsdale, NJ: The Analytic Press, pp. 101–120.

———— (1993b) Sándor Ferenczi's analysis of "R.N.": A critically important case in the history of psychoanalysis. *Brit. J. Psychother.*, 9:436–443.

———— (1994), A difficult ending: Ferenczi, "R.N.," and the experiment in mutual analysis. In: *100 Years of Psychoanalysis: Cahiers Psychiatriques Genevois, Special Issue*, ed. A. Haynal & E. Folzeder. pp. 217–223.

Fosshage, J. L. (1992), Psychoanalysis: Versions of blinis with sour cream. *Contemp. Psychother. Rev.*, 7:119–133.

Foucault, M. (1984), *The Foucault Reader*, ed. P. Rabinow. New York: Pantheon.

Fox, R. P. (1984), The principle of abstinence reconsidered. *Internat. Rev. Psycho-Anal.*, 11:227–236.

Frankel, J. B. (1993), Collusion and intimacy in the analytic relationship. In: *The Legacy of Sándor Ferenczi*, ed. L. Aron & A. Harris. Hillsdale, NJ: The Analytic Press, pp. 227–248.

Freud, S. (1900), The interpretation of dreams. *Standard Edition*, 4 & 5. London: Hogarth Press, 1953.

———— (1905), Fragment of an analysis of a case of hysteria. *Standard Edition*, 7:3–122. London: Hogarth Press, 1953.

———— (1910), The future prospects of psychoanalytic therapy. *Standard Edition*, 11:141–151. London: Hogarth Press, 1957.

———— (1912), Recommendations to physicians practicing psychoanalysis. *Standard Edition*, 12:109–120, London: Hogarth Press, 1958.

———— (1913), On beginning the treatment. *Standard Edition*, 12:121–144. London: Hogarth Press, 1958.

———— (1914), Remembering, repeating and working through. *Standard Edition*, 12:145–156. London: Hogarth Press, 1958.

———— (1921), Group psychology and the analysis of the ego. *Standard Edition*, 18:65–143. London: Hogarth Press, 1955.

———— (1923), The ego and the id. *Standard Edition*, 19:3–66. London: Hogarth Press, 1961.

———— (1933), Sándor Ferenczi. *Standard Edition*, 22:227–229. London: Hogarth Press, 1964.

Friedman, M. (1994), *The Healing Dialogue in Psychotherapy*. Northvale, NJ: Aronson.

Fromm, E. (1960), Psychoanalysis and Zen Buddhism. In: *Zen Buddhism and Psychoanalysis*, ed. D. T. Suzuki, E. Fromm & R. DeMartino. New York: Harper & Row.

———— (1964), *The Heart of Man*. New York: Harper & Row.

Gabbard, G. O. (1992), Commentary on "Dissociative Processes and Transference–Countertransference Paradigms" by J. M. Davies & M. G. Frawley. *Psychoanal. Dial.*, 2:37–47.

———— (1994), Commentary on papers by Tansey, Hirsch, and Davies. *Psychoanal. Dial.*, 4:203–213.

———— (1995), Countertransference: The emerging common ground. *Internat. J. Psycho-Anal.*, 76:475–486.

———— & Wilkinson, S. M. (1994), *Management of Countertransference with Borderline Patients.* Washington, DC: American Psychiatric Press.

Gergen, K. (1991), *The Saturated Self.* Basic Books.

———— (1994), *Realities and Relationships.* Cambridge, MA: Harvard University Press.

Gerson, S. (1995), The analyst's subjectivity and the relational unconscious. Presented at the spring meeting of the Division of Psychoanalysis (39), American Psychological Association, Santa Monica, CA.

Ghent, E. (1989), Credo: The dialectics of one-person and two-person psychologies. *Contemp. Psychoanal.*, 25: 169–211.

———— (1990), Masochism, submission, surrender. *Contemp. Psychoanal.*, 26:108–136.

———— (1992a), Foreword In: *Relational Perspectives in Psychoanalysis*, ed. N, J. Skolnick & S. C. Warshaw. Hillsdale, NJ: The Analytic Press, pp. xiii–xxii.

———— (1992b), Paradox and process. *Psychoanal. Dial.*, 2:135–160.

———— (1992c), What's moving, the train or the station? *Contemp. Psychother. Rev.*, 7:108–118.

———— (1993), Wish, need, and neediness: Commentary on Shabad's "Resentment, Indignation, and Entitlement." *Psychoanal. Dial.*, 3:495–508.

———— (1994), Empathy: Whence and whither? *Psychoanal. Dial.*, 4:473–486.

———— (1995), Interaction in the psychoanalytic situation. *Psychoanal. Dial.*, 5:479–491.

Gill, M. M. (1982), *The Analysis of Transference, Vol. I.* New York: International Universities Press.

———— (1983a), The point of view of psychoanalysis: Energy discharge or person? *Psychoanal. Contemp. Thought*, 6:523–552.

———— (1983b), The interpersonal paradigm and the degree of the therapist's involvement. *Contemp. Psychoanal.*, 1:200–237.

———— (1984), Transference: a change in conception or only in emphasis? A response. *Psychoanal. Inq.*, 4:489–524.

———— (1987), The analyst as participant. *Psychoanal. Inq.*, 7:249–259.

———— (1993), Interaction and interpretation. *Psychoanal. Dial.*, 111–122.

———— (1994), *Psychoanalysis in Transition.* Hillsdale, NJ: The Analytic Press.

———— (1995), Classical and relational psychoanalysis. *Psychoanal. Psychol.*, 12:89–108.

Gill, M. & Hoffman, I. Z. (1982), *Analysis of Transference, Vol. II.* New York: International Universities Press.

Goldberg, A. (1986), Reply to Philip M. Bromberg's discussion of "The Wishy-Washy Personality." *Contemp. Psychoanal.*, 22:387–388.

Goldner, V. (1991), Toward a critical relational theory of gender. *Psychoanal. Dial.*, 249–272.

Goldstein, E. G. (1994), Self-disclosure in treatment: What therapists do and don't talk about. *Clinical Soc. Work J.*, 22:417–433.

Gorkin, M. (1987), *The Uses of Countertransference.* Northvale, NJ: Aronson.

Gray, P. (1994), *The Ego and the Analysis of Defense.* Northvale, NJ: Aronson.

Greenacre, P. (1954), The role of transference: Practical considerations in relation to psychoanalytic therapy. In: *Emotional Growth. Volume 2.* New York: International Universities Press, pp. 627–640.

Greenberg, J. R. (1981), Prescription or description: Therapeutic action of psycho-analysis. *Contemp. Psychoanal.*, 17:239–257.

———— (1986), Theoretical models and the analyst's neutrality. *Contemp. Psychoanal.*, 22:87–106.

———— (1987), Of mystery and motive. *Contemp. Psychoanal.*, 24:689–704.

———— (1991), *Oedipus and Beyond*. Cambridge, MA: Harvard University Press.

———— (1995), Self-disclosure: Is it psychoanalytic? *Contemp. Psychoanal.*, 31:193–205.

———— & Mitchell, S. A. (1983), *Object Relations in Psychoanalytic Theory*. Cambridge, MA: Harvard University Press.

Greenson, R. R. (1967), *The Technique and Practice of Psychoanalysis*. New York: International Universities Press.

Groddeck, G. (1923), *The Book of the It*. London: Vision Press, 1950.

Grolnick, S. (1990), *The Work and Play of Winnicott*. Northvale, NJ: Aronson.

Grosskurth, P. (1986), *Melanie Klein: Her World and Her Work*. New York: Knopf.

Grotjahn, M. (1966), Georg Groddeck. In: *Psychoanalytic Pioneers*, ed. F. Alexander, S. Eisenstein & M. Grotjahn. New York: Basic Books.

Grubrich-Simitis, I. (1986), Six letters of Sigmund Freud and Sándor Ferenczi on the interrelationship of psychoanalytic theory and technique. *Internat. Rev. Psycho-Anal.*, 13:259–277.

Grünbaum, A. (1984), *The Foundations of Psychoanalysis*. Berkeley: University of California Press.

Guntrip, H. (1969), *Schizoid Phenomena, Object Relations and the Self*. New York: International University Press.

———— (1971), *Psychoanalytic Theory, Therapy, and the Self*. New York: Basic Books.

———— (1975), My experience of analysis with Fairbairn and Winnicott. In: *The Human Dimension in Psychoanalytic Practice*, ed. K. Frank. New York: Grune & Straton, pp. 49–68.

H. D. (1933), Diary entry for 9 March, In: *Tribute to Freud*. Manchester, UK: Carcanet Press, 1985.

Habermas, J. (1971), *Knowledge and Human Interests*. Boston: Beacon Press.

Harris, A. (1996), False memory? False memory syndrome? The so-called false memory syndrome? *Psychoanal. Dial.*, 6:155–187.

———— & Aron, L. (in press), Ferenczi's semiotic theory: Previews of postmodernism. *Psychoanal. Inq.*

Heimann, P. (1950), On countertransference. *Internat. J. Psycho-Anal.*, 31:81–84.

Hinshelwood, R. D. (1994), *Clinical Klein*. New York: Basic Books.

Hirsch, I. (1985), The Rediscovery of the advantages of the participant-observation model. *Psychoanal. & Contemp. Thought*, 8:441–459.

———— (1987), Varying modes of analytic participation. *J. Amer. Acad. Psychoanal.*, 15:205–222.

———— (1992), Extending Sullivan's interpersonalism. *Contemp. Psychoanal.*, 28:732–747.

———— (1993), Are intersubjectivity theory and interpersonal theory different? *Round Robin*, 9:25.

———— & Aron, L. (1991), Participant-observation, perspectivism, and counter-transference. In: *Psychoanalytic Reflections on Current Issues*, ed. H. B. Siegel, L. Barbanel, I. Hirsch, J. Lasky, H. Silverman & S. Warshaw. New York: New York University Press.

Hoffer, A. (1990), Ferenczi's search for mutuality: Implications for the free association method: An introduction. *Cahiers Psychiatriques Genevois* (special issue), pp. 199–204.

Hoffman, I. Z. (1983), The patient as interpreter of the analyst's experience. *Contemp. Psychoanal.*, 19:389–422.

———— (1987), The value of uncertainty in psychoanalytic practice. *Contemp. Psychoanal.*, 23:205–215.

———— (1990), In the eye of the beholder: A reply to Levenson. *Contemp. Psychoanal.*, 26:291–299.

———— (1991), Discussion: Toward a social-constructivist view of the psychoanalytic situation. *Psychoanal. Dial.*, 1:74–105.

———— (1992a), Some practical implications of a social-constructivist view of the analytic situation. *Psychoanal. Dial.*, 2:287–304.

———— (1992b), Expressive participation and psychoanalytic discipline. *Contemp. Psychoanal.*, 28:1–15.

———— (1992c), Reply to Orange. *Psychoanal. Dial.*, 2:567–570.

———— (1993), The intimate authority of the psychoanalyst's presence. *Psychol.-Psychoanal.*, 13:15–23.

———— (1994), Dialectical thinking and therapeutic action in the psychoanalytic process. *Psychoanal. Quart.*, 63:187–218.

———— (1995), Review essay; *Oedipus and Beyond* by J. Greenberg, *Psychoanal. Dial.*, 5:93–112.

Inderbitzin, L. B. & Levy, S. T. (1994), On grist for the mill: External reality as defense. *J. Amer. Psychoanal. Assn.*, 42:763–788.

Isakower, O. (1963), Minutes of the faculty meeting of the New York Psychoanalytic Institute, November 20.

Jacobs, T. J. (1986), On countertransference enactments. *J. Amer Psychoanal Assn.*, 34:289–307.

———— (1991), *The Use of the Self*. Madison, CT: International Universities Press.

———— (1995), Discussion of Jay Greenberg's paper. *Contemp. Psychoanal.*, 31:237–245.

Jones, E. (1957), *The Life and Work of Sigmund Freud, Vol. 3*. New York: Basic Books.

Joseph, B. (1989), *Psychic Equilibrium and Psychic Change*, ed. M. Feldman & E. B. Spillius. London: Routledge.

Kaplan, D. M. (1995), *Clinical and Social Realities*. Northvale, NJ: Aronson.

Kaufman, W. (1970), I and you: A prologue. In: *I and Thou* by M. Buber, New York: Charles Scribner's Sons, pp. 7–48.

Keller, E. F. (1985), *Reflections on Gender and Science*. New Haven, CT: Yale University Press.

Kernberg, O. F. (1965), Notes on countertransference. *J. Amer. Psychoanal. Assn.*, 13:38–56.

———— (1987), Projection and projective identification: Developmental and clinical aspects. In: *Projection, Identification, Projective Identification*, ed. J. Sandler. Madison, CT: International Universities Press, pp. 93–116.

King, P. & Steiner, R., ed. (1991), *The Freud-Klein Controversies: 1941–1945*. London: Tavistock: Routledge.

Klauber, J. (1981), *Difficulties in the Analytic Encounter.* London: Free Association Books.

Klein, M. (1932), *The Psycho-Analysis of Children.* Hogarth. Reprinted as *The Writings of Melanie Klein, Volume 2.* London: Hogarth Press, 1975.

———— (1946), Notes on some schizoid mechanisms. In: *The Writings of Melanie Klein, Vol. 3.* London: Hogarth Press, pp. 1–24.

Kohon, G. (1986), Countertransference: An independent view. In: *The British School of Psychoanalysis,* ed. G. Kohon. New Haven: CT: Yale University Press, pp. 51–73.

Kohut, H. (1971), *The Analysis of the Self.* New York: International Universities Press.

———— (1977), *The Restoration of the Self.* New York: International Universities Press.

———— (1984), *How Does Analysis Cure?* ed. A. Goldberg & P. Stepansky. Chicago: University of Chicago Press.

Kris, A. O. (1982), *Free Association.* New Haven, CT: Yale University Press.

Kvale, S. (1992), *Psychology and Postmodernism.* London: Sage.

Lacan, J. (1988), *The Seminar of Jacques Lacan, Book I,* ed. J. A. Miller (trans. J. Forrester). New York: Norton.

Lachmann, F. M. (1993), A self-psychological perspective on Shabad's "Resentment, indignation, entitlement." *Psychoanal. Dial.,* 3:509–514.

———— & Beebe, B. (1992), Reformulations of early development and transference: Implications for psychic structure formation. In: *Interface of Psychoanalysis and Psychology,* ed. J. Barron, M. Eagle & D. Wolitsky. Washington, DC: American Psychological Association, pp. 133–153.

———— & ———— (1995), Self psychology: Today. *Psychoanal. Dial.,* 5:375–384.

Langs, R. (1976), *The Therapeutic Interaction, Vol. I.* New York: Aronson.

———— ed. (1981), *Classics in Psychoanalytic Technique.* New York: Aronson.

Laplanche, J. & Pontalis, J. B. (1973), *The Language of Psychoanalysis.* New York: Norton.

Lasky, R. (1993), *Dynamics of Development and the Therapeutic Process.* Northvale, NJ: Aronson.

Leary, K. (1994), Psychoanalytic "problems" and postmodern "solutions." *Psychoanal. Quart.,* 63:433–465.

Lehrer, R. L. (1994), Some thoughts on self-disclosure and the danger-safety balance in the therapeutic relationship. *Psychoanal. Dial.,* 4:511–516.

Levenson, E. A. (1972), *The Fallacy of Understanding.* New York: Basic Books.

———— (1983), *The Ambiguity of Change.* New York: Basic Books.

———— (1987a), An interpersonal perspective. *Psychoanal. Inq.,* 7:207–214.

———— (1987b), Reply to Greenberg. *Contemp. Psychoanal.,* 24:704–707.

———— (1989), Whatever happened to the cat? Interpersonal perspectives on the self. *Contemp. Psychoanal.,* 25:537–553.

———— (1990), Reply to Hoffman. *Contemp. Psychoanal.,* 26:299–304.

———— (1991), Back to the future: The new psychoanalytic revisionism. *Contemp. Psychotherapy Rev.,* 6:27–43.

———— (1992), Help, I'm a captive in a psychoanalytic dialogue. *Contemp. Psychotherapy Rev.,* 7:133–138.

———— (1993), Shoot the messenger: Interpersonal aspects of the analyst's interpretations. *Contemp. Psychoanal.,* 29:383–396.

Levine, H. B. (1994), The analyst's participation in the analytic process. *Internat. J. Psycho-Anal.,* 75:665–676.

Lichtenberg, J. D. (1983), *Psychoanalysis and Infant Research*. Hillsdale, NJ: The Analytic Press.

——— (1989), *Psychoanalysis and Motivation*. Hillsdale, NJ: The Analytic Press.

Lieberman, E. J. (1985), *Acts of Will*. Amherst: University of Massachusetts Press.

Limentani, A. (1989), *Between Freud and Klein*. London: Free Association Books.

Lipton, S. D. (1977), Clinical observations on resistance to the transference. *Internat. J. Psycho-Anal.*, 58:463–472.

Little, M. (1951), Countertransference and the patient's response to it. *Internat. J. Psycho-Anal.*, 33:32–40.

——— (1957), "R"—the analyst's total response to his patient's needs. *Internat. J. Psycho-Anal.*, 38:240–254.

Loewald, H. W. (1960), On the therapeutic action of psychoanalysis. *Internat. J. Psychoanal.*, 41:16–33.

——— (1970), Psychoanalytic theory and the psychoanalytic process. In: *Papers on Psychoanalysis*. New Haven, CT: Yale University Press, 1980, pp. 277–301.

——— (1980), *Papers on Psychoanalysis*. New Haven, CT: Yale University Press.

——— (1986), Transference–countertransference. *J. Amer. Psychoanal. Assn.*, 34:275–287.

——— (1988), *Sublimation*. New Haven, CT: Yale University Press.

Lomas, P. (1987), *The Limits of Interpretation*. Northvale, NJ: Aronson, 1990.

Lowenstein, R. M. (1951), The problem of interpretation. *Psychoanal. Quart.*, 20:1–14.

Lum, W. B. (1988a), Sándor Ferenczi (1873–1933)—The father of the empathic-interpersonal approach. Part one: Introduction and early analytic years. *J. Amer. Acad. Psychoanal.*, 16:131–153.

——— (1988b), Sándor Ferenczi (1873–1933)—The father of the empathic-interpersonal approach. Part two: Evolving technique, final contributions and legacy. *J. Amer. Acad. Psychoanal.*, 16:317–347.

Mahler, M., S. Pine, F. & Bergman, A. (1975), *The Psychological Birth of the Human Infant*. New York: Basic Books.

Main, M., Kaplan, N. & Cassidy, J. (1985), Security in infancy, childhood and adulthood: a move to the level of representation. In: *Growing Points in Attachment: Theory and Research, Monographs of the Society for Research in Child Development, Serial 209*, ed. I. Bretherton & E. Waters. Chicago: University of Chicago Press, pp. 66–104.

Maroda, K. (1991), *The Power of Countertransference*. Chichester, New York: Wiley.

——— (1995), Show some emotion: Completing the cycle of affective communication. Presented at meeting of the Division of Psychoanalysis (39), American Psychological Association, Santa Monica, CA.

McConkey, K. M. (1992), The effects of hypnotic procedures on remembering: The experimental findings and their implications for forensic hypnosis. In: *Contemporary Hypnosis Research*, ed. E. Fromm & M. R. Nash. New York: Guilford, pp. 405–426.

McDougall, J. (1980), *Plea for a Measure of Abnormality*. New York: International Universities Press.

McGuire, W., ed. (1974), *The Freud-Jung Letters*, trans. R. Manheim & R. F. C. Hull. Princeton, NJ: Princeton University Press.

McLaughlin, J. T. (1981), Transference, psychic reality and countertransference. *Psychoanal. Quart.*, 50:639–664.

———— (1991), Clinical and theoretical aspects of enactment. *J. Amer. Psychoanal. Assn.*, 39:595–614.

Mead, G. H. (1934), *Mind, Self, and Society.* Chicago: Chicago University Press.

Megill, A., ed. (1994), *Rethinking Objectivity.* Durham, NC: Duke University Press.

Menaker, E. (1982), *Otto Rank: A Rediscovered Legacy.* New York: Columbia University Press.

Messer, S. B., Sass, L. A., & Woolfolk, R. L., ed. (1988), *Hermeneutics and Psychological Theory.* New Brunswick, NJ: The State University.

Micale, M. S. (1995), *Approaching Hysteria.* Princeton, NJ: Princeton University Press.

Miller, J. B. (1976), *Toward A New Psychology of Being.* Boston, MA: Beacon Press.

Mitchell, J. (1974), *Psychoanalysis and Feminism.* New York: Pantheon.

Mitchell, S. (1988a), *Relational Concepts in Psychoanalysis.* Cambridge, MA: Harvard University Press.

———— (1988b), The intrapsychic and the interpersonal: Different theories, different domains, or historical artifacts. *Psychoanal. Inq.*, 8:472–496.

———— (1991), Wishes, needs and interpersonal negotiations. *Psychoanal. Inq.*, 11: 147–170.

———— (1992), Response to Edgar Levenson's "Back to the Future: The New Psycho-analytic Revisionism," *Contemp. Psychother. Rev.*, 7:97–107.

———— (1993a), *Hope and Dread in Psychoanalysis.* New York: Basic Books.

———— (1993b), Reply to Bachant and Richards. *Psychoanal. Dial.*, 3:461–480.

———— (1995a), Interaction in the Kleinian and Interpersonal Traditions. *Contemp. Psychoanal.*, 31:65–91.

———— (1995b), Commentary on "Special Section: Contemporary Structural Psycho-analysis and Relational Psychoanalysis." *Psychoanal. Psychol.*, 12:575–582.

Modell, A. H. (1984). *Psychoanalysis in a New Context.* New York: International Universities Press.

Nagel, T. (1986), *The View From Nowhere.* New York: Oxford University Press.

Natterson, J. (1991), *Beyond Countertransference.* Northvale, NJ: Aronson.

Nicholson, L. J. (1990), *Feminism/Postmodernism.* New York: Routledge.

Ogden, T. (1979), On projective identification. *Internat. J. Psycho-Anal.*, 60:357–373.

———— (1986), *The Matrix of the Mind.* Northvale, NJ: Aronson.

———— (1989), *The Primitive Edge of Experience.* Northvale, NJ: Aronson.

———— (1994), *Subjects of Analysis.* Northvale, NJ: Aronson.

Olinick, S. L. (1969), On empathy and regression in service of the other. *Brit. J. Med. Psychol.*, 42:41–49.

Orange, D. M. (1992), Commentary on Irwin Hoffman's, "Discussion: Toward a Social-Constructivist View of the Psychoanalytic Situation." *Psychoanal. Dial.*, 2:561–565.

Ornstein, P. H. & Ornstein, A. (1995), Marginal comments on the evolution of self psychology. *Psychoanal. Dial.*, 5:421–426.

Panel (1992), Enactments in psychoanalysis (M. Johan, reporter). *J. Amer. Psychoanal. Assn.*, 40:827–841.

———— (1995a), Toward a definition of the term and concept of interaction (D. M. Hurst, reporter). *J. Amer. Psychoanal. Assn.*, 43:521–537.

———— (1995b), Interpretive perspectives on interaction (S. D. Purcell, reporter). *J. Amer. Psychoanal. Assn.*, 43:539–551.

Philipson, I. J. (1993), *On the Shoulders of Women.* New York: Guilford.

Phillips, A. (1988), *Winnicott*. Cambridge, MA: Harvard University Press.

—————— (1993), *On Kissing, Tickling and Being Bored*. Cambridge, MA: Harvard University Press.

Pick, I. B. (1985), Working through in the countertransference. *Internat. J. Psycho-Anal.*, 66:157–166.

Pizer, S. A. (1992), The negotiation of paradox in the analytic process. *Psychoanal. Dial.*, 2:215–240.

—————— (in press), Negotiating potential space: Illusion, play, metaphor and the subjunctive. *Psychoanal. Dial.*

Price, M. (1995), The illusion of theory: Discussion of R. D. Chessick's "Poststructural Psychoanalysis or Wild Analysis?" *J. Amer. Acad. Psychoanal.*, 23:63–70.

Protter, B. (1985), Symposium: "Psychoanalysis and Truth": Toward an emergent psychoanalytic epistemology. *Contemp. Psychoanal.*, 21:208–227.

Racker, H. (1968), *Transference and Counter–transference*. New York: International Universities Press.

Ragen, T. & Aron, L. (1993), Abandoned workings: Ferenczi's mutual analysis. In: *The Legacy of Sándor Ferenczi*, ed. L. Aron & A. Harris. Hillsdale, NJ: The Analytic Press, pp. 217–226.

Rank, O. (1929), *The Trauma of Birth*. New York: Harcourt, Brace.

—————— (1945), *Will Therapy and Truth and Reality*. New York: Knopf.

Reich, A. ed. (1973), *Annie Reich*. New York: International Universities Press.

Renik, O. (1993a), Countertransference enactment and the psychoanalytic process. In: *Psychic Structure and Psychic Change*, ed. M. Horowitz, O. Kernberg & E. Weinshel. Madison, CT: International Universities Press, pp. 135–158.

—————— (1993b), Analytic interaction: conceptualizing technique in light of the analyst's irreducible subjectivity. *Psychoanal. Quart.*, 62:553–571.

—————— (1995), The ideal of the anonymous analyst and the problem of self-disclosure. *Psychoanal. Quart.*, 466–495.

Resenau, P. M. (1992), *Post-Modernism and the Social Sciences*. Princeton, NJ: Princeton University Press.

Ricoeur, P. (1970), *Freud and Philosophy*. New Haven, CT: Yale University Press.

Rivera, M. (1989), Linking the psychological and the social: Feminism, poststructuralism, and multiple personality. *Dissociation*, 2:24–31.

Rorty, R. (1979), *Philosophy and the Mirror of Nature*. Princeton, NJ: Princeton University Press.

Rotenstreich, N. (1967), The right and the limitations of Buber's dialogical thought. In: *The Philosophy of Martin Buber*, ed. P. A. Schilpp & M. Friedman. La Salle, IL: Open Court, pp. 97–132.

Rothstein, A. (1995), Aspects of self-revelation and disclosure: Analyst to patient. Discussion. Presented at symposium of the New York Psychoanalytic Society.

Rudnytsky, P. L. (1991), *The Psychoanalytic Vocation*. New Haven, CT: Yale University Press.

Sameroff, A. J. & Emde, R. N., ed. (1989), *Relationship Disturbances in Early Childhood*. New York: Basic Books.

Samuels, A. (1985), *Jung and the Post-Jungians*. London: Routledge.

Sandler, J. (1976), Countertransference and role-responsiveness. *Internat. Rev. Psycho-Anal.*, 3:43–47.

—————— ed. (1987), *Projection, Identification, Projective Identification*. Madison, CT: International Universities Press, pp. 93–115.

————— Dare, C. & Holder, A. (1973), *The Patient and the Analyst*. London: Maresfield Reprints, 1979.

Sarup, M. (1993), *An Introductory Guide to Post-Structuralism and Postmodernism*, (2nd ed.). Athens: University of Georgia Press.

Schafer, R. (1983), *The Analytic Attitude*. New York: Basic Books.

————— (1992), *Retelling A Life*. New York: Basic Books.

Schon, D. (1983), *The Reflexive Practitioner*. New York: Basic Books.

Schwaber, E. (1981), Empathy: A mode of analytic listening. *Psychoanal. Inq.*, 1:357–392.

————— (1983), Listening and psychic reality. *Internat. Rev. Psycho-Anal.*, 10:379–392.

————— (1992), Countertransference: The analyst's retreat from the patient's vantage point. *Internat. J. Psycho-Anal.*, 73:349–362.

————— (1995), Toward a definition of the term and concept of interaction. *Internat. J. Psycho-Anal.*, 76:557–564.

Searles, H. (1975), The patient as therapist to his analyst. In: *Tactics and Techniques in Psychoanalytic Therapy, Vol. 2*, ed. P. Giovacchini. New York: Aronson, pp. 95–151.

————— (1979), *Countertransference and Related Subjects*. New York: International Universities Press.

Severn, E. (1933), *The Discovery of the Self*. London: Rider & Co.

Shengold, L. (1989), *Soul Murder*. New Haven, CT: Yale University Press.

Silberstein, L. J. (1989), *Martin Buber's Social and Religious Thought*. New York: New York University Press.

Singer, I. (1968), The reluctance to interpret. In: *The Use of Interpretation in Treatment*, ed. E. F. Hammer. New York: Grune & Stratton, pp. 364–371.

————— (1971), The patient aids the analyst. In: *In the Name of Life*, ed. B. Landis & E. Tauber. New York: Holt, Rinehart & Winston, pp. 56–68.

————— (1977), The fiction of analytic anonymity. In: *The Human Dimension in Psycho-analytic Practice*, ed. K. Frank. New York: Grune & Stratton, pp. 181–192.

Slavin, M. O. & Kriegman, D. (1992), Psychoanalysis as a Darwinian depth psychology: Evolutionary biology and the classical-relational dialectic in psychoanalytic theory. In: *Interface of Psychoanalysis and Psychology*, ed. J. Barron, M. Eagle & D. Wolitsky. Washington, DC: American Psychological Association, pp. 37–76.

Smith, B. L. (1990), The origins of interpretation in the countertransference. *Psychoanal. Psychol.*, 7:89–104.

Smith, H. F. (1993), Engagements in analysis and their use in self analysis. In: *Self-Analysis*, ed. J. W. Barron. Hillsdale, NJ: The Analytic Press.

Smith, M. B. (1994), Selfhood at risk. *Amer. Psychol.*, 49:405–411.

Spence, D. (1982), *Narrative Truth, Historical Truth*. New York: Norton.

————— (1993), The hermeneutic turn: Soft science or loyal opposition? *Psychoanal. Dial.*, 3:1–10.

Spezzano, C. (1993), *Affect in Psychoanalysis*. Hillsdale, NJ: The Analytic Press.

————— (1995), "Classical" versus "contemporary" theory. *Contemp. Psychoanal.*, 31:20–46.

Spillius, E. B. (1992), Clinical experiences of projective identification. In: *Clinical Lectures on Klein and Bion*, ed. R. Anderson. London: Tavistock.

Spitz, R. A. (1959), *A Genetic Field Theory of Ego Formation*. New York: International Universities Press.

Stanton, M. (1991), *Sándor Ferenczi: Reconsidering Active Intervention.* Northvale, NJ: Aronson.

Steiner, J. (1993), *Psychic Retreats.* London: Routledge.

Stern, D. B. (1983), Unformulated experience. *Contemp. Psychoanal.*, 19:71–99.

——— (1990), Courting surprise: Unbidden perceptions in clinical practice. *Contemp. Psychoanal.*, 23:484–491.

——— (1992), Commentary on constructivism in clinical psychoanalysis. *Psychoanal. Dial.*, 2:331–363.

Stern, D. N. (1983), Implications of infancy research for psychoanalytic theory and practice. In: *Psychiatry Update II*, ed. L. Grinspoon. Washington: American Psychiatric Association., pp. 8–12.

——— (1985), *The Interpersonal World of the Infant.* New York: Basic Books.

——— (1989), The representation of relational patterns: Developmental considerations. In: *Relationship Disturbances in Early Childhood*, ed. A. J. Sameroff & R. N. Emde. New York: Basic Books, pp. 52–69.

——— (1994), Conceptions of structure in interpersonal psychoanalysis. *Contemp. Psychoanal.*, 30:255–300.

Stolorow, R. (1992), Subjectivity and self psychology: A personal odyssey. In: *New Therapeutic Visions: Progress in Self Psychology, Vol. 8*, ed. A. Goldberg. Hillsdale: NJ, pp. 241–250.

——— (1995), An intersubjective view of self psychology. *Psychoanal. Dial.*, 5:393–400.

——— & Atwood, G. E. (1979), *Faces in a Cloud.* New York: Aronson.

——— & ——— (1992), *Contexts of Being.* Hillsdale, NJ: The Analytic Press.

——— ——— & Brandchaft, B. (1994), *The Intersubjective Perspective.* Northvale, NJ: Aronson.

——— ——— & Ross, J. (1978), The representational world in psychoanalytic therapy. *Internat. Rev. Psycho-Anal.*, 5:247–256.

——— Brandchaft, B. & Atwood, G. E. (1987), *Psychoanalytic Treatment.* Hillsdale, NJ: The Analytic Press.

Strachey, J. (1934), The nature of the therapeutic action of psychoanalysis. *Internat. J. Psycho-Anal.*, 15:127–159.

Sugarman, A. & Wilson, A. (1995), Introduction to the section: Contemporary structural analysts critique relational theories. *Psychoanal. Psychol.*, 12:1–8.

Sullivan, H. S. (1938). Editorial. *Psychiat.*, 1:135–143.

——— (1953), *The Interpersonal Theory of Psychiatry.* New York: Norton.

——— (1954), *The Psychiatric Interview.* New York: Norton.

Summers, F. (1994), *Object Relations Theories and Psychopathology.* Hillsdale, NJ: The Analytic Press.

Surrey, J. L. (1985), The "self-in-relation": A theory of women's development. Work in Progress, No. 13. Stone Center, Wellesley College, Wellesley MA.

——— Kaplan, A. G. & Jordan, J. V. (1990), Empathy revisited. Work in Progress, Stone Center, Wellesley College, Wellesley, MA.

Suttie, I. D. (1935), *The Origins of Love and Hate.* London: Free Association Books, 1988.

Swales, P. (1986), Freud, his teacher, and the birth of psychoanalysis. In: *Freud: Appraisals and Reappraisals, Vol. 1*, ed. P.E. Stepansky. Hillsdale, NJ: The Analytic Press, pp. 3–82.

Symington, N. (1983), The analyst's act of freedom as agent of therapeutic change. *Internat. Rev. Psycho-Anal.*, 10:783–792.

———— (1990), The possibility of human freedom and its transmission (with particular reference to the thought of Bion). *Internat. J. Psycho-Anal.*, 71:95–106.

Symposium: What does the analyst know? (1993), *Psychoanal. Dial.*, Vol. 3, Nos. 1 & 2.

Symposium: Self psychology after Kohut (1995), *Psychoanal. Dial.*, Vol. 5, No. 3.

Tabin, J. K. (1993), Freud's shift from the seduction theory: Some overlooked reality factors. *Psychoanal. Psychol.*, 10:291–298.

———— (1995), A bit more light on Ferenczi and Freud. *Psychoanal. Psychol.*, 12:305–315.

Tansey, M. J. & Burke, W. F. (1989), *Understanding Countertransference*. Hillsdale, NJ: The Analytic Press.

Tauber, E. S. (1952), Observations on countertransference phenomena, the supervisor–therapist relationship. *Samiksa*, 6:220–228.

———— (1954), Exploring the therapeutic use of countertransference data. *Psychiat.*, 17:331–336.

Thompson, C. M. (1956), The role of the analyst's personality in therapy. In: *Interpersonal Psychoanalysis*, ed. M. R. Green. New York: Basic Books, 1964.

Tolpin, P. (1988), Optimal affective engagement: The analyst's role in therapy. In: *Learning From Kohut: Progress in Self Psychology*, Vol. 4, ed. A. Goldberg. Hillsdale, NJ: The Analytic Press, pp. 160–168.

Tower, L. E. (1956), Countertransference. In: *Essential Papers on Countertransference*, ed. B. Wolstein. New York: New York University Press, 1988.

Trevarthan, C. and Hubley, P. (1978), Secondary intersubjectivity: Confidence, confiders, and acts of meaning in the first year. In: *Action, Gesture, and Symbol*, ed. A. Lock. New York: Academic.

Wachtel, P. L. (1982). Vicious circles. *Contemp. Psychoanal.*, 18:259–272.

———— (1986), On the limits of therapeutic neutrality. *Contemp. Psychoanal.*, 22:60–70.

———— (1993), *Therapeutic Communication: Principles and Effective Practice*. New York: Guilford.

Wallerstein, R. S. (1988), One psychoanalysis or many? *Internat. J. Psycho-Anal.*, 69:5–22.

———— (1995), *The Talking Cures*. New Haven, CT: Yale University Press.

Watzlawick, P., Bavelas, J. B. & Jackson, D. D. (1967), *Pragmatics of Human Communication*. New York: Norton.

Weedon, C. (1987), *Feminist Practice and Poststructuralist Theory*. Cambridge: Blackwell.

Whiston, S. C. & Sexton, T. L. (1993), An overview of psychotherapy outcome research: implications for practice. *Prof. Psychol.: Res. & Pract.*, 24:43–51.

Wilner, W. (1975), The nature of intimacy. *Contemp. Psychoanal.*, 11:206–226.

Wilson, A. (1995), Mapping the mind in relational psychoanalysis: Some critiques, questions, and conjectures. *Psychoanal. Psychol.*, 12:9–30.

Winnicott, D. W. (1941), The observation of infants in a set situation. In: *Collected Papers*. New York: Basic Books, 1958, pp. 52–69.

———— (1949), Hate in the countertransference. *Internat. J. Psycho-Anal.*, 30:69–75.

———— (1951), Transitional objects and transitional phenomena. In: *Collected Papers*. New York: Basic Books, 1958, pp. 229–242.

———— (1954), Metapsychological and clinical aspects of regression within the psychoanalytical set-up. In: *Collected Papers*. New York: Basic Books, 1958, pp. 278–294.

———— (1954–1955), The depressive position in normal development. In: *Collected Papers*. New York: Basic Books, 1975, pp. 262–277.

———— (1958), The capacity to be alone. In: *The Maturational Process and the Facilitating Environment*. New York: International Universities press, 1965, pp. 29–36.

———— (1960), Ego distortions in terms of true and false self. In: *The Maturational Process and the Facilitating Environment*. New York: International Universities Press. 1965, pp. 140–152.

———— (1963), Communicating and not communicating leading to a study of certain opposites. In: *The Maturational Process and the Facilitating Environment*. New York: International Universities Press, 1965, pp. 179–192.

———— (1969), The use of an object. *Internat. J. Psycho-Anal.*, 50:711–716.

———— (1971a), *Playing and Reality*. Middlesex, UK: Penguin.

———— (1971b), *Therapeutic Consultations in Child Psychiatry*. New York: Basic Books.

———— (1986), *Holding and Interpretation*. London: Hogarth Press.

Wittgenstein, L. (1953), *Philosophical Investigations*. Oxford: Blackwell.

Wolfenstein, E. V. (1993), *Psychoanalytic-Marxism*. New York: Guilford Press.

Wolstein, B. (1964), *Transference*. New York: Grune & Straton.

———— (1975), Countertransference: The psychoanalyst's shared experience and inquiry with his patient. *J. Amer. Acad. Psychoanal.*, 3:77–89.

———— (1981), The psychic realism of psychoanalytic inquiry. *Contemp. Psychoanal.*, 17:399–412.

———— (1983), The pluralism of perspectives on countertransference. *Contemp. Psychoanal.*, 19:506–21.

———— (1988), Introduction. In: *Essential Papers on Countertransference*, ed. B. Wolstein. New York: New York University Press, pp. 1–15.

———— (1990), Five empirical psychoanalytic methods. *Contemp. Psychoanal.*, 26:237–256.

———— (1991), The Hungarian school. *Contemp. Psychoanal.*, 27:167–178.

———— (1994), The evolving newness of interpersonal psychoanalysis: From the vantage point of immediate experience. *Contemp. Psychoanal.*, 30:473–499.

Zeligs, M. A. (1957), Acting in. A contribution to the meaning of some postural attitudes observed during analysis. *J. Amer. Psychoanal. Assn.*, 5:685–706.

Zucker, H. (1989), Premises of interpersonal theory. *Psychoanal. Psychol.*, 6:401–419.

Index